A WORLD OF POSSIBILITIES

Cultural Inquiry

EDITED BY CHRISTOPH F. E. HOLZHEY
AND MANUELE GRAGNOLATI

The series 'Cultural Inquiry' is dedicated to exploring how diverse cultures can be brought into fruitful rather than pernicious confrontation. Taking culture in a deliberately broad sense that also includes different discourses and disciplines, it aims to open up spaces of inquiry, experimentation, and intervention. Its emphasis lies in critical reflection and in identifying and highlighting contemporary issues and concerns, even in publications with a historical orientation. Following a decidedly cross-disciplinary approach, it seeks to enact and provoke transfers among the humanities, the natural and social sciences, and the arts. The series includes a plurality of methodologies and approaches, binding them through the tension of mutual confrontation and negotiation rather than through homogenization or exclusion.

Christoph F. E. Holzhey is the Founding Director of the ICI Berlin Institute for Cultural Inquiry. Manuele Gragnolati is Professor of Italian Literature at the Sorbonne Université in Paris and Associate Director of the ICI Berlin.

A WORLD OF POSSIBILITIES
The Legacy of *The Undivine Comedy*

EDITED BY KRISTINA M. OLSON

ISBN (Hardcover): 978-3-96558-107-4
ISBN (Paperback): 978-3-96558-108-1
ISBN (PDF): 978-3-96558-109-8
ISBN (EPUB): 978-3-96558-110-4

Cultural Inquiry, 37
ISSN (Print): 2627-728X
ISSN (Online): 2627-731X

Bibliographical Information of the German National Library
The German National Library lists this publication in the Deutsche Nationalbibliografie
(German National Bibliography); detailed bibliographic information is available online at
http://dnb.d-nb.de.

In Europe, volumes are printed by Lightning Source UK Ltd., Milton Keynes, UK. See the
final page for further details.

Digital editions can be viewed and downloaded freely at: https://doi.org/10.37050/ci-37.

ICI Berlin Press is an imprint of
ICI gemeinnütziges Institut für Cultural Inquiry Berlin GmbH
Christinenstr. 18/19, Haus 8
D-10119 Berlin
publishing@ici-berlin.org
www.ici-berlin.org

Contents

Introduction
KRISTINA M. OLSON 1

ON METHOD

Possible Worlds and Reading Dante's *Commedia*: Suspension
of Disbelief (Coleridge, Horace, Tolkien, Cecco d'Ascoli) and
the Solvents of Narrative and History
TEODOLINDA BAROLINI 15

I. DETHEOLOGIZE TO NARRATIVIZE

The Intricate Weaving of *The Undivine Comedy*
H. WAYNE STOREY 51

The Undivine Comedy: Dante One and Multiple
ROBERTO ANTONELLI 65

Reasoning between Possibility, Fictional Reality, and Actuality:
A Case Study in Detheologizing the *Commedia*'s Conditionals
LAURA DINARDO 99

II. DETHEOLOGIZE TO HISTORICIZE

Detheologize to Historicize
NASSIME CHIDA 125

Teodolinda Barolini and the Signs of Newness in *The Undivine Comedy*
ALBERTO CASADEI 135

Dante's War: Exiles, *carestia*, and Conflict in the Florentine
Countryside, 1301–1304
GEORGE DAMERON 149

III. DETHEOLOGIZE TO RETHEOLOGIZE

Dante's Lucy in the Canon Law of Consent
GRACE DELMOLINO 183

Prophetic Models and Structures in an Undivine *Comedy*
GIUSEPPE LEDDA 209

Divining *The Undivine Comedy*: Reflections and Recollections
ZYGMUNT G. BARAŃSKI 223

IV. DETHEOLOGIZE TO DRAMATIZE

Dante and 'visibile parlare'
LINA BOLZONI 245

Ovidio senza Dio: Ovidian Myth and Sexual Violence in the
Commedia
JULIE VAN PETEGHEM 261

In Praise of Detheologizing
ELENA LOMBARDI 285

Heavenly Paradoxes and Their Pleasures
MANUELE GRAGNOLATI 299

V. DETHEOLOGIZE TO MODERNIZE

The Role of the Reader in Actualizing the *Commedia*
F. REGINA PSAKI 317

From Detheologizing to Decolonizing: Toward a Reading of
Dante and Alterity
AKASH KUMAR 339

Translating *The Undivine Comedy*
ROBERTA ANTOGNINI 349

EPILOGUE

On Reading *The Undivine Comedy* Thirty Years Later
JOAN FERRANTE 369

References 373
Notes on the Contributors 397
Index 401

Introduction

KRISTINA M. OLSON

Like many of the authors in this volume, I can remember the first time that I read *The Undivine Comedy*. It was the summer of 1999, right before I was to begin coursework at Columbia as a newly admitted graduate student, intent on continuing my studies of contemporary Italian poets — Amelia Rosselli, among others. I had completed two senior projects at Bard College in fulfillment of my bachelor's degree: one a partial translation of Rosselli's *Documento* (recently translated by our contributor Roberta Antognini) and the other a collection of my own poetry. At Bard, I had the great fortune of studying trans-lation and contemporary Italian literature with William Weaver and Stephen Sartarelli, both eminent translators. At Columbia, I planned to complete a dissertation on the figure of the beloved woman as a spiritual catalyst in modern Italian literature — Eugenio Montale's Clizia, for example, who was based upon Irma Brandeis (1905–1990), the *dantista* who taught at Bard College and who wrote *The Ladder of Vision* (1962). While the topic is dissimilar from the scholarship I would eventually publish, I now understand the trajectory of this interest which felicitously brought me to study Dante with Teodolinda Barolini.

As an undergraduate, I had worked for many years at the Stevenson Library. High in a second-floor alcove in the antiquated part of the

1

library, I spent several hours unpacking and reshelving — and reading — Irma Brandeis's personal library, most of her tomes marked with an 'Ex Libris' stamp depicting the Florentine *duomo*. Dante's poetry, it was first surmised by my naïve eye, held a fictional world that was in turn held and examined by another world, that of living scholars, translators, and poets intent on recreating it. In my senior year, I took one course on Dante with the medievalist Karen Sullivan, now Irma Brandeis Professor of Romance Literature and Culture, and was taken in more by the *Vita nuova* than by the *Commedia*, which we read only in part. I understood the *Vita nuova* then as a personal memoir of poetic craft and juvenile infatuation. Beatrice and Brandeis came to represent women whose intelligence and authority inspired poets in my young configurations of medieval literature and the study thereof. Like the special alcove where I was dismantling the Brandeis collection box by dusty box, I wanted to research these women and learn more about their historical, scholarly and poetic worlds.

In August 1999, I decided to prepare myself for fall courses by reading *The Undivine Comedy*. The preface struck me, especially its first two sentences: 'One thinks of strange things reading the *Commedia*: that Dante's spires of poetic life — terza rima — bear a resemblance to modern science's spires of biological life, DNA; that his long obsession with the new is echoed in current research on the brain, which shows that the new things that we live actually become who we are. Dante is no naturalist, but he is the ultimate realist, preoccupied with rendering reality — even surreality — in language, "sì che dal fatto il dir non sia diverso"'.[1] Here was a scholar who not only knew the world of Dante studies, but one who commanded a knowledge of Dante's craft that could decode its marvelous texture. Her pages reintroduced me to Dante as a human poet, a mortal *fabbro*. Her book did not just pull back the curtain of Dante's subtle narrative art but showed me how the curtain was made.

No longer in New York but in the land of *gente nuova* in northern Virginia, I now find myself in dialogue with my students at George

---

[1]   Teodolinda Barolini, *The Undivine Comedy: Detheologizing Dante* (Princeton: Princeton University Press, 1992), p. ix, hereafter *UDC*. Subsequent references given in parentheses in the main text.

Mason, a nearly minority-majority institution with a plural religious profile. Many of my students are Muslim; some have even come from Iran, where they are forbidden to read Dante. To present them with the *Commedia* solely as the reflection of a Christian afterlife would exclude a large population of the student body. In this context, the method of *The Undivine Comedy* is essential to bringing students to Dante and to making him accessible within their *forma mentis*. They understand the idea of a virtual reality and of world-building. For non-Christian students, *The Undivine Comedy* makes Dante's afterlife less forbidden, because they have been allowed to detheologize and thus do not feel that they are supposed to take his vision at face value. Though assigning my students *The Undivine Comedy* sometimes solicits the reaction of the pilgrim in front of the Gate of Hell — 'il senso lor m'è duro' — they develop the ability to pose critical questions about Dante's vision of the afterlife to gain both an appreciation of his mastery as well as confidence in their readerly skills. This is the spirit of detheologizing, as Barolini writes it: 'Detheologizing is not antitheological ... [but] a way of reading that attempts to break out of the hermeneutic guidelines that Dante has structured into his poem' (*UDC*, p. 17).

Those who have not had the privilege to study with Barolini in person can enjoy some of that experience when reading *The Undivine Comedy*. Her 350-page *lectura dantis* mirrors the sweeping, comprehensive approach that she adopts in the classroom: a guided, intense reading that leads to a deep knowledge of the text. Students at Columbia then also had the benefit of studying with Joan Ferrante, her advisor, whose broad perspectives of continental medieval literature and history in which she contextualized Dante's poetic project complemented Barolini's granular study of the text. I would not have traded my rigorous study with them for anything else.

From historical women who inspired men's verse, I had arrived in a sphere where women professed Dante with authority and command (imagine my surprise once I left the *nido* of Columbia). Barolini and Ferrante taught us to question the commonplaces of Dante criticism, to read 'against the grain', as Barolini likes to say. We could, and should, refute the facile binary of salvation and damnation, research Dante's sources and his historical contexts, and overturn the misogynist narratives in scholarship that regarded female characters. Beatrice was

'loquax', for Barolini, and even — in Ferrante's phrase — the priest
of an androgynous god.[2] My scholarly journey thus began once my
standard frameworks for literature had been overturned — once that
which was divine had become undivine. The 'brash, sometimes militant' thirty-something, to use Barolini's words in these pages, became
my beloved forty-something advisor, an *ammiraglio in poppa* (to re-
phrase *Purgatorio* 30.58), who indicated the new worlds of intellectual
inquiry through her rigorous pedagogy.[3] There were, and still are, *cose
nove* to be discovered.

~

I begin with this personal reflection because the essays that follow
are at once both personal and intellectual. While several authors in
this volume are former students of Barolini (Antognini, Chida, Delmolino, DiNardo, Gragnolati, Kumar, Van Peteghem), others are her
contemporaries and friends, including the first reviewers of the book
(Barański, Psaki). This volume is not the published proceedings of the
international symposium held at the Italian Academy for Advanced
Studies to examine the legacy of *The Undivine Comedy* thirty years after
its publication (2022). *A World of Possibilities* includes new scholarship
by luminaries in the field whose contributions widely attest to the
cross-disciplinary and international breadth of *The Undivine Comedy*'s
legacy.

Published by Princeton University Press in 1992, and in Italian as
La 'Commedia' senza Dio (Feltrinelli, 2003), *The Undivine Comedy* was
a clarion call for a paradigmatic shift in reading Dante's *Commedia*, as
Ferrante writes in the epilogue:

> Thirty years ago, I was stunned by the brilliance of this book, a
> brilliance that was based on the simple but startling approach

2   Teodolinda Barolini, 'Notes toward a Gendered History of Italian Literature, with
     a Discussion of Dante's *Beatrix Loquax*', in *Dante and the Origins of Italian Literary
     Culture* (New York: Fordham University Press, 2009), pp. 360–378. Joan M. Ferrante,
     Dante's Beatrice: Priest of an Androgynous God (Binghamton, NY: State University of
     New York Press, 1992).

3   Quotations from the *Commedia* are from Dante Alighieri, *La Commedia secondo
     l'antica vulgata*, ed. by Giorgio Petrocchi, Società Dantesca Italiana, Edizione Nazio-
     nale, 2nd rev. edn, 4 vols (Florence: Le Lettere, 1994).

of focusing not on what Dante says he is doing, but on what he actually does, on how he manipulates us, forcing us to respond in his terms. Rereading the book thirty years later, I am once again overwhelmed by the striking effectiveness of looking so closely at the tools Dante uses to do this, creating tension and suspense where none should exist, using difference to enable a narrative that claims to describe unity. I am still struck by how obvious some of her points seem once she has pointed them out, not to say by how readers wrapped up in larger concepts had failed to see the most basic tools with which Dante creates his universe. *The Undivine Comedy* remains the most impressive work on the artistry of a great poet.

Thirty-three years after the publication of *The Undivine Comedy*, this volume takes a critical look at the field of Dante Studies and interrogates how it has been reconfigured. Barolini's critical intervention, which she coins as 'detheologizing', is more rigorously understood as a form of methodological recalibration. It is not, as she and others here clarify, an abandonment of theology, but a refusal to let ingrained modes of interpretation dictate the field. The distinction is subtle but vital. Her book shifts the field beyond an overdetermined reliance upon the structure of damnation and salvation and into the narrative space where the wealth of the poem is more powerfully mined.

When *The Undivine Comedy* was released in 1992, its title provoked some controversy, as Barański and Storey recall here. Some mistook it for a rejection of Dante's religiosity, an affront to faith, or a secularization of sacred text. But as she has clarified, the title — chosen by Princeton University Press — was a provocation aimed not at theology, but at the critical establishment that did not question inherited interpretive frameworks. In Italy, the translated title *La 'Commedia' senza Dio* stirred similar anxieties. The title's 'undivine' pun was not iconoclastic but methodological. It invited readers to approach the *Commedia* not as a repository of theological dogma, but as a complex fiction, to which the study of narrative and history must be applied as solvents, as Barolini explains in her essay in this book.

The importance of *The Undivine Comedy* lies not merely in the abundant insights it offers — the poetics of the new; the figures of Ulysses and Geryon for narrative transition; the heavenly paradoxes of *più e meno*; the leaps of the sacred poem — but in her insistence that we read the text closely. As she writes in her essay for this volume, Barolini believed in 'modeling what it is to read critically, using critical tools that must include an understanding of Coleridge's suspension of disbelief — and therefore also include the critic's ability to suspend the suspension of disbelief'. This call to action reverberates throughout the essays collected here, which variously take up her narratological and historicizing lenses and her critique of our 'reliance on the grid of the *Commedia*'s structure and thematics'.

Organized into five thematic sections, *A World of Possibilities* traces the impact of *The Undivine Comedy* across multiple axes: narrative, historical, visual, and theoretical. The structure reflects the capaciousness of Barolini's book and the wide reach of its influence, expanding our sense of what 'detheologizing' can cultivate in our scholarship.

Following the two solvents described by Barolini in her methodological essay, the first sections of the book are dedicated to narratological and historicized readings of the *Commedia*. The section 'Detheologize to Narrative' includes contributions by H. Wayne Storey, Roberto Antonelli, and Laura DiNardo. In 'The Intricate Weaving of *The Undivine Comedy*', Storey reminds us that *The Undivine Comedy* is to be read in whole and not in part as it magisterially analyzes the unified narrative threads spanning the *Commedia*'s three canticles, resulting in a view of Dante's poem as 'whole cloth, uncut'. The essay concludes with an analysis and an addition to Barolini's reading of Saint Francis and Saint Dominic in the Sphere of the Sun to disentangle the complex 'layering of cultural affinities' and narrative strategies within the *Commedia*.

As Roberto Antonelli writes in '*The Undivine Comedy*: Dante One and Multiple', Barolini arrives at 'original discoveries thanks to a formal interpretation in which, as compared to her predecessors, "the form is never disengaged from the content" (*UDC*, p. 17)'. Extending Barolini's method, Antonelli demonstrates how Dante employs 'camouflaging' techniques to divert attention from his narrative artistry by leveraging the complex functions of the poem's great characters and its pervasive intertextual relations. What results is an additional, theatricalized narrative that engages the reader in moral and existential considerations, to which Antonelli turns our attention in his essay.

Laura DiNardo explores how Dante-poet utilizes conditional constructions (expressions like 'if p, then q') in the *Commedia* to 'inscribe possibility into the poem' in her essay, 'Reasoning between Possibility, Fictional Reality, and Actuality: A Case Study in Detheologizing the *Commedia*'s Conditionals'. She argues that Dante employs these linguistic structures to bridge fictional reality with actuality and possibility, asserting the poem's truthfulness through a precise semantic framework. The essay provides original readings of *Inferno* 9 and 27 to demonstrate how the poet's careful use of 'se' (if) manipulates the reader's understanding of possible worlds and the story's realism. By examining Dante's engagement with the philosophy of language, DiNardo suggests that the *Commedia* functions as a testing ground for the power of conditionals in bolstering its narrative as 'a nonfalse error, a non falso errore, not a fiction that pretends to be true but a fiction that IS true' (*UDC*, p. 13).

'Detheologize to Historicize', the second section of the book, contains essays by Nassime Chida, Alberto Casadei, and George Dameron. A line of inquiry whose seeds are planted in *The Undivine Comedy*, historicizing approaches to Dante's poetry are related to the critical project of Barolini's book in ways that were subsequently explained in her essay, 'Only Historicize'.[4] In 'Detheologize to Historicize', Chida claims that by moving beyond the poem's theological framework and focusing on its formal structures, scholars can more effectively assess its historical context. Historicizing allows for new interpretations that challenge traditional understandings, such as viewing Dante as a historian who manipulated events for his own narrative — as Chida demonstrates for Guido da Montefeltro and the Romagnol families of *Inferno* 27 and for Farinata's account of the Battle of Montaperti in *Inferno* 10.

'Teodolinda Barolini and the Signs of Newness in *The Undivine Comedy*' by Alberto Casadei discusses the poem as a 'non-false error' or a 'truth that has the face of a lie' vis-à-vis the assertion that Dante blends poetic invention with what he believed to be a genuine vision. The text revisits Barolini's evaluation of previous critical approaches

---

4   Teodolinda Barolini, '"Only Historicize": History, Material Culture (Food, Clothes, Books), and the Future of Dante Studies', *Dante Studies*, 127 (2009), pp. 37–54.

to Dante, such as those of Nardi and Singleton, and suggests that Dante's initial cantos of *Inferno* may reflect an earlier, evolving stage of his thought. Casadei emphasizes the need for an historically sensitive reading that appreciates the chronology behind the *Commedia*'s poetic composition.

George Dameron examines Dante Alighieri's involvement in Florentine politics and military actions, particularly his role in disrupting food supplies to Florence during his exile (1302–1304), a period of severe food scarcity, in 'Dante's War: Exiles, *carestia*, and Conflict in the Florentine Countryside, 1301–1304'. Dameron contrasts these actions with the ideals of good governance and communal nourishment that Dante espoused in the *Convivio* and the *Commedia*. His essay also explores the symbolism of food and hunger in Dante's writings, notably in the portrayal of Count Ugolino in *Inferno* 33, suggesting a possible self-reflection on Dante's part regarding his earlier participation in weaponizing food. Taking inspiration from 'Only Historicize', Dameron's approach emphasizes the importance of historical context in understanding Dante's poetry, an approach first encouraged for readings of this canto by Barolini in *The Undivine Comedy* (*UDC*, p. 97).

The next section, 'Detheologize to Retheologize', confronts the misguided perception that 'detheologizing' excludes theology from interpretations of Dante. This section demonstrates, on the contrary, that Barolini's approach can help bring into focus the poet's distinctive strategies of theologizing. Grace Delmolino's 'Dante's Lucy in the Canon Law of Consent' evinces Dante's original characterization of Lucy in the *Commedia*. Lucy's story played a prominent role in legal and theological discussions of rape and the will. Comparing Dante's poem with sources in Gratian and Aquinas, Dante's Lucia no longer appears as a mediating figure, but as an embodiment of authority.

Giuseppe Ledda's essay, 'Prophetic Models and Structures in an *Undivine Comedy*', expands upon chapter 7 of Barolini's book and its analysis of Dante's prophetic identity. Ledda argues that 'detheologizing' does not negate the religious dimension of Dante's work but rather uncovers the literary and poetic strategies used to construct the illusion of theological truth. Dante both aligned with and distinguished himself from the medieval visionary tradition through his unique prophetic self-fashioning in which he asserted his authority as a divinely inspired poet.

'Divining *The Undivine Comedy*: Reflections and Recollections' by Zygmunt G. Barański offers a personal reflection on the intellectual influence of Teodolinda Barolini, focusing on *The Undivine Comedy*. One of the first reviewers of the book, Barański explains the originality and significance of *The Undivine Comedy* in its challenge to established modes of interpretations. This essay celebrates *The Undivine Comedy*'s enduring influence on Dante scholarship and its pivotal role in shifting critical perspectives within American Dantism.

The section 'Detheologize to Dramatize' collects essays that treat the poet's role in visualizing fictional worlds, whether the images evoked on the Terrace of Pride or the scenes of rape from Ovid's *Metamorphoses*. Further, the poet renders corporeal and visceral the experiences of love in his poetry in ways that are pointedly erotic and distinctive from contemporary medieval literature. Lina Bolzoni's essay, 'Dante and "visibile parlare"', examines Dante's poetic and visual project on the Terrace of Pride. Taking inspiration from chapter 6 of *The Undivine Comedy*, Bolzoni explores Dante's vivid descriptions to make the unseen tangible and comprehensible to his readers, effectively competing with divine creation in his mimesis. She traces Dante's intentional blurring of boundaries between divine art and his own representation, acknowledging the risks of such a challenge to divine authority, and draws our attention to how the poet educates the reader to engage their senses and emotions.

In 'Ovidio senza Dio: Ovidian Myth and Sexual Violence in the *Commedia*', Julie Van Peteghem surveys how medieval readers, particularly Dante, interpreted sexual violence in Ovid's *Metamorphoses*, contrasting Dante's approach with prevailing medieval commentaries. While earlier commentators often allegorized or omitted explicit mentions of rape and sexual assault, focusing on moral or biological meanings, Van Peteghem demonstrates that Dante's *Commedia* confronts these themes differently, especially through the myth of Salmacis and Hermaphroditus. Dante diverged from the medieval tradition by portraying such violence more explicitly, even infusing sexualized imagery into his descriptions of transformation and punishment in the cantos of the thieves (*Inferno* 24–25).

Elena Lombardi's 'In Praise of Detheologizing' celebrates the liberating joy of rediscovering Dante after the publication of *The Undivine Comedy* and its call for a shift away from a traditional, 'fundamentalist' approach that treats it as divinely inspired truth. Lombardi champions Barolini's perspective as it challenged the long-held notion of Dante as a perfect, morally unwavering author. By embracing a detheologized reading of the *Commedia*, Lombardi suggests, scholars can move beyond rigid, predetermined interpretations to appreciate his human artistry.

Manuele Gragnolati reads the paradoxical nature of heaven as poeticized in Dante's *Paradiso* in his essay, 'Heavenly Paradoxes and Their Pleasures'. Starting from Barolini's analysis of the poem's 'jumping textuality' (*UDC*, chapter 10), Gragnolati explores the third canticle's embrace of unity alongside individual difference. Drawing on feminist and queer scholars such as Julia Kristeva and Leo Bersani, Gragnolati affirms that this textual experience reproduces the 'paradoxical pleasure not only of losing but also finding oneself'.

The final section of the book engages *The Undivine Comedy* as a theoretical lens through which one can analyze the poem's modern reception and translations. F. Regina Psaki's contribution, 'The Role of the Reader in Actualizing the *Commedia*', meditates upon how Dante's epic poem perpetuates itself through its readers. Psaki argues that Dante deliberately engages and forms his audience, transforming them from passive recipients into active 'soundboxes' where the poem's themes and linguistic innovations resonate and persist across generations. Modern translations, particularly those by Mary Jo Bang, exemplify this ongoing actualization, making the *Commedia* accessible and relevant to contemporary readers by bridging the gap between Dante's historical context and our own 'postmodern, post-9/11, Internet-ubiquitous present'.

'From Detheologizing to Decolonizing: Toward a Reading of Dante and Alterity' by Akash Kumar proposes that 'detheologizing' the poem opens it to 'decolonized' readings. Drawing inspiration from chapter 2 of *The Undivine Comedy*, Kumar encourages readers to challenge the ingrained Eurocentric and nationalist views of Dante, whose poetry embodies his 'love of difference'. Kumar draws our attention to the reception of Dante's poem by Caribbean poets Derek Walcott and

Lorna Goodison, whose adaptations foreground linguistic difference and political rebellion. Kumar also posits that Salman Rushdie 'combines a decolonizing and detheologizing approach to the *Commedia*'.

Translator of *La 'Commedia' senza Dio: Dante e la creazione di una realtà virtuale* (Feltrinelli, 2003), Roberta Antognini delves into the complex nature of translating scholarship, while reflecting on her experience translating *The Undivine Comedy*. She analyzes the figure of Geryon from the *Inferno* as a metaphor for the intricate process through which a new text emerges from its original. The embodiment of transition and the 'truth that has the face of falsehood', Geryon symbolizes the delicate balance translators must strike between fidelity to the source and creating a fluid target text.

This volume — *A World of Possibilities: The Legacy of 'The Undivine Comedy'* — emerges from the conviction that Barolini's work opened not a path but a field. That field has grown beyond the contours of any single method, and the essays collected here demonstrate just how widely her influence has reached: across continents, disciplines, and generations. I offer this book not as a Festschrift in the traditional sense, but as a constellation of encounters with the legacy of *The Undivine Comedy*: critical, methodological, pedagogical, and, most deeply, readerly and personal.

I heartily thank Manuele Gragnolati and Christoph Holzhey of ICI Berlin Press for their belief in this project from its earliest stages and their collaboration on the manuscript. Their editorial vision created the perfect home for this special volume. It is due to them and to Louisa Elderton and Claudia Peppel, who provided patient guidance in the book's production and creative design, that this book became a reality. My gratitude extends to Zygmunt Barański for his friendship and support, as ever, and to Martin G. Eisner, whose many contributions to our discussions on *The Undivine Comedy* inform this volume. Finally, my deepest thanks to Laura DiNardo who translated several essays in this volume, and to Bridget Pupillo who copyedited each essay with expertise and precision.

ON METHOD

Possible Worlds and Reading Dante's *Commedia*
Suspension of Disbelief (Coleridge, Horace, Tolkien, Cecco d'Ascoli) and the Solvents of Narrative and History

TEODOLINDA BAROLINI

In 1817, Samuel Taylor Coleridge, English poet, literary critic, philosopher, and theologian, published an autobiographical treatise on aesthetic theory in which he coined the now canonical phrase 'willing suspension of disbelief'. Outlining a project undertaken by him and William Wordsworth, in which Coleridge was assigned supernatural topics and Wordsworth everyday topics, he describes his own task thus:

> My endeavours should be directed to persons and characters supernatural, or at least romantic; yet so as to transfer from our inward nature a human interest and a semblance of truth sufficient to procure for these shadows of imagination that willing suspension of disbelief for the moment, which constitutes poetic faith.[1]

---

1 Samuel Taylor Coleridge, *Biographia Literaria*, 1817, Chapter 14, §1. See the edition *Biographia Literaria*, ed. by James Engell and W. Jackson Bate, 2 vols (Princeton: Princeton University Press, 1983), II, p. 6, now in *The Collected Works of Samuel Taylor Coleridge*, 16 vols (Princeton: Princeton University Press, 1969–2001), VII (1985), pp. 1–856 (p. 6).

The issue of how a poet transfers 'a semblance of truth' to the 'shadows of imagination', in order to procure for those shadows 'that willing suspension of disbelief for the moment, which constitutes poetic faith', is deeply relevant to the study of Dante. The issue of 'poetic faith' speaks directly to Dante and to the history of Dante criticism, which has traditionally responded to Dante's poem as though what it describes were empirically real.

Coleridge's essay on Dante in his 'Lecture X' shows considerable knowledge of *Inferno* and enthusiastic appreciation of Dante's poetry.[2] While on the one hand he does not think that Dante effects the combination of poetry with doctrine 'nearly as well as Milton' ('LX', p. 150), on the other hand he has great praise for Dante's poetry, which excels Milton's in matters of 'Style': with respect to Dante's 'Style — the vividness, logical connexion, strength and energy of which cannot be surpassed', writes Coleridge, 'in this I think Dante superior to Milton' ('LX', p. 151). Coleridge continues to enumerate 'Dante's chief excellences as a poet' ('LX', p. 151), proceeding to Dante's 'Images', 'taken from obvious nature' ('LX', p. 152), his 'profoundness', exemplified by *Inferno* 3 ('LX', p. 152), his 'picturesqueness', in which 'Dante is beyond all other poets, modern or ancient' ('LX', p. 153). To Dante's picturesqueness Coleridge connects a further category, 'the topographic reality of Dante's journey through Hell' ('LX', p. 155). The features of Dante's poetic craft highlighted by Coleridge, in particular its ability to create the 'topographic reality' of Hell, focus on precisely those elements used by Dante to trigger the 'willing suspension of disbelief' with respect to the supernatural.[3]

Whether or not Coleridge was conscious of being drawn toward features of Dante's poetry that aid in creating the willing suspension

---

2   See Samuel Taylor Coleridge, *Coleridge's Miscellaneous Criticism*, ed. by Thomas Middleton Raynor (Cambridge: Harvard University Press, 1936), pp. 131–90, hereafter 'LX'. Subsequent references given in parentheses in the main text. The 'Dante' section of 'Lecture X', dated to 1818, encompasses pp. 145–57.

3   Coleridge goes on to discuss 'Dante's power, — his absolute mastery over, although rare exhibition of, the pathetic' ('LX', p. 156) and concludes his list of Dante's excellences by stating: 'As to going into the endless subtle beauties of Dante, that is impossible' ('LX', p. 156). Coleridge read *Inferno* attentively: while the example of Dante's mastery of the pathetic leads him to the obvious choice of Francesca in *Inferno* 5, his example of one of the 'endless subtle beauties' is the far-from-obvious first tercet of *Inferno* 29 ('LX', p. 156).

of disbelief with respect to the supernatural, I am unequipped to say. I can say that the history of Dante scholarship has not taken Coleridge's remarkable formulation to heart, or even into consideration. Although the years have passed and the phrase first published by Coleridge in 1817 has become ubiquitous in the Anglophone context, it has not successfully migrated from the English literary tradition to that of other national literatures.

The English poet's phrase has become a well-worn trope among English speakers. As Michael Tomko writes in his book *Beyond the Willing Suspension of Disbelief: Poetic Faith from Coleridge to Tolkien*: 'The "willing suspension of disbelief" is a phrase, like Freudian slip or Pavlovian response, that has made the rare transition from high intellectual discourse to pop culture, appearing everywhere from television commercials to the floor of the US Congress.'[4] The 'willing suspension of disbelief', now accepted among English speakers as a commonplace, is nourished particularly in discussions among the makers of films and television shows and video games, in the context of their efforts at 'worldbuilding'. An interview with a director or a game creator will frequently produce Coleridge's phrase, along with a reference to 'worldbuilding', a term that, according to Wikipedia, 'was first used in the *Edinburgh Review* in December 1820',[5] shortly after the publication of Coleridge's 'suspension of disbelief'. Likewise, entertainment magazines contain advice on how to produce the suspension of disbelief in one's audience.[6]

Another text frequently cited along with Coleridge's 'suspension of disbelief' is Roland Barthes's 1968 essay 'L'Effet de Réel'.[7] Barthes's article on the reality effect is, alas, also a classic example of the silo effect, for it does not mention Coleridge. The concrete detail that makes

---

4 Michael Tomko, *Beyond the Willing Suspension of Disbelief: Poetic Faith from Coleridge to Tolkien*, New Directions in Religion and Literature (London: Bloomsbury Academic, 2016), p. 1.

5 See 'Worldbuilding', Wikipedia, 5 April 2025 <https://en.wikipedia.org/wiki/Worldbuilding> [accessed 11 April 2025].

6 See, for example, an instruction to the would-be director in Suzy Woltmann, 'How to Make Audiences Suspend Their Disbelief', *Backstage*, 18 April 2023 <https://www.backstage.com/magazine/article/suspension-of-disbelief-75754/> [accessed 11 April 2025].

7 Roland Barthes, 'L'Effet de Réel', *Communications*, 11 (1968), pp. 84–89.

the reader experience the 'real' is exemplified with a detail from a novel of Flaubert and a brief discussion of the Alexandrians and their cultivation of ekphrasis. The semiotician's is fundamentally a rhetorical approach, and he never cites Coleridge's more philosophical discussion. None of this is surprising; we are all drawn to what we know best. In *Beyond the Willing Suspension of Disbelief*, Tomko minutely discusses responses of literary theorists and scholars of English literature to Coleridge's formulation, focusing in particular on scholars of Shakespeare and drama: 'Finally, aesthetic illusion raises pressing political questions. What are the dangers of believing in an aesthetic illusion, of being charmed by Prospero?'.[8]

To a Dante scholar, much of what these critics discuss seems far more relevant to Dante than to Shakespeare. The idea that 'the poet or dramatist has the powers not of a creator, but of the Creator'[9] reminds me of how I end the first chapter of *The Undivine Comedy*: 'What follows is an attempt to analyse the textual metaphysics that makes the *Commedia*'s truth claims credible and to show how the illusion is constructed, forged, made — by a man who is precisely, after all, "only" a *fabbro*, a maker ... a poet'.[10] We will come back to the issue of the author-creator when we reach Tolkien's theory of the 'sub-creator'. For now, let us note again the results of the silo effect. Despite a note in which Tomko says, à propos a comment of Walter Abrams, that 'Dante is a locus classicus of this debate',[11] there is no engagement in Tomko's book with Dante or with a debate on Dante. Given that the reception of the *Commedia* shows that its critics succumb to the ideological premises of the poem in an acritical fashion, a more sustained infusion of the willingness to suspend the suspension of disbelief, to engage in what Tomko calls 'the willing resumption of disbelief', would be helpful to the progress of Dante studies.[12]

---

8   Tomko, *Beyond*, p. 7.
9   Ibid., p. 9.
10   Teodolinda Barolini, *The Undivine Comedy: Detheologizing Dante* (Princeton: Princeton University Press, 1992), p. 20, hereafter *UDC*. Subsequent references given in parentheses in the main text.
11   Tomko, *Beyond*, p. 16, note 6.
12   Tomko's third and final chapter is titled 'The Willing Resumption of Disbelief', pp. 109–44.

It did not occur to me when I was writing *The Undivine Comedy* in the late 1980s that I should overtly stipulate the importance of Coleridge's formula for my interpretive practice. Rather, I took it for granted and embedded it in my analysis. The first use of Coleridge's phrase in *The Undivine Comedy* hails from the theoretical first chapter, 'Detheologizing Dante: Realism, Reception, and the Resources of Narrative'. The importance of Coleridge's formula for my thinking is clear, because this sentence is a manifesto regarding the basic premises of the book: 'The history of the *Commedia*'s reception offers a sustained demonstration of our narrative credulity, our readerly incapacity to suspend our suspension of disbelief in front of the poet-creator's masterful deployment of what are essentially techniques of verisimilitude' (*UDC*, p. 16). My second reference to the suspension of disbelief occurs in the context of a discussion of what I dub 'the Geryon principle'.[13] Noting that the episodes featuring the hybrid monster Geryon are 'the most exposed weapons in a massive and unrelenting campaign to coerce our suspension of disbelief' (*UDC*, p. 61), I comment that this is 'a campaign that the history of the *Commedia*'s reception shows to have been remarkably successful' (*UDC*, p. 61). My last reference to Coleridge's formulation belongs to chapter 7's discussion of visions:

> But Dante differs from other medieval visionaries in at least one fundamental respect, namely, the immensity of his poetic gift: a gift that, paradoxically, induces subconscious suspensions of disbelief in his readers on the one hand and prevents them from taking him seriously as a visionary on the other. (*UDC*, p. 143)

Given that dreams and visions are one of the most obvious 'supernatural' elements in Dante's poem, the context indicates again the degree to which Coleridge speaks to the core issues of reading and interpreting the *Commedia*.

Horace's *Ars Poetica* offered Dante a handbook on writing fiction, a narrative primer that openly and immediately tackles the topic of readerly belief. Horace begins his little treatise by emphasizing the

---

13   For the Geryon principle, see *UDC*, pp. 15, 60, 90, 98, and 271, note 33.

need to avoid writing about things that are so unnatural they cannot command audience belief, such as a human head on a horse's neck:[14]

> Humano capiti cervicem pictor equinam
> iungere si velit, et varias inducere plumas
> undique collatis membris, ut turpiter atrum
> desinat in piscem mulier formosa superne,
> spectatum admissi risum teneatis, amici?

> (If a painter chose to join a human head to the neck of a horse, and to spread feathers of many a hue over limbs picked up now here now there, so that what at the top is a lovely woman ends below in a black and ugly fish, could you, my friends, if favored with a private view, refrain from laughing?) (*Ars Poetica*, 1–5)[15]

These verses must have hit Dante forcibly; they are, indeed, the Roman author's version of the Geryon principle. Dante's monster Geryon is a hybrid of a just man's head on a serpent's trunk with a lion's hairy arms and paws and a scorpion's tail: he is as unnatural and unbelievable as Horace's evocation of a human head on a horse's neck that is covered with multi-coloured plumage and ends in the tail of a black fish.

There are clear points of overlap between Horace's unbelievable monster with its fish's tail and Dante's unbelievable monster with his scorpion's tail. Most notable to me is Horace's reference to 'varias [...] plumas' ('feathers of many a hue') in verse 2, which finds an echo in Dante's description of the colourful textile designs — the rhetorical colours — that embroider Geryon's flanks:

> lo dosso e 'l petto e ambedue le coste
> dipinti avea di nodi e di rotelle.

---

14   Zygmunt Barański notes that 'by the fourteenth century any reference to or excerpt from the description of the monster at the beginning of the *Ars Poetica* would have been associated with the basic rules of poetic composition, in particular, "quid vitandum, deinde quid tenendum sit" ("what to avoid, then what to adhere to")'; see 'Magister satiricus: Preliminary Notes on Dante, Horace and the Middle Ages', in *Language and Style in Dante*, ed. by John C. Barnes and Michelangelo Zaccarello (Dublin: Four Courts Press, 2013), pp. 13–61 (p. 19).

15   Horace, *Satires, Epistles and Ars Poetica*, ed. and trans. by H. Rushton Fairclough, Loeb Classical Library, 194 (London: William Heinemann, and Cambridge, MA: Harvard University Press, 1970).

Con più color, sommesse e sovraposte
non fer mai drappi Tartari né Turchi,
né fuor tai tele per Aragne imposte.

(his back and chest as well as both his flanks
had been adorned with twining knots and circlets.
   No Turks or Tartars ever fashioned fabrics
more colorful in background and relief,
nor had Arachne ever loomed such webs.)
(*Inf.* 17.14–18)[16]

Returning to the same point about artists and authors who insist on outrageous and unnatural — 'supernatural' — elements in their works, Horace repeats his earlier admonition with new examples: 'The man who tries to vary a single subject in monstrous fashion, is like a painter adding a dolphin to the woods, a boar to the waves' (*Ars Poetica*, 29–30).

Horace and Dante, however, describe themselves quite differently with respect to reader response. Dante presents himself as hyper-sensitive to potential readerly criticism while Horace displays an urbane and somewhat callous wit. Thus, the arrival out of the abyss of the unbelievable monster Geryon leads not to the imagined laughter of Horace's readers but to a very Dantean meditation on the imagined shame — *vergogna* — that will necessarily be incurred by an author who insists that he is telling the truth when what he is saying cannot be believed:

Sempre a quel ver c'ha faccia di menzogna
de' l'uom chiuder le labbra fin ch'el puote,
però che sanza colpa fa vergogna;
   ma qui tacer nol posso; e per le note
di questa comedìa, lettor, ti giuro,
s'elle non sien di lunga grazia vòte,
   ch'i' vidi per quell' aere grosso e scuro
venir notando una figura in suso,
maravigliosa ad ogne cor sicuro [...]

---

16   Quotations from the *Commedia* are from Dante Alighieri: *La Commedia secondo l'antica vulgata*, ed. by Giorgio Petrocchi, Società Dantesca Italiana, Edizione Nazionale, 2nd rev. edn, 4 vols (Florence: Le Lettere, 1994). Translations into English, with modifications at times for clarity, are from Dante Alighieri, *The Divine Comedy*, trans. by Allen Mandelbaum, 3 vols (Berkeley: University of California Press, 1980–82).

(Faced with that truth which seems a lie, a man
should always close his lips as long as he can —
to tell it shames him, even though he's blameless;
    but here I can't be still; and by the lines
of this my Comedy, reader, I swear —
and may my verse find favor for long years —
    that through the dense and darkened air I saw
a figure swimming, rising up, enough
to bring amazement to the firmest heart [...])
(*Inf.* 16.124–32)

Perhaps the most important for Dante of Horace's lessons is 'Either follow tradition, or invent what is self-consistent' (*Ars Poetica*, 119). Dante chose to invent consistently. And he does so realistically, thus hewing to another Horatian precept: 'Fictions meant to please should be close to the real' (*Ars Poetica*, 338).

    Coleridge's famous formulation has been applied far beyond the 'supernatural, or at least romantic' category for which it was designated, but it has not been systematically invoked with respect to Dante, who actually describes the supernatural. In the context of the interpretation of the *Commedia*, a text that deals precisely and realistically with the supernatural, we need to be more persistent in modelling, for new generations of readers, what it is to read critically, using critical tools that include Coleridge's suspension of disbelief. While, as Tomko shows, scholars of English literature engage in a discussion of the perils of suspending disbelief, a suspension that can make one more gullible to political propaganda, scholars of Italian literature have traditionally not given the matter much thought, certainly not with respect to Dante's poem. Thus, the article 'Worldbuilding' in English Wikipedia begins its 'History' section with Dante ('One of the earliest examples of a fictional world is Dante's *Divine Comedy*, with the BBC's Dante 2021 series describing it as "the first virtual reality"'), and then moves on to English authors who discuss fantasy and to Tolkien's essay 'On Fairy-Stories'.[17] It is noteworthy that the article 'Worldbuilding' in Italian Wikipedia follows the English version precisely until it comes to 'History' ('Evoluzione del worldbuilding'), where it omits Dante

---

17   'Worldbuilding', Wikipedia.

completely and moves directly to the English fantasy authors and to Tolkien's 'On Fairy-Stories'.

Many have seen points of contact between Dante and Tolkien, but this group does not include Tolkien himself, who does not mention Dante in his much-cited essay 'On Fairy-Stories'. To both Tolkien's essay and his omission of Dante I will return, because I believe there is much we can learn from Tolkien's failure to acknowledge his medieval precursor. We see a willingness to acknowledge the general kinship between Dante's work and that of fantasy writers in a project like *The Palgrave Encyclopedia of the Possible*, a work to which I was invited to contribute in May 2021. The charge was to examine 'how your topic relates to the possible/possibility', and the result was my essay on 'the possible *Divine Comedy*'.[18] Very suggestive was the working Table of Contents that the editor had included with his invitation, showing me a world in which many of the subjects listed were rich in Dantean themes (e.g., Counterfactual Thinking, Determinism, Dialogism, Dreams, Ecstasy) and in which Dante was included alongside fantasy writers like Asimov and Tolkien. However, the finished *Encyclopedia* was disappointing in this regard, since it contains almost no authors, omitting even the essential poet of the possible, Ovid. Coleridge is not mentioned, and the phrase 'suspension of disbelief' appears only in my essay.

Although I was unacquainted with the field of possible studies, I was primed to accept the invitation to contribute to *The Palgrave Encyclopedia of the Possible* by my familiarity with the concept of possible worlds. Indeed, I had recognized the value of this concept for Dante studies in *The Undivine Comedy*, which refers nine times to the 'possible world' that Dante is creating, three times in the methodological first chapter.[19] The most significant of the usages in chapter 1 is another manifesto moment, like the one cited above for 'suspension of disbelief': 'The *Commedia* makes narrative believers of us all. By this I mean that we accept the possible world (as logicians call it) that Dante has invented; we do not question its premises or assumptions

18   Teodolinda Barolini, 'The Possible *Divine Comedy*', in *The Palgrave Encyclopedia of the Possible*, ed. by Vlad P. Glăveanu (Cham: Palgrave Macmillan, 2022), pp. 437–44.

19   The expression 'possible world' occurs in *UDC* on pages 15, 16, 18 (chapter 1), 22, 35, 46 (chapter 2), 98 (chapter 4), 188 (chapter 8), and 219 (chapter 10).

except on its own terms' (*UDC*, p. 16). All art in all time is engaged
in creating virtual realities, but not all art is equal, in this respect as
in others. Ovid writes that art conceals its own art — 'ars adeo latet
arte sua' (*Metam.* 10.252) — and in the *Commedia* Dante masterfully
conceals his artfulness, building his possible world through manifold
and continuous narrative micro-strategies that conceal themselves and
surreptitiously take hold of the reader's mind. For the genius of Dante's
poetry is (also) 'its ability to construct a textual metaphysics so en-
veloping that it prevents us from analyzing the conditions that give rise
to the illusion that such a metaphysics is possible' (*UDC*, p. 20).

Chapter 1 of *The Undivine Comedy*'s ten chapters is titled 'Detheologizing Dante' and explains detheologizing as a method of reading (I
shall elaborate on detheologizing as a method further on). The subtitle,
'Realism, Reception, and the Resources of Narrative', focuses on what
we must take into consideration in order to suspend the suspension of
disbelief and thereby to arrive at a proper appreciation of *how* Dante
forged his realism: 'In this chapter I will trace, in broad outline, the
history of our recent handling of what I take to be the fundamental
question for all readers of Dante's poem: How are we to respond to
the poet's insistence that he is telling us the truth?' (*UDC*, p. 4). In
the spirit of that query, the first chapter analyses the major twentieth-
century criticism devoted to Dante's modes of signifying, explaining
why I consider the issue of truth claims to be the common denominator
that subtends previous discussions and pointing to the parallelisms
in the positions of two scholars from different critical traditions, the
Italian Nardi and the American Singleton: 'it is my belief that Nardi's
contributions regarding "Dante profeta" and Singleton's regarding the
Commedia's use of the allegory of theologians are essentially complementary. [...] These two traditions are in effect parallel ways of
discussing the one central issue of the poet's truth claims' (*UDC*, p. 5).

Revolving around the ancient dichotomy of Dante-*poeta* versus
Dante-*theologus*, the first chapter of *The Undivine Comedy* offers an
expansive examination of critical theories regarding Dante's modes of
signifying, moving from Nardi and Singleton to Auerbach, Hollander,
Padoan, Spitzer, and Freccero, among others, and invoking Augustine
along the way: 'Augustine discredits the common misapprehension
that a "prophet" cannot also be a "poet", that one who is inspired

need not also attend to the "how" of language and rhetoric' (*UDC*, p. 11). The discussion lingers on the so-called allegory of poets versus the allegory of theologians because this terminology dominated the twentieth-century debate on Dantean allegory in North America. The critical lexicon derives from the *Convivio*'s terminology for allegorical signifying: on the one hand, allegory of poets is man-made and invented, what we call personification allegory; on the other hand, allegory of theologians is intrinsic, historically based, and divine, what we — following Auerbach — call figural allegory. This issue is reprised in chapter 7, which turns to the *Commedia*'s relationship to vision literature and discusses Dante's dense interweaving of both modes of allegory — personification allegory and figural allegory — in the procession of the earthly paradise (see *UDC*, p. 158).

The successive nine chapters seek to analyse what Dante created, focusing on the particular tools in the poet's toolkit of realism. These tools are necessarily made of language: tropes, elements of rhetoric, as in the chart appended at the end of chapter 9, 'The Heaven of the Sun as a Meditation on Narrative', where I show how Dante balances the rhetorical tropes used to create the illusion of equality in the eulogies of Saints Francis and Dominic (*Paradiso* 11 and 12). Dante's toolkit is massively metapoetic, including addresses to the reader (the classic essays by Auerbach and Spitzer are discussed in chapter 1) and ekphrasis, most evidently on display in *Purgatorio* 10–12 and analysed in chapter 6, 'Re-presenting What God Presented: The Arachnean Art of the Terrace of Pride'. The Table of Contents below shows the trajectory from the theoretical first chapter to three chapters devoted to *Inferno* (chapters 2–4), three chapters devoted to *Purgatorio* (chapters 5–7), and three chapters devoted to *Paradiso* (chapters 8–10). *The Undivine Comedy* thus proceeds through the *Commedia* thematically and chronologically, following the order of the poem itself:

CHAPTER 1
    Detheologizing Dante: Realism, Reception, and the
    Resources of Narrative

CHAPTER 2
    Infernal Incipits: The Poetics of the New

CHAPTER 3
Ulysses, Geryon, and the Aeronautics of Narrative Transition

CHAPTER 4
Narrative and Style in Lower Hell

CHAPTER 5
Purgatory as Paradigm: Traveling the New and Never-Before-Traveled Path of This Life/Poem

CHAPTER 6
Re-presenting What God Presented: The Arachnean Art of the Terrace of Pride

CHAPTER 7
Nonfalse Errors and the True Dream of the Evangelist

CHAPTER 8
Problems in Paradise: The Mimesis of Time and the Paradox of *più e meno*

CHAPTER 9
The Heaven of the Sun as a Meditation on Narrative

CHAPTER 10
The Sacred Poem Is Forced to Jump: Closure and the Poetics of Enjambment

The Undivine Comedy is at the core a narratological and rhetorical study, a book that analyses the poet's narrative techniques and his techniques of verisimilitude. Thus, it offers a sustained analysis of what I present as two alternating narrative modes. The narrative or default mode is discursive (encompassing philosophical expositions), logical, linear, 'chronologized', and intellective; it is the narratological backbone of the *Commedia* as a 'realistic' journey that presents 'le vite spiritali ad una ad una' ('the lives of spirits, one by one'; *Par.* 33.24). The anti-narrative or lyrical mode, on the other hand, is non-discursive, non-linear or circular, 'dechronologized', and affective; it is used for the oneiric, the visionary, and the mystical. This mode is labelled by Dante as the 'jumping' poetics that provides the title of chapter 10 of *The Undivine Comedy* ('The Sacred Poem Is Forced to Jump: Closure and the Poetics of Enjambment') and that is announced in *Paradiso* 23: 'e così, figurando il paradiso, | convien saltar lo sacrato poema' ('And thus, in representing Paradise, | the sacred poem has to leap across; *Par.* 23.61–62). These two narrative modalities, each aligned with a particular set of tropes, together constitute the narratological skein of the *Commedia*. The poet alternates between them, in varying degrees according to *cantica*, as explained in this passage from the end of chapter 7:

> Looking at the *Commedia* as a whole, we could say that the *Inferno* is composed mainly in the straightforward 'realistic' manner, with the significant exception of the first part of canto 1; it is important to remember that Dante chooses to begin his narrative journey with a harbinger of alternatives to his dominant mode. The *Purgatorio* introduces longer 'nonrealistic' passages, concentrated in the sections devoted to the dreams, the reliefs, the visions, and so forth; while in the *Paradiso* the ecstatic visionary mode comes into its own, and the proportion of text devoted to it increases. (*UDC*, p. 164)

Paradiso is the *cantica* in which the anti-narrative mode comes to the fore. Recently I synthesized, unpacked, and expanded *The Undivine Comedy*'s reading of the alternating narrative modes of *Paradiso* in the essay 'The One and the Many as Philosophical and Narratological Key to *Paradiso*', where I included the following chart:[20]

The Narrative Modes of *Paradiso*

Narrative or Discursive Mode	Anti-narrative or Lyrical Mode
Aristotelian *procedere*: 'Or s'i' non procedesse avanti più' (*Par.* 13.88)	Augustinian *circolare*: 'Così la circulata melodia | si sigillava' (*Par.* 23.109–10)
Linguistic 'disagguaglianza' (*Par.* 15.83)	Linguistic 'equalità' (*Par.* 15.74)
The default mode: Discursive, logical, linear, 'chronologized', intellective	Non-discursive, non-linear or circular, 'dechronologized', affective

20 Teodolinda Barolini, 'The One and the Many as Philosophical and Narratological Key to *Paradiso*', in *Letteratura permanente. Poeti, scrittori, critici per Giorgio Ficara*, ed. by Igor Candido, Chiara Fenoglio, Raffaello Palumbo Mosca, Giulia Ricca, and Daniele Santero (Milan: La nave di Teseo, 2022), pp. 127–51. In Italian: 'L'Uno e i Molti quale chiave filosofica e narratologica alla lettura del *Paradiso*', in Barolini, *Il vento di Aristotele. Saggi danteschi* (Milan: La nave di Teseo), pp. 103–26.

Characterized by narrative that has an identifiable diegetic line, the use of technical philosophical language, e.g. *solutio distinctiva*, syllogisms; similes that function as small narratives	Characterized by 'jumping' and 'time-stopping' techniques, e.g. exclamations, metaphoric language, affective similes, enjambment, chiasmus, hysteron proteron, verbal repetition, neologisms, ineffability topoi
Aristotelian: Time Is Before and After	Augustinian: Present Is an Indivisible Instant
Examples: *Par.* 24, *Par.* 32 From non-discursive mode of *Paradiso* 23 to discursive mode of *Paradiso* 24	Examples: *Par.* 23, *Par.* 33 From discursive mode of *Paradiso* 32 to non-discursive mode of *Paradiso* 33

Perhaps the most important use of 'possible world' in *The Undivine Comedy* belongs to chapter 8, the first of the *Paradiso* chapters, 'Problems in Paradise: The Mimesis of Time and the Paradox of *più e meno*'. In this passage I equate the ability to step outside of the possible world of the *Commedia* with the act of 'detheologizing': while the idea that the blessed souls stage the hierarchy of the heavens for the pilgrim's benefit 'is acceptable within the possible world of the *Commedia* (i.e. at the level of its plot), if we step outside of that world — if we detheologize our reading — then we realize that the hierarchy is a means of allowing the last canticle to exist' (*UDC*, p. 188). This sentence from chapter 8 takes us back to chapter 1, where we find a straightforward explanation of what I mean by 'detheologizing':

> The chapters that follow propose a detheologized reading of the *Commedia*. This is not to say that they eschew theology. Detheologizing is not antitheological; it is not a call to abandon theology or to excise theological concerns from Dante criticism. Rather, detheologizing is a way of reading that attempts to break out of the hermeneutic guidelines that Dante has structured into his poem, hermeneutic guidelines that result in theologized readings whose outcomes have been overdetermined by the author. Detheologizing, in other words, signifies releasing our reading of the *Commedia* from the author's grip, finding a way out of Dante's hall of mirrors. In order to accomplish this, I privilege form over content [...]. (*UDC*, p. 17)

Some of the critical misprisions engendered by the title *The Undivine Comedy* might have been avoided had readers with strongly religious views taken seriously the above passage, with its accurate and sincere insistence that 'detheologizing is not antitheological'. No one who reads the *Paradiso* chapters of my book could believe that the author of *The Undivine Comedy*, who builds so much of her argument on Thomas Aquinas's 'distinctio et multitudo rerum est a Deo' — 'the difference and multiplicity of things come from God' (*Summa Theologiae* 1a.47.1) — could be 'against theology'.

Detheologizing is a method, a way of reading. It should not be controversial, as, very surprisingly to me, the title of *The Undivine Comedy* became. *The Undivine Comedy* is a witty title, one that I gladly accepted when it was suggested by the Editorial Board of Princeton University Press. It neatly captures a key point of the book: the *Commedia* is a text written by a man, not by God, and we can best honour the extraordinary man who wrote it by unravelling *how* he did it. Let us put to one side those who took umbrage at what they apparently took as the antireligious nature of the title, a position that displays a lack of intellectual openness and also, very likely, a willingness to criticize what one has not read. My own critique of the English title is that it does not do enough to inform the reader that detheologizing is a method, the *pars destruens* — the solvent — that then allows one to construct a new way of reading. Moreover, the new way of reading, the *pars construens*, not at all represented in the English title, embraces nine of the ten chapters of the book. This, in my view, is the major deficit of the English title: both parts of the title speak to the *pars destruens*, the method, and no part of the title speaks to the nine-tenths of the book that are devoted to showing what we can discover when we apply the method — when we detheologize our reading.

The structural economy of my book is better communicated by the Italian translation of 2003,[21] and in particular by the balance of the two parts of its title: the main title, *La 'Commedia' senza Dio* ('The Commedia without God'), offers a faulty statement of the *pars destruens*, and the subtitle, *Dante e la costruzione di una realtà virtuale* ('Dante and the

---

21 *La 'Commedia' senza Dio. Dante e la creazione di una realtà virtuale*, trans. by Roberta Antognini (Milan: Feltrinelli, 2003).

construction of a virtual reality') offers an accurate statement of the *pars construens*. I do not at all care for La *'Commedia' senza Dio*, a title chosen by the press, Feltrinelli, as *The Undivine Comedy* was chosen by Princeton. Shorn of the English edition's play on words, La *'Commedia' senza Dio* is too stark and does in fact seem to be making an argument that is not at all mine. I did what I could, without success, to resist the choice. I am very proud, on the other hand, of my contribution of the Italian subtitle, *Dante e la costruzione di una realtà virtuale*, which to my knowledge is the first articulation of the now obvious fact that Dante constructed our premier virtual reality.

However, there lies a huge and irreducible chasm between the *Commedia* and fantasy fiction, between Dante and today's creators of virtual realities. A virtual reality that is explicitly couched within and based upon the tenets of one the world's great revealed religions poses a much more complex critical problem than that posed by most fantasy fiction (or indeed by Shakespeare), given that in such a case the response to the work of art — the suspension of disbelief that it provokes — is inescapably conflated in the minds of many readers with their actual belief in their actual religion. The result of the combined synergy of possible world with actual religion is a 'reality effect' that is far beyond what literature on its own can conjure. The religious content of the *Commedia* has thus understandably produced a massive challenge to the reader's critical ability to manage the poem's fiction, indeed to accept that the poem is a fiction. It is immeasurably more difficult to read a text critically, to suspend one's suspension of disbelief, when that text connects itself authoritatively, and in manifold compelling ways, to the reader's real lived religious experience.

We now turn to Tolkien and his essay 'On Fairy-Stories', which has garnered a remarkably acritical treatment from its readers, who seem to treat it more like Tolkien's fiction than like a critical essay. I find quite unpersuasive, and also quite ungenerous, Tolkien's discussion of the suspension of disbelief, in which he never names Coleridge. He cites Coleridge's precept in quotation marks and uses it as a foil against which to construct his own arguments in defence of 'Fantasy': 'Children are capable, of course, of *literary belief*, when the story-maker's art is good enough to produce it. That state of mind has been called "willing suspension of disbelief".[22] It is interesting, too, that Tolkien never mentions Dante in 'On Fairy-Stories', given that he, a medievalist, obviously knew of Dante, a writer who was so important to his friends and fellow Inklings C. S. Lewis and Charles William. Why might Tolkien choose not to mention the *Divine Comedy*? In my view, Dante's work fits Tolkien's critical categories about the 'creator' and 'sub-creator' much too well.[23] Here is the full passage that immediately follows Tolkien's citation of Coleridge's 'willing suspension of disbelief', where Tolkien outlines the relationship between what he calls the Primary World and the Secondary World:

> That state of mind has been called 'willing suspension of disbelief'. But this does not seem to me a good description of what happens. What really happens is that the story-maker proves a successful 'sub-creator'. He makes a Secondary World which your mind can enter. Inside it, what he relates is 'true': it accords with the laws of that world. You therefore believe it, while you are, as it were, inside. The moment disbelief arises, the spell is broken; the magic, or rather art, has failed. You are then out in the Primary World again, looking at the little abortive Secondary World from outside. ('OFS', p. 60)

Tolkien downgrades the work of art — and the suspension of disbelief that the work of art generates, both belonging to what he calls in the above passage 'the little abortive Secondary World' — in comparison to what he goes on to call 'the genuine thing': 'But this suspension of disbelief is a substitute for the genuine thing, a subterfuge we use when condescending to games or make-believe, or when trying (more or less willingly) to find what virtue we can in the work of an art that has for us failed' ('OFS', p. 61).

Dante likewise downgrades the human work of art in comparison to God's art. We know this, and we understand that such downgrading

---

22 J. R. R. Tolkien, 'On Fairy-Stories', *The Tolkien Reader* (New York: Ballantine Books, 1966), pp. 31–99 (p. 60), hereafter 'OFS'. Subsequent references given in parentheses in the main text. For the record, as a lover of Tolkien's fantasy fiction in my youth, I was taken aback by his lack of generosity toward Coleridge when I discovered it in writing this essay.

23 Tolkien, who was averse to allegory and a champion of history, was in fact far closer to Dante as a narrator than he was to Lewis. See p. xv of Tolkien's 'Foreword to the Second Edition' of *The Fellowship of the Ring*, in J. R. R. Tolkien, *The Fellowship of the Ring*, 2nd edn (Boston: Houghton Mifflin, 1966).

is built into Dante's ideological premises. Dante is actually more open than Tolkien about both his ideological premises and about the ways in which he himself, as creator, is likely to flout them. This flouting takes shape as the Ulysses theme of the *Commedia*, analysed first in chapter 3 of *The Undivine Comedy*, 'Ulysses, Geryon, and the Aeronautics of Narrative Transition', and subsequently never absent from my reading. Chapter 6, 'Re-presenting What God Presented: The Arachnean Art of the Terrace of Pride', is particularly relevant to this part of our discussion, since it analyses Dante's wilful transgression of the medieval mimetic hierarchy to which he offers explicit allegiance. At the top of the hierarchy is God, the creator. Under God are, first, nature, which imitates God, and, second, human art or techne, which imitates nature.[24]

Discussions of Tolkien's critique of Coleridge seem to shy away from acknowledging Tolkien's ideological premises, and therefore from acknowledging that Tolkien's religious belief results in self-servingness about his own authorial enterprise, and that this self-serving element ultimately distorts Tolkien's argument. For Tolkien's demotion of the Secondary World — the work of art and the feelings that it generates — with respect to the Primary World — 'the genuine thing' and the feelings that it generates — occurs not in a neutral venue but in the context of an apologia for 'Fantasy', the one kind of writing that according to him has access to 'the genuine thing': 'Fantasy is made out of the Primary World' ('OFS', p. 78). While most artists can at best create 'a little abortive Secondary World' ('OFS', p. 60) that will pale in comparison to the 'genuine thing' ('OFS', p. 61), and that will therefore result in disenchantment and awakening to disbelief at the inevitable failure of the magic spell ('You are then out in the Primary World again, looking at the little abortive Secondary

---

24   For Dante's articulations in the *Commedia* of the mimetic hierarchy — comprising God, nature, and art, in that order — see *Inferno* 11.99–105 and *Purgatorio* 10.32–33. An earlier statement, very similar in its expression of the hierarchy to that found in *Purgatorio* 10, is in *De vulgari eloquentia*: 'So uncurable man, persuaded by the giant Nimrod, presumed in his heart to surpass with his art not only nature, but also nature's maker, who is God' (*Dve* 1.7.4). For the original text with Italian translation see Dante Alighieri, *De vulgari eloquentia*, ed. and trans. by Mirko Tavoni, in *Opere*, dir. by Marco Santagata, 3 vols (Milan: Mondadori, 2011–), I: *Rime, Vita nova, De vulgari eloquentia* (2011), pp. 1067–1547 (p. 1086). English translation mine.

World from outside'; 'OFS', p. 60), 'Fantasy' is different, for 'Fantasy is made out of the Primary World' ('OFS', p. 78).

What is 'the genuine thing', for Tolkien? His designations of the Primary World and the Secondary World are precise analogues to Dante's hierarchy of God the creator imitated by nature and art, which in Tolkien's system would be called sub-creators. Tolkien's genuine thing refers therefore to that which is created by the only true creator, God. Tolkien overtly states the religious basis of his thinking in the latter portions of his essay. When he claims that 'Fantasy is made out of the Primary World', Tolkien is giving himself as a fantasy writer a more direct conduit to the primary world and to the genuineness and realness of the original creator than that possessed by other kinds of writers. When he claims that fairy-stories must have happy endings ('*eucatastrophe*', 'OFS', p. 85), he is aligning them with Christianity, as he ultimately clarifies: 'I would venture to say that approaching the Christian Story from this direction, it has long been my feeling (a joyous feeling) that God redeemed the corrupt making-creatures, men, in a way fitting to this aspect, as to others, of their strange nature' ('OFS', p. 88). God thus arranged for the Gospels to contain a fairy-story: 'The Gospels contain a fairy-story, or a story of a larger kind which embraces all the essence of fairy-stories' ('OFS', p. 88). It is worth noting that all of these features that Tolkien claims for himself and for his own writing are also claimed by Dante, a 'scribe' who takes dictation with respect to the 'genuine things' he saw.[25] Dante's authorial stance, analysed in *The Undivine Comedy*, proves useful for understanding Tolkien's authorial stance in 'On Fairy-Stories'.

The feeling that I get from reading or witnessing great art may or may not be, as Tolkien says, a substitute for the genuine thing. It is certainly a substitute, in some way, for the natural thing, but is it less genuine? I do not understand why Tolkien's grounding of his concept of the genuine thing in religious belief goes unmentioned, and why his essay's findings are cited so often as evident and obvious truths. Why is there so little critical resistance or reference made to Tolkien's own

---

25   This ongoing trope is perhaps most emphatically stated in *Paradiso* 10.27, where Dante refers to 'quella materia ond' io son fatto scriba' ('that material of which I am the scribe').

religious belief as the explicit context of his arguments? At any rate, the feeling that great art produces in me feels true, and fulfilling, and does not accord with Tolkien's condescending and tendentious description of suspension of disbelief as 'somewhat tired, shabby': 'This suspension of disbelief may thus be a somewhat tired, shabby, or sentimental state of mind, and so lean to the "adult"' ('OFS', p. 61). Tomko paraphrases Tolkien on this point, explaining that the suspension of disbelief 'is not only the result of bad creating in poorly constructed art whose flaws inevitably disenchant, but also of bad believing'.[26]

Bad believing? This extraordinary phrase brings us to the crux of the matter as I see it (though not discussed by Tomko). It is difficult to avoid the suspicion that Tolkien's condescending attitude toward Coleridge, an author whom he uses as a foil for his whole argument, derives directly from his own position of simultaneous superiority in and defensiveness about his religious belief. Indeed, he does not hesitate to claim that this religious belief endows his fantasy and fairy-stories with a direct connection to the Primary World itself: 'The "fantastic" elements in verse and prose of other kinds, even when only decorative or occasional, help in this release. But not so thoroughly as a fairy-story, a thing built on or about Fantasy, of which Fantasy is the core. Fantasy is made out of the Primary World [...]' ('OFS', p. 78). Was Tolkien dismissive of Coleridge because Coleridge was a fellow believer who, in his view, did not believe well enough? Was Coleridge, for Tolkien, a bad believer? Because Coleridge was, like Tolkien, a thorough-going believer, whose work is imbued with religious and theological thought, he is the more worthy of our respect and gratitude for having formulated what Tomko calls 'an attempted *via media*'.[27]

Suspension of disbelief is, in any case, unavoidable; nor would we want to avoid it. Quite the opposite, for suspension of disbelief is pleasurable: it is the great gift of art, the essential mechanism that allows the reader to experience the pleasure of existing mentally in possible worlds different from her own. Suspension of disbelief is what allows us to be 'entertained', in the etymological sense of 'held', from Latin *tenere*: we are held in a frame of mind that allows us to succumb to

---

26   Tomko, *Beyond*, p. 54.
27   Ibid., p. 44.

the pleasure of possibilities not otherwise available to us. When Dante tells us, his readers, 'e ritegna l'image, | mentre ch'io dico, come ferma rupe' ('hold onto that image | while I speak, like a steadfast rock'; *Par.* 13.2–3), he is using 'hold onto that image' in precisely this sense: he is giving instructions in visualizing and holding onto the elements of the very abstract possible world of paradise that he is endeavouring to narrate.[28] But it is also of the utmost importance to be able to suspend suspension of disbelief, if we are to engage in critical analysis of a work of art and of how it procures its effects upon its audience.

In *The Undivine Comedy* I use the tools of narratology and rhetoric along with a running consideration of the *Commedia*'s reception in order to expose the ways in which the poem's basic thematic grid — damnation versus salvation, bad versus good — conditions our hermeneutic responses. Let me illustrate by once again sharing a personal experience, this time an anonymous reader's report commissioned in 1977 by *PMLA* with respect to my essay 'Bertran de Born and Sordello: The Poetry of Politics in the *Divine Comedy*'.[29] In my memory I conserved the relevant part of the report as follows: 'Why doesn't the author state that Bertran is in hell because he's bad, and Sordello is in purgatory because he's good?' Recently, because of the conference on *The Undivine Comedy* that led to the creation of this volume, I dug up the dossier of correspondence devoted to the *PMLA* article, and I discovered that my memory was not so far off. The report, dated October 31, 1977, forcefully declares a requirement of full suspension of disbelief when it comes to the *Commedia*. Nothing less than full allegiance to the possible world constructed by Dante is acceptable:

> Not once does the writer of the essay state that Bertran de Born is in Hell because he freely selected to do evil things, mortal sins, and that Sordello is in Purgatory, among the saved, because he freely selected to put God before the deification of the world. Had the author taken into consideration this

---

28 See Teodolinda Barolini, '*Paradiso* and the Mimesis of Ideas: Realism versus Reality', *SpazioFilosofico*, 8 (2013), pp. 199–208, repr. in Barolini, *Dante's Multitudes: History, Philosophy, Method* (Notre Dame, IN: Notre Dame University Press, 2022), pp. 121–36 (esp. pp. 133–34).

29 This became my first published work on Dante: Teodolinda Barolini, 'Bertran de Born and Sordello: The Poetry of Politics in Dante's *Comedy*', *PMLA*, 94.3 (1979), pp. 395–405.

simple fact stressed by both Aristotle and St. Thomas he would not have had any reason to believe that Dante 'enlarges' or 'diminishes' the figure of a poet in the treatment of the two characters.

Nowhere in this reader's response is there any acknowledgement that the *Commedia* is a fiction. Instead, it is treated as self-evident that the *Commedia* is not a fiction, that it tells truth. Singleton's famous formula that 'the fiction of the *Divine Comedy* is that it is not a fiction', had made no inroads into the reader's consciousness, although Singleton's book containing that phrase was published in 1954[30] (in fairness, as I have learned, it is very difficult to reroute a deeply entrenched centuries-old critical tradition). This is why an approach that focuses on the nature of narrative is the first, primary, solvent of my book. The comment from the above reader's report may seem too crass and simplistic to serve as a useful index of the critical zeitgeist, but in fact its utility lies in the honesty with which it reveals a critical mindset that is still pervasive. It was very useful to me because it taught me that if one discusses critical problems that are not fully coordinated with the plot's overdetermined grid of damnation and salvation, one may encounter resistance, or indeed hostility. That fact in itself seemed worth studying.

That *PMLA* reader's report from 1977 did not cause me to realize that I would write *The Undivine Comedy*. It did, however, begin to crystallize a set of insights that eventually led to a method of reading I call 'detheologizing', a word that has definitely engendered hostility. My coinage 'detheologizing' was a riff on Derridean 'deconstruction', whose vogue we had just lived through when *The Undivine Comedy* was published in 1992; indeed, in my persistent naïveté, I worried that I would be critiqued for so obvious a calque. Far from advocating the removal of theology, I instead advocated not adhering to the template provided by theology in analysing the text: 'my point is that on the representational front the poem is neutral; in the mimetic realm collocation does not imply value, as it does in the thematic sphere' (*UDC*, p. 19). I was advocating a more formalist — narratological —

---

30   Charles S. Singleton, *'Commedia': Elements of Structure* (Cambridge, MA: Harvard University Press, 1954), p. 62.

approach, because I was interested in focusing on *how* 'The *Commedia* makes narrative believers of us all' (*UDC*, p. 16).

Narratological analysis is the key solvent applied in *The Undivine Comedy*, and we have not yet exhausted its capacities for adding depth to our readings. Here I offer in example a new analysis of the narrative flashback in which Virgilio narrates Beatrice's previous arrival in limbo and urgent solicitation of aid for the pilgrim. This event, narrated in *Inferno* 2, occurred at the same time as the pilgrim's attempt to bypass the she-wolf, an event narrated in *Inferno* 1. The temporal coincidence is noted in instalments in *Inferno* 2: Virgilio tells Dante that Beatrice described him as 'impedito | sì nel cammin' ('so impeded in his path'; *Inf.* 2.62–63) that he required aid immediately, referring in the present tense to 'questo 'mpedimento ov' io ti mando' ('this impediment toward which I send you'; *Inf.* 2.95). Subsequently, Virgilio confirms that he arrived just in time to save Dante from 'quella fiera' ('that beast'), namely the she-wolf: 'd'inanzi a quella fiera ti levai | che del bel monte il corto andar ti tolse' ('I snatched you from the path of the fierce beast | that barred the shortest way up the fair mountain'; *Inf.* 2.119–20).

A diagram of these events requires two narrative lines that converge. One line represents the events that Dante-pilgrim experiences first-hand, starting in *Inferno* 1, as they are recounted to us by Dante-narrator. The other line represents events that the pilgrim does *not* experience first-hand, but that nonetheless occur in the possible world of the poem. Thus, the second narrative line includes *all* the events that occur within the possible world of the *Commedia*, including the 'off-screen' meeting of Virgilio and Beatrice as narrated in the flashback of *Inferno* 2. The opening up of possibilities not previously accounted for within the possible world that the poet narrates is a genial move on Dante-author's part: *his* possible world is not foreclosed by the narrative, and is always capable of revealing new possibilities. Our poet will later affirm that there are things that his poem does not care to narrate: 'altro parlando | che la mia comedìa cantar non cura' ('talking of things | my comedy does not care to sing'; *Inf.* 21.1–2).

These two narrative lines converge when the pilgrim and Virgilio meet in *Inferno* 1. To aid readers in visualizing my narratological

analysis, I offer the below timeline, which illustrates the relationship
between these two sets of events and the moment of convergence:[31]

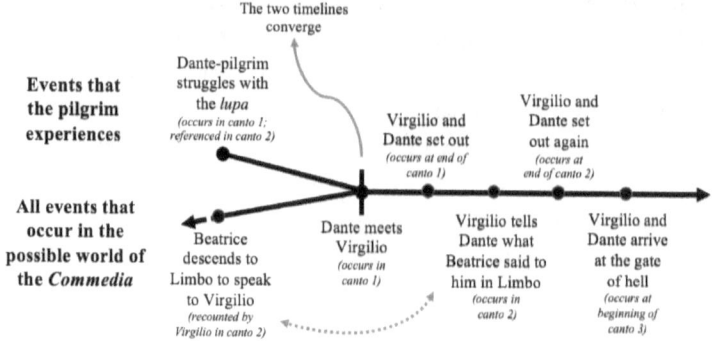

Dante-Poet Constructs a Narrative Pre-History

The outcome of all this narratological complexity is that the pilgrim and the readers have access to a crucial piece of the pilgrim's
pre-history. But why choose to narrate in so complex a fashion? I believe that Dante chooses this method because it suggests a possible
world of apparent infinite lifelike density: a possible world full of before times, after times, and lateral times — of possibilities that the poet
has simply not chosen to narrate.

In the wake of *The Undivine Comedy* I began reflexively to distinguish between theologized and detheologized readings. Expressions
that make use of the shorthand 'theologized' and 'detheologized' became more common in my writing: in my commentary on Dante's early
lyrics, it became natural for me to write of the ways in which Dante
created the theologized texture of his poems. For instance, in discussing the canzone *Donne ch'avete intelletto d'amore*, I explain that 'I prefer
to speak of the canzone as "theologized" rather than "theological",
because Dante is endowing his courtly discourse with a theologized
patina, not engaging in a careful use of theology'.[32] More recently, I

---

31   My thanks to Laura DiNardo for her subtle rendering of the narrative analysis in her
      design.

32   Dante Alighieri, *Dante's Lyric Poetry: Poems of Youth and of the 'Vita Nuova'* (1283–
      1292), ed. by Teodolinda Barolini (Toronto: University of Toronto Press, 2014),

have become even more synthetic, referring in essays to 'theologized eros' or to 'the logic of theologized courtliness'.[33] These are shorthand ways of conjuring historical movements like the creation of the *stil novo* and the signifying practices of a canzone like *Donne ch'avete* or of a book like the *Vita nuova*.

History has always been present in Dante commentaries, but I was interested in the historical vistas that open up after detheologizing, as I explained in the essay 'Only Historicize' (whose title is based on E. M. Forster's 'Only connect'):

> Of course, Fredric Jameson's 'always historicize' dates back to 1981. But fields have their own histories. As has been pointed out in the context of African American literary studies: 'At a time when theorists of European and Anglo American literature were offering critiques of Anglo-American formalism, scholars of black literature, responding to the history of their own discipline, found it "radical" to teach formal methods of reading'. There are good reasons that Dante scholarship, following its own particular trajectory, has been slow to reach this point: lack of historicizing has been an abiding feature of Dante exegesis, an essentializing tradition in which the entry 'Inferno' in the *Enciclopedia Dantesca* does not even gesture toward the history of the idea of hell.[34]

The essentializing nature of Dante studies is manifest in the article 'Inferno' in the *Enciclopedia Dantesca*,[35] where hell has no history prior to Dante (or after him). The article discusses only Dante's *Inferno*, situated in a historical vacuum. Contrary to that essentializing tendency, I explain how detheologizing allowed me to see new possibilities of

---

p. 178. Similarly in the Italian edition of 2009: 'È preferibile parlare di canzone "teologizzata" invece di canzone "teologica" perché non si tratta dell'uso accurato di un discorso teologico quanto della volontà di teologizzare un discorso cortese'; see Dante Alighieri, *Rime giovanili e della 'Vita Nuova'*, ed. by Teodolinda Barolini, with notes by Manuele Gragnolati (Milan: Rizzoli, 2009), p. 303.

33   The phrase 'theologized eros' belongs to my essay 'Archeology of the *Donna Gentile*', in *Dante's Multitudes*, pp. 225–42 (p. 235); 'the logic of theologized courtliness' belongs to 'The Case of the Lost Original Ending of Dante's *Vita Nuova*: More Notes Toward a Critical Philology', in *Dante's Multitudes*, pp. 287–97 (p. 295). Similar language moves into *Il vento di Aristotele*, the Italian translation of *Dante's Multitudes*.

34   Teodolinda Barolini, '"Only Historicize": History, Material Culture (Food, Clothes, Books), and the Future of Dante Studies', *Dante Studies*, 127 (2009), pp. 37–54 (p. 37).

35   *Enciclopedia Dantesca*, ed. by Umberto Bosco, 6 vols (Rome: Istituto dell'Enciclopedia Italiana, 1970–1978).

historicizing: 'We have to find ways to get traction in dealing with an overdetermined hermeneutic template engineered by the author to prescribe our readings. For me this traction came through "detheologizing" — a narrative approach that cleared the way for historicizing'.[36] When I reprinted the essay 'Only Historicize' in my book *Dante's Multitudes*, I extended the discussion, taking the opportunity to emphasize 'the binary damnation/salvation that conditions our readings' and to illuminate detheologizing as a method that 'works by detaching our interpretive practice from the theologized thematic grid of hell versus heaven, thus allowing us to make connections that the overdetermined template occludes'.[37]

Forster's 'Only connect' is evoked in the last clause above, 'thus allowing us to make connections that the overdetermined template occludes'. Yet — and this is the crucial point — however much we as a critical tradition have accepted the occlusion, the limitation imposed by the overdetermined template of the otherworld binary of damnation and salvation, the *Commedia* itself is not and never has been so limited. The *Commedia* contains worlds of possibilities beyond that basic binary template of good versus bad. Detheologizing allowed me to see some of those worlds of possibility, the untapped potential for historicizing.[38] All human ideas have histories, a truth whose relevance to Dante studies I experienced again recently, when I wrote an essay on Dante's limbo, a theological concept that was effectively 'reformed' out of existence in 2007, when John Paul II commissioned a report titled in English *The Hope of Salvation for Infants Who Die Without Being Baptized*. As a result, we witnessed a significant historical and theological change in real time, nothing less than a second harrowing of hell.[39]

---

36   Barolini, '"Only Historicize"', *Dante Studies*, pp. 37–38.

37   Teodolinda Barolini, '"Only Historicize": History, Material Culture (Food, Clothes, Books), and the Future of Dante Studies', repr. in Barolini, *Dante's Multitudes*, pp. 3–21 (p. 4).

38   A list of possible future topics is included in 'Only Historicize', in Barolini, *Dante's Multitudes*, p. 16; some are already being treated by former students.

39   The orthodox Catholic limbo ceased to exist because unbaptised infants are no longer denied the possibility of salvation. Dante's heterodox limbo needs to continue existing in order to provide a mitigated damnation for the virtuous pagans whom he alone included in that space. See 'Dante's Limbo and Equity of Access: Non-Christians, Children, and Criteria of Inclusion and Exclusion, from *Inferno* 4 to *Paradiso* 32', in Barolini, *Dante's Multitudes*, pp. 58–81.

Historicizing also uncovers worlds of historical nuance, worlds of human frailty and social injustice. Detheologizing my reading of Francesca da Rimini was a key turning point in my critical practice. In the essay 'Dante and Francesca da Rimini: Realpolitik, Romance, Gender', I relocated the interpretive discourse, detaching it from the theologized grid of damnation and salvation.[40] I analysed Francesca's history and the place of the poet Dante Alighieri in her history, building a historicized reading that takes into consideration her status as a dynastic wife in a ruthless political game. As a result of studying historians' research on Francesca, I was able to bring to prominence information which Torraca and other historians of Romagna long knew, but which had never been factored into mainstream literary criticism on *Inferno* 5, namely that Dante is the first to tell Francesca's story, that he is her historian of record. All this is irrespective of her place in the poem. Once we have established that Francesca would have been lost to history were it not for Dante (a fact not present in commentaries), one wonders: why is being damned in the fiction more important than being 'saved' — kept alive — in the consciousness of generations of human beings? To me the fact that Dante brought Francesca to life in our minds and in our cultures (we think of the unstaunchable flow of cultural artifacts inspired by *Inferno* 5) is infinitely more worthy of note than the fact that he places her in hell in his fiction. This interpretive possibility, and the need to historicize not only Francesca the person but also the story that Dante tells about her, became visible through detheologizing.

These remarks are rooted in ancient problems, and are inherent in the ancient dichotomy of Dante-*theologus* versus Dante-*poeta*. I have come to believe that one of Dante's contemporaries understood these hermeneutic problems as well as anyone in our Dantean critical history. I refer to Cecco d'Ascoli, the astrologer and professor in Bologna's faculty of medicine who was the Salieri to Dante's Mozart. Cecco was not a poet, although in some way he aspired to be one; his *Acerba* is philosophy in crude vernacular verse, showing that he did have

---

40   Teodolinda Barolini, 'Dante and Francesca da Rimini: Realpolitik, Romance, Gender', orig. *Speculum*, 75 (2000), pp. 1–28, repr. in Barolini, *Dante and the Origins of Italian Literary Culture* (New York: Fordham University Press, 2006), pp. 304–32.

aspirations to communicate in something other than Latin treatises. He openly resents the fact that Dante wrote poetry that entertains his readers while simultaneously daring to engage authoritatively in philosophy and theology. I have written on Cecco d'Ascoli's attacks on Dante, in which he denounced Dante as a flawed believer, a follower of determinism who was insufficiently committed to free will, and as a flawed practitioner and philosopher of love.[41] Cecco also denounced Dante as a dishonest and untruthful poet.

Cecco's battle with Dante was quixotic in the extreme, for he achieved no public recognition as a rival of Dante during his lifetime; the rivalry seems to exist mainly in his own head. Nonetheless, Cecco's analysis is astute. Perhaps his intense resentment and feelings of rivalry rendered him hyper-intuitive regarding the nature of Dante's project. Thus, when Cecco misogynistically derides Dante for respecting the intellect of women and thereby thinking that he can find the Virgin Mary in the streets of Ravenna — 'Maria va cercando per Ravenna | chi crede che in donna sia intellecto' ('He who believes that there is intellect in women is searching for Mary in Ravenna'; *Acerba* 4.9.4401–2])[42] — he understands Dante's project in ways that few did before the critical advances of the first half of the twentieth century. For Dante's bold embrace of an incarnational and figural poetics tells us that, *pace* Cecco, we *can* find the divine (Maria/Beatrice) in the quotidian (Ravenna/Florence):

> To search for the Virgin Mary — the transcendent — in the streets of Ravenna is, in effect, Dante's project. From the time of the *Vita Nuova*, Dante's endeavor was to search for the divine in the quotidian, for Christ in his lady, and to imbue his lyric poetry with this quest. When Dante was searching for Christ in the streets of Florence, when he was finding the divine in

---

41 See both essays now in Barolini, *Dante's Multitudes*: 'Contemporaries Who Found Heterodoxy in Dante: Cecco d'Ascoli, Boccaccio, and Benvenuto da Imola on Fortuna and *Inferno* 7.89', pp. 45–57; 'Dante and Cecco d'Ascoli on Love and Compulsion: The Epistle to Cino, *Io sono stato*, the Third Heaven', pp. 243–65.

42 For these verses and Cecco's misogynist attack on Dante's desire to instruct women, as expressed in his canzone *Doglia mi reca*, see Teodolinda Barolini, '*Sotto benda*: The Women of Dante's Canzone *Doglia mi reca* in the Light of Cecco d'Ascoli', *Dante Studies*, 123 (2005), pp. 83–88. For the *Acerba*, I cite Cecco d'Ascoli (Francesco Stabili), *L'Acerba* (*Acerba etas*), ed. by Marco Albertazzi, 3rd edn (Lavis: La Finestra, 2016). Translations are mine.

a young Florentine woman named Beatrice, 'she who gives beatitude', he was doing the equivalent of searching the streets of Ravenna for the Virgin Mary. We have only to exchange 'Beatrice' for 'Maria' and 'Firenze' for 'Ravenna' to see how profoundly Cecco d'Ascoli understood Dante's project.[43]

Cecco believed that Dante had used deeply unfair methods to win his status and fame. Close to the end of *Acerba*, in the thirteenth and final chapter of book 4 (the final book 5 contains only two *capitoli*), Cecco returns to Dante, defining his philosophical poetry as the opposite of Dante's *Commedia*. Dante's poem is nothing more than the singing of frogs, writes Cecco, the singing of a poetic fantasist engaged in feigned — fictional — vanities:

> Qui non se canta al modo de le rane!
> Qui non se canta al modo del poeta
> che finge, imaginando, cose vane.

> (Here one does not sing in the way of frogs! Here one does not sing in the way of the poet who feigns, imagining, vain things.)
> (*Acerba* 4.13.4669–71)

In the next two stanzas of *Acerba*, the philosopher goes on to list characters from *Inferno*, compiling a catalogue of names and events that belong to canti ranging from *Inferno* 5 to *Inferno* 33:

> qui non vego Paulo né Francesca,
> de li Manfredi non vego Alberigo,
> e de li amari fructi la dolce esca:
> del Mastin vechio e novo da Veruchio
> che fece de Montagna, qui non dico;
> né di franceschi lo sanguigno muchio.

> Non vegio el Conte che, per ira et asto,
> ten forte l'arcivescovo Rugiero,
> prendendo del so ceffo fiero pasto;
> non veggio qui squadrare a Dio le fiche.
> Lasso le ciance e torno su nel vero:
> le fabulle me fôn sempre inimiche.

> (Here I do not see Paolo nor Francesca, I do not see Alberigo of the Manfredi clan, who plucked bitter fruit with sweet bait.

---

43   Barolini, 'Contemporaries', p. 47.

Of the old and new Mastiffs of Verrucchio and what they did
to Montagna, here I do not speak, nor of the French and their
bloody heap.

I do not see the Count who, in anger and bitterness, holds
tightly to archbishop Ruggero, taking from his head a cruel
feast; I do not see here the figs being flashed at God. I leave
gossipy talk and return up to the truth. Fables were always my
enemies.) (*Acerba* 4.13.4675–86)

Cecco's list contains not only names mentioned in *Inferno*, but also
precise echoes of Dante's text, taken from *Inferno* 25–33.

In the order of Cecco's presentation, we find the following names
and textual references in the above stanzas: the lustful Paolo and
Francesca from *Inferno* 5; the traitor Alberigo dei Manfredi, with the
echo of Dante's 'frutta del mal orto' ('fruit of an evil garden'; *Inf.*
33.119) in the 'amari fructi' ('bitter fruit'; *Acerba* 4.13.4677) which
Alberigo used to kill his guests (*Inf.* 33.118–20); the Malatesta tyrants of Rimini, both the original founder of the dynasty, Malatesta
da Verrucchio and his first-born son Malatestino, called 'mastiffs' by
Dante and now by Cecco, who also echoes Dante in denouncing their
treatment of Montagna di Parcitade (*Inf.* 27.46–48). Immediately following, in verse 4680, Cecco cites *Inferno* 27.43–45 and the carnage
wrought by Guido da Montefeltro upon French forces in the siege of
Forlì: Dante's 'di Franceschi sanguinoso mucchio' ('and made a bloody
heap out of the French'; *Inf.* 27.44) is cited verbatim by Cecco with
'di franceschi lo sanguigno muchio' (*Acerba* 4.13.4780). In the next
stanza, Cecco devotes three verses to the infamous story of Count
Ugolino, the traitor from *Inferno* 32–33, who is pictured holding the
head of his enemy Archbishop Ruggieri and indulging in the 'fiero
pasto' (*Acerba* 4.13.4683) of the first verse of *Inferno* 33: 'La bocca sol-
levò dal fiero pasto' ('That sinner raised his mouth from his fierce meal';
Inf. 33.1). Ugolino is followed by Cecco's one-verse compression of
the first tercet of *Inferno* 25, where, in language used by Dante and
copied by Cecco, the thief Vanni Fucci flashes God with an obscene
and blasphemous gesture called 'le fiche' ('the figs'; *Inf.* 25.2; *Acerba*
4.13.4784).

Because of his flagrant use of precise textual echoes from *Inferno*,
Cecco d'Ascoli shows us that he has read Dante's poem very well. He

finds particularly galling the charismatic nature of these characters whom he takes the trouble to name and to cite — characters who in their polysemous and infinitely variable speech are, in my opinion, precisely the croaking frogs whose song he has just indicted as the song of the *Commedia*.[44] In other words, Dante wrote in the manner of frogs because Dante gave life in his verse to various and diverse characters, each endowed with a voice. The *Inferno*'s genial ability to ventriloquize these many and diverse human voices is what Cecco condemns as the 'modo de le rane' — the 'manner of the frogs' (*Acerba* 4.13.4669).[45] Diverse as they are, these characters are all Italians of some notoriety who populate Dante's text, and who (Cecco might think) exert an unfair fascination on potential readers, much like that exerted by celebrities featured in gossip magazines today. Cecco notes that *he*, unlike Dante, does not engage in gossip: 'Lasso le ciance' (*Acerba* 4.13.4685). Characters of this sort do not populate *Acerba*, a poem that here he characterizes both for what it does *not* do — it does not sing like a frog and is not based on the fictions of a fabulist — and what it *does* do, which is to tell the truth: 'Lasso le ciance e torno su nel vero: | le fabulle me fôn sempre inimiche' ('I leave gossipy talk and return up to the truth. | Fables were always my enemies'; *Acerba* 4.13.4685–86).

In Cecco's scathing caricature, Dante is said to write poetry in the way of frogs, and to use his imagination to write fictions about vain things, while he, Cecco, leaves behind frivolous talk and fables and dwells in the truth. Dante's sin is to write fiction, while also daring to claim that he tells truth. Cecco fiercely resents Dante's ability to entertain his readers with charismatic characters who converse with the poet-narrator so compellingly and so variously: one after another, 'le

---

44   The Malatesta tyrants of *Inferno* 27 are the only characters in Cecco's list who do not speak in *Inferno*.

45   In a reading that I find fully compatible with mine, Giuseppe Ledda takes 'il modo de le rane' as attacking Dante's prophetic claims. He follows Gorni in considering the frog reference an echo of the *Apocalypse* on false prophets: 'Cecco, di contro, gli attribuirà in modo memorabile proprio l'emblema metaletterario delle rane, colpendo in particolare le pretese profetiche e salvifiche della poesia di Dante, attraverso un'allusione, opportunamente messa in luce da Guglielmo Gorni, al passo dell'Apocalisse in cui il sintagma "in modum ranarum" è attribuito al falso profeta'; see Giuseppe Ledda, *Il bestiario dell'aldilà: gli animali nella 'Commedia' di Dante* (Ravenna: Longo, 2019), p. 154.

vite spiritali ad una ad una' ('the lives of spirits, one by one'; *Par.* 33.24)
speak and reveal their different characters to the poet as he undertakes
his journey through a fantasy universe. It is the *Inferno*'s brilliant and *fictional* dialogism that Cecco indicts in the phrase 'modo de le rane': the
way of the frogs is poetry that ventriloquizes the utterances of a multi-
tude of charismatic characters, all devised by the fiction-mongering
but truth-claiming 'poeta | che finge, imaginando, cose vane' ('poet
who feigns, imagining, vain things'; *Acerba* 4.13.4670–71).

Dante, in other words, has the unfair advantage, and the protective
cover (alas, poor Cecco was burned at the stake in 1327), of writing
fiction. Dante was not a *theologus*, Cecco is saying; he was merely a
poeta.[46] Cecco's attack on *Inferno* is a highly sophisticated recognition
of what Dante has in his toolkit that advantages the poet over the
philosopher-theologian. Dante's unfair advantage, Cecco is saying, is
that he writes fiction and employs dramatic narrative in order to cause
readers to engage in the willing suspension of disbelief. For all that
Dante writes fictions and Cecco instead writes truth (in his view),
Cecco has realized that Dante's readers respond to his fiction as though
he wrote truth. And Cecco shows us in this very passage that he,
too, responds to the power of Dante's fiction (although with greater
self-awareness than most of Dante's readers): by internalizing Dante's
poetry, remembering and citing Dante's language, Cecco indicates that
he experiences the pull of Dante's narratives, the pull of the 'real'.

The Undivine Comedy seeks to analyse Dante's genial ventriloquiz-
ing fiction and its brilliant methods of procuring 'that willing suspension of disbelief for the moment, which constitutes poetic faith'. I hope
in this essay to have given you some idea of what I thought I was doing
when I wrote *The Undivine Comedy*, why I thought it was important,
and how it changed my subsequent critical practice. I confess to some
nostalgia for the brash thirty-something person I was when I wrote
that book, which, like my son (by far the greater of the two *mirabilia*),
entered the world in my long-ago fortieth year. I was indeed brash, even
militant. But it makes me happy to read *The Undivine Comedy* now, in
this more prudential and somewhat cynical time, and to see that I was

---

46   For the idea that Dante's fictions protected him from the charge of heresy, see *UDC*,
     pp. 6, 143.

so fully committed to what I took to be my mission as a scholar and a humanist. My goal was to discuss why Dante scholars suspended their disbelief all too well, and then to embrace the *how* of the *Commedia*, analysing the narratological and rhetorical tools that Dante employs in order to bring his characters, and his possible worlds, to life.

In making connections to Coleridge and to Tolkien, to Horace and to Cecco d'Ascoli, I have endeavoured to throw some fresh light on the deep and murky methodological abyss into which, at the end of *Inferno* 16, Virgilio throws the knotted cord with which he summons the fantastic, the unknown, the supernatural. It is the very cord with which the pilgrim had been girded, with which he had attempted to snare the *lonza*, thus adding even more mystery to the cryptic passage. Obeying his master's command, Dante passes the cord to Virgilio; Virgilio then summons Geryon and the whole issue of belief palpably into the *Commedia* (here called for the first time by its name). It is no coincidence that, much textual time and space later, in *Purgatorio* 27, Virgilio conjures the full measure of their journey together with a carefully chosen synecdoche. He exhorts Dante to remember Geryon, the supernatural beast on whose back ('sovresso Gerïon') the travellers flew down into the abyss:

> Ricorditi, ricorditi! E se io
> sovresso Gerïon ti guidai salvo,
> che farò ora presso più a Dio?
>
> (Remember, remember! If I guided you
> to safety even upon the back of Geryon,
> then now, closer to God, what shall I do?)
> (*Purg.* 27.22–24)

In Geryon the poet summons the textual mystery at the heart of the *Commedia*: 'ciò ch'io attendo e che il tuo pensier sogna' ('what I await and what your thought is dreaming'; *Inf.* 16.122). It is a mystery that still inspires awe in me, awe for a very genuine thing, and a desire to understand, to the best of my ability, how it was made.

I. DETHEOLOGIZE TO NARRATIVIZE

The Intricate Weaving of *The Undivine Comedy*

H. WAYNE STOREY

I seem to remember that Teo and I were introduced to one another in 1977 by the erstwhile librarian of the Paterno Library, Bob Connolly, long before the building's renovation and back when the Paterno contained the core of the Italian Department's collection of books and journals that were studied at desks and tables for long hours by graduate and undergraduate students.[1] It was my first year at Columbia, the year I landed on the shores of the Upper West Side from the University of Florence; Teo was finishing her dissertation and would soon be Berkeley-bound. Our paths would not cross again, at least in any meaningful way, until some nine years later when Tibor Wlassics was organizing the first issues of his renegade journal *Lectura Dantis* and asked me to review *Dante's Poets* (1984). Published in 1988, the review found its way to Teo and we started a conversation that has lasted over

---

1   Originally delivered 21 October 2022 at Columbia University's Italian Academy for Advanced Studies for the conference 'The Undivine Comedy Thirty Years Later', I have attempted to maintain the talk's more conversational tenor, adding only some explanations and notes. A brief history of the Casa Italiana and some photos of scenes from its pre-renovation Paterno Library are included on the website of the Italian Academy <https://italianacademy.columbia.edu/>. For a more detailed history, see Barbara Faedda, *From Da Ponte to the Casa Italiana. A Brief History of Italian Studies at Columbia University* (New York: Columbia University Press, 2017).

thirty years, at first every week or so on the phone, and after that by email, lunches and dinners for one conference or another, shared with colleagues and our families. That collaboration produced volumes such as *Dante for the New Millennium* (2003) and *Petrarch and the Textual Origins of Interpretation* (2007), more than a few conferences, and even companion essays in the first issue of Francesco Benozzo's journal *Philology*.[2] But that collaboration has been perhaps even more significant in helping to shape intellectual directions, especially those of journals on which we served as editors and board members. When *Dante Studies* was disowned by the State University of New York Press, we found it a new editorial home, moving it to the same press that would publish our *Dante for the New Millennium*: Fordham University Press. Later, when *Dante Studies* fell further and further behind in issuing its annual volumes, we devised a series of guest-editors to bring the journal more rapidly up to date.[3] Teo's contributions to *Textual Cultures* and *Medioevo letterario d'Italia*, both journals with a philological focus, helped to expand their definitions of textuality and examine how the lines between philological and literary criticism were far more fungible and interrelated than most had proposed.[4] That collaboration continues to this day as it started off: the perhaps unlikely *sintonia* between a codicologist/philologist and a literary critic/historian, at times with two different perspectives.

I raise these memories not as a demonstration of the privilege of friendship but as part of what Teo herself would call 'the historical record' of *The Undivine Comedy*.[5] For I believe that back in the late

---

2   Teodolinda Barolini, 'Critical Philology and Dante's *Rime*', *Philology*, 1.1 (2015), pp. 91–114; H. Wayne Storey, 'A Note on Boccaccio's Dantean Categories, or, What's in a Book? *libro, volume, pistole, rime*', *Philology*, 1.1 (2015), pp. 115–19.

3   The first of these issues was a 2006 collection of essays devoted to the topic 'Dante and the Malaspina Seven Centuries after his Sojourn in Lunigiana (1306–2006)', *Dante Studies*, 124 (2006), and was guest edited by H. Wayne Storey and Michelangelo Zaccarello.

4   For example, Teodolinda Barolini's essay 'The Case of the Lost Original Ending of Dante's *Vita Nuova*: More Notes Toward a Critical Philology', *Medioevo letterario d'Italia*, 11 (2014), pp. 37–43, directly confronted the critical-interpretative nature of some of early Italian literature's supposedly philological proposals that crossed the line into critical interpretation, all the while claiming to be 'neutral' because of their philological methodology.

5   Teodolinda Barolini, *The Undivine Comedy: Detheologizing Dante* (Princeton: Princeton University Press, 1992), hereafter *UDC*. Subsequent references given in parentheses in the main text.

1980s, well before its publication, I might have been one of the earliest benefactors of the book's insights. I did not read any early drafts of chapters, though I knew Teo was writing and then later working on proofs. We might have discussed the title and certainly later the translation's title. But many of those same discussions led me through impasses in the second part of *Transcription and Visual Poetics*, so that I acknowledged in print that *Transcription* would never have been finished without those conversations with Teo.[6] Some of our discussions were about the nature of narrative and poetics, voice and rhetorical constructions; other times we talked about Guittone and even about the influence of Guido Cavalcanti on Bob Dylan, both of us independently sure that he appears in 'Tangled Up in Blue'. Like many of our generation, we had both been raised intellectually with a big dose of works like Scholes and Kellogg's *Nature of Narrative*, Frank Kermode's *The Sense of an Ending*, of course Auerbach's *Mimesis*, and, later, the essays in the 1984 *Yale French Studies* volume (67) *Concepts of Closure* (edited by David Hult), a volume I would review in 1990 in *Romance Philology*. But for me at the core of our conversations were often questions and observations that lingered about the multiple topics and approach of *Dante's Poets*, a book that so many of us, including the prize committees of the Medieval Academy of America and the Modern Language Association, had found innovative and compelling. In her treatment of Dante's engagement with ancient poets (and the narrative trajectories of their histories) of the caliber of Guittone d'Arezzo, Guido Guinizzelli, Arnaut Daniel, and Virgil, from the *Vita Nova* to the *Commedia*, Teo interrogated the implications of multiple poetics in Dante's re-creation of history, or — to be more precise — historiography. And at the core of that writing and rewriting is authority, the role of authoritative voice in the creation of narrative. If I had to write my 1988 review of *Dante's Poets* all over again, it would focus on the rhetorical structures and essential problem of authority in narrative. But Teo saved me this hypothetical task by writing *The Undivine Comedy*. If Conley's 1988 translation of Certeau's *L'Écriture de l'histoire* had gathered more notice, she could have easily entitled those ten chapters

---

6   H. Wayne Storey, *Transcription and Visual Poetics in the Early Italian Lyric* (New York: Garland, 1993), p. xviii.

and appendix 'The Dantean (Re)Writing of History and Narrative' as
a parallel exegesis of Dante's creation of narrative authority from multiple quadrants of his *Commedia*. Admittedly, this hypothetical and —
let's face it — inelegant title would have saved the book the distracting
and useless controversy that 'detheologizing Dante' raised, if not a tidal
wave, certainly a rumbling din of misperception that she was taking
God out of the *Commedia*: a response I never understood since a calm
reading of the entire book made it clear that the extraction of the divine
from the *Commedia* — pace Trissino evviva le *Terze Rime* di Pietro
Bembo e Aldo il Romano — was not anywhere in her agenda. The
controversy risked obfuscating not only the interpretative brilliance of
the whole book's contribution of a multifaceted exposition of narrative
and poetic authority that played out across individual chapters and in
the sweep of an exegesis that runs from chapter 2 on incipits in the
Inferno and chapter 3's 'Aeronautics of Narrative Transition' to the
Appendix's analysis of the essential notion of narrative transition 'How
Cantos Begin and End'. Obviously the dry Certeauesque title would
have listed toward the derivative, and in my decades of friendship with
Teo, I can tell you that there is nothing derivative in her thinking. Teo
charts new paths; she doesn't follow those of others. As her subsequent
works have verified, she loves to interrogate the philosophical system
of poetry and poetics and Dante's willingness — to use her words —
to go against the grain of that system with his eclecticism and to create
a new kind of authority, an authority at the juncture between art and
philosophy. Not to my mind alone, the proposal to 'detheologize' the
Commedia was to posit the poetic/philosophical dilemma of entering
and then closing off — concluding in words, space, and time — the
infinite. This Teo does by introducing us in chapter 2 to the philosophical essential instilled within the poetics of human newness, against the
problem that Boethius posed centuries before of the singular whole-
ness of all already known in the mind of the divine. And after an array of
analyses of the components of that poetics, she concludes with a final
meditation on transition and closure, both time-driven and imperfect,
like the human vision they encapsulate, both literally represented by
defective *terze rime*, the incipit missing its B rhyme to initiate the narrative's *concatenation* and the final rhyme of each canto missing its third
rhyme to shut down the artificial structure of the canto itself. Only the

repeated final rhyme of the three canticles, in *stelle*, enjoys a closure in a multiple of three that spans the entire work.

In chapter after chapter, *The Undivine Comedy* demonstrates the diverse facets and implications of Dante's creation of narrative authority within the problematic contexts tied both to theological and classical *topoi* such as Hell and Paradise and especially in the realm officially recognized by the Church only in the late thirteenth century: Purgatory. Teo investigates key moments in the text to answer the question of how the writer of the *sacrato poema* must wrestle control of authority but with the imperfect human voice of the initiate who must nevertheless be the narrative's *fabbro*.

Nowhere is the intricate task of *The Undivine Comedy* more nuanced and yet more resilient in its analysis of Dante's creation of his own authoritative voice than at the center of her study, chapter 6, 'Representing What God Presented'. In many ways it is the rhetorical and methodological key to *The Undivine Comedy*. Chapter 5 reminds us that the climb into Purgatory is the very definition of new narrative and the untrodden path in classical literature. But as we all remember, Dante sets himself the task of going beyond art and nature, violating — as Teo reminds us — the principles of mimesis (*UDC*, p. 122). Fair enough, no mean task. But she is quick to remind us that the three reliefs of the first terrace have their supernatural materiality of seemingly being alive and seemingly speaking precisely because they have been made by 'Colui che mai non vide cosa nova' ('The One who never saw anything new'; *Purg.* 10.94).[7] About this 'visibile parlare' Dante tells us it is new to us humans because it has never been seen in our world ('novello a noi perché qui non si trova', 'but we, | who lack its likeness here, find novelty'; *Purg.* 10.96). This is the same newness to which

---

7   Except where noted, citations from the *Commedia* are taken from Dante Alighieri, *Le opere di Dante. Testo critico della Società Dantesca Italiana*, ed. by Giuseppe Vandelli (Florence: R. Bemporad & Figlio, 1921). When possible, English translations of the *Commedia* come from Dante Alighieri, *The Divine Comedy*, trans. by Allen Mandelbaum, 3 vols (Berkeley: University of California Press, 1980–82). However, Mandelbaum used the 1966–67 Petrocchi edition for his translation rather than the earlier Vandelli edition. Moreover, by necessity, Mandelbaum's translation adopts great flexibility in rendering Dante's syntactic structures in English, at times expanding beyond even the limits of the *terzina* (see *Purgatorio* 10.106–08, which begins in his English in v. 105, creating an enjambment not in Dante's original). In both cases I supplement Mandelbaum's translation to render accurately the Italian verses.

she has introduced us in chapter 2, the new that 'novum aliquid atque intentatum artis' ('has never been tried in art'; *De vulgari eloquentia* 2.13.13)[8] that operates, she reminds us, in direct contrast to the angels in *Paradiso* 29, whose sight is never interrupted by the new ('non [...] interciso da novo obietto', 'never intercepted | by a new object'; v. 80). Dante's willingness to coin such a syntagm to render artistically what is divine and inimitable art that supersedes nature itself draws upon the unfolding of narrative in time and movement. In fact, both terms fuse activities in time and movement — perception and speech — to create a kind of *impossibilium* of the senses (visible orality), what Teo described as a 'fourth dimension'. It is, of course, narrative for which we have been prepared in Dante's descriptions of the *intagli* that extend through two senses: sight and sound, then eyes and nose, all systematically tempered by the verb *parere* to reclaim the poet's authority, reminding us that his are the eyes that witness and 'transcribe' and through which we too see and hear these new truths unfold: 'Gli occhi miei ch' a mirare eran contenti, | per veder novitadi ond' e' son vaghi' ('My eyes, which had been satisfied in seeking | new sights — a thing for which they long'; *Purg.* 10.103–04). Yet it is Dante's pivot in the very next *terzina* (vv. 106–08) that does something truly extraordinary: the narrator of this intense experimentation in perception breaks the spell he is casting by turning to us, his readers, to remind us of God's authority not only in the realm of the reliefs' superhuman perfection that God ('lo fabbro loro', 'their maker'; v. 99) has created and that he is now poetically rendering, but of God's command of their corrective moral message (the *proponimento*), to which we should not be too tired to pay attention:

> Non vo' però, lettor, che tu ti smaghi
> di buon proponimento per udire
> come Dio vuol che 'l debito si paghi.

---

8   Pier Vincenzo Mengaldo in his edition of the *D.v.e.* in Dante Alighieri, *Opere di Dante*, ed. by Franca Brambilla Ageno and others (Florence: Polistampa, 2012) numbers the lines in 2.13 differently than Pio Rajna did in the 1921 edition, but this part of the text clearly constitutes a first addendum against repeated rhyme ('rithimi repercussio') unless the poet is attempting that which has never been done, adopting for himself as it turns out (in the sonnet 'Amor, tu vedi ben che questa donna') the cultural right of the knight on the day he attains the rank ('ut nascentis militia dies'). English translation mine.

(But I would have you not, reader, be deflected from
your good resolve by hearing from me now
how God would have us pay the debt we owe.)
(*Purg.* 10.106–08)

Not since the Barbi-Vandelli debate on *smagare/dismagare* has this passage garnered the kind of attention it deserves.[9] The subtle physicality
of *smagarsi* (from the Old Occitan *esmaiar*) and the notion of a reader
potentially too tired or distracted from the effort needed to comprehend Dante's artistic 'fourth dimension' run up against the authority
of the moral proposal (*proponimento*) that 'Dio vuole': that is, that
humans pay their debt of pride through humility.[10] The contrast is
jarring. In few places do we see such a clear rhetorical reminder from
Dante that authorities have their realms. And Dante's authority extends
over the realm in which he creates a text for us to read, the realm of
artificio, a term Dante uses only once and precisely in *Purgatorio* 12
and that Teo glosses masterfully and is here worth recalling:

> The figured ground is imitated by the figured text, which
> now launches into its own *artificio*, the acrostic whose *arti-
> ficiosità*, frequently criticized, is in fact intended to imitate
> divine *artificio* [...] indeed, it should be noted that the words
> Dante chooses to build the *artificio* of *Purgatorio* 12 reflect
> the terrace's visual (*vedere*) and representational (*mostrare*)
> thematics, with the result that the acrostic is not an arbitrary
> appendage but is fully integrated into the text. (*UDC*, p. 127)

9   For the methodological contexts of these debates, the most useful points of departure
     are still Giuseppe Vandelli, 'Note sul testo critico della *Commedia*', *Studi Danteschi*, 4
     (1921), pp. 39–84; 6 (1923), pp. 45–98; 7 (1923), pp. 47–95; and Michele Barbi 'Per il
     testo della *Divina Commedia*', in Barbi, *La nuova filologia e l'edizione dei nostri scrittori
     da Dante al Manzoni* (Florence: Sansoni, 1938; facsimile repr. Florence: Le Lettere,
     1993), pp. 1–34. For the wider context of Barbi's editing of Dante, see also my own
     essay: H. Wayne Storey, 'Michele Barbi, curatore di testi danteschi', *Studi Danteschi*,
     85 (2020), pp. 45–67. On the interpretations of and debate regarding *dismagare* and
     smagare, see Antonietta Bufano, 'Smagare', in *Enciclopedia Dantesca*, ed. by Umberto
     Bosco (Rome: Istituto della Enciclopedia Italiana, 1970) <https://www.treccani.it/
     enciclopedia/smagare_(Enciclopedia-Dantesca)/> [accessed 31 May 2025].
10   Giuseppe Vandelli reads the address to the reader as more of a reference to 'Dante
     personaggio' than the reader. See Dante Alighieri, *La Divina Commedia. Testo critico
     della Società Dantesca Italiana*, ed. by Giuseppe Vandelli with revised commentary by
     Giovanni Scartazzini (Milan: Hoepli, 1928), *ad loc.*

The *signum moralis* is made flesh by the poetic text that recreates the four dimensions that — in spite of our disbelief — command our attention, the very opposite of the effect of being *smagati*.

I confess that in my own reading and especially in my teaching I leaned heavily and often on this chapter, frequently delving into the rhetorical constructs of textual materiality with which Dante conveyed the processes of flight (*Inferno* 17), morphing (*Inferno* 25) and most obviously in the textual representation of carvings that speak and smell but also call upon their viewers/readers to grasp their divine moral significance. Teo's lucidity on the topic of the layering of textual and moral authority spoke as well to my students. But *The Undivine Comedy* required a wholly different operation when it came to applying its readings. This was not the operation of consulting many *lecturae Dantis* and commentaries to reassess sources and to formulate a new and perhaps more accurate or nuanced reading. The mastery of *The Undivine Comedy* is not a source for dipping into here and there to see what Teo thought about this episode or this term or verse. Rather its mastery lies in its integral and systematic interpretation of an artistic and rhetorical rationale upon which Dante hammered his *sacrato poema* into existence. Chapter 6 can stand alone, but until you read and integrate chapters 2 through 5 and add 7 to 10 into the interpretative context of Teo's 'poetics of the new' and how it works in Dante's new narrativity, you cannot grasp the breadth and intellectual precision of the poet's taking on the task of textually visualizing the divine *exempla* of talking stone that is more real than the original historical figures they re-present. Nor can we understand the narratological contrast of *Paradiso*, which she describes in chapter 8 as the 'dechronologizing of narrative' and 'struggle against the linearity of narrative [that] dramatizes the very temporality it can never evade' (*UDC*, p. 166), without Teo's meditation on 'difference' and her exegesis on *Paradiso* 29.81's 'per concetto diviso' ('interrupted concept') in chapter 2. From that meditation stems her key explanation of Dante's struggle and the inherent 'problems in Paradise' as a function of language being 'a differential medium, unable to express simultaneity' (*UDC*, p. 167), a deeply inherent defect of language with which Dante knows he must contend and sets about early and often in the canticle to bend and reshape language and the new ways we must understand it to meet the challenge he faces.

Some years ago I ran aground on a curious variant in the Heaven of the Sun in the Landiano manuscript (Piacenza, Biblioteca Comunale, Passerini Landi, MS 190), the last verses of *Paradiso* 12 regarding the 'spirito profetico' ('prophetic spirit') of the 'calavrese abate Giovacchino' ('Calabrian Abbot Joachim', Joachim of Flora, ca. 1145–1202). The figure of Gioacchino had, as we remember, haunted the Franciscans from the *chartae* of manuscripts annotated by Franciscan enthusiasts of Joachim of Flora to the pages of Salimbene's *Chronicles* (where ownership of Gioacchino's works got you a severe condemnation from the conservative Franciscan gadfly from Parma) and ultimately to the suppression of the Joachite Franciscans in the first 35 years of the fourteenth century so well documented by David Burr.[11] I was especially perplexed by the internecine tensions among *dantisti* of the caliber of Michele Barbi and the historian Raoul Manselli surrounding the question of Dante's 'Franciscanism'.[12] I knew that if I wanted to have a better idea of the intricate narratives that bind Saint Francis and the Franciscans to Dante's philosophical and poetic orientations in the *Commedia*, I would have to become more than conversant with Teo's ninth chapter on the Heaven of the Sun. These are the cantos, we recall, in which Dante announces, especially in *Paradiso* 10, two addresses to the reader and two authoritative voices (or better, in this case, authoritative hands): the master artist who creates the universe (God) and the copyist (Dante) who must transcribe with all his skill, intellect, and knowledge 'quella materia' ('that matter'; *Par.* 10.27).

Included in that 'text' are the lives of Francis and Dominic not recounted by Dante as a biographer but by Dante's invented voices,

---

11 David Burr, *The Spiritual Franciscans: From Protest to Persecution in the Century after Saint Francis* (University Park: The Pennsylvania State University Press, 2001). Often overlooked is the spread of Joachim's ideas and the attribution of radical Franciscan doctrine to Joachim in Franciscan commentaries of prophetic books of the Bible; see Robert Moynihan, 'The Development of the "Pseudo-Joachim" Commentary "Super Hieremiam": New Manuscript Evidence', *Mélanges de l'École française de Rome, Moyen-Age*, 98 (1986), pp. 109–42.

12 For the historical, critical and textual implications of Dante's Franciscan leanings, see H. Wayne Storey, 'Franciscan Controversies and Paradigms in Dante', *Medieval Perspectives*, 24 (2009), pp. 1–22.

respectively, of the Dominican Thomas Aquinas and the Franciscan Bonaventure, their speeches rendered, as a notary might do, by the poet. The question of rhetorical layering in the discourses of *Paradiso* 10–12 that report numerous narratives instilled in the saints' lives and their praise and the criticism of their orders remains for me one of the most intricate interweavings of voice and narrative trajectory of the *Commedia* and certainly of Teo's discussion of those numerous layers. Dante's 're-historicization' not only of the saints' lives but also of their orders' ethos and socio-political trajectories is effectively a re-invention of the unfolding of narrative truth through Dante's fiction, his imagined witnessing — like John of Patmos (both scribe and wit-ness) — of the two saints narrating histories within the very fluid contexts especially of the papal treatments of strict Franciscan sects underway since the reign of Boniface VIII and continuing even past Dante's death. These are dizzying stratifications that rebound among the historical, the ethical and the poetic, all of which Teodolinda charts and analyses with insights that extend to other passages of Dante's works.

Teo formulates her exploration of these cantos' rhetorical dens-ity on the narrative problems inherent in the philosophical parity of Francis and Dominic and the necessary difference in the unfolding of their and their narrators' (Thomas's and Bonaventure's) unfolding narratives:

> By making Thomas and Bonaventure into narrators, Dante highlights narrative itself as an issue and also throws into sil-houette his own narrative problems as artificer of this text. Thomas and Bonaventure are not only presenters; they are also representers. (*UDC*, p. 195)

At the heart of Dante's narrative acrobatics is the impossible narra-tive construction that Dante gives to Thomas: 'De l'un dirò, però che d'amendue | si dice l'un pregiando' ('I shall devote my tale to one, because | in praising either prince one praises both'; *Par.* 11.40–41). As Teo reminds us, parity is impossible in the sequentiality of narrative: 'Despite the disclaimers, parity is breached when one saint's story is recounted first' (*UDC*, p. 201). She is careful to distinguish Thomas as an excellent narrator, a solid practitioner of difference (*UDC*, p. 205).

But in the end, in words that guide the entirety of *The Undivine Comedy*, Thomas's temporal/narrative path 'is a miniversion of the temporal/ narrative path followed by the reader of the *Commedia* as a whole, the discursive analogue to the journey in which the pilgrim is taken "per lo ciel, di lume in lume" and is shown "le vite spiritali ad una ad una"' (*UDC*, p. 206; references to 'from light to light in Heaven' in *Par.* 17.115 and 'the lives of spirits, one by one' in *Par.* 33.24).

What can we gather, then, from Bonaventure's rhetoric in his speech on the 'corrupted doctrine' of Franciscans like Ubertino da Casale and Matteo d'Acquasparta and his subsequent presentation of his companions in the second garland of saints? Is Dante imitating the moderate Franciscan party line through the well-known conservatism of Bonaventure while adhering in other places to the Joachite Franciscan line of a Peter John Olivi? If simultaneity is impossible to realize narratologically, how does the writing of Bonaventure's discourses affect Dante's plan for Thomas's narratives? Equally critical is the problem of squaring Dante's intellectual and ethical alliances and sympathies with the narrative trajectories of *Paradiso* 10–12. Teo's linkage of prophecy and narrative/anti-narrative structures of *Paradiso* 11 and 12 crystalizes the contrastive and risky discourses of prophecy in Dante's poem, clarifying Dante's poetic and ethical confidence in wading into bold assessments of pivotal cultural figures, such as Bonaventure and Thomas Aquinas, not to mention Joachim of Flora, who themselves weave narratives that historicize and portend in voices created, in Teo's words, by 'God's scribe' (*UDC*, p. 216), Dante: 'By making Thomas and Bonaventure into narrators, Dante highlights narrative itself as an issue and also throws into silhouette his own narrative problems as artificer of this text. Thomas and Bonaventure are not only presenters; they are also representers' (*UDC*, p. 195).

So when we encounter the Calabrian abbot Joachim of Flora — author of intricately interpretative and prophetic texts, especially his *Concordia novi ac veteris testamenti* and his *Expositio in Apocalypsim*, that would resound profoundly in Franciscan commentaries and in the ethical stands of Olivi and Ubertino — among the second circle of flashing lights of wisdom, the *sapienti*, we are surprised. Joachim is a figure of such controversy that his inclusion is already problematic for readers in the first half of the fourteenth century and beyond. But

Dante goes one step further and describes the Cistercian monk as 'di spirito profetico dotato' ('who had the gift of prophetic spirit'; *Par.* 12.141). As we recall from *Inferno* 19 and especially 20, prophecy beyond the prophetic books of the Bible can be tricky business and easily stray into false prophecy and a desire 'to see too far ahead' ('veder troppo davante'; *Inf.* 20.38). Dante's positive designation of such a dangerous figure as Joachim and his gift of prophecy must have put many early readers of the *Commedia* on edge. It certainly gave the original 1336 copyist of the early and famous Landiano codex pause. Though the preceding two rhymes are *Donato* and *lato*, the original copyist grammatically extends the gift of prophetic vision across all of Bonaventure's companions in the garland with the change of *dotato* to *dotati*:

> Natan profeta il metrapoliano
> crisostomo et anselmo, et quel donato
> c' a la prim'arte degnò porre mano.
> Rabano è qui et lucemi dallato
> il calabrese abate Giovachino
> di spirito profetico do tati[13]

In addition to the exemplar the copyist follows, regular norms and features dictate the transcription that he or she is expected to produce beyond the consistent formation and pacing of letters, the standards of scribal *ductus*. Medieval punctuation of the *Commedia* was limited in manuscripts, and the use of majuscules occurred mostly at the beginning of verses or, as here, of a terzina (thus the N of *Natan* and the R of *Rabano*). Thus the majuscule G of *Giovachino* suggests special attention to the figure who is — as we remember — more than announced by name. And, as we can well imagine, rhyme is one of the copyist's principal guides, especially when there are questions as to the *lectio* of a verse. The announcement of the presence of *Giovachino*, followed by Dante's bold, pro-Franciscan view of the Cistercian, might well have

---

13   My transcription of *Paradiso* 12.136–41, from c. 79ʳ of MS 190, renders the original stratum of the first copyist. A second hand corrects the *i* of *dotati* by making the *i* into an *o* (see also Giorgio Petrocchi, 'Radiografia del Landiano', *Studi Danteschi*, 35 (1958), pp. 5–27). I maintain the manuscript's spelling, spacing, majuscules and minuscules and punctuation, adding only limited diacriticals to distinguish two verbs (*degnò, è*) and two elisions (*c' a la, prim'arte*). The comma after *anselmo* is questionable since some medieval copyists anticipated the conjunction *et* with a virgule (/) as here.

disrupted more than the copyist's pace and adherence to the preceding rhyme (*do tati*). Still in the period when papal suppression of the Joachite Franciscans, the first copyist of the Landiano manuscript breaks with the rhyme scheme to defuse the potentially heretical assignment of prophecy solely to Joachim and to extend it potentially to all of Bonaventure's companions. Here more than ever, Teo's exegesis of the narratological and rhetorical systems of *Paradiso* 10–12 had become an eloquent guarantee of the ambiguities necessarily inherent in Dante's layering of the cultural affinities that could — in their unfolding, and in the dual strata of Bonaventure's voice and Dante script — both censure Joachites and so uniquely eulogize Joachim.

Once the initial controversy died down — for some of us it never started — it became clear that Teodolinda Barolini's *The Undivine Comedy* proposed a new paradigm. In the place of episodic analysis she demonstrated a command of the narrative threads woven by Dante's singular artistic authority. Teo demonstrates as never before — nor since, frankly — the rhetorical and structural mechanics of Dante's 'poetics of the new' founded on the richness and limitations of narrative. *The Undivine Comedy* left us immediately with a new challenge: to see the *Commedia* whole cloth, uncut, within and outside its editorially mechanical infrastructure, the reflection of a single mind on diverse cultural trajectories that constituted the intricate and multiple narratives of Florence's *exul immeritus*. From that moment in 1992 the fabric of the moral and poetic vision of humanity's condition reflected in the trope of the afterlife and the true complexity and breadth of Dante's narrative in the *Commedia* were now spread before us.

Thank you, Teo.

The Undivine Comedy
Dante One and Multiple
ROBERTO ANTONELLI

In chapter 1 of *The Undivine Comedy: Detheologizing Dante*, Teodolinda Barolini starts from Bruno Nardi's position, according to which 'those who consider Dante's vision and the poet's rapture to heaven as literary fiction distort the sense'.[1] She then evaluates the critical controversies that have resulted from Nardi's claim, in all their articulations and consequences, both in Europe and in North America:

> In this chapter I will trace, in broad outline, the history of our recent handling of what I take to be the fundamental question for all the readers of Dante's poem: How are we to respond to the poet's insistence that he is telling us the truth? Logically prior to this query stands another that we cannot answer, but on which we may speculate: Did Dante himself believe in the literal truth of those things for which he claims literal truth? (*UDC*, p. 4)

Barolini first of all underscores how 'the American *querelle* regarding the allegory of poets versus the allegory of theologians' had led to 'an impasse in which the question of Dante's truth claims has been

---

1 Bruno Nardi, quoted in Teodolinda Barolini, *The Undivine Comedy: Detheologizing Dante* (Princeton: Princeton University Press, 1992), p. 4, hereafter *UDC*. Subsequent references given in parentheses in the main text.

effectively put to one side', also due to an 'acritical assumption of
allegiance to Charles Singleton's teachings' (*UDC*, p. 5). Singleton
had claimed, on the basis of the presumed authenticity of the Epistle
to Cangrande, that Dante followed the allegory of theologians in the
Commedia.

Barolini, however, was convinced 'that Nardi's contributions regarding "Dante profeta" and Singleton's regarding the *Commedia*'s use
of the allegory of theologians are essentially complementary' (*UDC*,
p. 5). Indeed, as she notes:

> Since Singleton, in the wake of Erich Auerbach, emphasizes the
> validity of the literal sense as historically true, and the issue of
> Dante as *profeta* ultimately goes beyond the specific prophecies
> within the text to encompass the much larger problem of the
> poet's view of himself as a teller of truth, these two traditions
> are in effect parallel ways of discussing the one central issue of
> the poet's truth claims. (*UDC*, p. 5)

> At this point, the parallels between Nardi and Singleton be-
> come more evident [...] Nardi is as determined a defender of
> the literal sense of the *Commedia* as is Singleton; like Singleton,
> he is deeply aware of the significance of the Epistle to Can-
> grande as a hermeneutic document. But their approach to
> the document could not be more different. While Singleton
> grounds his defense of the *Commedia*'s literal sense in an ap-
> peal to the Epistle to Cangrande — 'The allegory of the *Divine
> Comedy* is so clearly the "allegory of theologians" (as the Letter
> to Cangrande by its example says it is) that one may only won-
> der at the continuing efforts made to see it as the "allegory of
> poets"' — Nardi refuses to acknowledge the Dantesque pater-
> nity of much of the Epistle because he thinks that it treats the
> poem's literal sense as mere *fictio*. (*UDC*, pp. 6–7)

Personally, I do not believe there is the slightest doubt about the
authorship of the Epistle, and, like Singleton, I am astonished at the
inane perpetuation of the *querelle*. In my opinion, critical response
to the Epistle qualifies as an example of the phenomenon, studied
by Barolini in a recent book, of an apparently philological debate
that in fact is not philological but hermeneutical.[2] Barolini (believing

---

2   Teodolinda Barolini, 'La *Vita nuova* e il caso del finale originario perduto', in Barolini,
     Il vento di Aristotele. Saggi danteschi (Milan: La nave di Teseo, 2024), pp. 349–59 (first

the Epistle to Cangrande to be by Dante, but all in all indifferent to the question) did not include the debate over the Epistle among her examples (all well chosen, in my opinion) of faux-philological debates that demonstrate the need for 'Critical Philology': a philology that privileges first and foremost what exists over what does not exist.

Dante certainly considered himself a poet-prophet. He says so himself, several times, and legitimizes the claim through Cacciaguida (*Par.* 15–17) and then through Saint Peter (*Par.* 27) after his preparatory investiture as poet-theologian thanks to his successful exams with Saints Peter, James, and John (*Par.* 24–26). But this claim, which Benedetto Croce rejected for fear of introducing 'into Dante's genius too great an excess of dementia',[3] is in reality the very foundation of the *Commedia*: precisely for the purposes of the self-legitimization of the truth of the text, Dante could never have done without it, as Singleton himself brilliantly put it in a now iconic phrase: 'the fiction of the *Divine Comedy* is that it is not a fiction'.[4] It is a formula shared by Barolini who, however, once again following Nardi, does not extend the consensus 'to the suggestion that Dante himself thought his poem a fiction in any simple sense' (*UDC*, p. 11). For Barolini, 'Dante self-consciously used the means of fiction — poetic and narrative strategies — in the service of a vision he believed to be true, thus creating the hybrid he defined a "truth that has the face of a lie" — "un ver c'ha faccia di menzogna"' (*UDC*, p. 11). In other words, Dante championed the use of rhetorical techniques in the service of a divinely inspired message. As Barolini points out, Augustine had clearly stated this in the *De doctrina christiana*, citing the authority of Saint Paul to legitimize its use: 'In other words, Augustine discredits the common misapprehension that a "prophet" cannot also be a "poet", that one who is inspired need not also attend to the "how" of language and rhetoric' (*UDC*, p. 11).

---

publ. as Barolini, 'The Case of the Lost Original Ending of Dante's *Vita Nuova*: More Notes Toward a Critical Philology', *Medioevo letterario d'Italia*, 11 (2014), pp. 27–44), and 'Filologia critica e le Rime di Dante', in Barolini, *Il vento di Aristotele*, pp. 361–83 (first publ. as Barolini, 'Critical Philology and Dante's Rime', *Philology*, 1.1 (2015), pp. 91–114).

3   Benedetto Croce, *La poesia di Dante*, 2nd rev. edn (Bari: Laterza, 1921), p. 6.

4   Charles S. Singleton, *'Commedia': Elements of Structure* (Cambridge, MA: Harvard University Press, 1954), p. 62.

How. This is the basis of all research in *The Undivine Comedy*, which is completely original and new (not by chance do I use one of the key terms that Barolini privileges in Dante's poetic construction): 'In sum, I suggest we accept Dante's insistence that he is telling the truth and move on to the consequences, which we can only do by accepting that he intends to represent his fiction as credible, believable, true' (*UDC*, p. 13). There is one condition, however. We must not read the poem

> through the lens of its own fiction treated as a dogma. When we approach the poem in this way, treating its fiction as objective reality, we neglect to remember that Dante is a creator and that his system of classification, for all its apparent objectivity, is a representation (and a rather arbitrary and idiosyncratic one at that) designed to promote the illusion of objectivity. [...] Once more, the conniving specularity of the 'ver c'ha faccia di menzogna' has cast its spell, leading us to pay its creator the ultimate compliment of forgetting that he is indeed creating the world he describes. (*UDC*, pp. 15–16).

All literary works, great and small, are always based on a tacit pact of verisimilitude between author and reader. But there is also a hierarchy between one work and another, based on the degree of verisimilitude achieved by the reader: the level of interpenetration and therefore of aesthetic results. The *Commedia*, a work created in a particular historical environment and with particular religious beliefs quite distant from us, has achieved a sort of miracle:

> The *Commedia* makes narrative believers of us all. By this I mean that we accept the possible world (as logician call it) that Dante has invented; we do not question its premises or assumptions except on its own terms. We read the *Commedia* as Fundamentalists read the Bible, as though it were true, and the fact that we do this is not connected to our religious beliefs, for on a narrative level, we believe the *Commedia* without knowing that we do so. The history of the *Commedia*'s reception offers a sustained demonstration of our narrative credulity, *our readerly incapacity to suspend our suspension of disbelief in front of the poet-creator's masterful deployment of what are essentially techniques of verisimilitude.* (*UDC*, p. 16, italics mine)

This is an outcome that was explicitly and emphatically foreseen and desired by the author Dante himself, not for nothing a poet-prophet in his aspirations and scriptural achievements. Implicitly, and with great caution but ultimately with great clarity, he establishes himself as a new Savior, well beyond any previous vision or journey into the afterlife, and he proposes his work as a new book for the salvation of humanity, right from the second canto of the *Inferno*. In contrast to all — or almost all — other Dante scholars, Teodolinda understood this well: she understood that to say 'Io non Enëa, io non Paulo sono' ('I am not Aeneas, not Saint Paul'; *Inf.* 2.32) is to say exactly the opposite, to say that he is the new Aeneas and above all the new Paul.[5] And even more: he is chosen by God to resolve the crisis of his time and to save humanity, undertaking the path that would lead him to surpass every pagan author (starting with his own guide, Virgil), and every other literary genre, including that highest, the epic, in order to found a new genre, the 'poema sacro' (*Par.* 25.1).

If we therefore want to understand the poem more fully, we must try to understand its creative mechanisms, the said and the unsaid, the rhetorical choices, the *form*:

> Therefore, the formal reading that follows differs from earlier formal readings, essentially stylistic, in that, in my reading, *form is never disengaged from content*; it never slips the traces of the ideology it serves. It is precisely in the ideology of the form that we can perceive the means through which Dante controls his readers and shapes their readings, and that we can locate the wellsprings of his mimetic art. (*UDC*, p. 17, italics mine)

It is necessary, we could also say, to break down the text as a complex system to understand how it was made in its *multiple* appearances and textures. Or, in Barolini's terminology, it is necessary to 'detheologize' it:

> We must detheologize our reading if we are to understand what makes the theology stick. For the final irony of our tradition of Dante exegesis is that, as a direct result of our *theologus-poeta* dichotomy, and frequently in the name of preserving the

---

5   Quotations from the *Commedia* are from Dante Alighieri: *La Commedia secondo l'antica vulgata*, ed. by Giorgio Petrocchi, Società Dantesca Italiana, Edizione Nazionale, 4 vols (Milan: Mondadori, 1966–67). English translations, with modifications at times for clarity, come from Dante Alighieri, *The Divine Comedy*, trans. by Allen Mandelbaum, 3 vols (Berkeley: University of California Press, 1980–82).

> poetry, *we have obscured its greatness by accepting uncritically its directives and its premises, its 'theology'*. To the extent that we read as the poet directs us to read we have not fully appreciated the magnificence of his direction. To the extent that we hearken always to what Dante says rather than take note of what he has done, we treat him as he would have us treat him — not a poet, but as an authority, a 'theologian'. (*UDC*, p. 17, italics mine)

Mutatis mutandis, we can follow Barolini in considering what Gian Biagio Conte called 'a philology of the narrative structure'.[6] Conte was, not coincidentally, one of the first to write about poetic memory and the relations among poets as 'allusive art', according to the formula of Giorgio Pasquali, or, better, to use the prevailing terminology of intertextuality. This is another of the methodological motors with which Barolini has journeyed across the *Commedia*, arriving at original discoveries thanks to a formal interpretation in which, as compared to her predecessors, the 'form is never disengaged from the content' (*UDC*, p. 17).

Is it possible to extend Barolini's method by focusing on other aspects of a 'philology of the narrative structure' (*UDC*, p. 17)? This will be my endeavour here. For instance, we might consider further analyses of the ways in which Dante constructs the poetic text, so that, as in Barolini's proposal, we can recognize other forms of 'camouflaging' through which Dante diverts our attention, causing us to lose fundamental elements of the discourse and its modalities of developing. I will try to do so by examining two aspects of the text that are parallel but in reality strongly interconnected: the function of the great characters of the poem (Dante, Virgil, Beatrice) and the function of intertextual relations, seen not episodically but as a great structural machine producing a further meaning, a second meaning parallel to the first, but hidden.

First of all, who are Dante, Virgil and Beatrice, really? In 'Dante', we have come to distinguish two 'functions' for some time now (thanks to the intuitions of Charles Singleton and, more specifically, of Gianfranco Contini in terms of encounters with the poets)[7]: the author

---

6   Gian Biagio Conte, *Il genere e i suoi confini* (Turin: Stampatori, 1980), p. 112.

7   Gianfranco Contini, 'Dante come personaggio-poeta della *Commedia*', in Contini, *Un'idea di Dante* (Turin: Einaudi, 1976), pp. 33–62.

and the character. However, the notable consequences of this critically important distinction regarding the structure, the narration and the formalization and dramatization of the discourse have not been fully developed, since it has never been systematically analyzed throughout the poem, along with the identity and function of Virgil and Beatrice. The result of the failure to analyze systematically this narrative function is to lose the necessarily dialectical and changeable development of the characters, from canticle to canticle. Here, therefore, is a gap between what Dante says and what he instead sets in motion in the poem.

Right at the beginning of the poem he says 'I'. This I-character, in addition to representing itself as a 'we' ('*nostra* vita') and thus speaking on behalf of all human beings, is also revealed at the same time as the one who narrates, the I-narrator. From a narratological perspective this distinction is as important as the one between 'existential I' and 'transcendent I', better known and more often discussed but not fully developed in its narratological function:[8]

> Nel mezzo del cammin di *nostra* vita
> *mi ritrovai* per una *selva oscura*,
> ché la diritta via era smarrita.
>   Ahi quanto *a dir* qual era *è cosa dura*
> esta selva selvaggia e aspra e forte
> che nel pensier rinova la paura!
>   Tant'è amara che poco è più morte;
> ma *per trattar* del ben ch'*i'* vi trovai,
> *dirò* de l'altre cose ch'*i' v'* ho scorte.
>
>   (When I had journeyed half of our life's way,
> I found myself within a shadowed forest,
> for I had lost the path that does not stray.
>   Ah, it is hard to speak of what it was,
> that savage forest, dense and difficult,
> which even in recall renews my fear:
>   so bitter — death is hardly more severe!
> But to retell the good discovered there,
> I'll also tell the other things I saw.)
>   (*Inf.* 1.1–9; italics mine)

The narrator is evidently the protagonist of the story, though playing two roles: he is the character and at the same time the representative of

---

8   Ibid.

all human beings (and therefore, in some way, the representative of all readers of the work), as well as the narrator: 'per trattar […] dirò' (*Inf.* 1.8–9). The fact that the character also represents all humanity adds a further element to the dialectic between the two functions since it places the reader, as represented by the I-character, in a structurally interactive position with the text, especially in relation to the dialectic between the I-character and the I-narrator. Because of this dialectic, the work is not closed or circumscribed in a religiously-based vision, but is rather open to the life experiences of the 'existential'-I, to the contradictions of the characters he meets, and above all to the readers. While the I-narrator knows everything about the journey and describes the situations and the characters according to the divine judgment already known to him, the I-character and actor (who is representative of all of us) can — and does — express emotional or intellectual positions different from those of the narrator (and different, therefore, implicitly, from divine judgment). The two perspectives often place before the reader a dilemma or a question.

The reader is the third fundamental interlocutor of the poem, along with the character and narrator, because she or he is often called upon to take a position — indeed, to cast the deciding vote. The narrator often addresses the reader to admonish her or him, to call her or him as a witness, but above all to involve the reader directly in the production of the text and in its truth, both explicitly and implicitly, when a difference of opinion emerges between the penitent traveler and the narrator. It is for the reader that the *Commedia* was written and also organized structurally in its dialogic form and its dramatization or *actio*: a dramatization that is a necessary tool to distinguish the poem from a moral treatise or sermon. It is on the reader that the future destiny of the work will depend, and Dante-*auctor* is perfectly aware of this.

Consequently, through the institutionalization of differences of opinion and through the structural use of dialogism and dramatization, the *Commedia* always calls to its readers, even today, and it will continue to call to them in the future. It calls to its readers quite aside from their ideology or affiliation. It calls on us to think and to make decisions about the punishments and merits apportioned by God in the afterlife — punishments and merits that have obviously been allocated by the narrator — and to hold opinions on good and evil. This is an author who, rooted as he is in a well-defined historical time and space, nonetheless has found a way to address problems that are still current. If it is true that a key of Dante's construction is, as Auerbach proposed, the idea of *figura* as a truthful completion in the afterlife of what has appeared and appears to the world, it is equally true that if Dante had not 'theatricalized' his journey and his encounters with the damned, the saved, and the blessed through the dialectic between narrator and character, the reader would not have been placed in a position to react in such an active way.

As a result of the theatricalized journey, every encounter with the souls is in fact a dialectical encounter between the consciousness of the individual historical I-character, on the one hand, and, on the other hand, his placement in the afterlife according to divine judgment, as decided by the *auctor* (Dante-narrator), and as acted out and experienced by Dante-character. The *contrapasso* is the knot that visually connects the two moments, making them memorable, sometimes in a spectacular way. Dante in this way creates the conditions for an organically *interactive* reader, a reader who is implicitly forced, subtly but inexorably, to take part and to question herself and the world. The I-character becomes a penitent pilgrim on the path to salvation in exactly the same way, interactively, through the encounters with souls, with their vices and virtues, and with the punishments and rewards decided by God.

On the one hand, Dante-narrator scripts for his Dante-character the stages of a long penitential journey (today we could say a psychoanalytic journey), with respect to his own history and that of the world. On the other hand, the reader is also constantly and strategically summoned to the same self-analytic journey with respect to the various punishments and rewards. The reader is summoned in a subtle and implicit way, not narratively declared but, in reality, extremely open, precisely because of the co-presence, quite often, of two possible judgments: that of God and that represented by Dante-character. The polysemy in the Epistle to Cangrande and according to Christian biblical exegesis, which Dante rightly and necessarily claims for the interpretation of the *Comnedia*, should not be applied only to the coexistence of a literal and an allegorical meaning, but also to the pos-

sible plurality of value judgments that are 'objectively' offered to the
reader, precisely because each *figura* includes a before and an after, an
earthly man and a soul that represents the completion rather than the
cancellation of that earthly man, even after the divine judgment.

Whether or not Dante consciously foresaw it or pursued it, this is
in any case the inevitable result of his culture and his structural choices,
which make the *Commedia* an open work, infinitely rereadable and re-
interpretable, whatever its literal meanings: according to divine justice,
the individual character's previous historicity and his eternal destiny
come to coincide and determine a constant co-presence of possible
interpretations by the reader ('quidquid recipitur ad modum recipien-
tis recipitur' states a famous scholastic proverb, certainly known to
Dante). If we look closely, it is a system of an implicit verisimilitude
inherent in the *fictio*, precisely because the same *fictio* is continuously
and almost inadvertently placed before us to judge, its values inevitably
experienced as our own.

Dante's idea of justice, one of the fundamental cornerstones of the
Commedia,[9] is therefore almost always presented as highly problematic, even in the text's most definitive and straightforward statements,
as it is always filtered through the ultimate goals of the work. Among
these goals the narrator's affirmations with respect to the injustices of
the world are certainly central. Indeed, the question of justice is always
problematic because it too is always entrusted to the reader's point of
view.

Let us take one of the most famous and studied cases, the canto
of Paolo and Francesca in *Inferno* 5.[10] Since the time of Francesco
De Sanctis, there has been discussion about Dante's attitude towards
Francesca. Here we must apply the distinction discussed above, between Dante-character and Dante-narrator. We should specify, as has
not often been done, that we are interested in the attitude of Dante-
narrator, given that Dante-character, who is at the first stage of his
penitential journey, is so emotionally involved in the encounter, right
from the beginning — 'pietà mi giunse, e fui quasi smarrito' ('pity

---

9　　Roberto Antonelli, 'In limine, tra *auctor* e *agens*: Francesca da Rimini', in *Dante
　　　poeta-giudice del mondo terreno* (Rome: Viella, 2021), pp. 85–103.

10　　Ibid.

seized me, and I was like a man astray'; *Inf.* 5.72); 'affettüoso grido'
('loving cry'; *Inf.* 5.87); 'c'hai pietà del nostro mal perverso' ('you
have pitied our atrocious state'; *Inf.* 5.93) — that at the end he falls
'come corpo morto cade' ('as a dead body falls'; *Inf.* 5.142). If attention
had been paid to the distinction between Dante-narrator and Dante-
character, many conflicting interpretations could have been avoided,
for they are interpretations entirely tainted by the idea that there is only
one 'Dante' in the poem.

In this case, it is particularly evident, as Contini proposed, that the
historicity of the Dante-character and the historicity of the Francesca-
character, both followers, albeit in different ways, of the doctrine of
courtly love, overlap for much of the encounter (Francesca speaks with
the words of Guinizzelli and Dante).[11] The result is to leave Dante-
traveller no other solution than to faint before the fatal consequences
of the love poetry he had so dearly loved — and in whose tenets he had
believed so thoroughly. And it is equally evident that Dante-narrator
plays a completely different role, as does Virgil.

That Francesca maintains a strong relationship with her 'beautiful
body' and is at the same time well aware, through the 'tortures' that
she suffers, of the sin by which her destiny is eternally fixed, is evident
throughout canto 5: verse 135, 'questi, che mai da me non fia diviso'
('this one, who never shall be parted from me'), is certainly to be interpreted as 'the eternal and tragic duration of that moment [i.e. the
moment of the kiss on the mouth] [...] in which they chose their
destiny.'[12] However, it is significant that the reading *sia* (rather that
fia) was already 'widespread' (as Petrocchi notes) in the manuscript
tradition (in fact, it is found in 72 of the 150 manuscripts examined
by Edward Moore).[13] The variant *sia* introduces a further element of
attachment to Francesca's 'earthly' thought process, which we encounter in the *Lectura Dantis* of the great Italian actor Roberto Benigni, who
with *sia* glossed the correct reading, *fia* ('sarà'). The variant *sia* is, in any

---

11   Contini, 'Dante come personaggio-poeta'.

12   For Chiavacci Leonardi's commentary see Dante Alighieri, *Commedia*, ed. with com-
     mentary by Anna Maria Chiavacci Leonardi, 3 vols (Milan: Mondadori, 1991–97), i:
     Inferno (1991), p. 164.

13   Edward Moore, *Contributions to the Textual Criticism of the 'Divina Commedia'* (Cam-
     bridge: Cambridge University Press, 1889), p. 290.

case, not so strange as it has seemed to some, since even *fia* or 'sarà' can be interpreted, and has been interpreted, in two contradictory ways.

I do not think that all the above confusion, manifesting itself even at the textual and exegetical level, should be considered a coincidence: the confusion results from the double exegetical level entrusted on the one hand to the *figura* and on the other to the *auctor-agens* of the poem. We encounter the same issue in other very famous episodes that critics have racked their brains over (from Farinata to Ulysses and beyond), where Dante's judgment seems to be torn between the magnanimity and greatness of the damned souls on the one hand and the harsh divine judgment on the other. This doubleness places before the reader an impossible and perpetually amphibological choice, which occurs because the text exists within a double register of values that are ultimately compressed into a unitary but structurally distinct figure: the narrator/character.

This is also what happens, *mutatis mutandis*, with respect to those characters whose divine destinies Dante, covered by the exceptionalism of being a traveler by grace and divine investiture, diverts from the normative point of view. The author removes some characters from the divine destinies that were considered most obvious, had the author wanted to conform to the legal criteria of *fama/infamia* accepted by his contemporaries. This is the case of Buonconte da Montefeltro, Cunizza da Romano and many others, perhaps also Brunetto Latini, certainly Boniface VIII. Unexpected clemency or unexpected punishment, in other words, are the dictates of a divine justice that reaches us solely through the word of Dante-narrator. These unexpected judgments overturn the judgments of men and implicitly take us back to the construction of Dante-character and to the legal condemnations that Dante Alighieri himself suffered — condemnations that he considered unfounded and unjust.

The 'lagrimetta' that saves Buonconte from hell, the revelation of Pope Nicholas III regarding the future damnation of Pope Boniface, and the many occurrences of 'forse' (perhaps) that hang over the narrative: these are all features of the poem that have a distinct function and purpose. Like the characters Francesca, Farinata, Cavalcanti, Ulysses and so many others, although certainly for different reasons, these features all have a common purpose, which is the narrator's need to have at his disposal both a clear set of rules (the moral order of the three kingdoms) and the possibility of the *exception*.[14] This is the judicial freedom that he grants himself, ordinarily as *auctor* but sometimes also as *agens* (think for example of the anger manifested by the penitent traveler against Filippo Argenti or Bocca degli Abati and Branca Doria). This judicial freedom extends at least as far as human free will, in its struggles with divine justice.

Are we discussing what holds for Dante, or what holds for us today? In fact, it is unnecessary to decide between these hermeneutic possibilities. In all literary texts these hermeneutic possibilities are always co-present and are a guarantee of timeless vitality, as well as the reason that a work succeeds in remaining a constant presence in the global canon. The concept of *figura* renders this co-presence even more a factor in the *Commedia*: it is the doubleness that, from a Christian perspective, is inherent in every human being and therefore in the meaning of every human's existence. This doubleness is in fact already to a certain extent foreseen by the author. The author-character and the reader are surprisingly equal in the *Commedia*, for the reader is also called to judge and to act freely, according to the example provided by the work itself and by its author, beyond what is expressed by the narration in the literal and linear sense.

Thus, in addition to freedom and justice, the *Commedia* also generates a sort of equality that is both moral and critical: if for Dante and his system it was possible to throw popes into hell and save those who were pre-convicted in the court of public opinion, why is the same not possible for the reader, or for the contemporary student? For this reason, if we look closely, the *Commedia* is defined in the Epistle to Cangrande with resolute self-awareness as belonging to the *genus phylosophie* — the genus of philosophy — that practices 'morale negotium, sive ethica' (the business of morals, namely ethics; *Ep.* 13.16).[15] The Epistle in

---

14   Gennaro Sasso, 'L'*ananke* di Ulisse', in Sasso, *Ulisse e il desiderio* (Rome: Viella, 2011), pp. 15–120 (p. 38).

15   All quotations from the Epistle to Cangrande are from Dante Alighieri, *Epistola XIII*, in Dante, *Opere minori*, ed. by Giorgio Brugnoli, 2 vols (Milan and Naples: Ricciardi, 1979–88), II (1988), pp. 598–643. English translations from Dante Alighieri, *Dante to Cangrande: English Version*, trans. by James Marchand <https://faculty.georgetown. edu/jod/cangrande.english.html> [accessed 21 May 2025].

this instance as well shows an extraordinary acuity and relevance with respect to the meaning of the text.

Dante made his fiction a work of individual and collective self-analysis but also, and above all, he made his fiction a work of (self-)reparation: a reparation that he grants himself as narrator (and author) for the in-justices of Florence and the world, and for the in-famy that had been heaped upon him.[16] With his writing, he creates the conditions for his own just fame in the city of God, and he overcomes the politics of the city of men, creating an alternative world, one that is moreover guaranteed by God (thus anticipating, in fact, the romantic notion of the writer-creator). At the same time, he has brought into being a reader who is programmatically summoned (sometimes even explicitly, in the course of the poem, with literal appeals to the reader) to participate in the same narrative mechanism: the reader too is part of the program that intends to 'removere viveres in hac vita de statu miserie et perducere ad statum felicitatis' ('remove those living in this life frome the state of misery and to lead them to the state of bliss'; *Ep.* 13.15). This is a constant human desire, not only in times of historical crises (as in the age of Dante, and in our own), but also in individual crises — which is to say it is a desire that exists always.

From the narratological point of view, special attention should also be paid to the male deuteragonist, Virgil, the Latin poet born 'sotto 'l buono Augusto | nel tempo de li dèi falsi e bugiardi' ('under the good Augustus | in the time of the false and lying gods'; *Inf.* 1.71–72), as he presents himself. Virgil is immediately recognized by the I-character as his own *auctor*. But who is Virgil really, as a narrative function?

As he immediately proposes, and as is universally recognized, Virgil is Dante's guide — 'io sarò tua guida' ('I shall guide you'; *Inf.* 1.113) — in the journey to escape from the wild forest (ll. 91–93). He is at the same time also the one who knows; he is the 'famoso saggio' ('famous sage'; *Inf.* 1.49). He is wise not only as a historical figure, and as the 'altissimo poeta' ('most high poet'; *Inf.* 4.80), the author of the poem that the *Commedia* will have to surpass, but as the one who knows the first two kingdoms in which Dante-penitent will have to travel. His

---

16   Justin Steinberg, *Dante and the Limits of the Law* (Chicago: University of Chicago Press, 2013).

function, according to Cesare Segre's terminology,[17] is certainly that of the 'Adiuvante-accompagnatore' ('helper-companion') who has been sent by God with plenipotentiary powers (or almost plenipotentiary powers, given some of Virgil's misadventures along the way), as in other journeys and visions of the afterlife. In reality, Virgil represents much more. He is an agent-character who on the one hand represents the narrator, but who can also announce the future of Dante-character, as well as his own replacement by a successor guide who will lead Dante to the blessed folk: 'un'anima [...] più di me degna' ('a soul more worthy than I'; *Inf.* 1.122).

As the author of the greatest pagan epic poem, singer of the Empire through which 'Cristo è romano' ('Christ is a Roman'; *Purg.* 32.102), and predecessor of Dante in the narration of the afterlife, it is obviously no coincidence that Virgil represents the narrator in the action and the unfolding of events, while also playing the role of 'God's plenipotentiary'. Virgil is immediately declared by Dante-character, with perfect and almost ludic correspondence to the narrative facts, to be 'mio autore' ('my author'; *Inf.* 1.85): Virgil is representative of the narrator and of the ultimate *Auctor*, God, as well as of himself as *auctor* of the *Aeneid*.

The figure of Virgil offers, therefore, a rather complex tangle, one that is difficult to manage by Dante-author and difficult to understand even for the reader, beyond the simple literal meaning. Endowed with multiple narrative and dramatic possibilities, Virgil is a real and polysemic character, completely new. On the one hand, Virgil is the deuteragonist, participant and supporter in the vicissitudes of Dante-character (even to the point of showing his own weaknesses), a guide on whom the attention of critics has justly concentrated. On the other hand, Virgil is also a teacher and — as a representative of the narrator — the first judge and critic of the traveler's behaviour. Most importantly, he is a participant, minor with respect to Dante but equally fundamental, in the implicit dialectic that runs through the entire poem. This is the dialectic between Dante-character and Dante-author, a dialectic present in all the episodes — and they are many — in which

---

17   Cesare Segre, 'Viaggi e visioni d'oltretomba fino alla *Commedia* di Dante', in Segre, *Fuori dal mondo* (Turin: Einaudi, 1990), pp. 25–48 (pp. 31–32).

we see a conflict between the experience, desires, and implicit attitudes of Dante-character and the final judgments of God.

Only in this way will Dante-character be able to respond to the special divine grace that granted him this extraordinary journey to the afterlife; whether it was a vision or a dream is obviously of no importance — God knows, as St. Paul had already said. Dante-character therefore inevitably participates in a conflict in which he is the loser, he *must* be the loser, regardless of the opinion of Virgil himself, who at times seems to share the feelings of his charge (as in the episode of Paolo and Francesca, see below, especially verses 78–79). But this situation objectively creates a problem and a possible gap with respect to the reader's reactions, which are inevitably open, as demonstrated by the reactions of critics over the centuries. And, in any case, such a gap is a sure guarantee of the verisimilitude of the story.

It is through Virgil that the narrator can continuously communicate essential elements of the story and of the souls encountered. Because of Virgil, he can do so without intervening in the first person, as happens instead with the addresses to the reader (not coincidentally all of a metatextual nature). We can see this use of Virgil starting from the first great encounter, the one with Paolo and Francesca:

> Poscia ch'io ebbi 'l mio dottore udito
> nomar le donne antiche e' cavalieri,
> pietà mi giuse, e fui quasi smarrito.
> I' cominciai: 'Poeta, volentieri
> parlerei a quei due, che 'nsieme vanno,
> e paion sì al vento esser leggeri'.
> Ed elli a me: 'Vedrai, quando saranno
> più presso a noi; e tu allor li priega
> per quello amor che i mena, ed ei verranno'.
>
> (No sooner had I heard my teacher name
> the ancient ladies and the knights, than pity
> seized me, and I was like a man astray.
> My first words: 'Poet, I should willingly
> speak with those two who go together there
> and seem so lightly carried by the wind',
> And he to me: 'You'll see when they draw closer
> to us, and then you may appeal to them
> by that love which impels them. They will come.')
> (*Inf.* 5.70–78)

The names of the great lovers of the protagonist's literary world can only be recognized through the guide. It is the guide, too, who understands Dante-penitent's distress and indicates to him the modality of communication that he should employ. It is precisely through a direct question from Virgil that the reader learns what could not be perceived otherwise except through a direct intervention by the narrator. In this way, the reader learns of the deep distress caused in Dante-character by the sudden death of the two sinful lovers, a death that — because it was sudden — was therefore without remedy: "'l *modo* ancor m'offende' ('how it was done still wounds me'; *Inf.* 5.102). Such a death is very far from the penitential journey that Dante-character is experiencing through encounters like the one with Paolo and Francesca and the recognition of their common emotional journey:

> Quand' io intesi quell'anime offense,
> china' il viso, e tanto il tenni basso,
> fin che 'l poeta mi disse: 'Che pense?'
> Quando rispuosi, cominciai: 'Oh lasso,
> quanti dolci pensier, quanto disio
> menò costoro al doloroso passo!'
>
> (When I had listened to those injured souls,
> I bent my head and held it low until
> the poet asked of me: 'What are you thinking?'
> When I replied, my words began: 'Alas,
> how many gentle thoughts, how deep a longing,
> had led them to the agonizing pass!')
> (*Inf.* 5.109–14)

Through Virgil, the narrator can avoid boring explanations regarding the order of *Inferno* (canto 11) and *Purgatorio* (canto 17), as well as many other necessary explanations, giving the afterlife of the *Commedia* a completely original structure and legitimacy. The law that regulates the penalties of the sinners, the *contrapasso* (*Inf.* 28.142), fits as if into a perfectly clear and transparent machine, offering the reader an easy means to understand the whole process and a further sense of participation in the events. Through Virgil, Dante-narrator can allow himself to correct implicitly Dante's experience as a lyric poet, as in the discourse on love of *Purgatorio* 18; it is also through Virgil that the author clarifies to the reader the difference between the various types of love. Through Virgil, Dante-narrator will be able to penetrate

Dante-character's desires (even beyond his explicit requests), without the narrator's or the character's direct intervention: 'Però a la domanda che mi faci | quinc' entro satisfatto sarà tosto, | e al disio ancor che tu mi taci' ('And so the question you have asked of me | will soon find satisfaction while we're here, | as will the longing you have hid from me'; *Inf.* 10.16–18). Further on, Virgil adds: 'Volgiti! Che fai? | Vedi là Farinata che s'è dritto: | da la cintola in sù tutto 'l vedrai' ('Turn round! What are you doing? | That's Farinata who has risen there — | you will see all of him from the waist up'; *Inf.* 10.31–33). This procedure occurs elsewhere as well, as long as Virgil is present.

Precisely because Virgil is the *auctor* of reference, master and 'father', Dante-narrator implicitly places himself as the one who will surpass his father and his guide. For his guide is just a guide, albeit a very high one, chosen precisely because he is the greatest pagan poet ('altissimo poeta'; *Inf.* 4.80). Statius, the Christian Virgil, has many of the functions previously allotted to Virgil. For Dante-character, Statius is the new master, the one who incorporated all the epic and pagan poetry through Virgil, and thus goes beyond Virgil. The *Commedia* will therefore not be epic like the pagan *Aeneid*, 'l'alta mia tragedìa' mentioned by Virgil in *Inferno* 20.114, nor even *comedìa*, as the poet immediately after calls his own poem in *Inferno* 21.2 (confirming the use of *comedìa* in *Inferno* 16.129). These are two terms that significantly are used only in the *Inferno*; ultimately, in *Paradiso* the poem will instead be designated a 'poema sacro' (*Par.* 25.2), a 'sacrato poema' (*Par.* 23.62): a new genre which incorporates all previous genres and draws from contemporary sacred representations, in the same way that the journey-vision, as Segre points out, has certainly drawn from similar, much more modest previous works of journeys and visions.[18]

The *Commedia* boasts a remarkable theatricality that is organic to the structure and narration of the poem, although little noted and discussed by commentators. Thanks to the dialectic between character and narrator, and between character and guides (above all Beatrice, then of course Virgil, but also Statius and the various saints of *Paradiso*), theatricality provides a fundamental narratological grid of the *Commedia*, in which are progressively situated all the other *dramatis*

---

18   Segre, 'Viaggi e visioni', p. 40.

personae of the great theatre of humanity: consisting of humanity both historical and contemporary to Dante-narrator and Dante-character.

The *Commedia*'s use of theatricality includes very subtle nuances in which, for example, Virgil is a guide, the 'highest poet', the author of the 'highest tragedy', and at the same time a veiled competitor. He is one to whom Dante-character addresses himself with almost excessive deference, immediately followed by an implicit surpassing of his guide and master:

> E io: 'Maestro, i tuoi ragionamenti
> mi son sì certi e prendon sì mia fede,
> che li altri mi sarien carboni spenti.
> Ma dimmi, de la gente che procede,
> se tu ne vedi alcun degno di nota;
> ché solo a ciò la mia mente rifiede'.
>
> (And I: 'O master, that which you have spoken
> convinces me and so compels my trust
> that others' words would only be spent coals.
> But tell me if among the passing souls
> you see some spirits worthy of our notice,
> because my mind is bent on that alone'.)
> (*Inf.* 20.100–05)

In quoting his own work in response and declaring that Dante had carefully read it — 'e così 'l canta | l'alta mia tragedìa in alcun loco: | ben lo sai tu che la sai tutta quanta' ('a certain passage | of my high tragedy has sung it so; | you know that well enough, who know the whole'; *Inf.* 20.112–14) — Virgil confirms his own role as an active deuteragonist in a dialectic with the primary narrator and protagonist, Dante. And he does this just before his protégé distances himself from the 'high' tragedy of his *auctor* by defining his own work as a *comedìa* at the beginning of *Inferno* 21.

Once again, here we find a complex interplay that thickens the poetic text while at the same time establishing precise theological implications: two travellers, coinciding with two narrators, who at the end of *Inferno* 4 resume their journey together, leaving behind all the other great pagan authors. But only one will make the journey to the end. The narrator will reserve for Virgil the task of proclaiming Dante's purification, not by chance after meeting Statius (the 'Christian' Virgil), the classical 'comic' authors of the second classical canon

in *Purgatorio* 22, and the vernacular poets who are friends or in some
way interconnected with the travelling protagonist:

> e disse: 'Il temporal foco e l'etterno
> veduto hai, figlio; e se' venuto in parte
> dov' io per me più oltre non discerno.
>
> Tratto t'ho qui con ingegno e con arte;
> lo tuo piacere omai prendi per duce;
> fuor se' de l'erte vie, fuor se' de l'arte.
>
> Vedi lo sol che 'n fronte ti riluce;
> vedi l'erbette, i fiori e li arbuscelli
> che qui la terra sol da sé produce.
>
> Mentre che vegnan lieti li occhi belli
> che, lagrimando, a te venir mi fenno,
> seder ti puoi e puoi andar tra elli.
>
> Non aspettar mio dir più né mio cenno;
> libero, dritto e sano è tuo arbitrio,
> e fallo fora non fare a suo senno:
>
> per ch'io te sovra te corono e mitrio'.
>
> ('My son, you've seen the temporary fire
> and the eternal fire; you have reached
> the place past which my powers cannot see.
>
> I've brought you here through intellect and art;
> from now on, let your pleasure be your guide;
> you're past the steep and past the narrow paths.
>
> Look at the sun that shines upon your brow;
> look at the grasses, flowers, and the shrubs
> born here, spontaneously, of the earth.
>
> Among them, you can rest or walk until
> the coming of the glad and lovely eyes —
> those eyes that, weeping, sent me to your side.
>
> Await no further word or sign from me:
> your will is free, erect, and whole — to act
> against that will would be to err: therefore
>
> I crown and miter you over yourself.)
> (*Purg.* 27.127–42)

At that same moment Virgil announces the imminent arrival of Beatrice, whose beautiful eyes will replace him as celestial guide, and who
appears to Dante first in ancient guise, as an 'antica fiamma' ('ancient
flame'; *Purg.* 30.48), just at the moment in which Virgil completes his
function within the poem. From pagan philosophical wisdom and the
cardinal virtues we pass to divine wisdom and the theological virtues:

E lo spirito mio, che già cotanto
tempo era stato ch'a la sua presenza
non era di stupor, tremando, affranto,
    sanza de li occhi aver più conoscenza,
per occulta virtù che da lei mosse,
d'antico amor sentì la gran potenza.
    Tosto che ne la vista mi percosse
l'alta virtù che già m'avea trafitto
prima ch'io fuor di püerizia fosse,
    volsimi a la sinistra col respitto
col quale il fantolin corre a la mamma
quando ha paura o quand'elli è afflitto,
    per dicere a Virgilio: 'Men che dramma
di sangue m'è rimaso che non tremi:
conosco i segni de l'antica fiamma'.
    Ma Virgilio n'avea lasciati scemi
di sé, Virgilio dolcissimo patre,
Virgilio a cui per mia salute die'mi;

    (Within her presence, I had once been used
to feeling — trembling — wonder, dissolution;
but that was long ago. Still, though my soul,
    now she was veiled, could not see her directly,
by way of hidden force that she could move,
I felt the mighty power of old love.
    As soon as that deep force had struck my vision
(the power that, when I had not yet left
my boyhood, had already transfixed me),
    I turned around and to my left — just as
a little child, afraid or in distress,
will hurry to his mother — anxiously,
    to say to Virgil: 'I am left with less
than one drop of my blood that does not tremble:
I recognize the signs of the old flame'.
    But Virgil had deprived us of himself,
Virgil, the gentlest father, Virgil, he
to whom I gave my self for my salvation;)
(*Purg.* 30.34–51)

But Beatrice is also the very first narrative element in the poem; she is
the promoter of the whole story, the one who had requested Virgil's
intervention through the intercession of the Virgin. At the same time
Beatrice is the one who will bring the poem's meaning to its conclusion.
She is the woman whose death in the *Vita nuova* had initiated a decisive

process,[19] one that was then interrupted and resumed in the *Commedia*, and whose presence will ensure the protagonist's repentance and therefore his success and ascent to the heaven of the Empyrean up to God. But now Beatrice also takes on a new function, which goes well beyond the functions of guide: 'Everyone realizes that Beatrice is she and is not she. It is she, the ancient one, as the trembling of Dante's veins at the mere feeling of her presence demonstrates; but she is also distant, veiled, wrapped in clouds of flowers thrown by angelic hands, welcomed by sacred songs'.[20]

In the three final cantos of *Purgatorio*, the narrative path and the allegorical meaning are intertwined in an almost inextricable way, generating a particular density of the text, which calls the reader to that exegetical effort that Augustine had already indicated as strongly aesthetic in one of the books most meditated on by Dante, the *De doctrina christiana* (2.6.7–8). Beatrice clearly represents divine wisdom when she arrives dressed in the colors of the three theological virtues: 'sovra candido vel cinta d'uliva | donna m'apparve, sotto verde manto | vestita di color di fiamma viva' ('a woman showed herself to me; above | a white veil, she was crowned with olive boughs; | her cape was green; her dress beneath, flame-red'; *Purg.* 30.31–33). Beatrice's fundamental function in the *Commedia* is to carry the banner of Love, maintaining a significance that she possessed throughout Dante's literary life (a literary life that she herself sums up in *Purgatorio* 31.52–63). She states this function explicitly to Virgil right from the beginning: 'I' son Beatrice che ti faccio andare | vegno del loco ove tornar disio: | amor mi mosse, che mi fa parlare' ('For I am Beatrice who send you on; | I come from where I most long to return; | Love prompted me, that Love which makes me speak'; *Inf.* 2.70–72).

Beatrice is organically linked, as we know, to the very foundational principles of the poem and of Dante's spiritual and poetic life. But above all she is an essential narrative connection between *before* and

---

19   Roberto Antonelli, 'La morte di Beatrice e la struttura della storia', in *Beatrice nell'opera di Dante e nella memoria europea (1290-1990)*, Atti del Convegno internazionale, Napoli 10–14 dicembre 1990, ed. by Maria Picchio Simonelli, Amalia Cecere, and Mariarosaria Spinetti (Florence: Cadmo, 1994), pp. 34–56.

20   Dante Alighieri, *Commedia*, commentary by Anna Maria Chiavacci Leonardi, II: *Purgatorio* (1994), p. 877, translation mine.

after, a fundamental narratological element that allows the character and the reader to begin to understand more clearly the meaning of the life and the penitential journey of a man who represents all humanity (the famous 'nostra' in the first verse) but who is *above all himself*. He is the poet whose life and literary career Beatrice recalls at the decisive moment, when she leads him to complete repentance and therefore to salvation:

> Tuttavia, perché mo vergogna porte
> del tuo errore, e perché altra volta,
> udendo le serene, sie più forte,
>> pon giù il seme del piangere e ascolta:
> sì udirai come in contraria parte
> mover dovieti mia carne sepolta.
>> Mai non t'appresentò natura o arte
> piacer, quanto le belle membra in ch'io
> rinchiusa fui, e che so' 'n terra sparte;
>> e se 'l sommo piacer sì ti fallio
> per la mia morte, qual cosa mortale
> dovea poi trarre te nel suo disio?
>> Ben ti dovevi, per lo primo strale
> de le cose fallaci, levar suso
> di retro a me che non era più tale.
>> Non ti dovea gravar le penne in giuso,
> ad aspettar più colpo, o pargoletta
> o altra novità con sì breve uso.
>> Novo augelletto due o tre aspetta;
> ma dinanzi da li occhi d'i pennuti
> rete si spiega indarno o si saetta.

> (Nevertheless, that you may feel more shame
> for your mistake, and that — in time to come —
> hearing the Sirens, you may be more strong,
>> have done with all the tears you sowed, and listen:
> so shall you hear how, unto other ends,
> my buried flesh should have directed you.
>> Nature or art had never showed you any
> beauty that matched the lovely limbs in which
> I was enclosed — limbs scattered now in dust;
>> and if the highest beauty failed you through
> my death, what mortal thing could then induce
> you to desire it? For when the first
>> arrow of things deceptive struck you, then
> you surely should have lifted up your wings
> to follow me, no longer such a thing.

No green young girl or other novelty —
such brief delight — should have weighed down your wings,
awaiting further shafts. The fledgling bird
   must meet two or three blows before he learns,
but any full-fledged bird is proof against
the net that has been spread or arrow, aimed.)
(*Purg.* 31.43–63)

Beatrice is therefore also the one who will have to assume the role of
harsh judge (*Purg.* 30.58–81); unlike Virgil, she anticipates for the living protagonist the final judgment of God. In this way she underlines
once again one of the fundamental aims of the poem, the affirmation
of justice. Above all, she also supports the fundamental truth claims
of the *Commedia*, as the direct witness of the earthly history of the
protagonist and his path to salvation:

   questi fu tal ne la sua vita nova
virtüalmente, ch'ogne abito destro
fatto averebbe in lui mirabil prova.
   Ma tanto più maligno e più silvestro
si fa 'l terren col mal seme e non cólto,
quant'elli ha più di buon vigor terrestro.
   Alcun tempo il sostenni col mio volto:
mostrando li occhi giovanetti a lui,
meco il menava in dritta parte vòlto.
   Sì tosto come in su la soglia fui
di mia seconda etade e mutai vita,
questi si tolse a me, e diessi altrui.
   Quando di carne a spirto era salita,
e bellezza e virtù cresciuta m'era,
fu' io a lui men cara e men gradita;
   e volse i passi suoi per via non vera,
imagini di ben seguendo false,
che nulla promession rendono intera.
   Né l'impetrare ispirazion mi valse,
con le quali e in sogno e altrimenti
lo rivocai: sì poco a lui ne calse!
   Tanto giù cadde, che tutti argomenti
a la salute sua eran già corti,
fuor che mostrarli le perdute genti.
   Per questo visitai l'uscio d'i morti,
e a colui che l'ha qua sù condotto,
li preghi miei, piangendo, furon porti.

> Alto fato di Dio sarebbe rotto,
> se Letè si passasse e tal vivanda
> fosse gustata sanza alcuno scotto
>   di pentimento che lagrime spanda.

>   (he, when young, was such — potentially — that any
> propensity innate in him would have
> prodigiously succeeded, had he acted.
>   But where the soil has finer vigor, there
> precisely — when untilled or badly seeded —
> will that terrain grow wilder and more noxious.
>   My countenance sustained him for a while;
> showing my youthful eyes to him, I led
> him with me toward the way of righteousness.
>   As soon as I, upon the threshold of
> my second age, had changed my life, he took
> himself away from me and followed after
>   another; when, from flesh to spirit, I
> had risen, and my goodness and my beauty
> had grown, I was less dear to him, less welcome:
>   he turned his footsteps toward an untrue path;
> he followed counterfeits of goodness, which
> will never pay in full what they have promised.
>   Nor did the inspirations I received —
> with which, in dream and otherwise, I called
> him back — help me; he paid so little heed!
>   He fell so far there were no other means
> to lead him to salvation, except this:
> to let him see the people who were lost.
>   For this I visited the gateway of
> the dead; to him who guided him above
> my prayers were offered even as I wept.
>   The deep design of God would have been broken
> if Lethe had been crossed and he had drunk
> such waters but had not discharged the debt
>   of penitence that's paid when tears are shed.)
> (*Purg.* 30.115–45)

Beatrice will thus supervise Dante's decisive liberation from sin, leading him to reflect on and repent for everything that had distanced him
from her (*Purg.* 30.118–41 and 31.43–60) and appearing to him in her
new and even more stunningly transformative guise (*Purg.* 31.82–90).
She also completely recapitulates the internal story of the *Commedia*,
through the contrast between the penitential 'ch'io caddi vinto' ('I

fell, overcome') of *Purgatorio* 31.89 and *Inferno* 5's 'caddi come corpo morto' ('I fell as a dead body'; l. 142):

> Sotto 'l suo velo e oltre la rivera
> vincer pariemi più sé stessa antica,
> vincer che l'altre qui, quand'ella c'era.
>   Di penter sì mi punse ivi l'ortica,
> che di tutte altre cose qual mi torse
> più nel suo amor, più mi si fé nemica.
>   Tanta riconoscenza il cor mi morse,
> *ch'io caddi vinto*; e quale allora femmi,
> salsi colei che la cagion mi porse.
>
> (Beneath her veil, beyond the stream, she seemed
> so to surpass her former self in beauty
> as, here on earth, she had surpassed all others.
>   The nettle of remorse so stung me then,
> that those — among all other — things that once
> most lured my love, became most hateful to me.
>   Such self-indictment seized my heart that I
> collapsed, my senses slack; what I became
> is known to her who was the cause of it.)
> (*Purg.* 31.82–90; italics mine)

Because of the multiplicity of roles and thematic aspects that she embodies, Beatrice still represents perhaps the most debated and mysterious critical node of the *Commedia*. She is a woman who reveals to Dante, thanks to her own death, the love-*charitas* that he follows from the *Vita nuova* to *Paradiso*; she is also revealed wisdom and guardian of divine justice in the world (*Purg.* 31.86–87). Finally, she is the first of the commissioners of the poem, alongside Cacciaguida and Saint Peter, part of the necessary completion of the journey:

> Qui sarai tu poco tempo silvano;
> e sarai meco sanza fine cive
> di quella Roma onde Cristo è romano.
>   Però, in pro del mondo che mal vive,
> al carro tieni or li occhi, e quel che vedi,
> *ritornato di là, fa che tu scrive.*
>
> (Here you shall be — awhile — a forest dweller;
> but you shall be with me — and without end —
> Rome's citizen, the Rome in which Christ
>   is Roman; and thus, to profit that world which
> lives badly, watch the chariot steadfastly

and, when you have returned, transcribe
what you have seen.)
(*Purg.* 32.100–105; italics mine)

Precisely because of her polysemy, because of the multiplicity of her
functions, which are apparently so transparent but at the same time so
elusive, Beatrice is the necessary link to Dante's introspection and self-
awareness throughout the poem, not only at the top of *Purgatorio*. She
is perhaps the highest literary representation of the paradise-woman in
all romance lyric poetry, although Beatrice herself denies that identity
in a gently ironic statement to Dante, who has just been overcome by
the light of her smile: 'Volgiti e ascolta; | ché non pur ne' miei occhi
è paradiso' ('Turn to him and listen — for | not only in my eyes is
paradise'; *Par.* 18.20–21). Here he refers to her new function as guide
in *Paradiso*: a woman not of this world. The narrator therefore proposes
her as the ultimate aspiration to the divine, since paradise includes
Beatrice as part of its 'forma general', to which she returns after having
exhausted her function as a poetic and theological guide:

> La forma general di paradiso
> già tutta mïo sguardo avea compresa,
> in nulla parte ancor fermato fiso;
>   e volgeami con voglia rïaccesa
> per domandar la mia donna di cose
> di che la mente mia era sospesa.
>   Uno intendëa, e *altro* mi rispuose:
>
> (By now my gaze had taken in the whole
> of Paradise — its form in general —
> but without looking hard at any part;
>   and I, my will rekindled, turning toward
> my lady, was prepared to ask about
> those matters that inclined my mind to doubt.
>   Where I expected her, another answered:)
> (*Par.* 31.52–58; italics mine)

The other ('altro') of verse 58 signals the absence of Beatrice, now
distant but very close in spirit. In this way Dante is able also to affirm
her function as the guarantor of his hope for future salvation; for the
protagonist, this is certainly the essence of the character of his lady. She
was also the guarantor of the faith with which he had declared himself
filled at his examination by Saint Peter in *Paradiso* 24, a faith that has
supported him up to this point:

> O donna in cui la mia speranza vige,
> e che soffristi per la mia salute
> in inferno lasciar le tue vestige,
>
> di tante cose quant' i' ho vedute,
> dal tuo podere e da la tua bontate
> riconosco la grazia e la virtute.
>
> Tu m'hai di servo tratto a libertate
> per tutte quelle vie, per tutt' i modi
> che di ciò fare avei la potestate.
>
> La tua magnificenza in me custodi,
> sì che l'anima mia, che fatt' hai sana,
> piacente a te dal corpo si disnodi.
>
> (O lady, you in whom my hope gains strength,
> you who, for my salvation, have allowed
> your footsteps to be left in Hell, in all
>
> the things that I have seen, I recognize
> the grace and benefit that I, depending
> upon your power and goodness, have received.
>
> You drew me out from slavery to freedom
> by all those paths, by all those means that were
> within your power. Do, in me, preserve
>
> your generosity, so that my soul,
> which you have healed, when it is set loose from
> my body, be a soul that you will welcome.)
> (*Par.* 31.79–90)

The *other* — Beatrice's successor in the guiding and narrative function, Saint Bernard — will be the one who will pray to the Virgin Mary, from whom the help for the sinner lost in the dark forest had originally come: 'Donna è gentil nel ciel che si compiange' ('In Heaven there's a gentle lady who weeps'; *Inf.* 2.94). The special function of the Madonna is remembered agaom at the end of the poem: 'La tua benignità non pur soccorre | a chi domanda, ma molte fïate | liberamente al dimandar precorre' ('Your loving-kindness does not only answer | the one who asks, but it is often ready | to answer freely long before the asking'; *Par.* 33.16–18). The special function of the Virgin Mary thus concludes the penitent's journey in a circular fashion, before the final vision of God: of that Love that had moved and continues to move Beatrice along with the sun and the stars.

The role and literal and allegorical function of the great co-protagonists (Dante, Virgil and Beatrice, but the discussion could be extended at least to Statius and Saint Bernard), therefore constitute the plot of a narration that also leads to the less superficial layers of the text. But there is also another systematic narrative plotline, perhaps even more important, which builds a second level of meaning throughout the poem, thanks to dense references that connect characters, themes and situations — ones that are close by, and also very distant. This is the real challenge addressed to the reader, who is called upon to identify those characters, themes and situations, to reconstruct their logic and to participate in a higher exegetic and aesthetic level. Dante also establishes a sort of hierarchy among the readers, as revealed in the famous prologue of *Paradiso* 2, beginning 'O voi che siete in piccioletta barca' ('O you who are within your little bark'; *Par.* 2.1).

All the episodes and the hundreds of figures that populate the poem are in fact united, memorized and strengthened thanks to a technique, the *memoria verborum*, called the 'allusive art' by some Italian critics and by others intertextuality, to whose importance Barolini has repeatedly called attention. Together with the *memoria rerum*, it constitutes a principle that is not only structuring but also narratological and aesthetic. It contributes powerfully to creating a denser meaning of the poem, detaching it from common language and establishing a second level of narration, beyond the literal one.

For particularly important speeches and themes, Dante frequently uses not only numerological correspondences and the three 'appointed' places of a work: that is, the beginning, the middle and the end of each canticle and of the various cantos (as rhetoric taught). He also uses the golden ratio of the poem and of the individual cantos for the same purpose. He establishes correlations and interpretative references between corresponding cantos of each canticle, reserving, as is well known, the sixth and seventh cantos for political argumentation (Ciacco in the *Inferno*, the negligent princes in *Purgatorio*, Justinian in *Paradiso*), the fifteenth and sixteenth cantos for the poem's fundamental ethical-political principles (Brunetto Latini in *Inferno*, Guido del Duca/Marco Lombardo in *Purgatorio*, Cacciaguida in *Paradiso*), and the twenty-seventh cantos — this last case being particularly interesting because Dante uses these cantos to highlight the progressive affirmation of himself as a poet-prophet.

In *Inferno*, canto 27 is dedicated to Boniface VIII, inventor of the Jubilee, a simoniac journey as opposed to the true spiritual journey

of the traveller Dante, who in *Paradiso* 27 is sacredly invested with
the function of poet-prophet by Peter and set to work against 'quelli
ch'usurpa in terra il luogo mio' ('He who on earth usurps my place';
Par. 27.22), that is, Boniface himself. The last example in particular
can be full of further allusive and semantic meanings, since it seems
evident that Dante's true Jubilee journey is precisely a journey in and of
memory, an interior journey, as opposed to the Jubilee, an entirely ex-
terior journey, which for Dante is moreover heretical. The Jubilee was
proclaimed by Boniface in *his* Rome, which in the eyes of Saint Peter
had become a sewer, 'cloaca' (*Par.* 27.25). The rhyme *-aca*, as in *cloaca*,
is used, throughout the entire poem, only in *Paradiso* 27 and *Paradiso*
16, at the moment of the celestial investiture by Saint Peter and, earlier,
at the moment of the earthly investiture in Dante's meeting with his
ancestor Cacciaguida, in the three central cantos of *Paradiso* (cantos
15–17). Moreover, Cacciaguida in *Paradiso* 17.51 uses a rhyme, *-erca*,
of which there is only one other occurrence in the *Commedia*, in the
previous canto (*Par.* 16.61), with repetition of the same rhyme series
(*noverca: merca: cerca*). In this way, Dante connects the mercantile
and corrupt infernal city of Florence to simoniacal and corrupt papal
Rome, which in *Paradiso* 27.46–60 will be a *cloaca* precisely because
it is a place where the Christian people experience division and where
the sacred is subjected to corruption and commerce.

Dante also uses the retrograde principle: for instance, the treatment of Fortune-Providence in the seventh canto of the *Inferno* is
repeated in *Paradiso* 27, which is seven cantos from the end of the
poem. Further subtle correspondences also occur, which might appear
to be fantasies of modern criticism if they did not correspond perfectly to a rhetorical art that was learned at school during the medieval
period and continued to be practiced throughout life in continuous
ruminatio. Memory-work became almost second nature, even in the
creative phase of the *dispositio*: 'Dandi sunt certi quidam termini, ut
contextus verborum, qui est difficillimus, continua et crebra meditatio,
partis deinceps ipsas repetitus ordo coniungant' ('It is necessary to
provide secure points of reference so that the coherent connection
of words, which is very difficult, is aided by continuous and assidu-

ous meditation, and that the order of words, recalled from memory, connects the various parts').[21]

What is the purpose of so many symmetries and correspondences? Through such references, as well as through intertextual allusions, which are based on echoes provided by memory-work, Dante directs the reader to connect his journey and his encounters into a unitary vision. The recalls and the allusions offer him the thread to retrace his thought and his musical resonances,[22] well beyond the purely literal or episodic meaning, and not limited to individual cantos. The poem is stratified in a network of references each of which strengthens the other, also at a subliminal level. Not all readers will be able to grasp the individual echoes (and even today new ones are continually being discovered), but in many cases the phonic reference activates the semantic one (and vice versa), as Contini had intuited.[23] Contini did not, however, connect the discovery and theorization of 'verbal criticism' to the *memoria verborum* and to procedures already technically known to Dante through rhetoric, and therefore critically verifiable beyond the *divinationes* of individual critics.[24]

Verbal references and correspondences will not always be events due to programmatic choices and to the intentional use of the procedures of *memoria verborum*; there are numerous places in which the

---

21   *Inst. or.* 11.2.28. All quotations from M. Fabi Quintiliani, *Institutionis oratoriae libri XII*, ed. by Michael Winterbottom, 2 vols (Oxford: Oxford University Press, 1985). Translation mine.

22   In *De vulgari eloquentia* Dante defines poetry as 'fictio rethorica musicaque poita' ('a verbal invention composed according to the rules of rhetoric and music'; 2.4.2). Quotes and English translations from the *De vulgari eloquentia* are from Dante Alighieri, *De vulgari eloquentia*, trans. by Steven Botterill (Cambridge: Cambridge University Press, 1996).

23   Gianfranco Contini, 'Filologia ed esegesi dantesca', in Contini, *Un'idea di Dante*, pp. 133–42.

24   On the fundamental role of rhyme and rhyming series in the construction of the poetic text (but in this case still without connections to the *ars memoriae*), see Roberto Antonelli, 'Rima equivoca e tradizione rimica nella poesia di Giacomo da Lentini, 1. Le canzoni', in *Bollettino del Centro di studi filologici e linguistici siciliani*, 13 (1977), pp. 20–126; and Roberto Antonelli, 'Tempo testuale tempo rimico. Costruzione del testo e critica nella poesia rimata', *Critica del testo*, 1 (1998), pp. 177–201. An in-depth analysis of serial rhyme used in the *Commedia* can be found in the introduction of Arianna Punzi, *Rimario della 'Commedia'* (Rome: Bagatto, 2001), pp. 13–52, the first rhyming dictionary organized by rhyming series. Relevant and anticipatory analyses on Dante's rhyming series (*Reimbildungen*) are found in Giorgio Brugnoli, 'Ancor che fosse tardi', in Brugnoli, *Studi danteschi*, 3 vols (Pisa: Edizioni ETS, 1998), I, pp. 133–39.

rhyming correspondence does not have significant value and refers
to an interdiscursive or intermemorial situation.[25] At the same time,
it cannot always be a coincidence that in corresponding cantos of
the same canticle Dante rhymes the same word or the same series of
rhymes or that in approximately ninety cases in the *Commedia* the
same rhyming word is used in the same verse, exactly as each canticle
is closed by the rhyme word 'stelle'.

For example, in a famous verse in *Purgatorio* 24, Dante uses the
rhyme-word 'penne': 'Io veggio ben come le vostre penne | di retro
al dittator sen vanno strette, | che de le nostre certo non avvenne' ('I
clearly see how your pens follow closely | behind him who dictates,
and certainly | that did not happen with our pens'; *Purg.* 24.58–60).
It is not unlikely that in a very close canto, *Purgatorio* 27, where we
find the same word in rhyming position — 'al volo mi sentia crescer
le penne' ('I felt my wings was growing for the flight'; *Purg.* 27.123)
— Dante reuses the rhyme-word 'penne' with allusive purposes, given
the apparent discursive continuity: from the superiority of stilnovistic
and Dantean poetry over its predecessors in *Purgatorio* 24, we move, in
Purgatorio 27, to the poet's ascent to the earthly paradise and to earthly
happiness, and therefore to his superiority over all his predecessors.
Almost as a culmination of a journey centered on feathers and wings,
we find 'penne' again at the end of the poem, in *Paradiso* 33.139, where
it also serves as a reminder of the wings of Ulysses's impossible 'folle
volo': 'de' remi facemmo ali al folle volo ('we made oars into wings for
the mad flight'; *Inf.* 26.125) in the last verses of the *Commedia*. Dante
again uses the rhyme that throughout the poem had emphasized the
superiority of his own poetic experience ('penne'), now to recognize
his own momentary inadequacy in the face of the difficulty of fully
representing the mystery of God:

> tal era io a quella vista nova:
> veder voleva come si convenne
> l'imago al cerchio e come vi s'indova;
>   ma non eran da ciò le proprie penne:
> se non che la mia mente fu percossa
> da un fulgore in che sua voglia venne.

---

25   Roberto Antonelli, 'L'intertestualità contesa: intertestuale, interdiscorsivo, interme-
     moriale', in *Mélanges en l'honneur de Mariella Di Maio*, ed. by Valentina Fortunato
     (Soveria Mannelli: Rubbettino, 2019), pp. 15–24.

(so I searched that strange sight: I wished to see
the way in which our human effigy
suited the circle and found place in it —
    and my own wings were far too weak for that.
But then my mind was struck by light that flashed
and, with this light, received what it had asked.)
(*Par.* 33.136–41)

Dante sometimes uses the same series of rhymes in interrelated episodes within the *Commedia,* or between the *Commedia* and the works
of the characters involved. The most striking case of the second type
has long been noted and is found in *Inferno* 10, with respect to the
rhyming series *nome: come: lume,* which intertextually refers to Guido
Cavalcanti's canzone *Donna me prega.*[26] However, it should also be
noted that they are significantly surrounded by other series of equal
intratextual value (the adjacent *ingegno: vegno: disdegno* and *meco:
cieco: teco*).[27] The same will happen in other places that are fundamental to the relationship between Dante and his romance predecessors,
that is to say between Dante and his own work, revisited in the light of
the memorial and penitential journey represented in the *poema sacro.*

Here we see an art of memory that is extended even beyond the
traditional limits of ancient rhetoric, since Dante was able to insert into
the ancient *ars* techniques of the new romance poetry, at the service of
a discourse that aspired to unite 'cielo e terra' ('heaven and earth'; *Par.*
25.2). He therefore needed poetry, not prose, and he needed the bond
that united poetry and theology. This bond existed not only for Dante,
but from the time of the first prophets, according to a famous definition
of the contemporary yet distant Albertino Mussato: 'Quisquis erat
vates, vas erat ille Deus' ('Whoever was the prophet, the vessel was
God').[28]

---

26 For terminology and critical use see Roberto Antonelli, 'Rima equivoca e tradizione
    rimica'; and Roberto Antonelli, 'Tempo testuale tempo rimico'.

27 Gianfranco Contini, 'Filologia ed esegesi dantesca' and 'Cavalcanti in Dante', in Con-
    tini, *Un'idea di Dante,* pp. 113–42 and 143–57; Giorgio Brugnoli, 'Ancor che fosse
    tardi', pp. 133–39; Roberto Antonelli, 'Tra Farinata e Guido Cavalcanti', in Antonelli,
    Dante poeta-giudice del mondo terreno (Rome: Viella, 2021), pp. 93–96.

28 Mussato, *Epistola* 7.15–21, in Albertino Mussato, 'Épîtres métriques sur la poésie', in
    Écérinide, épîtres métriques sur la poésie, songe, ed. and trans. by Jean-Frédéric Chevalier
    (Paris: Les Belles Lettres, 2000), pp. 37–39. Translation mine.

The choice of poetry and not prose, which seems so obvious to us in hindsight (like the choice of the vernacular over Latin, which was not obvious at the time either, as we are reminded by the controversy with Giovanni del Virgilio), in fact responds to a strategic and far-sighted choice. That choice reflects the logic of taking on a prophetic voice (that of the poet-theologian, as Boccaccio will immediately recognize) and taking on the role of custodian of cultural memory. Let us remember Quintilian again: 'Even well-composed speeches will guide the memory with their structure. In fact, just as we learn verses more easily than a prose speech, so of prose speeches we learn better those that are well connected to each other than those that are not. Thus, it happens that even speeches that seemed improvised can be repeated word for word'.[29]

The *Commedia* is also this: the reduction of earthly time, of all history, to text and memory, to the long short-circuit in which past, present and future, the I-We/Dante, *figura* of all humanity, are arranged according to an *a priori* path of which Dante-author is the responsible director and creator, but above all, as he wanted, the *Poet*.

---

29   Quintilian, *Inst. or.* 11.2.39: 'Etiam quae bene composita erunt memoriam serie sua ducent: nam sicut facilius versus ediscimus quam prorsam orationem, ita prorsae vincta quam dissoluta. Sic contigit ut etiam quae ex tempore uidebantur effusa ad uerbum repetita reddantur.' Translation mine.

Reasoning between Possibility, Fictional Reality, and Actuality
A Case Study in Detheologizing the *Commedia*'s Conditionals

LAURA DINARDO

The *Commedia* is a fictional construction that seeks to establish itself as a true object, and one that represents the world as it indeed is, through a persistent preoccupation with the possible. The reader is introduced to the central role of possibility in the poet's construction of the afterlife almost immediately in *Inferno* 1. In his very first directive as newfound guide, Virgil asserts to the pilgrim in a rather straightforward manner that if he wishes to leave the dark wood, he must take another path: 'A te convien tenere altro vïaggio | [...] se vuo' campar d'esto loco selvaggio' ('It is another path that you must take, | [...] if you would leave this savage wilderness'; *Inf.* 1.91–93).[1] With these words, Dante-poet opens an alternate pathway to resolve the narrative and physical impasse experienced by the pilgrim at the *Commedia*'s beginning and, in doing so, establishes the motivation for the entire

---

1   All citations from the *Divina Commedia* are drawn from Dante Alighieri, *La Commedia secondo l'antica vulgata*, ed. by Giorgio Petrocchi, Società Dantesca Italiana, Edizione Nazionale, 2nd rev. edn, 4 vols (Florence: Le Lettere, 1994). English translations come from Dante Alighieri, *The Divine Comedy*, trans. by Allen Mandelbaum, 3 vols (Berkeley: University of California Press, 1980–82).

poem. This notion of possibility is explicitly signalled to the reader on the part of Dante-poet through the use of the adjective 'altro': *another* means, a different journey, will be needed in this instance. He further embeds the importance of possibility into his presentation of this different journey through his appeal to a distinct linguistic structure that establishes the conditions by which escape will be possible: the hypothetical or the conditional, introduced in the formula 'if p, then q' (or vice versa, in this instance).[2] Virgil states unquestioningly: *If* the pilgrim wishes to make it out alive, he must enter into the possible world that is the poet's construction of hell, purgatory, and heaven, thus asserting a clear condition and its real consequent should he follow through on the advice.

This opening appeal that, as stated above, serves to motivate the entire fictive journey that is the *Commedia*, quickly establishes the poem's relationship to possibility by intertwining it with the narrative foundations of the text. The *altro viaggio* through the three realms of the afterlife is then constructed and authenticated across the ninety-nine cantos that follow as Dante asks us to buy into the truth of his narrative using poetic structures that create a bridge between the world of the text and the actual world. It also provides early indication of the stakes of embedding a constructed reality and its relation to possibility in the capabilities of language. For ultimately any question of the truth of the poet's words and the world he seeks to create is one of meaning, or semantics. As Dante seeks to represent reality in language, he continually encodes meaning into his verses that can then be evaluated by the reader as true or false, and in doing so makes evident a key component of the philosophy of language he constructs across his work.

In its simplest sense, semantics can be defined as 'the meaning of words and sentences'.[3] Additionally, this question of meaning elicited via an appeal to semantics is also inherently tied to issues of truth and reference as '[...] any theory of meaning will have to describe what

---

2   My analysis will predominantly utilize the terminology of 'conditional' constructions, however it may at times be interchanged with its alternate, 'hypothetical' constructions.

3   The definition of semantics is from A. P. Martinich and David Sosa, Introduction to *The Philosophy of Language*, 6th edn (New York: Oxford University Press, 2013), p. 2.

is and what is not a meaningful expression as well as the systematic relations between words and what they mean'.[4] Possibility enters into philosophical and linguistic theories of meaning through the framework of possible worlds, which have been the subject of intense study beginning around the turn of the twentieth century and have gained steam especially in the most recent fifty years.[5] Evolving out of its early employment by Leibniz, the expression has come to be loosely understood as those worlds different than our own, in which other events or actions could or could have occurred (I will further define how we can understand the notion of 'possible worlds' in the context of this analysis below).[6] It has become especially prevalent in the philosophy of language thanks to its application in semantics and modal logic, with a particular focus in the late twentieth century on conditional statements. Within the literary context, narrative possibility has concomitantly been explored in the most recent century through the rise of theories related to world building and the 'willing suspension of disbelief' inherent to fiction.[7]

---

4   Ibid., p. 2.

5   To understand the depth and breadth of concerns related to possibility and possible worlds, one need look no further than the recently published *Palgrave Encyclopedia of the Possible*, ed. by Vlad P. Glăveanu (Cham: Palgrave MacMillan, 2022), with its 263 entries.

6   For an overview of the derivation of 'possible worlds' from the theories of Leibniz, see Benson Mates, 'Leibniz on Possible Worlds', in *Leibniz: A Collection of Critical Essays*, ed. by Harry G. Frankfurt (Garden City, NY: Anchor Books, 1972), pp. 335–64. Although, as Mates notes, 'the concepts of "possible world" employed by modern investigators are quite different from that of Leibniz himself' (p. 335). For an example of the turn of its application to semantic theory, see Saul Kripke, *Naming and Necessity* (Malden, MA: Blackwell Publishing, 1981).

7   This conception of narrative possibility arises out of the coinage of 'willing suspension of disbelief' on the part of Samuel Taylor Coleridge in Chapter 14 of *Biographia Literaria*, ed. by James Engell and W. Jackson Bate, 2 vols (Princeton: Princeton University Press, 1983), now in *The Collected Works of Samuel Taylor Coleridge*, 16 vols (1969–2001), VII (1985), pp. 1–856. For an overview of the literary theoretical stakes of a discussion of possibility, see also within this volume Teodolinda Barolini, 'Possible Worlds and Reading Dante's *Commedia*: Suspension of Disbelief (Coleridge, Horace, Tolkien, Cecco d'Ascoli) and the Solvents of Narrative and History'. For an example of how the philosophical framework of possible worlds has been applied to narrative theory in more recent decades, see Marie-Laure Ryan, *Possible Worlds, Artificial Intelligence, and Narrative Theory* (Bloomington & Indianapolis, IN: Indiana University Press, 1991).

As it relates to Dante, the issue of possibility has long been tied to the larger stakes of the *Commedia*, as well as to the questions it asks of its readers, through a preoccupation with establishing the truth claims of the poem. In the opening chapter of *The Undivine Comedy*, 'Detheologizing Dante: Realism, Reception, and the Resources of Narrative', Teodolinda Barolini cogently outlines and then engages with the status of this question in the field of Dante studies at the time of the book's publication. The central issue confronting readers, as she reminds us, is: 'How are we to respond to the poet's insistence that he is telling us the truth?'.[8] Her analysis in the chapters that follow has proved foundational in the response it provides by demonstrating exactly how the poet constructs the text at a narrative level such that 'we accept the possible world [...] that Dante has invented' through the deft employment of strategies that allow us to implicitly consent to its reality and realism, thereby establishing 'a fiction that IS true' (*UDC*, pp. 16 and 13).[9] Building on Barolini's approaches to the text, I contend we can also look to Dante's technical employment of the linguistic structure of the hypothetical or the conditional as another tool utilized by the poet to assert the *Commedia*'s composition as a true object that represents the world as it indeed is — one that relies on the poet's engagement with philosophy of language as a mechanism to get at these truths. Introduced within the poem through Dante's use of the small but powerful word 'se' or 'if', this crucial conjunction opens pathways for the reader to imagine or consider various narrative, theological, or logical possibilities that clarify the stakes of the actual poem. We can see the work of the conjunction 'se' in action, for example, if we return to Virgil's words in *Inferno* 1, for its employment sets up the conditions whereby an alternate pathway — a journey through Dante's possible world of hell, purgatory, and heaven — is presented to resolve his narrative dilemma.

---

8   See Teodolinda Barolini, *The Undivine Comedy: Detheologizing Dante* (Princeton: Princeton University Press, 1992), p. 4, hereafter *UDC*. Subsequent references given in parentheses in the main text.

9   For a discussion of how those narrative and poetic strategies utilized in the *Commedia* then extend to engage with the notion of possibility, see Teodolinda Barolini, 'Divine Comedy', in *The Palgrave Encyclopedia of the Possible*, pp. 437–44.

The conjunction 'se' is not an unfamiliar one across the works of Dante. In fact, as the entry on 'Se' in the *Enciclopedia Dantesca* notes, it appears '76 times in the *Vita nuova*, 120 in the *Rime*, 278 in the *Convivio*, and 578 in the *Commedia*, for a total of 1052 occurrences in the canonical works'.[10] Of these occurrences, the most prominent use of 'se' is found in the *periodo ipotetico* or the conditional construction as presented above, which follows the formula 'if *p*, then *q*' and demonstrates some form of entailment between two propositions — the antecedent (*p*, also known as the protasis) and the consequent (*q*, also known as the apodosis) — that establishes a relation to the actual world.[11] However, as Ugo Vignuzzi highlights in this entry, Dante's use of the term also includes syntactic and semantic functions beyond the hypothetical, due to the ability of the Italian to inscribe into the same lexical item concepts that exist separately in languages such as English.[12] For example, Dante utilizes 'se' across his works with multiple additional functions. It can have a delimiting capacity, as well as function in an emphatic, causal, optative, desiderative — which Vignuzzi notes is 'peculiare del fiorentino due-trecentesco' ('particular to Florentine of the 1200s and 1300s') —, concessive, and exceptional ('tranne, eccetto che') manner.[13] Dante also at times uses 'se' as a stand in for 'quasi' ('almost') when paired with 'come', or in a line of indirect questioning. Nevertheless, the preponderance for its employment in conditional constructions, alongside its sustained presence

---

10   See Ugo Vignuzzi, 'Se (sed)', in *Enciclopedia Dantesca*, ed. by Umberto Bosco, 6 vols (Rome: Istituto dell'Enciclopedia Italiana, 1970–78), v (1976), pp. 112–17 (p. 112): '76 volte nella *Vita Nuova*, 120 nelle *Rime*, 278 nel *Convivio*, e 578 nella *Commedia*, per un complesso di 1052 occorrenze nelle opere canoniche [...]'.

11   Ibid.: 'l'impiego più diffuso della congiunzione è quello nel periodo ipotetico, dove introduce l'elemento logicamente condizionante (la protasi, appunto) con una precisa concatenazione causale ("X, allora Y"), cui si unisce la specificazione ulteriore della "possibilità" (reale o ipotetica) di tali premesse, e quindi di tutto il complesso di fatti affermati' ('the most diffuse use is that in the *periodo ipotetico*, where it introduces the logically conditioning element (indeed, the antecedent) with a precise causal concatenation ("X, therefore Y"), to which is added the further specification of "possibility" (real or hypothetical) of such premises, and therefore of the entirety of affirmed facts'). Translation mine.

12   This flexibility of 'se' still exists in modern Italian today.

13   The list here and in the following sentence derives from Vignuzzi, 'Se (sed)', pp. 113–17. His comment regarding the particularity of the desiderative use of the conjunction as deriving from Dante's historical context can be found on p. 115.

particularly in the *Commedia* where it occurs on average five times per canto, demonstrates the centrality of this conjunction in the poem on both a narrative and linguistic level as it creates avenues for the reader to imagine and reason about the relation between the pilgrim's experiences and the world of the poet.

This contribution looks to early moments in the *Commedia* as a case study in how Dante-poet exploits the notion of possibility to important narrative ends, utilizing conditional constructions to assert the truth value of the reality and the realism that he seeks to evince and to nuance his own theory of the meaning within the text.[14] In doing so, I follow Barolini in employing a detheologized approach to analysing the interrelated concepts of possibility and reality as they appear in the poem. This foundational methodology, which serves to move beyond theologized readings of the text (or rather 'a way of reading that attempts to break out of the hermeneutic guidelines that Dante has structured into his poem'), is one she establishes early in *The Undivine Comedy* (*UDC*, p. 17). Importantly, Barolini's method provides us with the ability to stand outside 'Dante's hall of mirrors' through a 'privileg[ing of] form over content' (*UDC*, p. 17). In this vein, I will utilize three related notions of possibility/reality as they appear in the poem as the basis of my argument and as an interpretive tool to step outside of the worlds that Dante has so carefully crafted for his readers, his 'hall of mirrors'. In naming their layers explicitly, I will then be able to demonstrate how the poet masterfully establishes and then exploits the relations between them. Where exactly one should draw the line between broader notions of the real and the possible is contestable. In the context of the present analysis, therefore, I do not seek to demarcate the two definitively or make a claim to their ontology. Rather, I aim to acknowledge and analyse the layers and interactions between the worldviews that Dante proposes.

---

14   My use of the term 'truth value' in this analysis points toward the technical semantic notion where utterances are evaluated as true or false and therefore assigned a truth value. That is, while the term exhibits similarity to the notion of 'truth claims' coming out of narrative theory, it seeks to position itself as distinct from this tradition in its more philosophical application. See *UDC*, chapter 1 for a synthesis of how scholars have discussed the 'truth claims' of Dante's work over the centuries.

The first notion I seek to establish for its employment in this essay is that of the 'actual world'. Different individuals have different viewpoints on the world, which are informed by and encompass their historical and physical realities, but also importantly their belief systems. Therefore, I will define the actual world as that which Dante the historical poet inhabits. This actual world includes his own historical and physical realities and — crucially here — also includes and takes into consideration the Christian belief system that underpins his view of the actual. This world will be designated as the 'real'. I call it the real not because I assert that it is uncontestably real, but rather that it is the worldview Dante is reasoning from, a base world that encompasses his beliefs.

The second notion I seek to define is that of the fiction of his text, which exists as a unique possible world governed by the terms established across the three canticles. This unique possible world is distinct because, while it is informed by the belief systems and historical realities of Dante's actual world, it exists as a separate fictional entity governed by its own organizational principles and structures and contains its own events and individuals. These elements may be shaped by the Christian worldview derived from Dante's actual world (the real), but they are also a manifestation of a unique set of facts and possible belief worlds that governs how such events, characters, and structures would interact in a given context. This world I will assert is the 'fictional reality'.[15] Therefore, while the existence of an afterlife is itself a part of what I will define as the real, given the diffusion of a

---

15 My definition of 'fictional reality' takes inspiration from philosopher David Lewis's understanding of how to evaluate truth claims in fiction, which will be discussed further in relation to *Inferno* 27 (See David Lewis, 'Truth in Fiction', *American Philosophical Quarterly*, 15.1 (1978), pp. 37–46). The paradoxical nature of the terminology I employ here is, as mentioned earlier, consistent with how I believe Dante views his own constructed possible world — one that is fictional but also asserts itself as true. Using the label 'fictional reality' I therefore acknowledge the philosophical implications of calling a fiction a reality. However, my terminology also acknowledges the narratological matrix of 'fictional truth' that exists in both Dante and literary studies more broadly, gestured toward already in this analysis. See, for example, Barolini's discussion from chapter 1 of *The Undivine Comedy* cited above: 'A further paradox furnishes the poet's definition of his poem: the *Commedia* is a nonfalse error, a *non falso errore*, not a fiction that pretends to be true but a fiction that IS true' (*UDC*, p. 13). We can further note that Barolini's Dantean analysis of fictional reality/fictional truth belongs to the current of heightened narratological and semiotic interest that

Christian eschatology underpinning Dante's worldview, the fact that
Minos serves as the guard to the second circle of hell and determines
where newly arrived souls will end up is a particularity that is confined
to the fictional reality.

Finally, a third notion with which the poet engages is simply possibility itself, which allows him to hypothesize what could be or could
have been in relation to the real and/or the fictional reality of the text
using a possible worlds framework. Within the critical tradition, there
has been a tendency to conflate these three distinct layers as I explicate
them here, often claiming an equivalence especially between Dante's
actual world and his fictional reality such that they come to singularly
represent *the real* itself, rather than examining how he structures these
notions as highly technical entities that position themselves in relation
to one another. Utilizing these three established frameworks, I provide
a preliminary assessment of the narrative importance of conditional
constructions in the poem, according to the relation of possibility
to the real and/or the fictional reality, such that we are more clearly
able to see Dante's reliance on these distinct linguistic structures to
construct and consent to the *Commedia*'s truth.

I will begin by assessing the ways in which Dante-poet explicitly signals to the reader the role and the importance of conditional
structures within the text, showing how he isolates and elevates the
construction in *Inferno* 9. It is in this early example that we will see
both his awareness of the inherent possibility inscribed in conditionals,
as well as the way in which their employment serves to buttress the
fictional reality of the narrated journey. I will then turn to *Inferno* 27
to examine more specifically how the poem's employment of conditionals helps situate the fictional reality of the text in dynamic relation
to both possibility and actuality with the help of the frameworks of
contemporary philosophy of language and its approaches to possible
worlds. This episode can then serve as a template for conceptualizing
how Dante-poet's own frequent deployment of linguistic structures
that nuance this relationship between possibility and reality highlight
just how aware he is of the capabilities of one to encode meaning

---

includes works such as Michael Riffaterre's aptly named *Fictional Truth* (Baltimore:
Johns Hopkins University Press, 1990).

about the other. I argue using *Inferno* 27 that, by parsing conditional constructions as a dynamic interplay between the abovementioned forms of possibility and reality, we can observe a technical claim to the truth value of the poet's work and thus to his attention to semantics within the text. Moreover, we are able to more clearly see how the construction contributes to the dual mandate of the *Commedia* as a true object that represents the world as it indeed is.

ESTABLISHING POSSIBILITY: *INFERNO* 9

I turn first to *Inferno* 9, where Dante-poet provides the reader with an early key to understanding the potential of 'se' as a vehicle for possibility within the poem. By staging what happens when one isolates the utterance of a conditional itself, we can observe in this episode how Dante is able to dramatize the construction's ability to encode possibility, for better or for worse, into the meaning of words.

The opening of *Inferno* 9 is critical to the development of the *Commedia*'s narrative in that it represents an early moment of uncertainty within the poem, specifically as it relates to the successful progression of the journey ahead. In earlier cantos of *Inferno*, such as the crossing of the Acheron in *Inferno* 3 and the passage by Minos in *Inferno* 5, any impediment to the travellers' path was met with assurance and easy resolution on the part of Virgil, inaugurating a pattern for the reader whereby the success of the journey and its divine status were taken as a given. For the first time in *Inferno* 8 and the episode's continuation into *Inferno* 9, the established narrative structure is resisted: Virgil and Dante-pilgrim find themselves having been denied entrance into the gates of the city of Dis and, as a result, the pilgrim begins to doubt the abilities of his guide and the sanctioned nature of his travels.

As the two await a sign of help to resolve their narrative impasse, Virgil utters a series of disconnected statements in which he puts into words the doubt that has been building since the previous canto: '"Pur a noi converrà vincer la punga", | cominciò el, "se non…Tal ne s'offerse. | Oh quanto tarda a me ch'altri qui giunga!"' ("'We have to win this battle", he began, | "if not… But one so great had offered help. | How slow that someone's coming to see me!'"; *Inf.* 9.7–9). Importantly, at this critical narrative juncture — the first moment in the text where the

certainty of the journey is placed in question — Virgil begins to express
a conditional statement regarding what might happen if aid does not
come swiftly, signalled by the employment of an antecedent 'se non'
(v. 8), before cutting himself off from the consequent and switching
course. More specifically, he only begins to establish the conditions of
possibility related to the success of the journey in his statement; he
does not flesh them out fully or arrive at a conclusion regarding that
which the possibility would entail. The very nature of the conditional
is never fully expressed before it is denied as impossible. As Anna
Maria Chiavacci Leonardi notes in her commentary, this denial of
the consequent is never unpacked explicitly within the dialogue, but
instead must be supplied by the reader and pilgrim alike:

> la reticenza non è spiegata; il lettore, proprio come il Dante
> personaggio, deve supplire con la sua immaginazione. Eviden-
> temente essa esprime una esitazione in Virgilio, integrabile
> dalle parole che seguono [...].
>
> (the reticence is not explained; readers, just like Dante-pilgrim,
> must compensate with their imagination. Evidently this reti-
> cence expresses a hesitation in Virgil, which can be inserted
> from the words that follow [...]).[16]

While Virgil foregoes the second half of his conditional formula 'if p,
then q', those two small words alone — 'se non' — alongside Virgil's
own rebuttal in the verses shortly after, 'Tal ne s'offerse. | Oh quanto
tarda a me ch'altri qui giunga!' (vv. 8–9), allow Dante-pilgrim to begin
to imagine outcomes that await them if help does not arrive. These
linguistic signals also allow Dante-poet to dramatize the process of
making meaning in conversation in the verses that follow.

In the context of the present analysis, we can note how these three
early verses foreground the work that the conditional is doing to set up
the dialogic interaction that follows in the canto, for the mechanism by
which meaning is made in this episode is presented as a complex interaction between the unfinished conditional and the rebuttal to these

---

16   See Dante Alighieri, *Commedia*, ed. with commentary by Anna Maria Chiavacci Leo-
     nardi, 3 vols (Milan: Mondadori, 1991–97), I: *Inferno* (1991), *ad loc*. For a more recent
     reading of Virgil's cut-off speech, see J. C. Wiles, '"Se non..." (*Inf* 9.9) and "I vostri
     mali..." (23.109): Interpretative Issues of Infernal *Aposiopesis*', *Annali d'italianistica*,
     39 (2021), pp. 205–27.

words all carried out on the part of Virgil as guide. As Chiavacci Leonardi's commentary highlights, it is only by proceeding in the narrative that Dante-pilgrim, and the reader alongside him, is able to supply the remainder of the conditional statement: the consequent is concluded based on how quickly Virgil denies its potential implications. Moreover, the isolation of the antecedent, 'se non' (v. 8), allows Dante-poet to underscore the power of possibility itself in the context of a narrative structure that inherently tends toward a singular resolution. *If* aid does not arrive, the journey might not go as planned. These cut-off words, then, whose effects on the pilgrim are staged throughout the rest of the exchange, do double duty within the construction of the narrative in the poem. From a world-building perspective, they resist the singular path that is the pilgrim's journey, seeding doubt in its foregone conclusion. Importantly, though, they do so by staging possibility itself to allow the pilgrim and reader to imagine the various ways that the narrative could be diverted.[17]

We can therefore see firsthand how this notion of possibility works to reinforce the poet's fictional reality in this moment in *Inferno* 9. By staging doubt regarding what *could* happen if aid does not arrive via a cut-off conditional (explicitly labelling it a 'parola tronca' ('broken phrase'; v. 14), the poet asks the reader to buy into the truth of the path on which Dante-pilgrim is travelling. He does so by creating avenues to consider the journey as one in which success is not a given, thus calling its status as a foregone conclusion into question. The introduction of this possibility then allows the reader to buy more deeply into the fiction that is the *Commedia*, therefore upping the poem's truth value. The result of this buy-in becomes even more important in the context of Dante's enactment of a theory of meaning or semantics within the poem because it then serves as consent to the power that inscribing possibility into language holds in bolstering reality, and therefore its assertion of truth. The poet seems highly aware of the ability of 'se' to

---

17   See Nicolò Crisafi, *Dante's Masterplot and Alternative Narratives in the 'Commedia'* (Oxford: Oxford University Press, 2022), in particular chapter 2, 'Alternative Endings and Parallel Lives' for an important recent contribution that engages with similar questions of possibility in the context of the teleology of the poem, positioning narrative alternativity as manifested in hypothetical constructions as one mechanism by which 'Dante exposes the conditions of possibility of his autobiographical masterplot as such' (p. 85).

access this relation in the context of the narrative in that he isolates and dramatizes its use by cutting the conditional off from its consequent. Thus, he is able to effectively stage how the conjunction alone works to construct possibility, establishing its use in his language theory as a constituent component of the truth value of the poem itself. We will never actually know what the second half of Virgil's cut-off statement would look like, however the mere signalling of the possible through a particular conjunction — 'se non' — is enough to activate fear within the pilgrim and to create narrative suspense for the reader such that the journey's inevitable success becomes all the more believable.

THE STUDY OF CONDITIONALS PAST AND A CONTEMPORARY FRAMEWORK

Having established this distinct connection between conditionality and possibility that Dante constructs in *Inferno* 9, as well as the import- ance of its impact on the narrative and its truth value, we can now turn to contextualizing the poet's employment of conditionals to then bet- ter evaluate them throughout the *Commedia*. I begin by noting that the study of conditional constructions is not foreign to the field of Dante studies, or its points of contact in the discipline of historical linguistics. Gianluca Colella's monograph *Costrutti condizionali in italiano antico*, for example, has undertaken the important historical-linguistic project of tracing the development of and categorizing the use of conditional constructions in early Italian literature, which includes a discussion of Dante in light of his employment of conditionals in the argumentative structure of the *Convivio*.[18] Colella demonstrates how the use of this particular linguistic structure in the poet's philosophical treatise, much like in *Monarchia*, is largely modelled off earlier Latin forms that serve to establish and verify premises in a scholastic vein.[19] As his study relates to how conditionals can figure in narrative formulations, and specifically in dialogue, he turns instead to Boccaccio's *Decameron*.

---

18   See Gianluca Colella, *Costrutti condizionali in italiano antico* (Rome: Aracne, 2010), Section 9.3.2, 'L'argomentare del *Convivio*'.

19   In particular, he notes how within the *Convivio*, 'la costruzione condizionale permette di connettere la domanda alla risposta' ('the conditional construction allows the connection of the question to the answer'). Colella, *Costrutti condizionali*, p. 231, translation mine.

The *Enciclopedia Dantesca*, cited earlier in this essay, also includes two important entries related to conditionals. Both the entry on 'Se', as well as one specifically dedicated to the 'Periodo ipotetico' serve predominantly to catalogue the poet's various uses of the conjunction itself and the conditional construction.[20] In the latter in particular, Franca Brambilla Ageno categorizes the different types of conditionals in the poet's works and gestures toward their narrative impact. She begins by noting that a highly common conditional in Dante is that of the type discussed from *Inferno* 1, in which the antecedent and the consequent are both in the indicative mood such that the statement serves as 'una concatenazione di fatti che "suole" verificarsi, che ha luogo tutte le volte che si verifica l'ipotesi' ('a concatenation of facts that "customarily" occurs, that happens every time that the hypothesis is verified').[21] Interestingly, her succinct description of these indicative conditionals provides additional credence to the relation between reality and possibility gestured toward in the *Inferno* 1 example and asserted in this essay: Virgil introduces the possible world of the poem, the 'altro viaggio' ('other path'; *Inf.* 1.91), in a structure that establishes a factual relation. If Dante wishes to exit the dark wood, he must travel through the three realms of the afterlife. The fact that the afterlife is presented as a 'verifiable' consequent, encoded via the use of an indicative conditional, underscores its existence as a true object.

Brambilla Ageno also notes a high density of what she terms 'true' hypotheticals ('il periodo ipotetico vero e proprio'),[22] or those in which one can observe the subjunctive in the antecedent and the conditional in the consequent. Dante's use of this formula, she asserts, does not always indicate impossibility, but rather seems to get at different forms of possibility:

> Presso Dante, l'alto numero di p[eriodi] ipotetici con protasi al cong[iuntivo] e apodosi al cond[izionale] può suggerire molte considerazioni sia sulla capacità costruttiva che regge periodi vasti e complessi e nello stesso tempo saldi e simmetrici come

---

20   See Vignuzzi, 'Se (sed)'; and Franca Brambilla Ageno, 'Periodo ipotetico', Appendix to *Biografia, Lingua e stile, Opere*, in *Enciclopedia Dantesca*, ed. by Bosco, VI (1978), pp. 408–24.

21   Brambilla Ageno, 'Periodo ipotetico', p. 409, translation mine.

22   Ibid., p. 417.

architetture classiche; sia sulla ricchezza fantastica, che non
solo conferisce concretezza ed evidenza a un mondo immagina-
rio, ma varia tale rappresentazione col riferimento (anche nella
protasi di p[eriodi] ipotetici) a immagini di altra sfera [...].

(In Dante, the high number of conditional constructions with a
protasis [antecedent] in the subjunctive and an apodosis [con-
sequent] in the conditional can suggest many considerations
both with respect to Dante's capacity to construct, a capacity
that supports vast and complex sentences that are at the same
time firm and symmetrical as in classical architecture; as well
as with respect to the richness of his fantasy, which not only
confers concreteness and evidence on an imaginary world but
varies such representation with referral (even in the protasis of
the conditional) to images from another realm [...]).[23]

Brambilla Ageno gestures toward something important in her observation that these forms of the conditional — what in English are termed
counterfactuals or subjunctive conditionals — ground the poet's statements regarding his imaginary world in concreteness and evidence.
How exactly the construction does so is the point of departure for
the present analysis. As I have shown thus far, scholars of Dante have
observed both the importance of possibility in the construction of
the *Commedia* as a whole, as well as certain linguistic features such
as the conditional that may contribute to its centrality within the text.
However, a next important step in this discussion is to analyse how
these linguistic features do indeed contribute in a technical manner
to this established relation between possibility and reality, thereby
underscoring the truth of the poet's work. It is here that I believe the
employment of approaches from philosophy of language, and particularly those frameworks proposed in the most recent century, can be
useful.

I assert that Dante is utilizing the poem itself as a testing ground
for the ways the linguistic construction of the conditional taps into
various frameworks of possibility within the narrative to say something
about its ability to bolster the truth value of his fictional reality under
construction and open pathways to access the real. This performance
of the power of conditionals to inscribe possibility within the poem
presents an interesting counterpoint to ancient and medieval concerns

---

23   Ibid., translation mine.

about the construction, which largely focused on their appearance in logical argumentation. As noted also by Colella, Boethius and Abelard can be taken as prime examples of these earlier studies of the linguistic structure of conditionals. Boethius investigated their form in his *De hypoteticis syllogismis*; as the title of this work implies, his predominant interest was their relation to the syllogism and to Aristotelian logic.[24] Abelard, too, speaks of conditionals always in relation to the truth or falsity of statements.[25]

It is predominantly in modern philosophical investigation that we see a turn toward formalizing the connection between conditional constructions and various forms of possibility through a semantics of possible worlds. Therefore, I will turn to the contemporary discipline of philosophy of language to demonstrate further the robust and highly technical nature of Dante's thoughts on possibility and its ability to be encoded within the linguistic structures of poetry. Much work has been done in the previous century in the philosophy of language to conceptualize this semantic theory of possible worlds, which has then been applied to conditional constructions to demonstrate their effectiveness at tapping into that notion of possibility. One of the earliest and most important philosophers who utilized possible worlds to provide a working theory of conditional constructions was Robert Stalnaker. I propose that his 'A Theory of Conditionals' can be used with great effectiveness to unpack the implicit and explicit work that these structures are doing within the *Commedia*.

In his essay, Robert Stalnaker looks specifically to counterfactual conditionals to discuss the semantic and pragmatic issues that arise in analysing conditional statements and puts forth a theory for their evaluation. He writes that to establish the belief conditions of these sorts of statements, the process of evaluation is as follows: 'First, add the antecedent (hypothetically) to your stock of beliefs; second, make whatever adjustments are required to maintain consistency (without modifying the hypothetical belief in the antecedent); finally, consider

---

24   See Boethius, *De hypotheticis syllogismis*, ed. and trans. into Italian by Luca Obertello (Brescia: Paideia, 1969). For a succinct overview of these historical touchpoints, see Colella, *Costrutti condizionali*, p. 15.

25   See, for example, the fourth tractatus of Abelard's *Dialectica*, ed. by Lambertus M. De Rijk, rev. 2nd edn (Assen, Netherlands: Van Gorcum & Comp., 1970).

whether or not the consequent is then true.[26] However, he notes that while we may be able to assert a set of conditions under which we can determine the belief conditions of any statement of the structure 'if p, then q', we must also identify a mechanism by which we are able to assert the truth conditions of these constructions to provide credence to our beliefs. Specifically, we must appeal to the idea of possible worlds to move from belief to an evaluation of the truth conditions of a conditional statement. Stalnaker proposes the following framework to do so: 'Consider a possible world in which A is true, and which otherwise differs minimally from the actual world. *"If A, then B" is true (false) just in case B is true (false) in that possible world.*'[27] That is, to evaluate conditionals we must begin by establishing some sort of relation between a possible world in which the hypothetical under consideration were true and the actual world. We do so by employing a selection function to find the closest possible world in which the antecedent or if-statement is true, with otherwise minimal difference from the actual world, and evaluate if the consequent is also true at that world.

As indicated in this description, Stalnaker's theory of conditionals is important for its introduction of the concept of minimal difference between the actual world and possible worlds as a means to assert the truth value of a conditional statement, thus also introducing a hierarchy or ordering of possible worlds such that some might be closer to the actual world while others remain farther away, depending on the similarity of their characteristics. It is additionally useful to note that he positions this framework as largely a semantic one. The theory as it is presented explains an underlying linguistic concept, rather than the particularities of use of conditionals in everyday human speech. This semantic concept does have distinct pragmatic repercussions, in that he notes how the changes that each possible world undergoes are 'largely dependent on pragmatic considerations for their application.'[28] We will see in the discussion that follows how Dante too seems to be negotiating the bounds between semantic theory and pragmatic contexts of use in his own working understanding of conditionals in

---

26   Robert Stalnaker, 'A Theory of Conditionals', in *Studies in Logical Theory*, ed. by Nicholas Rescher (Oxford: Blackwell Publishing, 1968), pp. 98–112 (p. 102).

27   Ibid., p. 102, author's emphasis.

28   Ibid., p. 104.

the poem, for he takes the interaction between the two as part and parcel of his establishment of his fictional reality in the narrative, as well as its relation to accessing the real.

Toward the end of his discussion, Stalnaker highlights the importance — and at first glance the contradictory nature — that evidence plays in the assessment of the truth value of this linguistic structure. We might ask: Since conditional statements rely on an assessment of a possible world, which does not indeed exist, how can they be verified in the actual world? He relies once again on minimal difference to answer this question: 'It is because counterfactuals are generally about possible worlds which are very much like the actual one, and defined in terms of it, that evidence is so often relevant to their truth.'[29] This theory of conditionals leads Stalnaker to assert that the function of a conditional is that it '[...] provides a set of conventions for selecting possible situations which have a specified relation to what actually happens. This makes it possible for statements about unrealized possibilities to tell us, not just about the speaker's imagination, but about the world.'[30] As can be seen from this high-level overview, the notion of possible worlds is central to Stalnaker's theory of conditionals. Moreover, as he briefly suggests in his own conclusion, the theory of conditionals he develops also has real repercussions in the assertion of a relation to the actual world.[31]

Stalnaker's theory discussed here is one of the earliest that proposes a possible worlds framework for conditional statements and, as such, the tools and vocabulary employed therein are particularly productive for the clarity they provide in recognizing the fundamental components of the linguistic construction and its connection to possibility.[32] I believe that the methodologies provided by Stalnaker,

---

29   Ibid., p. 112.

30   Ibid.

31   As will be shown in the analysis that follows, this framework for conditional statements not only serves as a basis to establish relations between the possible and the real, but also how fiction figures into this discussion. See, for example, David Lewis's 'Truth in Fiction', cited earlier, which relies on similar correspondences between different possible worlds and the actual world as a means to establish the truth value of statements in the context of a fiction.

32   For an overview of how theories of possible worlds and of conditionals have evolved in recent decades, see Christopher Menzel, 'Possible Worlds', in *The Stanford Encyclope-*

and later by philosopher David Lewis who continued to nuance this framework of possible worlds as they relate to counterfactuals,[33] are particularly helpful in reconstructing how Dante might be theorizing a use of conditionals within the context of the *Commedia*. As the examples that I have discussed have shown, he similarly perceives this ability of conditionals to access the question of possibility and possible worlds and, across the poem, he is capitalizing on the connection between these linguistic structures and the idea of possibility for narrative buy-in. Thus, the poet's own use of the construction seems well positioned to benefit from this more contemporary approach. Moreover, his sustained employment of this linguistic structure at critical narrative moments contributes to the establishment of larger theories of meaning and use within the text.

DETHEOLOGIZING NARRATIVE POSSIBILITY AND FICTIONAL
REALITY: *INFERNO 27*

I now turn to one canto in particular — the pilgrim's encounter with Guido da Montefeltro in *Inferno* 27 — to highlight the conditional construction's ability to establish the fictional world of the *Commedia* specifically in relation to the possible and the real. In particular, we can observe that a counterfactual conditional introduces Guido's biographical discussion, which then leads to the recounting of the course of action that landed him in the eighth circle of hell. As will be shown, Guido's use of this conditional does double duty in the context of this narrative episode. It is not only our first indication of a seriously faulty logic on the part of the sinner, which gives credence to the erroneous reasoning that led to his actions recounted in the text, but, moreover, it embeds the complex notion of possibility in counterfactual form to assert a relation between possible worlds, including that of the poem's fictional reality. This relation that Guido's conditional establishes then allows Dante-poet to nuance how the rules of his construction of the

---

dia of Philosophy, ed. by Edward N. Zalta, Summer 2024 edn <https://plato.stanford.edu/entries/possible-worlds/> [accessed 9 June 2025]; and Willow Starr, 'Counterfactuals', in The Stanford Encyclopedia of Philosophy, ed. by Edward N. Zalta, Winter 2022 edn <https://plato.stanford.edu/archives/win2022/entries/counterfactuals/> [accessed 9 June 2025].

33   See David Lewis, *Counterfactuals* (Cambridge, MA: Harvard University Press, 1973).

underworld itself hinge on careful assessment of the distance between the actual world (the real) and the world of his fiction.

The exchange in *Inferno* 27 between the pilgrim, his guide, and Guido da Montefeltro opens with the yet-to-be-named sinner who greets the two travellers, noting that he heard Virgil speaking Lombard. The Roman poet then urges Dante-pilgrim to speak in this instance, given their interlocutor is Italian. After exchanging information regarding the current political state of Romagna, the narrative shifts from the urban to the personal and Dante-pilgrim requests to know the sinner's name. By way of response, he answers with an overture that couches his fear of revealing himself in two conditional statements:

> 'S'i' credesse che mia risposta fosse
> a persona che mai tornasse al mondo,
> questa fiamma staria sanza più scosse;
> ma però che già mai di questo fondo
> non tornò vivo alcun, s'i' odo il vero,
> sanza tema d'infamia ti rispondo'.
>
> ('If I thought my reply were meant for one
> who ever could return into the world,
> this flame would stir no more; and yet, since none —
> if what I hear is true — ever returned
> alive from this abyss, then without fear
> of facing infamy, I answer you'.)
> (*Inf.* 27.61–66)

The sinner, we come to learn, is Guido da Montefeltro; however, as he declares in these verses, he is only willing to identify himself as such if he can be assured that the individual speaking to him cannot return to the world of the living (and likely spread news of his story). His preamble is predicated entirely on conditional reasoning to arrive at this point.

Guido's first assertion in verses 61–63 — 'S'i' credesse che mia risposta fosse | a persona che mai tornasse al mondo, | questa fiamma staria sanza più scosse' — is a textbook case of a counterfactual conditional, with a subjunctive in the antecedent and a conditional in the consequent. Moreover, it is followed by an indicative conditional that rebuts the doubt seeded in the counterfactual, asserting as fact the belief that no one has ever returned from hell to the world above. Relying on precise linguistic structures and verb forms that reveal the sinner's apparent reasoning, the importance of this narrative moment is heightened by the fact that it is immediately clear to the reader that Guido's belief conditions and the truth he derives from them are utterly incorrect.

In his recent commentary to the *Commedia*, Nicola Fosca succinctly unpacks the incorrect logic that Guido da Montefeltro utilizes in this moment such that he arrives at false conclusions:

> in effetti il suo ragionamento è formalmente esatto, ma la premessa su cui si basa ('nessuno entra in *questo fondo*, nell'Inferno, e poi torna a vivere sulla terra') è materialmente erronea, e quindi porta ad una conclusione altrettanto erronea ('il mio interlocutore resterà qui e posso tranquillamente parlargli').

> (in effect, his reasoning is formally precise, but the premise on which it is based ('no one enters into this pit, in inferno, and then returns to live on earth') is materially incorrect, and therefore it leads to a further incorrect conclusion ('my interlocutor will remain here and I can calmly speak to him').[34]

I assert that, in addition to staging the use of faulty logic to arrive at incorrect premises and conclusions, Dante-poet is also tapping into the framework of possible worlds he observes within counterfactual conditionals to heighten the absurdity of Guido's statement in the context of the poem. The problem for Guido, the poet implies, is that he reasons using an incorrect relation between worlds.

Guido da Montefeltro's counterfactual seeks to establish a relation between a possible world and the base world from which he reasons, which has its foundation in beliefs derived from the actual world. However, as Dante-poet masterfully shows, what the sinner does not consider is how the world in which the pilgrim is travelling (that of the fictional reality in which Guido also happens to exist) is already different from the actual world he claims as his starting point — for

---

34   See Nicola Fosca, Commentary to the *Inferno*, in The Dartmouth Dante Project, 2025 <https://dante.dartmouth.edu/> [accessed 9 June 2025], author's emphasis. For an alternate reading whereby Guido da Montefeltro employs the conditional precisely because he knows Dante is living and wishes to have his story told in the world above, see Joseph Markulin, 'Dante's Guido da Montefeltro: A Reconsideration', *Dante Studies*, 100 (1982), pp. 25–40.

indeed, the world of the fiction *does* allow for a sanctioned individual to journey to the underworld in the flesh only to return to that of the living. Therefore, rather than simply asserting a belief about a possible world in which a distinct hell that can be journeyed to exists, calculated based on its distance to the actual world, the sinner must judge the relation taking into account the ways in which the *Commedia* has established a different rulebook for the afterlife.

We can begin to understand the full impact of Guido da Montefeltro's counterfactual and its subsequent rebuttal by turning to Stalnaker's theory of conditionals. We remember that to evaluate a counterfactual statement, we can utilize the following formula: 'Consider a possible world in which A is true, and which otherwise differs minimally from the actual world. *"If A, then B" is true (false) just in case B is true (false) in that possible world.'*[35] We can see that Guido da Montefeltro is staging an appeal to a similar framework in his own conditional as a means to assess the truth value of his belief. When he reasons, "'S'i' credesse che mia risposta fosse | a persona che mai tornasse al mondo, | questa fiamma staria sanza più scosse'" (*Inf.* 27.61–63), what he implies in his antecedent is: *If there exists a world in which* my interlocutor could return to the living. In that case, he would say no more.

Importantly, though, he continues in the indicative to highlight how this process of reasoning using another possible world (i.e., one in which someone could return above) leads him to conclude that this possible world couldn't exist: If what he knows about the actual world is true, this simply isn't possible. The inherent impossibility he expresses in his denial highlights his miscalculation: he did not consider all possible worlds accurately in his evaluation of the first conditional. His incorrect evaluation of possible worlds and his ultimate denial of their existence results in Guido's choice to speak.

What he fails to recognize is that the possible world in which an individual can return to the world above does indeed exist; it is the world he is living in himself. This is the fictional world of the poem, which has its own set of minimal differences from the actual world that must inform Guido's reasoning. Therefore, Guido's logic breaks down

---

35   Stalnaker, 'A Theory of Conditionals', p. 102, author's emphasis.

because he creates a relational framework between the wrong set of worlds. What he needs to do is judge the distance of his conditional from the fictional world of the poem, which holds different rules about travelling to and returning from the underworld, not the actual world. To do so correctly, he would need to utilize a slightly modified set of facts or evidence. In his own theory of conditionals, Stalnaker gestures toward issues of this nature in discussing the contingency of possible worlds and their need for evidence.[36] However, we can further specify this notion by turning to highly related frameworks in philosophy of language regarding truth in fiction to better understand how counter-factual reasoning can be employed specifically to determine the truth value of assertions about a fictional world. This additional nuance will allow us to then better understand how Guido's logic fails in such a particular way, as well as how Dante-poet can be seen as staking claim to the world of his fiction in relation to the real and the possible in this moment.

Earlier in this essay, I indicated how a possible worlds theory of conditionals allows one to assess the truth claims encoded within this linguistic structure. Interestingly, this framework of possible worlds developed for assessing the truth conditions of a counterfactual has been similarly applied to conceptualize the reasoning individuals must engage in to determine the truth conditions of fictional worlds. Phil-osopher David Lewis, whose own theory of conditionals very much builds on that of Stalnaker, puts forth this framework in his 'Truth in Fiction'.[37] The possible worlds theory of truth in fiction asserts that to establish the truth conditions of statements regarding a fictional world, we need to view them keeping in mind both the authorial assertions made about its existence (derived from the facts of the narrative), as well as the general background of 'belief worlds' on which the fic-tion operates. These 'belief worlds' can be defined as 'the beliefs that are overt in the community of origin of the fiction'.[38] Putting these components together, Lewis states that the truth value of a statement regarding fictional worlds can be determined by taking as fact authorial

---

36   Ibid., pp. 111–12.
37   See David Lewis, 'Truth in Fiction', *American Philosophical Quarterly*, 15.1 (1978), pp. 37–46.
38   Ibid., p. 44.

assertions about its existence against the backdrop of the overt belief worlds of the author's community of origin and then judging new information based on the relation of similarity between the fictional world and the possible world in which the new premises exist.[39] That is, rather than reasoning between the actual world and the possible, we must first accommodate the reality of the fictional world before establishing its new relation to possibility.

Utilizing the conceptual framework afforded by this notion of truth in fiction, we can more clearly understand how Dante-poet is theorizing the interaction between the actual world, the fictional world, and both of their relations to other possible worlds in his staging of this utterance on the part of Guido da Montefeltro. While Guido asserts a counterfactual conditional to assess the truth value between the actual world and a minimally different possible world, he fails to consider the relevant interactions between the facts and belief systems of that world in which one who lives could be standing in front of him, or rather the fictional world that is the *Commedia*. These factors that Guido disregards are however highly apparent to both the reader and Dante-pilgrim, for their truth is constantly reaffirmed across the poem, such that we are able to immediately spot the faulty logic of the sinner.[40]

Dante utilizes these conditionals in *Inferno* 27 as a mechanism to then set up a dense dialogic interaction that follows to highlight the breakdown of language and logic on the part of both Boniface VIII and Guido. However, the precise linguistic constructions discussed here that initiate Guido's tale specifically engage with possibility to establish the fictional world in relation to the actual and the possible, highlighting the importance of taking the rules of the world of the

---

39 Lewis states that 'a sentence of the form "In the fiction f, φ" is non-vacuously true iff, whenever w is one of the collective belief worlds of the community of origin of f, then some world where f is told as known fact and φ is true differs less from the world w, on balance, than does any world where f is told as known fact and φ is not true. It is vacuously true iff there are no possible worlds where f is told as known fact'. See Lewis, 'Truth in Fiction', p. 45.

40 They are reaffirmed, for example, each time the status of the pilgrim's body is discussed in hell. See *Inferno* 3 where the apparent (i.e., perceivable) nature of Dante's body, and therefore his status as living and distinct from the souls that populate *Inferno*, is acknowledged by Charon on the shores of the Acheron: 'E tu che se' costì, anima viva, | pàrtiti da cotesti che son morti' ('And you approaching there, you living soul, | keep well away from these — they are the dead'; *Inf.* 3.88–89).

fiction into consideration to accurately assess the truth value of claims asserted therein. In so clearly staging an incorrect application of a possible worlds framework by having a sinner miscalculate the role that the fiction plays in this sort of reasoning, Dante-poet gives credence to his own world and establishes it as a verifiable reality. By highlighting the inaccuracy of facts and belief systems that differ from those that comprise the world of the *Commedia* — he indicates they ultimately lead to erroneous conclusions — he elevates the truth of the fictional reality itself.[41]

Beginning with Dante's staging of the power of 'se' in *Inferno* 9, we have seen how conditionals contribute to the construction of the *Commedia* as a true object that represents the world as it indeed is. *Inferno* 27 then serves to highlight how the linguistic structure is employed as a key for the reader to situate the fictional reality of the text in dynamic relation to both possibility and actuality. Using these cantos as case studies, I contend that by parsing conditional constructions as an interplay between the abovementioned layers of possibility and reality embedded in the poem, we can observe a technical claim to its asserted truth value. Moreover, in foregrounding the poet's keen attention to a semantic claim to truth therewithin, we can more clearly see how linguistically encoded possibility contributes to Barolini's convincing affirmation of the *Commedia* as 'a fiction that IS true' (*UDC*, p. 13).

---

41 This move to elevate the truth of the fictional reality by highlighting as erroneous the belief systems that differ from it demonstrates interesting similarity to the poet's move in the intertextual domain to elevate the credibility of his own text by calling into question the texts of authors with whom he is in direct conversation, such as Virgil (for example in *Inferno* 13). On the use of intertextuality to establish truth claims, Barolini has noted: 'To study Dante's handling of his precursors is necessarily to study his truth claims, since he consistently formulates the difference between his poetry and that of his predecessors in terms of truth versus falsehood: he secures the credibility of his text by constructing situations designed to reveal the incredibility of his precursors' texts'. See *UDC*, p. 5 note 5. Her discussion of intertextuality and truth claims in *The Undivine Comedy* derives from Teodolinda Barolini, *Dante's Poets: Textuality and Truth in the 'Comedy'* (Princeton: Princeton University Press, 1984).

II. DETHEOLOGIZE TO HISTORICIZE

Detheologize to Historicize

NASSIME CHIDA

Francesco Torraca's early twentieth-century scholarship on Dante was notable for its historical detail. Torraca identified specific historical events and associated them with Dante's verse, locating many of Dante's manipulations of history by bringing divergences between Dante's account and the historical record to the reader's attention. In this vein, not as an example of a divergence but as a clarification of the historical record, Torraca pointed out that Dante is the only source for the story of Francesca.[1]

For almost a century following Torraca's work, Dante scholars avoided using history to interpret the *Commedia*.[2] During this period, the areas of Dante Studies where history would be used was in the time-honoured tradition of writing biographies of Dante, as well as in the philological work of collecting, editing, interpreting and distributing the extant documents relevant to his life, his reception, and the material production of his poem. Over the course of the twentieth century,

---

1   Francesco Torraca, *Il Canto v dell' 'Inferno'* (Rome: Nuova Antologia, 1902).
2   Elisa Brilli wrote of a hesitance among Dante scholars to use historical research following the foundational work carried out in the previous century. Nevertheless, she drew attention to some notable exceptions in her essay Elisa Brilli, 'Dante e la storia: gli studi storici nelle *Letture Classensi* (12 dicembre 2020)', in *Cinquant'anni di letture classensi: lingua, storia e modernità di Dante*, ed. by Giuseppe Ledda, special issue of *Letture Classensi*, 49 (2021), pp. 69–88, including philological work on Dante's religious context, his relationship with and representation of Florence, and the 1979 edition of his letters edited in part by the medieval historian Arsenio Frugoni.

six new biographies of Dante were written, none of which altered the long-established narrative of his life.[3]

In the new millennium, there was a surge in scholarship involving historical research, sometimes referred to as the 'historical turn' in Dante Studies. This historical turn is typically traced back to Carpi's 2004 book, *La nobiltà di Dante*, which challenged a number of previously settled questions about Dante's life.[4] In her survey of historical research in Dante Studies within the context of the publication *Letture Classensi*, Brilli highlighted two older works: Padoan's 1993 *Il lungo cammino del 'poema sacro'* and Pasquini's *Dante e le figure del vero. La fabbrica della 'Commedia'*, published in 2001.[5]

The Undivine Comedy was published in 1992. I wish to highlight here the fact that *historicizing* approaches to Dante, which are a part of the historical turn in Dante Studies, belong to the legacy of Teodolinda Barolini's concept of 'detheologizing' Dante. Within the corpus of Barolini's writing, the series formed by *The Undivine Comedy* in 1992 and the articles 'Dante and Francesca da Rimini' in 2000 and '"Only Historicize"' in 2009 represents a critical trajectory from detheologizing to historicizing.[6] In *The Undivine Comedy*, Barolini devised a

---

3   For an assessment of the biographical tradition in the twentieth and twenty-first centuries see Elisa Brilli, 'Dante's Biographies and Historical Studies: An Ouverture', *Dante Studies*, 136.1 (2018), pp. 133–42.

4   See Umberto Carpi, *La nobiltà di Dante* (Florence: Polistampa, 2004). Carpi's study focuses on Dante's engagement with his political contexts. It promoted the theory of an ideological shift over the course of Dante's exile. This work inspired a 2012 biography of Dante by Santagata, a new account of Dante's life that presented him as a political opportunist. See Marco Santagata, *Dante. Il romanzo della sua vita* (Milan: Mondadori, 2012). These books were in turn followed in 2015 by a biography by Inglese which, unlike Carpi and Santagata's accounts, was firmly grounded in both literary and documentary evidence. See Giorgio Inglese, *Vita di Dante. Una biografia possibile* (Rome: Carocci, 2015). These works coincided with the historical turn in Dante Studies.

5   The two works cited by Brilli are Giorgio Padoan, *Il lungo cammino del 'poema sacro'. Studi danteschi* (Florence: Olschki, 1993); Emilio Pasquini, *Dante e le figure del vero. La fabbrica della 'Commedia'* (Milan: Bruno Mondadori, 2001).

6   Teodolinda Barolini, *The Undivine Comedy: Detheologizing Dante* (Princeton: Princeton University Press, 1992), hereafter *UDC*. Subsequent references given in parentheses in the main text. See also Teodolinda Barolini, 'Dante and Francesca da Rimini: Realpolitik, Romance, Gender', *Speculum* 75.1 (2000), pp. 1–28 and Barolini, '"Only Historicize": History, Material Culture (Food, Clothes, Books), and the Future of Dante Studies', *Dante Studies*, 127 (2009), pp. 37–54, hereafter *OH*. Subsequent references given in parentheses in the main text.

new way of reading Dante, detheologizing, which among other things, offered a solution to the bind that was inhibiting the use of history to better understand Dante's writings. In 'Dante and Francesca da Rimini' she produced an example of the interpretations made possible by historicizing, which she explicitly traced back to detheologizing. In '"Only Historicize"' she invited young scholars to historicize Dante for themselves.

Historicizing is one among several approaches to Dante that uses history to enhance an understanding of the text. In the context of Dante Studies, the word immediately evokes Barolini's '"Only Historicize"', which in turn brings to mind two other texts; first, Fredric Jameson's 1981 injunction to 'always historicize' in *The Political Unconscious: Narrative as a Socially Symbolic Act*. Jameson's thesis was that narratives are socially symbolic acts that negotiate and symbolically resolve the contradictions inherent in social and political life; they should therefore be interpreted within their social and historical context. Second, '"Only Historicize"' also refers to E. M. Forster's novel *Howards End*, published in 1910, in which the protagonist Margaret Schlegel seeks to bridge the gaps between people of different social classes and to reconcile the intellectual and emotional aspects of life. Margaret's exhortation to 'only connect!' is used as an epigraph, and the passage is quoted at greater length within the article. The combination of these two references in the title '"Only Historicize"' suggests to me that restoring Dante's poem to its historical context need not undermine the view that the poem also transcends its context, and is thus exceptional. In Margaret's words, 'Only connect the prose and the passion, and both will be exalted' (*OH*, p. 38).[7]

To historicize the *Commedia* is to locate meaning in Dante's verse that can only be accessed by considering its historical context, understood on the basis of pre-existing and contemporary sources, as well

---

7   *OH*, continuing on p. 38: 'By "only historicize" I mean to invoke the well known injunction of E. M. Forster's *Howards End* and thus to exhort rather than to restrict: "Only connect! That was the whole of her sermon. Only connect the prose and the passion, and both will be exalted, and human love will be seen at its height. Live in fragments no longer. Only connect, and the beast and the monk, robbed of the isolation that is life to either, will die." The fact that Forster's plea also takes a stand that is profoundly against dualism makes it, in my view, all the more suited as a Dantean epigraph.'

as current historiography, on the assumption that, if the context is not restored, some aspects of the poem will become obscured over time, including in the time between the writing of the poem and the earliest commentaries. To historicize the *Commedia* is to confront the implications of the vast historiography on Dante's context that remains unexploited within Dante Studies. Barolini does this in 'Dante and Francesca', effectively participating in the historical turn before it was detected and named. Barolini discovered 'a specialized bibliography on the historical Francesca of great erudition' but found that it 'rarely factored into literary readings'.[8] Thus the fact that Dante was the only source for Francesca, highlighted by Torraca and reiterated in the *Enciclopedia Dantesca*, had not, she noted, informed subsequent readings of *Inferno* 5.

A significant part of the historiography on Dante's historical context has yet to inform critical readings of the *Commedia*, a fact I had the opportunity to substantiate for myself. In dealing with the Malatesta family's politics in 'Dante and Francesca', Barolini had noted the absence of interpretations of *Inferno* 27 that took into account Guido da Montefeltro's impact on Romagna. In 2021, I consulted the most cited history of medieval Romagna, published in 1965,[9] and found that the catalogue of Romagnol tyrants in *Inferno* 27, apparently unrelated to the second half of the canto featuring Guido da Montefeltro, became both a historical analysis of exceptional insight and an informed assault on Guido's personal military record, when read in light of the history of medieval Romagna and of the Montefeltro bloodline.[10] The failure to factor in historical information, latent in the first half of the canto, with respect to Guido da Montefeltro's story in the second half of the canto left a critical void that resembled the situation described by Barolini in 'Dante and Francesca'.

Historicizing does not involve confirming or questioning any given narrative of Dante's life, including the material conditions of the poem's production. When historicizing the *Commedia*, only the

---

8   Barolini, 'Dante and Francesca', p. 2.
9   Augusto Vasina, *I Romagnoli fra autonomie cittadine e accentramento papale nell'età di Dante* (Florence: Olschki, 1965).
10   Nassime Chida, 'Guido da Montefeltro and the Tyrants of Romagna in *Inferno* 27', *Romanic Review*, 112.1 (2021), pp. 97–119.

most uncontroversial facts about Dante's life serve to support an argument, meaning any event for which there is unambiguous first-hand documentary evidence, such as his exile and his letters, or the events included in Inglese's 'cronologia minima'.[11] Dante's own claims about his life are important to acknowledge when historicizing; however, these should be treated on a case-by-case basis with every effort made to maintain appropriate scepticism.[12] The uncertainty about Dante's life can be tolerated by not basing a given interpretation of the poem on either unproven biographical data or on Dante's own statements. For example, when historicizing *Inferno* 10, I found that while in 1302 Dante and the other exiles were accused of public crimes, in the time of Farinata and until 1267, mass exclusion was practiced on the basis of factional affiliation. To factor this information into a reading of *Inferno* 10 is to see that Dante inserted his own exile — and to some extent Guido Cavalcanti's exile, during which Guido became terminally ill during Dante's term as a prior — into the history of mass exclusion which he reconstructed over the course of the canto, in the form of a back and forth between the pilgrim and Farinata, the factional leader who inaugurated this very history in Florence and one of the first Ghibellines on record. Whether the accusations of corruption were grounded in truth or entirely fabricated is not relevant to this understanding of the canto, which shows Dante constructing a history of Florentine factionalism centred around moments of mass political exclusion, and presenting his own exile as a continuation of this partisan warfare, at a time of Guelf hegemony in Florence. The historical context thus shows Dante as a historian, who also used his poem to defend himself against accusations of corruption.

While historicizing, from a practical standpoint, relies on the scholarship of historians of medieval Italy and philologists of Italian literature, from a conceptual perspective it is made possible by detheologizing. In the first chapter of *The Undivine Comedy*, entitled 'Detheologizing Dante: Realism, Reception and the Resources of Narrative', Barolini took the necessary first step of deconstructing Dante's

---

11   Inglese, *Vita di Dante*.

12   Brilli called attention to the fact that over fifty percent of the sources for Dante's life are Dante's own statements, which scholars have preferred not to question even when there is counter-evidence. See Brilli, 'Dante's Biographies', pp. 137–38.

realism: 'Dante's realism causes critics to tend to "believe" Dante without knowing that they believe him, i.e, to pose their critical questions and situate their critical debates within the very presuppositions of the fiction they are seeking to understand' (*UDC*, p. 15). She then proposes to examine the 'formal structures that manipulate the reader' (*UDC*, p. 16) in service of Dante's realism, calling for a 'new formalism' which she describes as a 'formal method of reading' (*UDC*, p. 17), because the tools of new historicism would not work on a representation so successfully engineered to be perceived as objective reality, and on a poet whom readers have traditionally read as a theologian, sometimes without realizing it.[13] This method of reading is detheologizing.

The first traces of historicizing can be found in chapter 4 of *The Undivine Comedy*, where Barolini writes that *Inferno* 33 is 'steeped in the people and events that shaped Ugolino's politics, a politics whose central node was Sardinia, a Pisan possession' (*UDC*, p. 96). In '"Only Historicize"' Barolini refers back to *The Undivine Comedy*, noting that 'the implicit hermeneutic guidelines structured by Dante into his text determine, indeed, overdetermine, interpretation' (*OH*, p. 37), and that one way to deal with these is detheologizing, 'a narrative approach that cleared the way for historicizing' (*OH*, p. 38). In the 2022 revised edition of '"Only Historicize"', she offered additional language about detheologizing as a method: 'Detheologizing works by detaching our interpretive practice from the theologized thematic grid of hell versus heaven, thus allowing us to make connections that the overdetermined template occludes'.[14] This revision theorizes her approach, which had previously been described in a footnote: referring to her essay 'Dante and Francesca da Rimini', she wrote that detheologizing allowed her to go beyond the damned/saved binary imposed by the author: 'detheologizing allowed me to postulate interpretive categories more complex than '"Dante places Francesca in hell, so his view of her is negative,"

---

13 'To the extent that we hearken always to what Dante says rather than take note of what he has done, we treat him as he would have us treat him — not as a poet, but as an authority, a theologian' (*UDC*, p. 17). Dante is the subject of academic research carried out in theology departments as well as Italian or Romance Studies departments in the United States and in the United Kingdom.

14 Teodolinda Barolini, *Dante's Multitudes: History, Philosophy, Method* (Notre Dame, IN: University of Notre Dame Press, 2022), p. 4, hereafter *DM*. Subsequent references given in parentheses in the main text.

and thereby opened the way for a reconsideration of Dante's treatment of the dynastic wife' (*DM*, p. 321 note 3 to chapter 1).

Detheologizing is the conceptual leap required to assess the significance of context. A systematic identification of the historical figures and events described in the poem, even if supported by a meticulous review of available sources, such as that of Torraca, merely creates the illusion that one is viewing the poem through the lens of history, when in fact one is viewing history through the lens of the poem. As a result, the accumulation of historical context falls short of complicating a pre-existing understanding of the text. Instead, the poem generates interest in the historical context. This may go some way in explaining the reluctance of Dante scholars to use history to interpret the poem for a century after Torraca's scholarship, as well as the fact that so much historiography on Dante's context has yet to inform readings of his poem. Without the preliminary work of detheologizing the text, a discrepancy such as the one we see in the catalogue of tyrants of in *Inferno* 27 — where Scarpetta's rule over Forlì is anticipated by two years — is assumed to be the result of ignorance or bias, when there is counter-evidence for the former (Dante was a member of the exiled White Guelfs in the same year that they elected Scarpetta as their leader) and no concrete evidence for the latter.

To assess the significance of the historical context one needs, consciously or not, to detheologize the text. To do so is not to deny the moral dimensions of the poem but instead to look wilfully beyond Dante's categories so as to bring the full complexity of Dante's choices into view, since they include so much more than damnation and salvation. Returning to detheologizing in 'Dante's Sympathy for the Other', another example of her historicizing approach to the poem, Barolini writes: 'Which is more important: fictive damnation in a text or actual salvation in the historical record of human existence? To my mind, the answer is clear' (*DM*, p. 29). Torraca himself did not aspire to establish a new critical methodology nor to occupy a unique theoretical position, his primary objective was to democratize access to Dante, particularly in educational settings undergoing reforms at the time.[15]

---

15   See Carlo Dionisotti, 'Scuola storica', in *Dizionario critico della letteratura italiana*, ed. by Vittore Branca, 3 vols (Torino: Unione Tipografico-Editrice Torinese, 1973), III, pp.

Barolini's essay 'Dante and Francesca' self-consciously relies on Torraca's historical work, recovering his insight and reformulating it as the claim that Dante is Francesca's historian of record.

While Dante's representation of Francesca elicited an enduring interest in her, Dante's realism prompted readers to grapple with her damnation as though it were a fact, and hence remain firmly 'within the presuppositions of the fiction they are seeking to understand' (*UDC*, p. 15). This effect is operative whenever one consults the available historiographical sources on a particular character, only to renegotiate the ethics of their placement in one or the other section of Dante's afterlife, or only to determine why Dante has cast them in a particular light. As Barolini reminds her readers, 'If we stand outside the fiction of who is damned and who is saved — if, in my terms, we "detheologize" — we can see that Dante acted as the historian of record for Francesca da Rimini, and for many other women as well' (*DM*, p. 29).

Another effect of Dante's realism is that his manipulations of history are difficult to see, because the poem changed how the past was remembered. For example, Farinata became the most famous Uberti after *Inferno* 10, but before *Inferno* 10, the most famous Uberti was likely Pierasino Uberti, a leader of the Ghibelline regime in Florence that followed Montaperti and the only Uberti to be named in the letters of Charles I of Anjou. Dante gave the Uberti who was responsible for the first mass political exclusion in Florentine history a prominence that endured through the centuries, while the Uberti who was the leader of the Ghibelline regime under which Dante himself was born faded into obscurity. To historicize the text is not only to recover such a manipulation of history, but also to decipher it. On the basis that Farinata inaugurated a new era of mass political exclusion in Florence by orchestrating the first mass political exclusion in Florentine history, I argue that Dante reconstructed a history of Florentine factionalism in *Inferno* 10.[16]

352–61; Valerio Marucci, 'Introduzione', in Francesco Torraca, *Commento alla Divina Commedia*, 3 vols (Rome: Salerno, 2008), I, pp. 9–32; Valerio Marucci, 'Francesco Torraca e Dante', *L'Idomeneo*, 31 (2021), pp. 97–106.

16   Nassime Chida, 'Dante and the legacy of Montaperti', *Studj Romanzi*, n.s., 19 (2023), pp. 163–74.

Since detheologizing is the necessary first step in historicizing, interpretations obtained through historicizing are part of the legacy of *The Undivine Comedy*. Barolini's essay 'Dante and Francesca' is a clear example of what can be achieved by historicizing one of the most famous characters in the *Commedia*. A number of studies have historicized other aspects of the *Commedia* since then, exploring the relationship between Dante's narrative choices and the social and political realities of his time, including Kristina Olson's 2015 work on Dante and sumptuary laws in Florence, my 2021 reading of *Inferno* 27, Grace Delmolino's 2023 essay on legal temporality and liability, and research available on *Digital Dante*.[17] More studies like these are likely to emerge in the coming years.

---

17   Kristina M. Olson, 'Uncovering the Historical Body of Florence: Dante, Forese Donati, and Sumptuary Legislation', *Italian Culture*, 33.1 (2015), pp. 1–15; Chida, 'Guido da Montefeltro'; Grace Delmolino, 'Fraudulent Counsel: Legal Temporality and the Poetics of Liability in Dante's *Inferno*, Boniface VIII's *Liber Sextus*, and Gratian's *De penitentia*', *Speculum*, 98.3 (2023), pp. 727–62.

Teodolinda Barolini and the Signs of Newness in *The Undivine Comedy*

ALBERTO CASADEI

1.

Over thirty years after its publication, *The Undivine Comedy* continues to pose questions of fundamental importance, particularly in relation to exegeses of the poem that seek to be 'absolutist'.[1] Already in her short but dense Preface, Barolini offers some starting points for an interpretive framework, in which she underscores Dante's identity not as a naturalist but as a realist *tout court*. Among other things she calls

---

1   My analysis in this article will focus on Teodolinda Barolini, *The Undivine Comedy: Detheologizing Dante* (Princeton: Princeton University Press, 1992), hereafter UDC (subsequent references given in parentheses in the main text), but will keep in mind all of Barolini's other Dantean contributions, among which one in particular complements and specifies some hypotheses from the volume: 'Why Did Dante Write the *Commedia*? Or, The Vision Thing', *Dante Studies*, 111 (1993), pp. 1–8. I must also note in particular *Dante and the Origins of Italian Literary Culture* (New York: Fordham University Press, 2006), in which the Introduction's polemical stance against all unilateral visions of Dante's works underscores their constitutive eclecticism. See more recently Teodolinda Barolini, *Dante's Multitudes: History, Philosophy, Method* (Notre Dame, IN: Notre Dame University Press, 2022), with further important topics, including New Historicism, philology, and 'social and cultural difference'. So as not to overdo it in the notes, I will avoid proposing a long integrative bibliography on the themes discussed: this can be found in Alberto Casadei, *Dante oltre l'allegoria* (Ravenna: Longo, 2021), pp. 203–09.

attention to Auerbach's claim that the poem's theology is threatened by its poetic genius: the form becomes more determining than the content, or, better, it becomes the means by which that content (although reliant on Christian doctrine) is rendered *new*. The sacred poem is a 'Ulyssean adventure'; its reality does not correspond either to a truth already revealed, or to a fiction that pretends not to be a fiction, but rather locates itself in the realm of the 'non-false error' or of the truth that seems to be a lie while in fact it unmasks falsehoods. *The Undivine Comedy* tracks the creation of this 'detheologized' dimension, offering an introductory chapter followed by nine others, three for each canticle. I will concentrate here, due to spatial constraints, on some implications of the book's general structure and on its reading of the first cantos of *Inferno*.

In the initial chapter of her book, Barolini begins by arguing for the non-implausibility of Bruno Nardi's thesis on the status of Dante-prophet: this move is not to be discounted given that, in 1992, the whole of Dante studies considered Nardi's thesis with a certain dismissiveness. And yet strong reasons existed to re-evaluate it, for example on the basis of the poem's numerous truth claims, as well as the prophetic-apocalyptic dimension manifested in various epistles. However, Barolini's reconsideration of Nardi's essay depended on her posing a general question, all the while knowing how problematic this question was (and is): Did Dante believe in the truth that he claims to recount? In practice, her central concern was to find a *mode* of reading Dante's poem that does not result in tautology, stepping outside of its structural configuration to be able to interpret it.

Equally courageously, the chapter tackles Charles S. Singleton and the question of allegory, both of the poets or of the theologians, in relation to the Epistle to Cangrande. Authentic or not, the Epistle authorizes us to consider the credibility of the literal level of the text in a similar manner to how we consider the books of the Bible. Barolini plays a precision game, bringing to light, beyond their contrasting principles, the similarities between Nardi's position, which presupposes a correspondence between what is narrated and what is effectively granted as 'inspiration' to Dante-prophet, and Singleton's position, which defines the *Commedia* as a fiction that pretends not to be a fiction and holds that every aspect of the Dantean account must be read on a second allegorical (and theologically orthodox) level while accepting the truth of the literal first level. There exists, therefore, an *objective truth* in Dante's text, which is a literary and rhetorical construction that is modelled on either a vision or a theological pattern.

Fittingly, Barolini reflects at length on how Dantean 'truth claims' can be accommodated and condemns the forced division between *poeta* and *theologus*, as well as the inflexibility surrounding the issue of the non-authenticity of the Epistle to Cangrande. The true problem is to establish how — within the narrative construction of his poem — Dante positions himself regarding the substance of his account and its truth value. The reader is certainly primed for a reception mode that must be attentive to the levels of truthfulness problematized within the work itself. Noting insightfully the limits of various other interpretations that built upon these arguments (such as those of Robert Hollander, Giorgio Padoan, Peter Dronke, Peter Hawkins, etc.), Barolini arrives at an essential assumption in her interpretative framework by turning to Augustine (who did not exclude poetic abilities on the part of a prophet): 'In my opinion, Dante self-consciously used the means of fiction — poetic and narrative strategies — in the service of a vision he believed to be true, thus creating the hybrid he defined a "truth that has the face of a lie" — "un ver c'ha faccia di menzogna" (*Inf.* 16.124)' (*UDC*, p. 11). In short, there is no clear distinction between poetry and theological fiction, or between authentic inspiration and imposed structure: Dante is a prophet *and* a poet, one who achieves a 'non-false error', or rather 'a fiction that IS true' (*UDC*, p. 13).

At this point, some methodological reflections come to mind. As we have seen, Barolini demonstrated that, up to the early 1990s, the primary proposals regarding the truth claims of the *Commedia* were connected to its content and to the possible role of the 'real' Dante (Nardi), or to the hypothesis that the literal level must always be combined with allegorical significance to complete its meaning (Singleton). Both these propositions, in theory, emphasize the value of the text, and yet in practice they involve a radical removal of the poem's rhetorical and narrative aspects *in and of themselves*. Nardi, not coincidentally, is preoccupied with re-establishing the exact meaning of controversial passages (for example, the cord and Geryon in *Inferno*

16 and 17, Virgil's speech in *Inferno* 34, etc.), but not with the overall form of the narrative in the three canticles. Singleton, on the other hand, who believes in a general organization to be studied *a priori* by way of recognizable theological principles, avoids all 'novelistic' and thus effectively false aspects of the poem, considering them not pertinent to the overall truth that Dante wished to communicate. From this point of view, it was absolutely necessary to move toward a multifocal reading, which also took into consideration the figural-Auerbachian approach.

Barolini's gambit was that of finding footholds within Dante's narrative that allow us to discern and to understand its fundamental characteristics, which are then adequately interpreted and not simply paraphrased. Thus, if the term *comedìa* is introduced (*Inf.* 16.128) in a passage that explicitly establishes the problem of the 'ver c'ha faccia di menzogna' ('truth that has the face of a lie'; *Inf.* 16.124), such a connection must be considered essential, and must work together — creating a textual system — with the 'non falsi errori' ('non-false errors') of *Purgatorio* 15.117.[2] Both passages address the necessity that the reader consider as truthful that which may seem instead — on a superficial reading — erroneous or untruthful. In its subject matter and in its overall narrative journey, in fact, the *comedìa* establishes a more profound truth than the debatable truth of Virgil's *tragedìa*. Here we see how Barolini establishes an interpretation, rather than a simple paraphrase, of the explicit opposition between the two terms: *tragedìa* in *Inferno* 20.113 and *comedìa* in *Inferno* 21.2.

We are now in a position to establish a fundamental feature of Barolini's analysis: for her, the entirety of Dante's poem is cohesive to the point of allowing comparisons even at notable textual distances. At the same time one can move through a progressive discovery of its fundamentals by dealing with problems that present themselves as different each time, problems that the author was compelled to resolve while at the same time maintaining narrative credibility. For example,

---

2   All citations from the *Commedia* are drawn from Dante Alighieri, *La Commedia secondo l'antica vulgata*, ed. by Giorgio Petrocchi, Società Dantesca Italiana, Edizione Nazionale, 2nd rev. edn, 4 vols (Florence: Le Lettere, 1994). Translations into English, with modifications at times for clarity, are from Dante Alighieri, *The Divine Comedy*, trans. by Allen Mandelbaum, 3 vols (Berkeley: University of California Press, 1980–82).

the representational mode of *Paradiso* needed to prioritize the dialectic between the one and the many in a context that in theory should have been monistic, and therefore deprived of all possible narrative development, contrary to what had occurred in *Inferno* and *Purgatorio*. (I must note parenthetically that the brilliant Dantean theatrical reinterpretation of Romeo Castellucci, staged in Avignon in 2008, symbolically translated the first two realms of the afterlife but proposed a static installation for the third, demonstrating the difficulty mentioned above.) In other words, the level of truth that Dante's text offers does not lie in its contents (which however Barolini does not discount), nor in its literal account; it lies instead in the skilled construction of a narrative modality in which the reader is called to believe, via the same paradoxical terms indicated above and without any rigid pre-established norms.

In sum, 'because of its biblical and prophetic pretensions the *Commedia* poses the basic narrative issue of its truth value in aggravated form' (*UDC*, p. 14). It is necessary, however, to step outside of the hall of mirrors that Dante himself creates and therefore to read the poem without reaffirming its claim to divine status, aiming instead to recognize its narrative strategies (see *UDC*, pp. 17–18). From this point of view, an analysis of how the text is constructed is the only way to avoid the vicious hermeneutical circle that explains Dante with Dante's own ideology, thus rendering all features of the narrative always already coherent through the application of an *a priori* law, whether that law be allegory of the theologians or something else.

I believe that this move was and is, from a critical point of view, essential, even though, in the last thirty years, narrative interpretations of the poem have diminished rather than increased.[3] Many new studies have focused on content over method, either historical-biographical or philosophical-theological, and have generated numerous corrections to the theses of Nardi and Singleton. At the same time, even linguistic and rhetorical analyses, à la Auerbach or Contini, have been challenged in their assumptions: for example the supposed homology between

---

3   However, after Vittorio Russo, *Il romanzo teologico: Sondaggi sulla 'Commedia' di Dante* (Naples: Liguori, 1984), see the recent contribution of Nicolò Crisafi, *Dante's Masterplot and Alternative Narratives in the 'Commedia'* (Oxford: Oxford University Press, 2022), also for further bibliography.

stylistic solutions that are otherwise divergent, as in the case of the
Fiore and the *Divina Commedia*; or the supposed connection between
distant episodes of the *Commedia* that have been interpreted on the
basis of very loose allegorical-figural principles, perhaps elicited from
random signposts, such as the comparisons between the incident of
the Argonauts in *Paradiso* 2.16–18 and 33.96. We find risky attempts
to create bridges between religious and profane texts that are perhaps
known by Dante but not explicitly acknowledged; all this with the goal
of explaining — in the name of a supposed intertextuality — episodes
in the poem that instead require first and foremost to be correctly
placed in the narrative framework. In general, according to Barolini,
Dante's narrative must be explicated without turning to interpretative
paradigms that reduce it to an average text of its historical period (as
the first commentators did and, in my opinion, as did the author of
the Epistle to Cangrande). Nor should we flatten its principal strength,
that of not being subject to rigid blueprints, while still being structured
and at the same time invariably inventive.

2.

Fully recognizing the richness of the principles articulated by Barolini,
it is possible, at a distance of thirty years, to now add new considerations and to carry out further analyses that tackle the issue of
historicizing Dante's writing, a topic also very important in Barolini's
recent research (see note 1). We can take as an example those pages
that discuss the beginning of the poem in the chapter 'Infernal Incipits:
The Poetics of the New' (*UDC*, pp. 21–47). 'Newness' is a fundamental
element for Dante, who emphasizes it in various ways in all of his works,
up to the well-known figure of the 'ovis gratissima' in the first eclogue
sent to Giovanni del Virgilio (see *Eclogues* 2.58–62), which can be
interpreted correctly only if it is considered as the bucolic equivalent to
Dantean poetic inspiration, resistant to barriers and to what is already
known.

However, it may not be necessary to discern this general charac-
teristic already in the *incipit* 'Nel mezzo del cammin di nostra vita'
('When I had journeyed half of our life's way'; *Inf.* 1.1), which first
and foremost does not refer, as Singleton suggests, to the human con-

dition in and of itself. It is a rhetorically elevated formula (suggestive of the probable hypotext Isaiah 38:10) that introduces a protagonist who has just entered his thirty-fifth year: the adjective 'nostra' (our) is necessary (instead of 'mia' [my]) to indicate the expected duration of a human life, the seventy years that, for Dante, began in 1265. For those to whom the author's birth year was known, specifically among his Florentine audience, it then became possible to intuit that the year 1300 was being referred to, with a beginning *ab incarnatione* (March 25). If we hypothesize that the text addressed *in primis* his fellow citizens, as was already the case of the *Vita nuova* (knowledge of the *libello* is indispensable beginning with the *Commedia*'s second canto), we can better understand that the opening is not abstract but focused on characterizing the poet: the 'I' that comes to understand his sinful situation is not an 'Everyman' but rather the Dante already famous for the *Vita nuova*, where he makes known his special relationship with Beatrice. One who is saved by an exceptional otherworldly intervention and then undertakes a journey comparable only to that of Aeneas and Saint Paul is certainly not an Everyman, even if he is able to teach a great deal to each one of his readers.

Personally, I believe that Dante wrote the first four cantos of *Inferno* prior to exile, perhaps after a trip to Rome to take advantage of the indulgences for sins made available by that extraordinary event for all Christians that was the first Jubilee. Seeing as the cantos were later recovered and disseminated prior to any possible correction, as Boccaccio affirms on the basis of reliable witnesses (except for the number of cantos recovered), here the dominant framework could not be anything but the 'allegory of poets', in a narrative that is moreover marred by many incongruities with the later storyline. This does not take away from the fact that, as Barolini affirms, the beginning of the poem is 'a carefully constructed sequence of ups and downs, starts and stops' (*UDC*, p. 28), provided that the recognition of these attempts to escape the 'selva oscura' take into consideration the narration's actual limitations, as described above. Here there is no alternative to the allegory of the poets, which reveals the protagonist's inability to overcome his most pressing sins (leopard-lust and lion-pride), to which we can add, with particular emphasis, the wolf-cupidity. Against this backdrop a *Veltro* (greyhound) is evoked that is in part allegorical and in part auspiciously historical, though not the Emperor (who corresponds, if to anything, to the 'Cinquecento diece e cinque' ('Five Hundred and Ten and Five') of *Purgatorio* 33.43). We are very far, in any case, from a narrative that is already self-sufficient on its first, literal, level.[4]

Once more we see the need to consider carefully the characteristics that make up Dante's narration, hybrid as ever and capable of evolving. Whoever regards it as a monolithic poem, written from the first to the last verse without making any adjustments, does not understand its variations, for the text undergoes a radical modification between the first four cantos and the fifth, where narration infused with a historical background becomes paramount. Moreover, the *Commedia*'s beginning is quite congruous with a framework already traceable to Brunetto Latini's *Tesoretto*, in which an *alter ego* protagonist of the author loses the correct path, in his case after having come to learn of the loss of the Florentine Guelfs at Montaperti while he is traveling between Spain and France, and finds himself in a dangerous forest, where he then sees three terrible beasts but also receives precious teachings, especially thanks to Nature, a figure that brings us back to the works of Alain de Lille. No critic voices major concerns regarding the allegorical and fictitious foundations of this literary work, which has the benefit of being certified at the beginning by 'authentic' historical-biographical details (a feature not attested in similar texts).

While also following the Brunettian model, in the first four cantos Dante avoids precise self-references and ennobles his allegorical account by adhering in the third canto to the Virgilian model, interwoven with the biblical echoes possibly drawn from the *Visio Pauli* in one of its many versions. Therefore, with respect to the *Tesoretto*, the text is more elaborate, boasting a wealth of features that are not merely didactic. Nevertheless, the *Commedia*'s different stature (owing additionally to the extraordinary invention of interlocking and rhymed *terzine* that substitute for Brunetto's monotonous couplets of rhymed *settenari*) does not annul the strong initial similarity as to pattern with Brunetto's *Tesoretto*. Of course, Brunetto's text is situated on a plane

---

4   I will allow myself to point to some of my studies that refer to the considerations touched upon here in a more concise manner: Casadei, *Dante oltre l'allegoria*, pp. 33–70; and Alberto Casadei, 'Ancora sui canti fiorentini dell'*Inferno* (e ancora sul Veltro)', *Italianistica*, 52.2 (2023), pp. 11–32, with ample bibliography.

that is prevailingly moral and notional, given its intent to synthesize his encyclopaedic *Tresor*, while Dante's poem features, as Barolini has emphasized many times, both a strong Christian spirituality and respect for the great ancient pagan writers. Such respect is clearly demonstrated by his own positioning, in *Inferno* 4.102, as 'sixth' following the great poets already evoked in the famous twenty-fifth chapter (ed. Barbi) of the *Vita nuova*. The endorsement offered to Dante by the ancient poets derives from his new undertaking, that of creating a truly 'epic' poem of Christianity and employing the vernacular at its highest levels (by no means in the comic style). Here is the novel choice that leads Dante to finally exalt his protector, Beatrice, as he promised to do at the end of the *Vita nuova*: the criterion of 'newness', decisive in *The Undivine Comedy*, at this point in Dante's authorial trajectory is clearly reengaged (although not yet in the form that will sustain the text beginning in the fifth canto).

3.

Barolini similarly highlights those sections of cantos 2 and 3 related to the dialectic between fictional representation and the creation of 'non-false errors'. With respect to the manner of configuring higher judgment, in theory divine and in effect Dantean, the surprises of the narrative are and remain continuous. Moreover, they vary according to the type of reception that can be hypothesized for each. For example, among the neutrals there is only one person who is included without a name, a person who was identified as Celestine V already by the first and, in this instance, most trustworthy commentators. For Barolini, this identification does not prevent the text from contributing to his punishment by impeding certainty about his name. But, if the potential audience of readers was that of Florence in 1300, it is evident that this allusion would not fall flat, given that at this time all the White Guelfs knew that Pope Boniface VIII was by now allied to the Black Guelfs, and that this peril was caused by the scandalous abdication of his predecessor, Celestine V. The allusion, therefore, would strengthen the satisfaction of recognizing as condemned to Hell a character who was truly detested by Dante's political faction.

Recent studies of the Florentine context demonstrate that questions on the actual state of the otherworld were being tackled that relate to problems touched on in these first cantos and that create more than one aporia if we consider them as written after the fourth book of the *Convivio*. What theological foundation can there be for the neutral angels of *Inferno* 3.37–42, given that they are untenable according to the Bible and to the common exegesis regarding the angels' division into two groups after the rebellion of Lucifer (two groups who are mentioned again, without a nod to the neutrals, in *Paradiso* 29.49–54)?[5] Was the Dante who introduces this position, a position that is more bizarre than daring, perhaps not yet the systematic thinker of the treatise? Was he rather the still immature frequenter of the discussions of philosophers and theologians, who remained in Florence until 1301? In that case, we could hypothesize this young Dante's willingness to sustain an original position with respect to the existence of 'lukewarm' figures like those of *Apocalypse* 3:14–16, figures who are very appropriate for the ante-Hell of the pusillanimous. If one considers the historical genesis of the claim and the audience that Dante had in mind when he came up with neutral angels, a concept so out of tune with the argumentative modalities of the *Convivio*, it is perhaps acceptable to circumscribe the range of interpretations of the passage, evading the reductionism that impedes us in understanding the critical points of Dante's narrative.

4.

From investigations such as the ones summarized above, the specificity of the beginning of the poem emerges, also with respect to the allegorical modality that is then abandoned. But there are other questions that can be posed in line with new approaches, as Barolini has repeatedly done. I believe that we need to reconsider the meaning of the comic

---

5   On this complex question, after John Freccero, 'The Neutral Angels', in Freccero, *Dante: The Poetics of Conversion*, ed. by Rachel Jacoff (Cambridge, MA: Harvard University Press, 1986), pp. 110–18, see most recently Fabrizio Crasta, 'Gli angeli neutrali da Dante a Matteo Palmieri', *Lettere Italiane*, 67.1 (2015), pp. 5–25. Lorenzo Dell'Oso provides new evidence in relation to Florentine culture of the end of the thirteenth century with 'L'*Inferno* a Firenze? Su alcuni elementi teologici dei primi canti della *Commedia* (*Inf.* 1–4)', *Italianistica: Rivista di letteratura italiana*, 53.3 (2024), pp. 12–26.

style, in relation to the entire poem and to its truth that has the face of
a lie. By the same token, the tragic style of Virgil is positioned on the
side of falsity. But why rely on this guide and why reuse this model in
a collateral work such as the *Eclogues*? Virgil's knowledge is carried out
within the limits assigned to human reason,[6] and his work is nevertheless a point of reference that has long been considered superior with
respect to the infernal *comedìa*, which however is capable of evolving
in relation to the material treated. And it is indeed this evolution that
the reader will be obliged to follow closely, to the point of needing
to leave one's usual mode of interpretation behind to contemplate the
exceptional truths of the third canticle, almost as though sitting at a
desk in the library (see *Par.* 2.1–18 and 10.22–27). We might therefore propose that the poet's pact of truthfulness is one that embraces
variability, in continuity with the assertions of Barolini's work of 1992.

To return to the analysis of the first cantos of *Inferno*, the question
of Limbo and its castle for magnanimous souls in *Inferno* 4 merits its
own treatment. The rather ambiguous nature of the infernal 'lembo'
as Dante conceived it is already underscored in *The Undivine Comedy*,
and correctly so, given that it is populated primarily by non-baptized
souls who were not saved by Christ at the moment of his death and
resurrection: these are souls who led honourable lives and accrued
'onrata nominanza' ('honor of their name'; *Inf.* 4.76), and who therefore do not suffer active punishment but rather the impossibility of
satisfying their desire to see the true God. This is a state of exception,
one that is guaranteed by the 'nobile castello' ('exalted castle'; v. 106),
illuminated even though it finds itself in a circle of Hell. Here we have a
sort of medieval re-elaboration of Virgil's Elysian fields (and, to a lesser
degree, of the seat of the moral virtues in the *Tesoretto*). Altogether, as
has been noted since the first commentators, it is a rather contradictory canto with respect to various principles of the Christian faith, in
particular when even Muslims such as Avicenna, Averroes, and Saladin
are named among those residing in Limbo.

---

6   See most recently Paolo Falzone, 'Per Dante virgiliano', in *Dante e l'eredità dei classici*,
     ed. by Stefano Carrai, special issue of *Letture Classensi*, 51 (2023), pp. 31–60. Re-
     garding the interpretation of Virgil, see Barolini's intervention already in Teodolinda
     Barolini, *Dante's Poets: Textuality and Truth in the 'Comedy'* (Princeton: Princeton
     University Press, 1984), pp. 198–256, in particular 200–01 and 214.

Barolini has returned to this topic in her commentary on the entire poem and in a recent essay,[7] in which she highlights the exceptionality of Dante's Limbo, a place in the afterlife not imagined in the Bible but hypothesized by the Fathers of the Church and by theologians to resolve doubts regarding the destiny of children who die before baptism. The fate of these children is not of particular interest to Dante in *Inferno* 4, but will be recalled in the treatment of the placement of children within the Empyrean (see *Par.* 32.73–84, as well as *Purg.* 7.31–33). The destiny of those who are excluded from divine grace only on account of a lack of knowledge of Christ remains unclear. The exceptionality of Dante's Limbo, therefore, is not so much in the doctrinal-ecclesiastical choice of this place, but rather in Dante's need to contaminate it with another space: Limbo is the equivalent of the Elysian fields for great souls, who are in theory from any era or religion (Barolini would opt for the term 'multiculturalism').

This particular concession concerning the great souls of Limbo is clearly willed by Dante, since it is not corrected in the course of the poem (rather, Dante confirms his position in the additional lists of *Purg.* 22.97–114), and nevertheless it seems constructed on a precarious (although not deliberately transgressive) foundation as far as its theological lapses. What is most surprising is that, to take advantage of the doctrine relative to Limbo, Dante places in this circle two types of rather different 'guilty but not guilty' souls: children who die before baptism and are therefore in theory incapable of using reason or feeling actual desire, and adults who instead are unable *not* to feel the desire to reach God, once they learn the Christian truth. Therefore they live 'sanza speme' ('without hope'; *Inf.* 4.42), in a condition that is a sort of substitute for the true infernal punishment that, in as much as they are placed in Hell, they do nevertheless receive.

---

7   See Teodolinda Barolini, 'Non-Christians in the Christian Afterlife', Digital Dante (Columbia University Libraries, 2018) <https://digitaldante.columbia.edu/dante/divine-comedy/inferno/inferno-4/> [accessed 5 June 2025]. The essay, published first in Italian as 'Il Limbo di Dante e l'equità di accesso: non-cristiani, bambini, e i criteri di inclusione ed esclusiond, da *If* 4 a *Pd* 32', *Italianistica*, 50.1 (2021), pp. 49–64, was later expanded on in English as Teodolinda Barolini, 'Dante's Limbo and Equity of Access: Non-Christians, Children, and Criteria of Inclusion and Exclusion, from *Inferno* 4 to *Paradiso* 32', in *Dante's Multitudes*, pp. 58–81. For specific bibliography, I refer again to Casadei, *Dante oltre l'allegoria*, pp. 62–70.

Saint Thomas (*Summa Theologica*, Suppl. 69.6), in an observation that is often insufficiently noted, also posits two groups of Limbo-dwellers who were able to coexist in the same place: namely, the un-baptized children and the patriarchs. In 1300 this coexistence was no longer relevant because the patriarchs had long ago been transported to heaven by Christ, given that the *lumen gratiae* was able to work on them. But to substitute this category with that of non-Christians in general (see *Inf.* 4.30, almost a calque from *Aen.* 6.306), and of the great souls in particular, could not in any way appear plausible: one needed to hypothesize that God had reserved a sort of special treatment for these individuals, regardless of their behaviour, although not one of true grace.

Likewise in this case there are many signs that lead us to think that the entire concept of the 'nobile castello' dates to a time prior to the development of a true philosophical position on the part of Dante (for bibliography, see note 6). It is important, with Barolini, to emphasize the singularity of Dante's position on Limbo; at the same time, however, we must ask whether, as with the neutral angels, we find ourselves in front of an eccentric position that has a precise purpose (to show contempt for every type of pusillanimity), or whether it is more probable that these evident uncertainties are the sign of a very personal conviction that is however still *in fieri*. Perhaps this conviction took shape as a result of reading the *Nicomachean Ethics* (in particular 4.3), after which Dante formed the desire to safeguard the great souls, and in particular the five greatest poets of antiquity: Homer, Virgil, Ovid, Horace, and Lucan (who were previously named in *Vita nuova* 25) and after them the 'new' poet who is sixth (see *Inf.* 4.102). This choice of himself is indeed clear and audacious: he is ready to write the *epos* of the Christian afterlife, for the first time in the vernacular. This self-investiture is of fundamental importance, especially if it is detached, as it should be, from the problem of the comic style.

Many studies in recent decades have examined with great care the material dimension of Dante's works (moments and places of writing, expected audience, etc.). Although in many cases, only generic hypotheses can be formulated, it is a task that must at least be attempted, to avoid remaining within the single dimension of Dantean 'intratextuality', in which we gloss Dante with Dante. The task, as emphasized even recently by Barolini (see note 1), must be that of historicizing in ways that are more flexible and more dynamic than in the past. That said, the legacy of *The Undivine Comedy* remains strong, for it undertook to study the *inventio* and not just the *dispositio* of Dante's narrative. Such work must undoubtedly continue.

TRANSLATED BY LAURA DINARDO

Dante's War

Exiles, *carestia*, and Conflict in the Florentine Countryside, 1301–1304

GEORGE DAMERON[*]

In *Inferno* 32 and 33, the narrator-poet, Dante, encounters a flesh-eater. In the ninth circle (Cocytus) of the treacherous, in the second 'round' of those condemned for treachery against party or faction (Antenora), the narrator and his guide, Virgil, come upon a prominent Guelf nobleman, Ugolino della Gherardesca. As Ugolino is gnawing on the nape of Archbishop Ruggieri of Pisa, he recounts a story that is both poignant and horrifying. The prelate Ruggieri, who had condemned his former ally Ugolino (along with his sons) to die of starvation in the Torre della Fame in Pisa, suffers the infernal fate of being eaten himself by his erstwhile ally.[1] In chapter 4 of *The Undivine Comedy* ('Narrative and Style in Lower Hell'), Teodolinda Barolini observes that Ugolino

---

[*] The title of this essay pays homage to William Caferro's marvelous book, *Petrarch's War: Florence and the Black Death in Context* (Cambridge: Cambridge University Press, 2018).

1 For a recent reading of cantos 32 and 33 which highlights the role of 'political betrayal' as the cause of his punishment (rather than cannibalism), see Christiana Purdy Moudarres, 'Bodily Starvation and the Ravaging of the Will: A Reading of *Inferno* 32 and 33', *Viator*, 47.1 (2015), pp. 205–28. For the historical Ugolino della Gherardesca (and bibliography), see Donna Yowell, 'Ugolino della Gherardesca', in *The Dante Encyclopedia*, ed. by Richard Lansing (New York: Garland Publishing, 2000), pp. 839–41. See also Simonetta Saffiotti Bernardi and Umberto Bosco,

went about telling this story with a 'narrative cunning by which he hopes to elicit the pilgrim's sympathy'.[2] Indeed, 'the self-consciousness of the episode encompasses an authorial self-scrutiny as well' (*UDC*, 95). After all, the dream embedded in Ugolino's narrative with wild animals recalls the 'dreamscape' of *Inferno* 1, with its 'allegorical wolves and hounds' (*UDC*, 95), presumably signifying Ugolino's greed and bestiality. However, even if Ugolino is a 'good storyteller', Barolini writes, 'the poet asserts his own narrative authority over Ugolino's with extraordinary force and aggressivity, issuing the ferocious invective against Pisa' (*UDC*, 95). To understand the significance of Ugolino's story, therefore, an appreciation of the historical context within which it unfolded is necessary. Indeed, as Barolini noted in her discussion of the episode, the criticisms of both Pisa and Genoa issued by the poet in canto 33 are 'important to understanding the historical backdrop against which Ugolino betrayed and was betrayed' (*UDC*, 97).

'Authorial self-scrutiny', 'understanding the historical backdrop', 'betrayed and betrayal' — these are indeed crucial dimensions of a canto about which so much can still be written. In her recent book, *Dante's Gluttons: Food and Society from the 'Convivio' to the 'Comedy'*, Danielle Callegari explores this story, adding insights to an already extensive corpus of commentary on the two cantos. It is, however, part of a much broader enterprise on her part, as she examines closely the symbolic meaning of food and images of food in Dante's writings from his early works through the *Commedia*. Noting that previous 'indifference to food in Dante may also be due to a methodological bias against the use of material culture to read the poet's work',[3] Callegari observes

---

'Ugolino della Gherardesca, conte di Donoratico', in *Enciclopedia Dantesca*, ed. by Umberto Bosco (Rome: Istituto della Enciclopedia Italiana fondata da Giovanni Treccani, 1970) <https://www.treccani.it/enciclopedia/ugolino-della-gherardesca-conte-di-donoratico_(Enciclopedia-Dantesca)/> [accessed 18 May 2025]. All references to the text of the *Commedia* used for this essay are from Dante Alighieri: *La Commedia secondo l'antica vulgata*, ed. by Giorgio Petrocchi, Società Dantesca Italiana, Edizione Nazionale, 2nd rev. edn, 4 vols (Florence: Le Lettere, 1994). English translations come from Dante Alighieri, *The Divine Comedy*, trans. by Allen Mandelbaum, 3 vols (Berkeley: University of California Press, 1980–82).

2   Teodolinda Barolini, *The Undivine Comedy: Detheologizing Dante* (Princeton: Princeton University Press, 1992), p. 95, hereafter *UDC*. Subsequent references given in parentheses in the main text.

3   Danielle Callegari, *Dante's Gluttons: Food and Society from the 'Convivio' to the 'Comedy'* (Amsterdam: Amsterdam University Press, 2022), p. 18.

that the language of food functions in Dante's work promote his notions of good leadership. Dante 'establishes our responsibility to create
and sustain community through the act of nourishment and giving of
the self'.[4] Regarding the *Convivio* (1303–07) in particular, she writes:
'The gesture of feeding, to give food instead of keeping it for oneself,
afforded the opportunity to model good leadership by being a reliable
provider and inclined toward charity'.[5] The character of Ugolino in
cantos 32 and 33 represents the opposite of that model. Along with
other characters portrayed at the end of the canticle (Alberigo and
Satan), Ugolino represents 'a perfect contrast with the successful head
of the community, who is powerful through providing and enforcing
cohesion through communion in food'.[6] He is the negative archetype
of a civic leader.

The image of the character of Ugolino as 'betrayer and betrayed',
his association with the factionalism of his native city, his record of
previous service to his community, and his close connection of his
destiny with food ironically call to mind certain aspects of Dante's own
life. Indeed, at least on the surface, and perhaps only incidentally, the
historical Ugolino had something in common with Dante the poet. Of
course, unlike Ugolino (if we believe the story about him), Dante was
not a cannibal, even though he wrote about it in canto 33. Nevertheless,
there are some interesting parallels between the historical Ugolino (d.
1285) and the poet (d. 1321). When the Black Guelfs condemned
Dante as a traitor in 1302, he considered himself betrayed both by his
native city and by the faction of Guelfs. As Ugolino had once served
as *podestà* of Pisa for ten years, Dante had also served his city-state
in a variety of posts for at least seven years, including (and most importantly) as prior in 1300.[7] After returning to Pisa at the invitation
of his ally, Archbishop Ruggieri, Ugolino was betrayed and died in

---

4   Ibid., p. 14.
5   Ibid., p. 114.
6   Ibid., p. 116.
7   The primary guide for the chronology of Dante's life is taken from the 'Chronology'
     in *Dante in Context*, ed. by Zygmunt G. Barański and Lino Pertile (Cambridge: Cam-
     bridge University Press, 2015), pp. xx–xxiii; and Lino Pertile, 'Life', ibid., pp. 461–74.
     For specific details about Dante's life chronology, I draw upon Marco Santagata, *Dante:
     The Story of His Life*, trans. by Richard Dixon (Cambridge, MA: Harvard Belknap Press,
     2016).

prison. Condemned to death himself by his own factional enemies, Dante also faced the death penalty after 1302, but he escaped punishment because he never returned to Florence. Both were caught up in factional divisions. Finally, according to the Florentine-biased Pseudo-Brunetto Latini chronicle (c. 1300), the historical Ugolino roused the Pisans to anger for having allegedly brought about starvation at a time of grain abundance. This behaviour is precisely the opposite of the model of urban governance as apparently portrayed by Dante in the *Convivio*.[8] But as for Dante, surprisingly, his own actions in 1302 in support of the military campaigns against Florence aimed to limit if not end the ability of the city to import food, particularly grain. In that year he supported if not helped lead armed efforts to induce hunger in his native city during the most serious food (grain) crisis (*carestia*) in a generation. His activities stand in stark contrast to the model of civic governance that he apparently later developed in the *Convivio* and the *Commedia*.[9]

As this essay will argue, after many years of public service, the newly exiled Dante was directly engaged in aiding and abetting a military strategy in 1302–03 based on the use of food deprivation as a weapon of war. The Dante who wrote (but did not finish) the *Convivio* (1303–07) observed that good citizenship and leadership required providing sufficient nourishment for one's citizens. This was the same Dante who in 1302–03 helped lead and support military policies designed to deprive Florence of sufficient food during the Mugello war

---

8   The relevant passage from the chronicle of Pseudo-Brunetto Latini is quoted in both English and the original Italian in Callegari, *Dante's Gluttons*, pp. 105–06. Callegari notes that both Cook and Herzman use the text to argue in favour of Ugolino's cannibalism in their essay, William R. Cook and Ronald B. Herzman, 'Inferno xxiii: The Past and Present in Dante's Imagery of Betrayal', *Italica*, 56.4 (Winter 1979), pp. 377–83. On p. 378 of their essay, the authors quote the passage from Pseudo-Brunetto Latini's chronicle that relates to Ugolino's withholding of grain from the Pisans: 'This Count Ugolino was a man of such a type that he caused the people of Pisa to die of hunger and at this time although he had a great abundance of grain was so cruel that a staio of grain cost seven pounds.' They cite the source for the quote in David Herlihy, *Pisa in the Early Renaissance: A Study in Urban Growth* (New Haven: Yale University Press, 1958), p. 109.

9   As Callegari argues, Dante's progression from Ugolino to Alberigo and then to Satan offers 'a perfect contrast with the successful head of the community who is powerful through providing and enforcing cohesion through communion in food' (Callegari, *Dante's Gluttons*, p. 116).

(during summer and fall of 1302). How do we explain this apparent contradiction between actions taken in 1302–03 and the philosophical arguments advanced after 1303? It is not the aim of this essay to resolve this issue, as any response must be speculative. Dante left the armed struggle and the battlefield as early as the spring of 1303 or as late as the summer of 1304. Perhaps there is a dose of self-criticism and regret ('self-scrutiny') on Dante's part when he finished *Inferno* in 1315, evident in cantos 32 and 33 in the person of Ugolino? We can never know for certain. However, at the very least, this essay aims to renew attention to Dante's participation in military operations directed against Florence in 1302–03 that intended to induce hunger in the city. Unfortunately, as Guido Pampaloni observed many years ago when he published his findings on Dante's year of exile, the lack of sufficient documentation hampers the ability of the historian to answer all the questions and fill in the gaps.[10] Nevertheless, we know enough to conclude that Dante's role as a major participant in the wars by Ghibellines and White Guelf exiles against Florence seems to stand at variance with the philosophical positions regarding food, leadership, and governance that he apparently later promoted in his works after 1303.

For seven years (1295–1302), Dante had been a reliable and consistent participant in Florentine public life. Some of those duties either directly or indirectly included responsibilities associated with the urban grain supply. After his exile from Florence in 1302, his political activity continued, albeit in alliance with White Guelfs and Ghibellines engaged in a war against the Black Guelf faction then in control of Florence. After many years as a public servant with duties that at times concerned the urban food supply, Dante supported and

---

10 Santagata, *Dante*, p. 152; Guido Pampaloni, 'I primi anni dell'esilio di Dante', in *Conferenze Aretine 1965* (Arezzo: Academia Petrarca; Bibbiena: Società Dantesca Casentinese, 1966), pp. 133–47 (p. 144). Scholars hold differing views about when exactly Dante left the armed struggle. Pampaloni believes he left in the spring of 1303 (ibid., pp. 144–45), as did Robert Davidsohn, *Storia di Firenze*, trans. by Giovanni Battista Klein, 5 vols (Florence: Sansoni, 1960), IV, p. 325. For Santagata, Dante 'distanced himself from the theater of war' either after Niccolò da Prato's departure from Florence on June 10, 1304, or after the death of the pope on July 7 (Santagata, *Dante*, p. 172). Given the fact that Dante began the *Convivio* in 1303, abandoning the armed struggle in the spring of 1303 seems more plausible than leaving a year later in the summer of 1304.

helped lead military efforts in the countryside north and east of the city that intended, among various goals, to disrupt the supply of food to the city, particularly grain. The purpose, at the very least, was to drive up the urban price of grain and thereby encourage disorder to undermine the legitimacy of the new Black Guelf regime; at most, it aimed to induce hunger if not starvation within the city walls. In early 1302 Dante was one of several signatories of an agreement at San Godenzo in the Mugello valley north of Florence to indemnify members of the Ubaldini magnate family for any losses incurred from those military actions. Indeed, as a military leader and as a financial guarantor of those efforts, Dante was therefore an active participant and financial guarantor in a military strategy based on food deprivation: tactics that exacerbated an already severe *carestia* (grain shortage) in 1302–03. Not surprisingly, in March of 1302 the Black Guelf regime identified Dante as a traitor to Florence and to his party (the Guelfs).[11] For the writer who had completed the *Commedia* by 1321, however, it was Black Florence itself, allied with Pope Boniface VIII in 1302, that had been the 'betrayer' — to him, to his party, to his city.

What follows is a presentation of the historical context leading up to the time when Dante signed the indemnification agreement in June of 1302 at San Godenzo. It focuses specifically on the politics of food during the years of his public service and early exile (1295–1303). It does not add any new specific details to what we already know about Dante's life during those seven years; nevertheless, the evidence that Dante was a party to a military strategy based on inducing food depriv-ation is compelling and worth emphasizing. With his past experiences

---

11   Robert Hollander, *Dante: A Life in Works* (New Haven: Yale University Press, 2001) provides a very detailed chronology of the poet's life on pp. xi–xiv, as does Nick Havely, *Dante* (Maldon, MA, and Oxford: Blackwell, 2007), pp. xxi–xxvi. Santagata, *Dante*, chapter 3 covers Dante's public service between 1295 and 1301, as do Barański and Pertile, 'Chronology', pp. xxi–xxii, and Pertile, 'Life', pp. 464–66. For Dante's role at the conferences at Gargonza and San Godenzo, see Pampaloni, 'I primi anni', pp. 142–44; Santagata, *Dante*, pp. 144–57. For the first Mugello war from June through September 1302, see Santagata, *Dante*, p. 152. The text of the indemnification letter is published in Isidoro del Lungo, *Dino Compagni e la sua Cronica*, 3 vols (Florence: Le Monnier, 1879–87), II (1879), pp. 569–70. See below for details. For the severe *carestia* (food shortage) of 1302–03 and the disruption of grain shipments by White Guelf exiles and Ghibellines, see Giuliano Pinto, *Il libro del Biadaiolo. Carestie e annona a Firenze dalla metà del '200 al 1348* (Florence: Olschki, 1978), pp. 84–88.

as a public official engaged in food policies and as a military (cavalry) leader at the battles of Campaldino and Caprona in 1289, at San Go-denzo in 1302 Dante signed an indemnity agreement that effectively subsidized Ubaldini's efforts in the Mugello to use food deprivation as a weapon of war. Those efforts included a variety of strategies to hamper the delivery of grain to the city from Romagna, including tar-geting grain shipments, capturing Florentine *castelli*, and obstructing or disrupting the road infrastructure. In 1302–03 the ideal strategic goals of the White Guelf exiles and Ghibellines in the *contado* — aims that Dante not only supported but led — were to induce famine and inspire internal rebellion.[12] The rest of this essay will consist of three parts. A brief first section surveys the history of the political economy of grain and food crises from 1265 to 1295, coinciding with the first three decades of the poet's life. The second section highlights the seven years between 1295 and 1302, the period during which Dante assumed an active role in public service that included a close familiarity with the urban food supply (the *annona*). The third part examines two years, 1302 and 1303, the beginning of his exile and engagement in the mili-tary resistance to the new Black Guelf regime in Florence. Sometime in 1303 the poet abandoned the field of battle to resume his philosophical writing, beginning both the *Convivio* and *De vulgari eloquentia*.[13]

For the first decade of Dante's life (1265–75), as the population and size of Florence was growing rapidly, the Florentine city-state en-joyed reliable access to its principal source of food source: grain.[14] In fact, for most of the third quarter of the thirteenth century (c. 1250–c. 1275), grain harvests were generally favourable. Occasionally, how-

---

12   Pinto, *Il libro del Biadaiolo*, pp. 85–86; Santagata, *Dante*, pp. 150–52; Davidsohn, *Storia di Firenze*, IV, pp. 319–32.

13   For Dante's life in exile, see Pertile, 'Life', pp. 466–68. For the *Convivio* and *De vulgari eloquentia*, aside from Callegari, *Dante's Gluttons*, see Lino Pertile, 'Works', in *Dante in Context*, ed. by Zygmunt G. Barański and Lino Pertile (Cambridge: Cambridge University Press, 2015), pp. 483–88.

14   For a general overview of the political economy of grain from the twelfth to the mid-fourteenth century, see George Dameron, 'Feeding the Medieval Italian City-State: Grain, War and Political Legitimacy in Tuscany, c. 1150–c. 1350', *Speculum*, 92.4 (October 2017), pp. 976–1019 <https://doi.org/10.1086/693379>. For the period covered by this essay, c. 1250–c. 1330, see pp. 996–1007. See also Dameron, *Feeding the Medieval Italian City-State: Grain, Political Legitimacy, and War, c. 1100–1350* (Philadelphia: University of Pennsylvania Press, forthcoming).

ever, imports from afar were necessary. For example, although the city imported grain in 1271 from southern Italy and from Provence, for the most part Florence experienced no major interruption in its grain supply until the mid-1270s. Like most city-states in Tuscany, in the 1270s we first begin to see the emergence of the most significant public bureaucracies dedicated to insuring grain security. Such was the case for Florence, as managing imports from neighbouring regions to supplement domestic grain reserves became increasingly necessary. The first actual grain bureaucracy appeared in 1274, but it was apparently short-lived. Food security was increasingly becoming a major public policy priority for the government of the Florentine Commune, as grain harvests between 1275 and 1285 were increasingly inconsistent and difficult. For two years (1275–77), the city as well as the region of Tuscany experienced the first major grain shortage or dearth (*carestia*) of the second half of the thirteenth century. In response, the Parte Guelfa loaned funds to finance imports to the new (post 1267) government of the Primo Popolo, and the Kingdom of Naples exported many hundreds of *salme* of grain to Florence.[15] After the crisis of the mid-1270s, the grain magistracy created in 1274 disappeared from our sources for reasons unknown (though it was not uncommon in Tuscan communes for certain magistracies to pop up as needed and then disappear after the crisis that called them into being had dissipated).[16]

The 1280s and 1290s (and until 1295, when Dante turned 30) were important decades in the development of the poet's life and family. During those decades he married Gemma Donati (1285), his children

---

15   Pinto, *Libro del Biadiaolo*, pp. 80–81, 100–01, 107–09; Nicola Ottokar, *Il comune di Firenze alla fine del Dugento* (Turin: Einaudi, 1962), p. 110; Davidsohn, *Storia di Firenze*, III, pp. 104–05, 166–67. The license to export 800 *salme* of wheat from Sicily to Florence in 1276 by way of Pisa to meet the food needs of Florence is as follows: 'Cum ad supplicationem Potestatis, Consilii et Comuni Florentie, devotorum nostrorum eis concesserimus licentiam extrahendi de portubus licitis et statutis Sicilie, ad extractionem victualium deputatis, octingentas salmas frumenti ad salman generalem, ferendas per mare apud Pisas et deinde apud Florentiam pro usu et sustentatione hominum ipsius terre [...]'. *Documenti delle relazioni tra Carlo I d'Angiò e la Toscana*, ed. by Sergio Terlizzi (Florence: Olschki, 1950), pp. 398–99. For other export licenses to ship grain to Florence from Sicily, see ibid., pp. 397, 402–03, 404–05.

16   This first grain magistracy appears in the document Archivio di Stato di Firenze, *Diplomatico*, Santissima Annunziata, dicembre, 1274, hereafter *ASF*. For more information (and documentation) of this magistracy, see Ottokar, *Il comune di Firenze*, pp. 109–10; Davidsohn, *Storia di Firenze*, III, pp. 166–67.

were born (1287, 1289), he wrote two of his most important early lyrical works (the *Detto d'Amore* and *Fiore*, 1286–87), and his muse, Beatrice (wife of Simone dei Bardi), died in 1290. In June of 1289, to be precise, Dante served as a cavalry officer for Florence at the battle of Campaldino (and possibly Caprona on August 6, 1289) during its war with Arezzo. During this war (which lasted until 1293), Dante served in the cohort of *feditori*, a prestigious detachment of cavalry that usually spearheaded the attack.[17]

This was also an important decade and a half in the food history of Florence. By 1284, the urban government opted to create a new and more permanent magistracy, the *Sei della biada*, dedicated specifically to insuring food (grain) security for the city. This is the same year that a new loggia at Orsanmichele was begun, a short distance from Dante's home parish church, to provide a large and central location for the marketing of grain. When the married poet began his twenty-first year (1285–86), Florence and the rest of Tuscany experienced another severe grain shortage (*carestia*), far worse than the crisis of the mid-1270s. In order to deal with this crisis, the Commune unveiled several new initiatives to supplement domestic production and to encourage imports from the Senese and Romagna. These measures included the offer of bounties to anyone bringing grain from outside the city limits (*districtus*) to the urban market (1285), the establishment of a major urban granary or storehouse (*canova*, 1285), and the repair of road infrastructure with public funds provided the *Sei della biada* to facilitate grain deliveries to the Orsanmichele market (1286–87). The members of the new (1282) governing magistracy of the Commune, the priorate, approved in 1287 the creation of a new grain market at Monteluco della Berardegna in the *contado* to facilitate access to grain reserves from an agriculturally rich region of Tuscany. It was located on the periphery of two major grain producing regions, the Senese and the Aretino.[18]

---

17   Barański and Pertile, 'Chronology', p. xx; Pertile, 'Life', pp. 461–64; Santagata, *Dante*, chapters 1–2. For the battle of Campaldino, see Federico Canaccini, *1289: la battaglia di Campaldino* (Bari: Laterza, 2021). For Dante's role in the Aretine war, including Campaldino and Caprona, see Santagata, *Dante*, pp. 52, 61–62; and John Najemy, *History of Florence* (Malden, MA, and Oxford, UK: Blackwell, 2006), pp. 80–81.

18   Giovanni Villani, *Nuova Cronica*, ed. by Giuseppe Porta, 3 vols (Parma: Guanda, 1990–91), I, pp. 547, 576; Marchionne di Coppo Stefani, *Cronica Fiorentina di Marchionne di Coppo Stefani*, ed. by Niccolò Rodolico (Città del Castello: Lapi, 1903), p. 62 (rubric

On July 10, 1289, just a month after Campaldino, the newly elected magistrates of the *Sei della biada* successfully petitioned the powerful Consiglio del Capitano for funds to use at their own discretion to purchase grain and to pay the salaries of their small staff. In 1290 and 1291 the government defined more precisely the powers and duties of the *Sei della biada* regarding imports, grain purchases, and policing. By early 1291, for example, we learn that the magistracy of the *Sei* was empowered to arrange for grain imports, keep careful track of their governance procedures and records, and police (guarantee the security) of the urban grain supply (*annona*). All their duties, however, were to be conducted under the supervision of the principal magistracy of the priorate, and all their funds came from communal coffers. Although 1291 was not a year of *carestia* (harvests were apparently favourable from 1287 to 1295), there was sufficient concern on the part of the *Sei* regarding a shortage of grain — enough to prompt the import of at least 400 *staia* from Romagna and to enforce strict fines levied on violators of the export ban (*divieto*).[19] Immediately after Campaldino, therefore, it seems that communal leaders initiated certain measures through its grain magistracy (now half a decade old) to mitigate the vulnerability of the commune to threats to its grain imports during possible military operations. The areas of highest vulnerability to disruption were grain imports from the Aretino (upper Arno valley) and from across the Apennines from Romagna (through the Mugello valley).[20]

168, year 1286): 'Come fu grande carestia in Firenze ed in molte altre parti'; Pinto, *Il libro del Biadaiolo*, pp. 80–81, 107–09, 116, 122–23; Najemy, *History of Florence*, chapters 2–4 (for political and social background up to 1340). For the grain market at Orsanmichele, see ibid., pp. 54–55. In 1287 the Florentine government approved a market to be established at Monteluco della Berardegna, near the border with Siena and Arezzo. The purpose was to maximize the amount of grain from that region for Florence ('maxime pro copia grani et blade habenda', from Pinto, *Il libro del Biadaiolo*, p. 107, citing *ASF* Provvizioni Protocolli 1, c. 45r).

19   Pinto, *Il libro del Biadaiolo*, pp. 80–83, 101. Davidsohn notes that the Commune gave Guido da Polenta enough money to import 3,000 staia of grain to the city market (Orsanmichele). See Robert Davidsohn, 'Die Getreidepolitik, der Kommune', in Davidsohn, *Forschungen zur Geschichte von Florenz*, 4 vols (Berlin: Mittler und Sohn, 1896–1908), IV, pp. 307–15.

20   Giovanni Cherubini, 'L'approvvigionamento alimentare delle città toscane tra XII e XV secolo', in Cherubini, *Firenze e la Toscana (Scritti vari)* (Pisa: Ospedaletto, 2013), pp. 39–55 (especially pp. 42–46).

It was during this year, 1295, that Dante entered public service. Over the next six years, he served in several positions that either directly or indirectly involved the urban grain supply. His entry into public life came at the end of an especially productive phase of his artistic life, as the writer of lyrical (love) poetry. His entry into public life also coincided with the political ascendancy of the Cerchi, who were apparently his patrons, allies, or both. Though originally from the non-aristocratic *popolo*, gradually (and certainly by the time he was writing the *Commedia*) he came to be politically critical of both the *popolo* (whom he believed were flawed by envy and greed) and the aristocracy or magnates (for their factionalism). To be eligible to serve in the Commune, the governance of which was managed by the major guilds, one had to be registered as a member of a guild. Dante did join a guild in July of that year: the guild of doctors and apothecaries (*Medici e Speziali*). His political career in communal governance began — as was expected of any politician wishing to ascend the ladder of political office — with service on several communal councils. In November (1295) he appeared as a member of the Council of Thirty-Six (or *Consiglio speciale del Capitano del Popolo*) as a representative of his neighborhood (*sestiere*). A month later, he spoke before the council of the heads of the major guilds (the *Consiglio dei Capitudini*) on the issue of election reform regarding the priorate. In June of 1296 he assumed a role on the Council of One Hundred (*Consiglio dei Cento*), which normally met with the priors, and he spoke on several issues. He opposed welcoming Pistoian exiles into the city, spoke in support of certain anti-magnate proposals, and expressed an opinion regarding the relocation of a hospital in Piazza San Giovanni to make room for the new cathedral.

By 1297 the Donati faction, opponents of Dante's political patrons, the Cerchi, had returned to political dominance, and Dante dropped out of public life. Surviving records note that he made one more set of remarks in council in 1297.[21] This was the same year that coincided

---

21   Santagata, *Dante*, chapter 3 (especially pp. 93–96); Hollander, *Dante*, p. xii; Pertile, 'Life', pp. 464–65; Najemy, *History of Florence*, pp. 57, 62; Barański and Pertile, 'Chronology', p. xxi; Davidsohn, *Storia di Firenze*, IV, pp. 168–70; *Codice diplomatico dantesco*, ed. by Renato Piattoli (Florence: Libreria Luigi Gonnelli e figli, 1940), documents 56 and 79, pp. 62–64, 85–87. Starn offers a brief and concise overview of Dante's public

with a significant enhancement of the supervisory power of the priorate and the *Gonfaloniere della Giustizia* (Standard-bearer of Justice)
over the operations of the *Sei della biada*. Specifically, the priors and
the Standard-bearer of Justice were now invested with ultimate authority over the grain supply, superseding the *Sei della biada*. This did not
presumably mean that they were managing the day-to-day operations
of the grain supply process (the *annonaria*), but it did signal increased,
centralized oversight over the *Sei* by the principal organs of power,
the Signoria. These measures occurred two years after the passages
of the Ordinances of Justice of 1295, which enhanced the power of
the Signoria over many of the rural magnates (who themselves were
major producers of grain destined for urban markets). The priors and
the *Gonfaloniere della Giustizia* anticipated correctly in 1297 that 1298
would bring a poor harvest. It was indeed quite a mediocre year regarding grain. The *Sei* planned for the potential danger posed by the 1298
harvest and requested and received public funds to import supple-
mental grain. Imports continued into 1299, when the Bardi company
imported 2,000 florins worth of wheat from southern Italy with funds
from tolls dedicated to the *Sei* for imports.[22] Although Dante seems
to have dropped out of public life after 1297, he had already served as
a veteran of several government councils (one of which met with the
priorate) and had participated in significant discussions as a member
of the communal governing elite. He was no doubt familiar with the
workings of the *Sei della biada*, now more closely supervised from 1297
by both the priorate and the *Gonfaloniere della Giustizia*.

The half decade between 1297 and 1302 were decisive years
for both the commune and Dante's own personal fortunes. At least
three massive construction projects were underway: the new cathedral
(from 1296), the Palazzo dei Priori (1299), and the new circle of walls
(begun 1284, and continuing especially after 1299).[23] However, polit-

---

career. See Randolph Starn, *Contrary Commonwealth: The Theme of Exile in Medieval and Renaissance Italy* (Berkeley: University of California Press, 1982), p. 72.

22   Pinto, *Il libro del Biadaiolo*, pp. 80–83, 107–09, 115–17; Najemy, *History of Florence*, pp. 81–87; Davidsohn, *Storia di Firenze*, IV, pp. 97–98.

23   Richard Goldthwaite, *The Building of Renaissance Florence: An Economic and Social History* (Baltimore: Johns Hopkins, 1980), pp. 4–5; Najemy, *History of Florence*, pp. 87, 97–100.

ical and social conflict intensified during this half decade, fueled by the tension between the Cerchi faction of the Guelfs (White Guelfs, with which Dante was aligned) and the Donati faction. At the same time, the papacy aligned itself increasingly with the Donati faction (Black Guelfs) to leverage its own efforts at the time to dominate Tuscany, particularly Florence. During these tumultuous years (1297–1302), as a civic leader, the poet found himself in the middle of these escalating crises. Nevertheless, he continued to serve the Commune in a variety of ways, including, and most importantly, as prior between June 15 and August 15 of 1300. As Florence moved closer toward civil war and Dante toward eventual exile in early 1302, he assumed several responsibilities that were either indirectly or directly concerned with the security of the urban grain supply. Not only was there a growing political crisis, but there was also a food crisis that reached its peak in 1302, the same year as Dante's exile: a severe region-wide grain shortage (*carestia*) caused by heavy rains, followed by severe drought.[24]

The list of duties and responsibilities which Dante shouldered for the Commune in 1300 and 1301 is well known and will not be described in detail here. However, for the purposes of this essay, it is noteworthy that several of them — at least three, specifically — were either directly or indirectly food- (grain-) related. Perhaps most important was his service as prior between June 15 and August 15, 1300. As previously noted, the priors had ultimate responsibility for overseeing the grain supply and exercised supervisory control over the *Sei della biada*. In the year before his term began, in 1299, some regions of Tuscany were already suffering from a food emergency. In June of that year the *Consiglio generale* in Siena had declared a *charestia generalis* connected with all foodstuffs. By the next year, the Commune of Siena was requiring its ecclesiastical institutions to deliver

---

24   For a first-hand account of the political developments in Florence between 1295 and the end of 1301, see books 1 and 2 of Dino Compagni, *Dino Compagni's Chronicle of Florence*, trans. by Daniel Bornstein (Philadelphia: University of Pennsylvania Press, 1986), especially pp. 19–48; and Giovanni Villani, *Nuova Cronica*, II, pp. 29–109. For secondary accounts, see Najemy, *History of Florence*, pp. 88–93; Santagata, *Dante*, pp. 88–109; Hollander, *Dante*, p. xii; Davidsohn, *Storia di Firenze*, IV, chapter 1. For the 1302 *carestia* and food crisis, see Villani, *Nuova Cronica*, II, pp. 108–09; Pinto, *Il libro del Biadaiolo*, pp. 83–84, 105.

grain reserves to the city.[25] When Dante served as ambassador to San Gimignano on behalf of Florence in May of 1300 at a conference of White Guelfs, he had entered territory already suffering from serious food shortages. The aim of that meeting was to create a plan to push back against further papal encroachment in Tuscany. In this year of political and food-related crises, his opposition to expansionist papal policies toward Tuscany was steadfast. Even a year later in June of 1301 he was the only member of the *Consiglio dei Cento* to vote against any further Florentine aid to the papacy for its military war against the Aldobrandeschi in southern Tuscany. In addition, the years 1300 and 1301 coincided with some of the worst factional violence to date, resulting in a final split between White (anti-papal, *popolo*-leaning) and Black (pro-papal) Guelfs. Although Dante aligned with the former, during his two-month stint as prior in the summer of 1300, he and his colleagues tried to tamp down the escalating conflicts by exiling selected leaders of the two major factions. Seven members of the Cerchi faction (Whites) were banished to Sarzana, and eight members of the Donati factions (Blacks) were exiled to Città del Pieve. Among those exiled was Dante's pro-Donati friend, the poet Guido Cavalcanti. This effort at peace-making unfortunately failed in August and September. The Cerchi convinced the priorate to allow their leaders to return (but not the Donati). This cancellation of the exile of Cerchi leaders contributed to the decision on September 23 by Matteo Acquasparta, the papal legate in Tuscany and the Romagna, to excommunicate the government of Florence and to impose an interdict on the city. Emissaries from Florence, Siena, and Bologna went to Rome to seek resolution to the factional conflicts, and Pope Boniface VIII agreed to lift the interdict in exchange for an agreement by Florence to contribute to the papal war effort against the Aldobrandeschi.[26]

---

25   Davidsohn, *Storia di Firenze*, IV, p. 102, citing Archivio di Stato di Siena (ASS) Consiglio Generale 55, folio. 102. For Siena, see William M. Bowsky, *A Medieval Italian Commune: Siena under the Nine, 1287–1355* (Berkeley: University of California Press, 1981), pp. 203–04.

26   For a contemporary perspective on the origins and course of the Black-White feud, see Villani, *Nuova Cronica*, II, pp. 62–81. See also *Codice diplomatico dantesco*, ed. by Piattoli, document 73, pp. 80–82. For secondary accounts, see Davidsohn, *Storia di Firenze*, IV, pp. 154–56; Najemy, *History of Florence*, p. 91; Santagata, *Dante*, pp. 105–14, 131–37; Pertile, 'Life', p. 465; Havely, *Dante*, pp. xxiii–xxiv; Hollander, *Dante*, pp.

Differences over food policies, though never explicit, played a role in the factional tensions between Black and White Guelfs. The Blacks tended to follow policies sympathetic to the magnates, many of whom were urban or rural lords in possession of grain-producing lands. They preferred high grain prices in the city. The political base of the more *popolo*-oriented Whites, led by Vieri dei Cerchi, favoured lower food (especially grain) prices that were consistent with the interests of their own political base, the urban population. This may help explain why, in August of 1300, before Dante rotated off the priorate on August 15, the magistracy was seeking a military and diplomatic alliance with Guelf Bologna, a major source of grain imports for Florence. At least indirectly, and perhaps even directly, if such an alliance had succeeded, it would have had a significant positive impact on Florentine food security. It promised, for example, not only to provide Florence with a strong Guelf military ally as a hedge against further papal encroachment in Tuscany, but more importantly the agreement could help keep secure and safeguard the mountain passes and road arteries between Romagna and Florence that were so vital for the grain imports from the Romagna to Florence. Military and diplomatic cooperation between Florence and Bologna would therefore have helped ensure that exported Romagnolo grain would have had unobstructed and secure access to the Florentine market. This was especially important, as the Ubaldini magnate family still exercised considerable power in the Mugello valley and already had a long history of anti-Florence military activity in the hinterland between Romagna and Tuscany. Not surprisingly, these diplomatic efforts met with opposition from the pope's legate in Tuscany and the Romagna, Matteo Acquasparta. As Dante's biographer Marco Santagata noted, the alliance was to be formalized just ten days after Dante had left the priorate on August 15. Like previous priors' efforts at peace-making, however, this attempt at an alliance with Bologna fell victim to escalating internal political tensions and violence within Florence itself, and fierce opposition from the papacy.

---

xii–xiii; Barański and Pertile, 'Chronology', p. xxi. The long article by Guido Pampaloni, 'Bianchi e Neri', in *Enciclopedia Dantesca*, ed. by Umberto Bosco (Rome: Istituto della Enciclopedia Italiana fondata da Giovanni Treccani, 1970) <https://www.treccani.it/enciclopedia/bianchi-e-neri_(Enciclopedia-Dantesca)/> [accessed 19 May 2025] is still very relevant.

Its surrogates (the Black Guelfs) were on the political rise in mid- and late-August of 1300.[27]

Although Dante was no longer serving on the priorate, he continued to be an active participant in urban governance in the following year, 1301. In a meeting of the *Consiglio delle Capitudini* in April, for example, he spoke out as an 'advisor' or 'wise man' (*savio*) regarding advice about the procedures for the election of the priors. During his tenure as a member of the *Consiglio dei Cento* (April–September), while meeting jointly with the *Consiglio delle Capitudini*, he argued in June against extending the two-and-a-half-month end date for Florence to supply knights (*cavalieri*) for the papal war against the Aldobrandeschi in southern Tuscany. The request was made by the papal legate, Matteo d'Acquasparta, and it carried with it the recommendation of the priors. Later that same day, when the *Consiglio dei Cento* was meeting alone, Dante spoke out against it once more. By June 19, however, the proposal received majority support in the council. Dante's stance turned out to be the minority position. The White Guelfs seemed divided on the issue, and Dante sided with a vocal minority increasingly hostile to the apparent aims of Pope Boniface VIII to replace the Whites in government with his allies, the Blacks, and to bring Tuscany as a whole under the hegemony of the papacy.[28] Even though he represented a minority position at the time with regards to the issue of military aid to the papacy, he continued in the spring of 1301 to be chosen by civic leaders for positions of leadership. The second major grain-related post he assumed came in the spring of 1301 (his first was his service as prior).

In April of 1301 the members of the grain magistracy (*Sei della biada*) appointed him as chair (*officialis et superstans*) of a commission charged with the responsibility to supervise the road renovation, straightening, and extension of via San Procolo from the urban suburb of borgo Piagentino to the *torrente* (stream) of Affrico. Today the road corresponds to the via Pandolfini. In the early fourteenth century it was lined with houses, cottages, and small parcels of land, extending

---

27   Santagata, *Dante*, p. 114.
28   *Codice diplomatico dantesco*, ed. by Piattoli, documents 81, 82, 83, 84, pp. 92–96; Santagata, *Dante*, pp. 135–37; Hollander, *Dante*, p. xii; Davidsohn, *Storia di Firenze*, IV, pp. 197–98; Santagata, *Dante*, pp. 135–37; Pertile, 'Life', pp. 464–66.

beyond the urban walls into the eastern suburbs. The purpose of this project, among other commercial goals, was to facilitate the flow of grain and foodstuffs from the eastern suburb and beyond — the borgo Piagentino — to the urban market of Orsanmichele and to prevent obstructions along the route caused by local (presumably pro-Donati?) magnates. These food shipments came from the Valdarno di Sopra to the east of the city, corresponding roughly with the borderlands of the Aretino. The Signoria had ultimate authority over roads and bridges, but often that authority was delegated to the grain magistrates (as it was here). Dante's biographer, Santagata, argues that the *Sei* appointed Dante because he himself was a property owner near the borgo Piagentino (in the parish of Sant'Ambrogio) and therefore had a stake in the project. An additional argument that does not exclude Santagata's observation is that the *Sei* recognized Dante as an experienced leader who could be trusted to complete a project and as someone with previous experience as a prior whose principal responsibilities included supervision of the food supply and the grain magistracy (the point of the project). In addition, Dante had already established a record of opposition and hostility towards magnates.[29] Five months later in an urban council he spoke out once more against magnate interests. On September 13, 1301, in the *Consigli dei Cento e del Capitano* (meeting

---

29   *Codice diplomatico dantesco*, ed. by Piattoli, document 80 (April 28, 1301), pp. 87–92; Michele Barbi, *L'ufficio di Dante per i lavori di via S. Procolo* (Florence: Sansoni, 1921), pp. 89–110; Franek Sznura, *L'espansione urbana di Firenze nel dugento* (Florence: La Nuova Italia, 1975), pp. 50–51; Davidsohn, *Storia di Firenze*, IV, p. 200; Santagata, *Dante*, pp. 121–22. The document about the via San Procolo project was first published by G. Milanesi in 1869 (see Barbi, *L'ufficio di Dante*, p. 89). It specifically cites the need to secure the delivery of foodstuffs into the city by extending and making straight the via S. Procolo that headed toward the eastern suburb of borgo Piagentino and the Affrico (*torrente*). By so doing, the project also aimed to put an end to the noisy obstructionism and disorder caused by the magnates along the way. They were identified as a security threat to the food supply that entered the city from the eastern suburbs. The key passage, as reproduced by *Codice diplomatico dantesco*, ed. by Piattoli, p. 87 is the following: 'Exponitur coram vobis dd. sex officialibus positis pro comuni Florentie super reinveniendis iuribus comunis Florentie et viis mistendis et dirizzandis, quod via Sancti Proculi, que protenditur versus Burgum de la Piagentina, que est multum utilis et necessaria hominibus et personis civitatis Florentie, maxime propter vittualium copiam habendam et maxime eo quod populares comitatus absque strepitu et briga magnatum et potentum possunt securo venire per eandem ad dd. priores et vexilliferum iustitie cum expedit'. In Dante's day along the via S. Procolo were houses and small cottages ('domus, terrena sue casolaria in via Sancti Proculi'; Sznura, *L'espansione urbana*, p. 51).

jointly), Dante spoke out in favour of conserving the anti-magnate Ordinances of Justice from 1293 and 1295. For over half a decade they had elevated the political power of the *popolo* and excluded the magnates from the most important positions in the Commune.[30]

The third example of a food-related public service taken by Dante occurred while serving on the *Consiglio dei Cento*. It was also one of the final instances in which he spoke publicly in a communal council. On September 20, 1301, in the *Consiglio dei Cento*, meeting jointly with other councils, Dante spoke in favour of initiatives to construct new roads to guarantee access to products from the *contado*, including food (to provide the means of subsistence for the city: 'mezzi di suscitenza' in Davidsohn's words). Along with Lapo Saltarelli (of whom Dante will be sharply critical in *Paradiso* 15.126–29), he spoke in council in favour of letting Bologna transfer imported grain from Pisa through Florentine territory to Bologna. Not only did Dante acknowledge again in council the need to have a road infrastructure that facilitated the delivery of products from the *contado* (such as grain and other foodstuffs) to urban residents, but he also in this intervention demonstrated his ongoing sympathy for Guelf Bologna.[31]

The next four months in Florence were tumultuous as well as increasingly dangerous for anyone who was not a Black Guelf sympathizer. In October 1301, Charles of Valois, the pro-papal commander of a very sizeable military force, joined the exiled Donati at Siena. Anticipating direct political and military intervention by the papacy in Florence, Dante was part of a delegation sent to Rome on behalf of the Signoria to convince Pope Boniface VIII at the Lateran Palace to step back from encouraging and supporting a military incursion into Florence. The pope, however, demanded obedience, and the priors back in Florence acquiesced. The mission of the embassy had been undercut. While Dante remained in Rome, Charles of Valois and his soldiers entered Florence on November 1 with the help of Vieri dei Cerchi and the Black Guelfs. What followed was nothing short of a coup-d'état by the Black Guelfs, and by November 7 all major commu-

---

30   *Codice diplomatico dantesco*, ed. by Piattoli, document 86, pp. 97–98; Davidsohn, *Storia di Firenze*, IV, p. 199.

31   *Codice diplomatico dantesco*, ed. by Piattoli, document 87, pp. 98–99; Davidsohn, *Storia di Firenze*, IV, p. 201.

nal offices were in the hands of the pro-papal Blacks.[32] Subsequent to
the coup, the Blacks were now in control of the government. By the
end of 1302 the Black regime will have exiled around 600 people, condemned to death about 559, and either destroyed or confiscated the
properties of the exiles. Among those outside the city on November
7 (1301), whose property would later be subject to confiscation and
whose public career was over, was Dante Alighieri. He was in Rome
during the coup and chose never again to return to his native city.[33]

The year 1302 was a very fateful year for both the White Guelf-
Ghibelline alliance in exile and for Dante personally. In this year he
chose to join the armed struggle in the countryside against his native
city. By early 1302, Florentine territory was entering a worsening food
emergency (*carestia*) caused by excessive rains followed by drought.
Over the course of 1302, White Guelf exiles and Ghibellines in the
contado acted to undermine the legitimacy and power of the new pro-
Black regime in Florence by disrupting the flow of grain to the city
through military activity in the Mugello and upper Arno valley (Valdarno di Sopra). They struck at their enemies by disrupting roads,
besieging *castelli*, and blocking grain shipments to the city. Ghibelline Pisa, an enemy of the new communal regime, also helped by
obstructing deliveries at Porto Pisano in early 1302. Among many
other consequences, this compelled the merchant Giovanni di Marsi-
glia to seek an alternative port to unload his 2,000 *moggia*. Ghibelline
and White Guelf emissaries also petitioned the Commune of Genoa in
this same year to cease handling exports to Florence, and, concurrently,
pressured Pisan and Genoese ship captains to attack ships that carried
grain to Florence. In early 1302, during a worsening food emergency,
White Guelf exiles and their Ghibelline allies were therefore embark-
ing on a strategy to use food as a weapon of war against their Black
Guelf enemies in Florence. Repercussions against Dante and other
opponents of the new Black regime began as early as January. In late
January of 1302, Dante found himself and four other former priors

---

32   Compagni, *Dino Compagni's Chronicle*, pp. 22–52 (especially pp. 38–48); Najemy,
      History of Florence, pp. 88–93; Santagata, *Dante*, pp. 137–40; Pertile, 'Life', p. 466;
      Hollander, *Dante*, pp. xxii–xxiii.
33   Compagni, *Dino Compagni's Chronicle*, pp. 46–48; Santagata, *Dante*, pp. 138–42;
      Najemy, *History of Florence*, pp. 88–93.

accused in absentia of extortion, barratry, and ill-gotten gains; he was
fined 5,000 florins and barred from office for two years by the Florentine *podestà*, Cante dei Gabrielli da Gubbio. He would refuse to pay
and chose instead not to return to Florence. By not returning, he faced
confiscation of his property and death.[34] Also in 1302, the *podestà* of
Florence, as recorded in the *Libro del chiodo*, noted that several men
had been convicted for having journeyed to Genoa to stop grain shipments to Florence. Those cited included Lapo Saltarelli. The *podestà's*
statement clearly reveals the intentional aim of these emissaries, and it
also represents the general aims of the Guelf exile-Ghibelline alliance:
to bring about famine for Florence and its population ('predictam
civitatem Florentie et populum ipsius fame necare').[35]

Already by the end of January the Florentine priors, *podestà*, and
Capitano del popolo were deliberating what to do about the devastation
and revolts sparked by an alliance between the Pazzi and the Ubertini
in the Valdarno di Sopra. In February the two rural magnate families
had taken Treggiaia in the Valdarno, for example, located between Piantravigne (or Pian-tra-Vigne) and San Giovanni Valdarno.[36] However,
Dante's involvement in the armed struggle against Black-controlled
Florence most likely began no later than early March of 1302. We know
very little of his movements in the first half of 1302, but we know
enough to conclude that by June of that year he was fully engaged in the
struggle. Initially, the poet probably travelled from Rome to Siena, and
from there to Gargonza, according to Leonardo Bruni's biography. Located in the Val di Chiana in the grain-producing region of the Aretino

---

34 Giovanni Villani recorded the severity of the 1302 *carestia* in the usual way of contem-
    porary chroniclers: by recording the high price of grain: 'E nel detto anno fue gran
    caro di vittuaglia, e valse lo stato del grano in Firenze a la rasa soldi xxii di soldi [...]
    il fiorino d'oro'. Villani, *Nuova Cronica*, II, p. 109. For Dante's convictions, the grain
    politics of early 1302, and the activities of the White Guelf exiles and Ghibellines after
    the November 8 (1301) takeover of Florence by the Blacks, see Najemy, *History of
    Florence*, pp. 88–95; Pinto, *Il libro del Biadaiolo*, pp. 84–87; Hollander, *Dante*, p. xiii;
    and Santagata, *Dante*, pp. 143–44. Santagata, chapter 5 (especially pp. 149–73), covers
    the White Guelf-Ghibelline war against Florence. Davidsohn covers much the same
    ground regarding the military activities of the White exiles and Ghibellines and their
    efforts to cut off the supply of grain to Florence during Dante's first year of exile in
    1302; see Davidsohn, *Storia di Firenze*, IV, pp. 317–31.

35 Fabrizio Ricciardelli, *Il libro del chiodo*, Fonti per la storia dell'Italia medievale, Anti-
    quitates, 9 (Rome: Istituto Palazzo Borromini, 1998), pp. 152–53.

36 Davidsohn, *Storia di Firenze*, II, pp. 286–87.

not far from the White Guelf exile base at Arezzo, it was the site of a significant strategic planning conference of Ghibelline and White Guelf exiles for anti-Florence military activities. Pampaloni dated the conference sometime between January 27 (first condemnation of Dante) and March 10 (the second); Santagata dates it between February 10 (internment and final fines) and March 10. In any case, the conference at Gargonza essentially launched the armed struggle against Florence. Its *castello* was in the possession of the Pazzi and Ubertini, fierce and traditional Ghibelline opponents of the Florentine Guelfs. By March of 1302, a military campaign to hobble grain deliveries to Florence and to recapture Florentine *castelli* had already gotten underway. When, in early March, White exiles met with these Ghibelline leaders at Gargonza, they apparently formalized an alliance around a war strategy directed against Florentine *castelli* and possessions in the upper Arno valley, east of Florence. By April, that strategy was bearing fruit, and the exiles-Ghibelline enemies of Florence in the Arno valley were conducting military operations against Florentine interests in that region of Tuscany. Part of those activities included the obstruction of grain transports from the upper Arno valley to Florence, the capture of strategic *castelli*, and the disruption of the road infrastructure. Figline, a key grain market town for Florence, fell to the Pazzi and Ubertini. The Gherardini eventually took major *castelli* in the Chianti, Montagliari, and Brolio regions, allowing them to control the road infrastructure in the Greve and Pesa river valleys. Both valleys were major sources of grain for Florence. White exiles then used the *castello* of Montagliari (near Panzano in the Chianti) as a base from which to attack grain shipments from the south Tuscan port of Talamone to Florence through the Maremma Senese.

Dante's role in all of this is not clear, and the absence of adequate documentation does not allow us to confirm his presence at Gargonza. However, the best evidence that he was there comes from the fact that on March 10, the *podestà* of Florence, Cante dei Gabrielli, went much further in terms of penalties imposed on Dante than in January. He sentenced him and fourteen other White Guelfs to death for not having returned to Florence and for not having paid the fines as stipulated on January 27. An additional factor for the March decree was likely his attendance at the Gargonza conference. Indeed, historians Giovanni Cherubini and Guido Pampaloni both conclude that Dante was probably present at Gargonza, which most likely took place before the March 10 death penalty judgment. Not only was he there, Pampaloni argues, but he was also part of the leadership team planning military operations at the conference. In addition, he suggests, it was precisely this role at the conference that triggered the second condemnation of Dante (and others) by the Black Guelf-controlled government of Florence. Dante's modern biographer, Marco Santagata, also concludes that Dante was a participant at Gargonza. He notes that the death sentence imposed on Dante on March 10 is evidence of retaliation for his presence at the conference.[37] By early April, the military operations conducted by the White Guelf exiles and Ghibellines were already far along, creating conditions resembling civil war in the *contadi* of Florence and Pistoia. On April 5, the Florentine *podestà* Cante dei Gabrielli, therefore, issued another series of death sentences, also targeting White Guelf exiles, among others.[38]

As the rural magnates, the Ubaldini and the Adimari, were leading military operations in the Mugello to obstruct the delivery of grain from the Romagna to Florence in the south, exiles commanded by Naldo dei Gherardini were simultaneously targeting the road and *castello* infrastructure south and southwest of the city in the Val di Greve and Val di Pesa. For the Gherardini, both Montagliari and Montaguto (Val di Greve) in 1302 were centres of fierce resistance to Florence. From May 1, 1302, they intercepted grain transports headed for Florence from southern Tuscany along the Greve and Pesa river valleys. Those conducting the transports were either killed or taken prisoner for ransom. The exiles, under the command of Naldo dei Gherardini, also took the captured grain destined for Florence to their own *castelli*,

---

37 *Codice diplomatico dantesco*, ed. by Piattoli, documents 90, 91, pp. 103–09; Santagata, *Dante*, pp. 142–58; Starn, *Contrary Commonwealth*, pp. 50–52; Davidsohn, *Storia di Firenze*, IV, pp. 275–82, 280n, 317–18; Pampaloni, 'I primi anni', pp. 140–43; Pampaloni, 'Bianchi e Neri'; Giovanni Cherubini, 'Gargonza', in *Enciclopedia Dantesca*, ed. by Umberto Bosco (Rome: Istituto della Enciclopedia Italiana fondata da Giovanni Treccani, 1970) <https://www.treccani.it/enciclopedia/gargonza_(Enciclopedia-Dantesca)/> [accessed 19 May 2025]; Pertile, 'Life', p. 466. For White Guelf use of Montagliari as a base to attack grain shipments from Talamone, see Pinto, *Il libro del Biadaiolo*, p. 86.

38 Villani, *Nuova Cronica*, II, p. 108; Davidsohn, *Storia di Firenze*, IV, pp. 292–94.

and they sliced the hooves of the mules carrying the sacks of grain (to prevent them from being used again). In the rebellious Mugello, the White Guelf and Ghibelline alliance operated out of Ubaldini and Adimari *castelli* to harass the grain transports from the Romagna that were headed for Florence. As the historian Robert Davidsohn notes, this was all part of a grand strategy to bring hunger to the city during an already serious *carestia* and create conditions for an internal revolt that would bring members of the alliance back into power ('per affamare la città e provocare nel popolo assiliato dai bisogni una sollevazione che li avrebbe dovuti ricondurre in patria').[39]

During the spring of 1302 the heavy rains that had initially caused the *carestia* were ending, and what was to become a prolonged drought was now beginning. In April, Ghibelline exiles seized the strategic grain market in the upper Val d'Arno, Figline, wresting control from the signoria of Florence. In the upper Arno valley itself, Florentine military efforts, led by Cante dei Gabrielli, were concentrated on attacking the city's enemies at Piantravigne. From that location the alliance of Ghibellines and White Guelf exiles engaged in widespread warfare throughout the valley (in Villani's words, 'grande guerra nel Valdarno'). Though first without success, the Florentine army was eventually able to take Piantravigne in July only because Carlino dei Pazzi, its castellan, allegedly betrayed the *castello* to the Florentines for a bribe. Many years later, for this act of treachery, Dante — ever the supporter of the White Guelf-Ghibelline alliance against the Blacks — places Carlino in the second ring of Cocytus, Antenora, at the bottom of hell among those who betrayed their country or party (*Inf.* 32.68–69).[40] During those operations at Piantravigne, the exiled Whites and Ghibellines met again on June 8, this time north of Florence in the Mugello valley in Guidi territory. The site of the conference was the palazzo of the Guidi at San Godenzo, and Dante was there to represent the Whites

---

39   Villani, *Nuova Cronica*, II, pp. 108–10; Davidsohn, *Storia di Firenze*, IV, pp. 322–32 (quote on p. 328); Compagni, *Dino Compagni's Chronicle*, pp. 55–59; Starn, *Contrary Commonwealth*, pp. 49–52.

40   Villani, *Nuova Cronica*, pp. 86–87 (quote on p. 86); Compagni, *Dino Compagni's Chronicle*, pp. 55–56; Davidsohn, *Storia di Firenze*, IV, pp. 316–32; Santagata, *Dante*, p. 151.

along with Vieri dei Cerchi.[41] It marked a shift of the armed struggle from the south to the northeast. Representing the Ghibellines was Lapo degli Uberti, the nephew of Farinata, noted for his appearance in the *Commedia*. As a leader among the White exile organization (the *Universitas partis Alborum de Florentia*) in its governing body, the Council of Twelve, Dante lent his considerable letter-writing and rhetorical talents to the council as its secretary or registrar.[42]

At the San Godenzo conference, Dante joined thirteen others on June 8 to sign an agreement to indemnify the house of the Ubaldini for any losses incurred in its military operations against Florence in the Mugello and other mountainous regions north of the commune. Those assets at risk included the territory around the *castello* of Montaccianico and any ecclesiastical benefices lost to the Ubaldini from confiscation in retaliation by the pope.[43] The original document no longer exists, but the local notary, Giovanni di Buto, included the text in a later notarial protocol.[44] As both Robert Davidsohn and Guido

---

41   Davidsohn, *Storia di Firenze*, IV, pp. 319–22; Pampaloni, 'I primi anni', pp. 142–44.

42   Santagata, *Dante*, pp. 149–58, 408 note 15; Pertile, 'Life', p. 466.

43   Davidsohn, *Storia di Firenze*, IV, pp. 319–32; Pampaloni, 'I Primi anni' pp. 143–44; *Codice diplomatico dantesco*, ed. by Piattoli, document 92, pp. 109–10. Isidoro del Lungo edited and published the indemnification agreement in *Dino Compagni e la sua Cronica*, II, pp. 569–70. As noted in Davidsohn, *Storia di Firenze*, IV, p. 321, the text was transcribed into the notarial protocol (*segnatura antica*) of Giovanni di Buto, G, 366, f. 120. Apparently, water has blotted out the date. The notary included the text among the documents of 1309 (but after one from 1324). Giovanni di Buto da Ampinana was a notary who worked in the Mugello (Vespignano, Ampinana, San Godenzo) from 1299 to 1335. For reference to him, see George Dameron, *Florence and its Church in the Age of Dante* (Philadelphia: University of Pennsylvania Press, 2005), p. 253; and Emanuele Repetti, 'Ampinana', in *Dizionario geografico, fisico, storico della Toscana*, 6 vols (Florence: Presso l'autore e editore, 1833–46), I (1833), p. 82. There are twelve volumes of his notarial protocols for that period, from 1299 to 1335 (*ASF* Notarile Antecosimiano 9493–9503). On the basis of the online information regarding Giovanni di Buto da Ampinana at the Archivio di Stato di Firenze site, provided by the Associazione Amici dell'Archivio di Stato di Firenze, I can identify the protocol that includes the indemnification agreement as *ASF* Notarile Antecosimiano 9495. Unfortunately, I have not yet had the opportunity to see the original document myself in the archive.

44   The most relevant passage for this essay from the text of the indemnification agreement reads as follows: 'Dominus Torigianus, Carbone et Vieri de Circhiis; dominus Guillelminus de Ricasoli; dominus Neri, Bectinus Grossus, Bectinus et Nuccius domini Acceriti de Ubertinis; dominus Andreas de Gherardinis; Branca et Chele de Scolaribus; Dante Allegherii; Minus de Radda; Bectinus de Pazziis; Lapus, Ghinus, Taddeus et Azzolinus de Ubertis. Isti omnes, et quelibet eorum per se, omni deliberation pensata, promiserunt et convenerunt Lapo Bertaldi de Florentia, recipiente

Pampaloni have argued, by signing onto the agreement Dante lent the alliance his prestige and prominence to the campaign, even though he certainly did not have the financial assets equal to those of his aristocratic co-signatories. The events of the following two months reveal exactly what was being planned at San Godenzo. Between June and September 1302, the 'Mugello war' resulted in widespread destruction, particularly of *castelli* and farmlands (wheat fields), by Ubaldini forces. Among the locations targeted in the Mugello during the summer of 1302 were San Piero a Sieve and Gagliano, near Barberino. Both were market towns important for the grain trade, and both were on important highways linking Florence with the Romagna (the source of much of its imported grain). According to contemporary accounts, significant amounts of farmland were destroyed.

Though challenged, the Florentine Blacks were not, however, losing the war. In fact, they were growing stronger.[45] By mid-July, Florentine (pro-Black) forces began to 'turn the tables' on the Ubaldini and the exile armies. On July 15, the Whites finally suffered defeat in the Val d'Arno at Piantravigne. The Florentines then moved against the two remaining areas of the *contado* that had been targeted by their enemies: the Mugello and the Val di Greve (south of city). Florentine forces devastated several *castelli* of the Ubaldini (Santerno near Firenzuola, Santa Croce, San Martino a Lago near Scarperia, and another near Senni). Then, Florentine armies took the offensive in the Val di Greve and defeated the combined White-Ghibelline forces at Montagliari and Montaguto (Montagliari, as noted above, had been the base from which Whites were harassing grain transports to Florence

---

pro viro nobili Ugolino de Felicione et pro eius filius, et pro omnibus aliis de domo Ubaldinorum et pro quolibet eorum, omnia dampna interesse et expensas restituere satisfacere et emendare de eorum propriis bonis, quod vel quas predicti Ugolinus vel eius consortes incurrerent sue reciperent tam in bonis temporalibus quam etiam in benefitiis ecclesiasticis occasione novitatis sue guerre facte vel faciende per castrum Montis Accianichi, vel per aliquam aliam eorumdem fortilitiam seu fideles, vel per ipsosmet ad arbitrium eorum; sub pena duorum milium marcarum argenti. Isidoro del Lungo, *Dino Compagni*, II, p. 570.

45 *Codice diplomatico dantesco*, ed. by Piattoli, document 92, pp. 109–10; Compagni, *Dino Compagni's Chronicle*, pp. 55–57; Isidoro del Lungo, *Dino Compagni*, II, pp. 569–70; Santagata, *Dante*, pp. 151–58; Starn, *Contrary Commonwealth*, pp. 49–52; Pampaloni, 'I primi anni', pp. 143–44; Davidsohn, *Storia di Firenze*, IV, pp. 317–23.

from the south Tuscan port of Talamone).[46] However, Florentine armies were not always victorious. In fact, on August 17 the Commune suffered defeat at Montaccianico, the major Ubaldini possession in the Mugello. By the end of 1302 or early 1303, the Whites had moved their headquarters from Arezzo to Forlì, then a centre of power for the Ghibellines in the Romagna. Dante apparently joined them there.

The White Guelfs continued their military operations in the Mugello. According to Dino Compagni, White exiles in 1303 continued to wage total war in the Mugello between Montaccianico in the Mugello to Lastra on the Via Bolognese: 'The Whites rode from Monte Accenico to the area of Lasta, burning whatever they found.'[47] Along with their allies, however, during the launching of a second Mugello campaign in March of 1303, the White-Ghibelline-Ubaldini coalition nevertheless failed to take Pulicciano near Borgo San Lorenzo, and thereby lost the capacity to control a major route across the Apennines that could serve as a pathway from which to attack Florence. At this time in 1303 Dante left Tuscany for the Veneto, settling for at least ten months at Verona in the household of Bartolomeo della Scala (death c. 1304). There, still serving as a representative of the White government in exile, he worked unsuccessfully to convince Bartolomeo to join forces with the exiled White Guelfs, the Commune of Bologna, and other Romagnol communes in an anti-Florence alliance.[48]

Back in Florence, violence erupted in February 1304 as the Black Guelfs themselves split into two major factions led on one side by Rosso della Tosa and on the other by Corso Donati. On March 2 the papal cardinal legate, Niccolò da Prato, entered Florence amidst a population still facing high grain prices and weary of factional conflict. He had successfully helped to resolve the intra-Black factional violence, and by February he had intended to engineer a resolution to the conflict between White exiles and Ghibellines on one hand, and the Black Guelfs on the other. From Arezzo, still a White Guelf and Ghibelline headquarters where Dante was then apparently resid-

---

46 Villani, *Nuova Cronica*, II, pp. 86–87, 135–42; Pinto, *Il libro del Biadaiolo*, pp. 85–86; Davidsohn, *Storia di Firenze*, IV, pp. 322–32.

47 Compagni, *Dino Compagni's Chronicle*, p. 59.

48 Compagni, *Dino Compagni's Chronicle*, pp. 57–58; Davidsohn, *Storia di Firenze*, IV, pp. 321–25; Santagata, *Dante*, pp. 151–73; Pertile, 'Life', pp. 466–67.

ing, the poet wrote a letter in March or April to Niccolò da Prato on behalf of the captain of the White Guelf organization (Universitas) while preparations for a meeting were taking place. Eventually, twelve representatives of the Whites and Ghibellines met with twelve representatives of the Blacks in Florence. Unfortunately, the Black Guelfs set out to disrupt the peace-keeping efforts of the cardinal and created a climate of violence to undermine any agreement. On June 8, 1304, the cardinal counselled several major White families to leave the city, and he did so himself on June 10. This did not prevent the Blacks from torching hundreds of homes in the city centre, including many owned by the Whites. On July 7, 1304, Pope Benedict XI, horrified by the violence yet still seeking a peaceful solution, died after ordering the various parties to Perugia for a conference. Over a month later, on July 19 and 20, the White Guelfs, in an anti-Florence alliance with enemy communes (Arezzo, Pisa, Pistoia, Bologna), suffered a devastating defeat at La Lastra, just north of the city on the Via Bolognese.

By then, on both an artistic and a political level, Dante had already distanced himself from the White Guelf-Ghibelline alliance and from its military operations. He had already abandoned the armed struggle as early as the spring of 1303 or perhaps as late as after the departure of Niccolò da Prato on June 10 or right after the death of the pope a month later (July 7) in 1304. From July of 1304 to early 1306, now in Bologna, he apparently devoted most of his time to the composition of both the *Convivio* and *De vulgari eloquentia*. Indeed, it was earlier at Verona in 1303, benefiting from the intellectual riches of the Biblioteca Capitolare while he was negotiating with Bartolomeo della Scala to join the anti-Florence coalition, that Dante had begun writing the *Convivio*, or 'The Banquet'. A philosophical work about the natural desire for knowledge and wisdom, it relied on the metaphorical language of hunger and deprivation to designate the absence of those virtues.[49]

Several years later, following the Florentine defeat at Montecatini in 1315, the Florentine authorities offered amnesty to those eligible rebels (White Guelfs and Ghibellines) previously condemned to death.

---

49   Compagni, *Dino Compagni's Chronicle*, pp. 72–75; Villani, *Nuova Cronica*, II, pp. 135–40; Santagata, *Dante*, pp. 160–73; Pertile, 'Life', pp. 467–68; Hollander, *Dante*, pp. xiii–xiv.

The judge, Ranieri di Zaccharia da Orvieto, appointed by King Robert of Anjou, made a list, and among those on it was Dante. At the time he was probably completing the *Purgatorio* and writing *Monarchia*. In exchange for amnesty, the rebels were required to return, acknowledge guilt, and pay a fine. Dante opted not to accept the terms of the amnesty. As a result, the judge reaffirmed the death sentence (death by beheading) for Dante as well as his sons. A proclamation of permanent banishment followed on November 6. There was no turning back for Dante in 1315. As Lino Pertile has observed, by 1315 the *Commedia* (he was just beginning *Paradiso*) 'was a declaration of militant politics, which was fatally destined *not* to resolve the conflict between Dante and his birthplace but rather to exacerbate it'.[50] Dante's decision not to acknowledge any fault and not to accept the amnesty seems to confirm that in 1315 he still had no regrets for joining the armed struggle against Florence twelve years earlier.

In her 2009 essay for the Annual Report of the Dante Society in *Dante Studies*, '"Only Historicize": History, Material Culture (Food, Clothes, Books), and the Future of Dante Studies', Teodolinda Barolini lamented that the 'lack of historicizing has been an abiding feature of Dante exegesis'.[51] Her advice 'to the young Dante scholar', and presumably for the field in general, was simple: 'only historicize' (*OH*, p. 37). To 'historicize' Dante and arrive at a rich understanding of his cultural legacy, Barolini suggested, one might for example focus on food and food imagery in a text such as the *Convivio* (1303–04). Here material life — the consumption of food to remedy deprivation (hunger) — is vividly and metaphorically made apparent in the very title itself: *Convivio*, or the banquet. Regarding the aim of this vernacular philosophical treatise, Barolini observes that it 'is essentially an analysis of the forms of human deprivation, both spiritual and material, that the author is undertaking to redress' (*OH*, p. 39). Arguing from Aristotle, according to this interpretation, Dante observed that humans

---

50   *Codice diplomatico dantesco*, ed. by Piattoli, documents 114 and 115, pp. 153–57; Starn, *Contrary Commonwealth*, pp. 81–82; Santagata, *Dante*, pp. 300–01; Pertile, 'Life', pp. 472–73.

51   Teodolinda Barolini, '"Only Historicize": History, Material Culture (Food, Clothes, Books), and the Future of Dante Studies', *Dante Studies*, 127 (2009), pp. 37–54 (p. 37), hereafter *OH*. Subsequent references given in parentheses in the main text.

have a natural desire to know, to satisfy with knowledge the hunger that results from deprivation. *Convivio* itself serves as a 'banquet of knowledge', and food as metaphor becomes central to its meaning. Indeed, bread ('pane') itself, Barolini notes, represents symbolically 'the crumbs of knowledge from the table where the bread of the angels is served that Dante will dispense to those who have been knowledge-deprived' (*OH*, p. 39). Sources of material deprivation simply hamper our ability to live life to the fullest. As Barolini observes, 'Thus the obstacles to self-fulfilment begin for Dante with physical defects of the body, "difetti da la parte del corpo," which until very recently in human history posed insurmountable impediments to full participation in life' (*OH*, p. 40).

The images in the *Convivio* associated with food are rooted in real life: hunger, crumbs, food, deprivation, the communal table, bread, and satiety. Food and drink imagery are also certainly omnipresent in classical literature and philosophy, most famously in Plato's *Symposium*. As argued here, however, there may have been an additional context that contributed to Dante's focus on food and hunger imagery in his *Convivio*: a political one. When the poet began both the *Convivio* and *De vulgari eloquentia*, it was 1303, the last year of a significant food crisis (*carestia*) in Tuscany before 1329.[52] This was also the year (1303) that followed his attendance of the military planning conferences at Gargonza and San Godenzo. For seven years prior (1295–1302), Dante had been involved in one way or another in the governance of his native city. He had been the member of and participant in several of the most important councils in which grain transports were discussed, the overseer of a significant grain-related road project associated with the Florentine *annona*, an ambassador to the papacy and to San Gimignano, and the member of the most important urban magistracy that exercised authority over the urban grain supply, the priorate. During those seven years, among his many other roles, he was well experienced in the politics of food and the dangers of grain shortages for a city of 100,000. Any prior in 1300 —

---

52   In Tuscany, the food (grain) crisis of 1302–03 was followed by a good harvest in the summer of 1303. There were no major *carestie* or grain crises again until 1328–29 (Pinto, *Il libro del Biadaiolo*, pp. 87–88).

and Dante served for two months (June 15 to August 15) — knew that unlike the communes of Siena, Arezzo, and Colle, Florence was unable to feed its growing population of 100,000 from its own territory and was required to import grain, particularly from nearby Romagna, the Aretino (upper Arno valley), and distant Apulia.

Although we are hampered by a lack of documentation that can provide precise details about the nature of his collaboration with White Guelf exiles and Ghibellines in the countryside in 1302–03, we do know that with his participation in the armed struggle against Florence, Dante brought a legacy of experience and leadership in grain-related urban governance at the highest level. His leadership in those military efforts and his signature on the indemnification agreement signified a willingness to participate in a strategy built around food deprivation, directed at the city controlled by his enemies and from which he was now an exile. The upper Arno valley, the mountainous borderlands between Tuscany and Romagna, and the infrastructure of roads and *castelli* in the Greve and Pesa valleys — so vital to the Florentine food (particularly grain) supply — became the targeted zones for attack by the White-Ghibelline alliance meeting at Gargonza (March 1302) and San Godenzo (June 1302). By the spring of 1303 or summer of 1304, having decided to abandon the battlefield for the challenge of philosophy, Dante wrote about hunger in *Convivio* as a metaphor that signified the innate yearning for philosophical wisdom and knowledge. It is indeed ironic — if not perfectly understandable — that after leaving the field of battle and opting to turn his attention to philosophy and learning, the first work he wrote in exile, the *Convivio*, dealt with the epistemological themes of deprivation, relying on metaphors associated with food and hunger. The year before (1302) he began that work, inducing hunger had served as the end goal of a real-world war strategy in which he had played a part. Thirteen years after his exile had begun (1315), Dante completed the *Inferno*. The historical Ugolino (d. 1289), cited by the chronicler Pseudo-Brunetto Latini (c. 1300) as having intentionally starved his fellow Pisans, had become in the imagination of Dante the fictional character of Ugolino in cantos 32 and 33. Of this figure in the *Inferno*, Callegari writes: 'The count's gruesome gluttony in Hell is not only an ironic twist on the rejection of communion with Christ, but also a reminder of the agreement he broke with his people in choosing to let them starve while indulging in political factionalism'.[53] Thirteen years after Dante, the exiled political actor, had participated in and led military actions including the obstruction of grain supplies against Florence in 1302, he became the poet who now condemned Ugolino della Gherardesca (*Inferno* 32 and 33) to the ninth circle of hell, among those who had been treacherous against their own people.[54] One wonders if Dante himself was aware of the irony.

---

53   Callegari, *Dante's Gluttons*, p. 107.

54   Dante Alighieri, *The Divine Comedy*, trans. with commentary by Charles S. Singleton, 6 vols (Princeton: Princeton University Press, 1970–75), II (1970), pp. 606–12.

III. DETHEOLOGIZE TO RETHEOLOGIZE

Dante's Lucy in the Canon Law of Consent

GRACE DELMOLINO

For Teo

luce intellettüal, piena d'amore

Before I get to Lucy, the spirit of this volume moves me to record my profound intellectual and personal debt to *The Undivine Comedy*. At its core, this is a hymn to Teodolinda Barolini as a teacher who immerses us in the *gran mar* of the *Commedia*'s poetic, historical, theological, legal, and ethical depths, all of which flow from a reading of the poem in its entirety.

My first encounter with *The Undivine Comedy* was not as a scholar reading a ground-breaking work fresh off the presses, since I was three months old when the book came out. I read *The Undivine Comedy* two decades later, as a grad student taking Teo's Dante course at Columbia in 2012.[1] That chapter is still fresh in the book of my memory. I am in the second year of my PhD. The Dante class meets for two hours, twice a week — double the meeting time of a regular grad seminar — for a

---

1   The yearlong course is now available online as *The Dante Course*, Digital Dante, 2015–2016 <https://digitaldante.columbia.edu/the-dante-course> [accessed 2 June 2025].

full academic year. We read two cantos every class. I take advantage of a long break to prepare the reading beforehand; I get the $10 lunch special at a now-defunct sushi place directly across from Columbia's Morningside gate and linger there every Tuesday and Thursday to spend several hours with Dante. By mid-year, the servers know my order and start bringing me a hot green tea as soon as they see me sit down. In the lecture hall, Professor Barolini speaks directly from her densely annotated, rebound copy of the text, explaining Dante's poetry with the sparkling precision of Beatrice delivering her *infallibile avviso* in *Paradiso* 7 (a Beatrice dressed in pearls and enviably fashionable jackets). My experience of that class — truly a course in *how to read*, tested regularly by translations on demand in front of my classmates — is inextricably bound up in the other defining experience of my life that year, one of enormous personal loss after the death of my brother. What I remember most from studying the *Commedia* is not some sharp moment of insight into the nature of grief. It is the simple consolation of walking along the path of the text each day: two cantos per class, two classes per week, two semesters to reach 100 cantos, punctuated only by the absolute wringer that is the bluebook final exam.

To create a year-long course by close reading a single text is both a deeply medieval and a deeply radical pedagogy. In an age of shortening attention spans, few readers today ever have the opportunity to sit so long with a text. Few texts and few teachers can sustain that depth. Like her Dante course, Teodolinda Barolini's *Undivine Comedy* teaches a methodology of reading the poem as what it actually is, which is not so simple a process when its author is a sublime manipulator of our response to the text. The book and the course both yield a cornucopia of hermeneutic fruits. The root from which they grow is an uncompromising commitment to that process of clear-eyed reading. I present the pages that follow here in tribute to *The Undivine Comedy* as the unsurpassed methodological guidebook of Dante studies, and in honour of the many years of friendship and intellectual dialogue that came into my life because of that book and its author.

~

Reading the *Commedia* requires analysing the poem's narratological features, contextualizing it with history and theology and law and lyric, and seeing past what commentators have repeated for centuries without critical reflection. In the present chapter, I follow the path laid out in *The Undivine Comedy* and its sister essay "'Only Historicize'":[2] the path of detheologizing and historicizing, which is also the path of retheologizing. Dante studies needs a new and better theology — or rather, it needs a theology grounded in history. We must detheologize so that we do not read the *Commedia* uncritically as an instruction manual on how souls get placed into hell, and then we must retheologize by looking to actual theology to see how Dante intervenes — sometimes quite radically — in the ethical and philosophical questions that make up so much of medieval Christian thought. Consent is one such question. Consent sits at the intersection of theology and the law, for it is both a moral and a legal issue, with practical implications in the courts and eschatological implications in the afterlife. Lucia (St. Lucy) is a bridge from the *Commedia*, where she appears as a character, to the theological jurisprudence of consent in the Middle Ages, where she appears, well before Dante's poem was ever written, as a conceptual cornerstone for the treatment of rape, consent, and free will.

Dante's Lucia is an enigmatic figure in the *Divine Comedy*. Her structural position in the poem suggests that she is important: she appears three times, once in each canticle (*Inferno* 2, *Purgatorio* 9, *Paradiso* 32), at moments of threshold and transition along Dante's journey. But the standard glosses on Lucia are banal. Among early commentators, the Ottimo and Benvenuto da Imola allegorized Lucia as divine grace; modern commentaries generally give some version of this reading and few dwell further on Lucia.[3] Some have proposed that Lucia

---

2   Teodolinda Barolini, "'Only Historicize': History, Material Culture (Food, Clothes, Books), and the Future of Dante Studies', *Dante Studies*, 127 (2009), pp. 37–54.

3   The Ottimo and Benvenuto draw on Augustine to designate Lucia's role as *gratia cooperans*, moved by the *gratia operans* of the first 'donna' in *Inferno* 2's chain of grace. Other early commentaries had different (though similarly generic) allegories: Lucy as Prudence (Anonimo Selmiano), Lucy as 'uno intelletto profondo di divinità' (Jacopo della Lana), or Lucy as 'la divina clemenza, la divina misericordia, la divina benignità' (Boccaccio). L'Ottimo Commento (1333), glosses to *Inf.* 1 nota and *Purg.* 9.52; Benvenuto da Imola (1375–80), gloss to *Inf.* 2.94–96; Anonimo Selmiano (1337[?]), gloss to *Inf.* 2.102; Jacopo della Lana (1324–28), gloss to *Inf.* 2.97–99; Giovanni Boccaccio (1373–75), allegorical gloss to *Inf.* 2.52–120. I cite all commentaries from the

(whose name means 'light' from *lux* and whose iconography involves eyes) was Dante's personal saint because of the ophthalmological strain Dante once experienced, as recounted in *Convivio* 3.9.15.[4] Neither gloss gives much purchase on the passages where Lucia appears and the allegory strips Lucia of all specificity: any Christian saint might have equally well represented divine grace. This essay considers Saint Lucy beyond the pages of Dante's poem, moving through the saint's recorded legend and its use in Gratian's *Decretum* to contextualize Dante's mysterious Lucia.

Very few Dante commentators note that across medieval Latin versions of St. Lucy's life, including the *Golden Legend* and the *Speculum Historiale* that were widely read in the thirteenth and fourteenth centuries, the distinctive feature of Lucy's martyrdom is her physical resistance to gang rape and her verbal defence of the power of consent. In Gratian's *Decretum*, the foundational textbook of canon law completed around 1140 and still in vigorous use in Dante's time, Lucy is the first example cited in Gratian's analysis of rape.[5] The term Gratian uses for

---

Dartmouth Dante Project, 2025 <https://dante.dartmouth.edu/> [accessed 2 June 2025].

4   Many moderns attribute this connection between Lucia and Dante's eye troubles to Jacopo Alighieri, but I have not yet found a source who directly quotes what Jacopo said, nor can I turn up a relevant gloss in his commentary on *Inferno*. Graziolo in 1324 claims that Dante had a particular devotion to Lucia but does not connect this to Dante's eyesight: 'beata Lucia, in qua ipse Dantes in tempore vite sue habuit maximam devotionem, venit ad locum felicem in quo residebat ipsa domina Beatrisia' (gloss to *Inf.* 2.76–102). The relevant passage in the *Convivio* is: 'E io fui esperto di questo l'anno medesimo che nacque questa canzone, che per affaticare lo viso molto a studio di leggere, in tanto debilitai li spiriti visivi che le stelle mi pareano tutte d'alcuno albore ombrate. E per lunga riposanza in luoghi oscuri e freddi, e con affreddare lo corpo dell'occhio coll'acqua chiara, riunì sì la vertù disgregata che tornai nel primo buono stato della vista' ('And I experienced this in the same year in which I wrote this canzone, for by greatly straining my eyes through studious reading I weakened my vision so much that the stars seemed shrouded by a white haze. But by resting in dark, cool places and by cooling my eyes with clear water, I regained that deteriorated power and I returned to my earlier state of good vision'; *Convivio* 3.9.15). All quotes from Dante Alighieri, *Convivio*, ed. by Franca Brambilla Ageno (Florence: Le Lettere, 1995). Translations mine. Giorgio Padoan dismisses the *Convivio* reference as 'dato pressoché inutile in questo contesto' (Padoan 1967, gloss to *Inf.* 2.98). See also Rachel Jacoff and William A. Stephany, *Lectura Dantis Americana: Inferno II* (Philadelphia: University of Pennsylvania Press, 1989), pp. 30–31.

5   *Dec.* C. 32 q. 5. I cite the text from Gratian, *Decretum*, in *Corpus iuris canonici*, ed. by Emil Friedberg, 2 vols (Leipzig: B. Tauchnitz, 1879–81; repr. Graz: Akademische Druck- und Verlagsanstalt, 1959), I. Citations from the *Ordinary Gloss* are from the

rape is *vis* or 'violence', meaning sexual violation without the victim's consent, and for canon law the topic of rape becomes a broader ethical inquiry into the nature of violence, sin, guilt, and consent. Those topics have obvious weight for Dante, too. As Barolini notes, he treats the interplay of will and consent in the *Commedia* most prominently in *Inferno* 5 and *Paradiso* 3–4, a set of cantos tightly connected by the adaptation of *Nicomachean Ethics* 3.1 on voluntary and involuntary action (Aristotelian categories that the later canonists also applied to Gratian's quaestio on *vis*).[6] In the *Decretum*, Lucy is a legal example for the same conceptual issues Dante treats in *Inferno* 5 and *Paradiso* 3–4. But when Dante places Lucia in his poem, he divorces her from any explicit discussion of violence and consent, even though these are precisely the issues she brought up for the canonist Gratian, the theologian Aquinas, the hagiographer Jacobus de Voragine, the preacher Fra Giordano, and, in all probability, any medieval reader who possessed even a passing familiarity with her passion.[7]

Lucia's three appearances in the *Commedia* mark threshold moments in Dante's journey. *Inferno* 2 prepares Dante to enter the underworld (which he does in *Inferno* 3), *Purgatorio* 9 prepares Dante to

---

digitized version of the sixteenth-century *Editio Romana* available through UCLA under the directorship of Henry Ansgar Kelly: UCLA Digital Library Program, *Corpus juris canonici emendatum et notis illustratum*, 4 vols (Rome: Gregory XIII, 1582) <https://digital.library.ucla.edu/canonlaw/> [accessed 2 June 2025]. Translations of Gratian and the glosses are mine.

6   Teodolinda Barolini first observed in 1998 that Dante adapts Aristotle's example of a wind that carries a man away (involuntary action) into the whirlwind of the lustful (voluntary action falsely conceived of as involuntary action). Aristotle's other example, of someone being carried away 'by men who had him in their power', is reworked in *Paradiso* 3–4 with Piccarda and Constance. Barolini's more recent essay examines how closely Dante works with Aristotle and yet how profoundly Aristotle's ethics are disrupted by Dante's introduction of Christian free will. That second example bears on the case of Saint Lucy as well, who is *not* carried off by the men who attempt to take her. Teodolinda Barolini, 'Dante and Cavalcanti (On Making Distinctions in Matters of Love): *Inferno* 5 in its Lyric and Autobiographical Context', in Barolini, *Dante and the Origins of Literary Culture* (New York: Fordham University Press, 2006), pp. 70–101 (pp. 74–75); Teodolinda Barolini, 'Dante and Aristotle on Voluntary and Involuntary Action: *Nicomachean Ethics* 3.1 in *Inferno* 5 and *Paradiso* 3–5', *Textual Cultures*, 16.2 (2023), pp. 247–74 <https://doi.org/10.14434/tc.v16i2.36773>.

7   I will treat the first three of these thinkers directly in this essay; for analysis of Fra Giordano that provides important context for popular knowledge of Lucy in Dante's time and confirms that these features of her martyrdom were readily known, see Silvio Pasquazi, 'Il canto II dell'*Inferno*', in *Inferno: letture degli anni 1973–1976*, ed. by Silvio Zennaro (Rome: Bonacci, 1977), pp. 35–65.

enter purgatory proper (which he does in *Purgatorio* 10), and *Paradiso* 32 concludes the *Commedia*'s formula of soul-introduced-to-Dante-by-guide and finally prepares Dante to gaze upon the vision of God (which he does in *Paradiso* 33). Each time she appears at a moment of threat or uncertainty or potential transgression in Dante's journey along the straight path. Her role is mediator and conduit. Her characterization is feminine and lyric: she is one of 'tre donne benedette' ('three blessed ladies'; *Inf.* 2.124) who care for Dante in the court of heaven; she appears amidst flowers (*Purg.* 9.54); she has beautiful eyes (*Purg.* 9.62); she is the mover of Beatrice ('Lucia, che mosse la tua donna', 'Lucia, who moved your lady'; *Par.* 32.137).[8] Had Dante not named this lady as 'Lucia' in each of these three cantos, no one would ever have been able to identify her as Saint Lucy. But Dante insists on her name. That name can lead us to Lucy's textual history before Dante's poem, where we find not a generic allegory of grace, but the story of a woman saint whose words on the power of consent became a keystone for the treatment of rape in medieval Christian law and theology.

In Jacobus de Voragine's *Golden Legend* (*Legenda Aurea*), one of the most popular hagiographical collections of the Middle Ages, Saint Lucy is an emblem of rectitude. Her name, etymologically linked to the Latin *lux* (light), expresses constancy and straightness:

> Habet etiam diffusionem sine coinquinatione, quia per quaecunque immunda diffusa non coinquinatur; rectum incessum sine curvitate, longissimam lineam pertransit sine morosa dilatione. Per hoc ostenditur, quod beata virgo Lucia habuit decorem virginitatis sine aliqua corruptione, diffusionem caritatis sine aliquo immundo amore, rectum incessum intensionis in Deum sine aliqua obliquitate, longissimam lineam divinae operationis sine negligentiae tarditate. Vel Lucia dicitur quasi lucis via.

> (Light also has radiation without contamination, because no matter how unclean may be the places where it radiates, it is

---

8   Quotations from the *Commedia* are from Dante Alighieri: *La Commedia secondo l'antica vulgata*, ed. by Giorgio Petrocchi, Società Dantesca Italiana, Edizione Nazionale, 2nd rev. edn, 4 vols (Florence: Le Lettere, 1994). English translations come from Dante Alighieri, *The Divine Comedy*, trans. by Allen Mandelbaum, 3 vols (Berkeley: University of California Press, 1980–82), with some alterations to emphasize literal readings.

not contaminated; it goes in straight lines, without curvature, and traverses the greatest distances without losing its speed. Thus we are shown that the blessed virgin Lucy possessed the beauty of virginity without trace of corruption; that she radiated charity without any impure love; her progress toward God was straight and without deviation, and went far in God's works without negligence or delay. Or the name is interpreted 'way of light'.) (*Legenda aurea*, 'De Sancta Lucia virgine')[9]

In general terms, the association of light-love-motion from the *Legenda aurea* fits neatly with *Inferno* 2's intertwining of love and movement ('amor mi mosse', 'love moved me'; *Inf.* 2.72) and Lucy's opposition to negligence ('sine negligentiae tarditate') also fits with her role in transitioning Dante out of the late repentant in *Purgatorio* 9. More importantly, though, the abstract qualities represented by her name take tangible form in the account of her life. Most Dante commentaries gloss her as a fourth-century Syracusan martyr; very few indicate that there is anything more to her story.[10]

Accounts of Saint Lucy's life tell that she vows her virginity to God, angering the man she was supposed to marry, and her jilted groom reports her as a Christian to the consul Paschasius.[11] Paschasius taunts her repeatedly, to which she responds each time in defence of herself

---

9   I cite the Latin from Jacobi A Voragine, *Legenda Aurea*, ed. by Johann Georg Theodor Graesse (Vratislavia: Koebner, 1890). Translations, sometimes modified for literalism, are from Jacobus de Voragine, *The Golden Legend: Readings on the Saints*, trans. William Granger Ryan (Princeton: Princeton University Press, 2012).

10   Edward Moore, in an essay dedicated entirely to Lucia, does not go into any detail about her legend other than to note briefly that she is 'the Syracusan martyr Lucia who suffered under Diocletian c. 300' (Edward Moore, 'Sta. Lucia in the Divina Commedia', in Moore, *Studies in Dante, Fourth Series: Textual Criticism of the 'Convivio' and Miscellaneous Essays* (New York: Haskell House, 1917; repr. 1968), pp. 235–55 (p. 245)). This is typical: the term 'rape' never appears in commentaries on Dante's Lucia and only rarely in the scholarship. The entry on 'Lucia, santa' in the *Enciclopedia Dantesca* is very short and uses Dante's text to confirm Graziolo's 1324 gloss on Dante's devotion to Lucia: 'La devozione di D. per la santa è attestata dal figlio Iacopo e da Graziolo de' Bambaglioli [...] notizia confermata dallo stesso poeta che si dichiara fedele, cioè devoto di L.' (Agostino Amore, 'Lucia, santa', in *Enciclopedia Dantesca*, ed. by Umberto Bosco (Rome: Istituto della Enciclopedia Italiana fondata da Giovanni Treccani, 1970)<https://www.treccani.it/enciclopedia/santa-lucia_(Enciclopedia-Dantesca)/> [accessed 2 June 2025].

11   For close reading and plot summary of Lucy's passion, this essay uses the thirteenth-century *Legenda aurea*, a wildly popular hagiographical collection and a source available to Dante. Another popular source of saints' lives, the thirteenth-century *Speculum Historiale*, contains a very similar story of Lucy (14.2–3).

and God. Then, in an episode that is undoubtedly the highlight of her legend, Paschasius orders her dragged to a brothel so that she will be raped until the Holy Spirit leaves her:

> Paschasius dixit: 'cessabunt verba, cum perventum fuerit ad verbera.' Cui Lucia dixit: 'verba Dei cessare non possunt.' Cui Paschasius: 'tu ergo Deus es?' Respondit Lucia: 'ancilla Dei sum, qui dixit: "cum steteritis ante reges et praesides etc. Non enim vos estis etc."' Paschasius dixit: 'in te ergo spiritus sanctus est?' Cui Lucia: 'qui caste vivunt, templum spiritus sancti sunt.' Cui Paschasius: 'ego faciam te duci ad lupanar, ut ibi violationem accipias et spiritum sanctum perdas.'

> (Paschasius said: 'The sting of the whip will silence your lip!' To which Lucy said: 'The words of God cannot be stilled!' Paschasius: 'So you are God?' Lucy: 'I am the handmaid of God, who said to his disciples, "You shall be brought before governors and before kings for my sake, but when they shall deliver you up, take no thought how or what to say, for it is not you that speak but the Holy Spirit that speaks in you."' Paschasius: 'So the Holy Spirit is in you?' Lucy: 'Those who live chaste lives are the temples of the Holy Spirit.' 'Then I shall have you taken to a brothel', said Paschasius, 'your body will be defiled and you will lose the Holy Spirit.') (*Legenda aurea*, 'De Sancta Lucia virgine')

Paschasius threatens Lucy with sexual violence as a challenge to her faith and commitment to chastity. The consul sees chastity and virtue as features of the body, which can be taken away by forcible sex and the violence of men, but Lucy asserts that chastity belongs to the mind and therefore cannot be touched so long as she refuses to give her consent: 'non inquinatur corpus nisi de consensu mentis, nam si me invitam violari feceris, castitas mihi duplicabitur ad coronam. Nunquam autem voluntatem meam ad consensum poteris provocare' ('The body is not defiled unless by the consent of the mind, so if you have me violated against my will, my chastity will be doubled to my crown. Nor will you ever be able to provoke my will into consent'; *Legenda aurea*, 'De Sancta Lucia virgine'). When Paschasius brings in a crowd to carry Lucy off, the Holy Spirit fixes her so firmly in place that the men are unable to move her body. A thousand men, a thousand oxen, magicians, urine, fire, boiling oil — none can budge her. She continues speaking even after being stabbed in the throat and dies only once priests administer last rites. Lucy's forceful speech, and especially her words on consent, are the standout feature of her martyrdom.

The historical context of Saint Lucy — by which I mean that these accounts were historically available to Dante, not that they are true histories — shows a Lucy who embodies constancy and fortitude, demonstrated by actions and words as reported in her hagiography and her existence as a specific woman.[12] Like Beatrice, she cannot be reduced to only an allegory of her abstract qualities; she represents those qualities yet also maintains a reality and a historicity, because she existed beyond Dante's text. Silvio Pasquazi, in a 1977 *lectura* examining Fra Giordano's sermons on Lucy, argues that these qualities of fortitude and resistance would have been very familiar to a medieval audience.[13] Building on Pasquazi, Rachel Jacoff and William Stephany made the case in 1989 that Dante chose Lucia specifically because of her inflexible will, writing:

> The antiphon of the mass said on her day makes it her central attribute: 'Columna es immobilis, Lucia, sponsa Christi' ['You are a pillar immovable, Lucy, bride of Christ']. Her martyrdom testifies to the qualities Dante praises in the first sphere in the *Paradiso* when the difference between the absolute and the conditional will is clarified by Beatrice's discourse [...] Although Lucy's 'salda voglia' is the central feature of her legend, no commentator before Pasquazi so much as mentions it.[14]

I wish here to consider what it means that Lucy's fortitude derives its power from the specific threat of rape: that is, violence.[15] The Latin words of her legend are explicit. In the *Legenda aurea* Paschasius first

---

12   Others have noted that the three blessed ladies of *Inferno* 2, unlike the three beasts of *Inferno* 1, have some kind of indisputable historical dimensionality. See Moore, 'Sta. Lucia', p. 241; and Pasquazi, 'Il canto II dell'*Inferno*', p. 41: 'queste donne sono anzitutto reali [...] Dante le assume come soggetto di poesia, perché le ama e le venera nella loro realtà, e ama e venera in esse quei valori che esse portano e manifestano'.

13   'Dalle prediche di fra Giordano e dalla *Passio* risulta concordemente che per Dante come per i suoi contemporanei il carattere specifico di Santa Lucia fu la fermezza e costanza nel volere il bene e nell'attuarlo con tutte le forze, e la corrispondente inflessibile resistenza contro ogni male' (Pasquazi, 'Il canto II dell'*Inferno*', pp. 48–49).

14   Jacoff and Stephany, *Inferno II*, pp. 33–34.

15   To the extent that scholars and commentators have picked up on the readings advanced by Pasquazi and Jacoff and Stephany, it is usually to add 'fortitude' to the allegorical inventory of Lucia's significance, erasing the concrete details and textual history from which they extract only that general quality of fortitude. See, for example, Anthony

threatens to have her sexually violated ('ego faciam te duci ad lupanar,
ut ibi violationem accipias et spiritum sanctum perdas', 'I will have you
dragged to the brothel, so that you will be violated and lose the Holy
Spirit') and then commands pimps (*lenones*) to have a crowd of men
rape her to death ('invitate ad eam omnem populam et tamdiu illuda-
tur, donec mortua nuntietur', 'invite the whole crowd to her and let
them take their pleasure from her until she is dead'; *Legenda aurea*, 'De
Sancta Lucia virgine'). Gratian, the 'father of canon law', uses Lucy's
words to illustrate the force of consent in his legal analysis, drawing on
the powerful story of her attempted and thwarted rape. Aquinas brings
up St. Lucy in the *Summa Theologiae* when exploring the possibility
of a martyrdom based on the violence of rape alone, without death
(a possibility ultimately rejected insofar as 'it is not evident to men
whether [a woman] suffers this for love of the Christian faith, or rather
through contempt of chastity', though this hypothetical type of martyrdom is still conceivable 'on the sight of God, who searcheth the heart';
ST 2 2ae q. 124 a. 4, reply to objection 2).[16] For these two influential
Christian thinkers, Lucy is indelibly linked to the issues of violence
and consent. These concepts raise ethical questions with far-reaching
implications for the Christian doctrine of sin and free will, and they are
treated in the particular context of rape law.

Lucy's powerful defence of her will is the first example Gratian
cites in C. 32 q. 5 of the *Decretum*. Causa 32 is in the section of
the *Decretum* that deals with marriage; the causa has eight questions
that cover adultery, sexual issues, and marital separation. Question 5
picks up a portion of the main case narrative in which a certain man
'quemdam rogavit, ut vi uxorem opprimeret suam, ut sic eam dimittere
posset' ('asked another to assault his wife by force so that he could
dismiss her'). The question hones in on the issue of culpability in
rape, asking 'si ea, quae vim patitur, pudicitiam amittere comprobetur?'

K. Cassell, 'Santa Lucia as Patroness of Sight: Hagiography, Iconography, and Dante',
Dante Studies, 109 (1991), pp. 71–88 (p. 72). Robert Hollander, in his commentary
to *Purgatorio* 9.55, cites Pasquazi and Jacoff and Stephany while summing up their
contributions as an attempt 'to restore the importance of the cardinal virtue fortitude
in Dante's fashioning of the meaning of Saint Lucy.

16   English translation of the *Summa Theologiae* from Thomas Aquinas, *The Summa Theologiae of St. Thomas Aquinas*, trans. by the Fathers of the English Dominican Province,
2nd rev. edn (London: Washbourne, 1920).

('whether a woman who has suffered violence can be judged to have given up her chastity?').

To understand this question, we must understand how medieval law understood 'rape'.[17] Modern treatments of sexual consent juxtapose 'rape' and 'sex', where rape happens without consent and is therefore a crime while sex happens with consent and is therefore legally/ethically permissible. The medieval canonistic paradigm, by contrast, uses consent to theorize sex outside of marriage as an act that can be either criminal and blameworthy if done *with* consent (various forms of lust and illicit sex), or criminal on the part of the perpetrator but blame-free on the part of the victim if done *without* consent (*vis*).[18] Whereas the presence of consent during sex today usually transforms that sex into a moral good, medieval canon law calls attention to positive sexual consent in order to designate the sex as criminal and sinful, as in the crimes of *fornicatio* and *stuprum*. The progressive power of medieval consent lies in its *refusal*, in its capacity to protect the rape victim from accusations of lust and immorality.

---

17   Many critical treatments of 'rape in medieval law' become muddled by mistranslations and misunderstandings of *raptus*, a medieval term which is the etymological root of the word 'rape'. *Raptus* is legally defined as a crime of abduction, not a crime of forced coitus; the two may have frequently gone together in practice but they are still separate concepts in medieval law. The medieval term that best corresponds to what we mean today by 'rape' is *vis* or *per vim stuprum*. Those are the concepts that Gratian explores in C. 32 q. 5, while he treats *raptus* elsewhere in the *Decretum*. Atria Larson analyzes the common scholarly confusion between *raptus* and *vis* in order to argue that not only did medieval canon law treat rape as a serious offense, an author like Gratian might even be considered progressive in the emphasis he places on women's consent (Atria Larson, 'Lucretia (and Lucia) and the Medieval Canonists: Guilt, Consent, and Chastity in the Early Canonistic Jurisprudence of Rape', *Law and History Review* (2025, forthcoming)).

18   The conception of lust as consensually immoral sex is a specific manifestation of the broader Christian doctrine of free will. Gregory the Great writes, in a passage that presages the *contrapasso* of *Inferno* 5: 'And we "shut the doors", when we restrain forbidden lusts; and so whereas our consent set open these doors of carnal concupiscence, it forced us to the countless evils of our corrupt state. And so now we henceforth groan under the weight of mortality, though we came thereunto by our own free will, in that the justice of the sentence against us requires thus much, that what we have done willingly, we should bear with against our will' (*Moralia in Job*, 4.26.47). English translation from Gregory the Great, *The Book of the Morals of St. Gregory the Pope, or an Exposition on the Book of Blessed Job*, trans. and ed. by John Henry Parker, 3 vols (London: Rivington, 1844). Gregory is an important author in *Dec.* C. 32 q. 5, providing c. 13 in that *quaestio* as well as *De pen.* D. 2 c. 23, which the Ordinary Gloss attaches to C. 32's discussion of culpability via wilful self-subjugation to sensual desire (see below).

In response to the question of whether a woman bears any guilt
for committing the sin of lust if she has been raped, Gratian answers
clearly in the negative, citing Lucy in his preliminary comments:

> Quod autem pudicitia uiolenter eripi non possit, multorum
> auctoritatibus probatur. Est enim uirtus animi, que uiolentiam
> non sentit. Corpori namque uis infertur, non animo. Unde,
> quamuis corpus uiolenter corrumpatur si pudicitia mentis ser-
> uetur illesa, tamen castitas duplicatur. Sicut B. Lucia fertur
> dixisse Pascasio. 'Si inuitam me feceris uiolari, castitas michi
> duplicabitur ad coronam'. De sensibus enim et uoluntatibus
> iudicat Deus.
>
> (Many authorities prove that chastity cannot be snatched away
> by violence. For it is a virtue of the mind, which does not
> feel violence. Violence is done to the body, not to the mind.
> Thus, if untainted chastity of the mind is observed even while
> the body is violently corrupted, chastity is even doubled. Thus
> Saint Lucy is to have said to Paschasius: 'If you will have me
> violated against my will, my chastity will be doubled to my
> crown'. For God judges according to senses and wills.) (*Dec.*
> C. 32 q. 5 d.a.c. 1)[19]

Question 5 affirms the idea, articulated by Lucy herself in her *vita*, that
'nunquam coinquinatur corpus nisi de consensu mentis' ('the body
is not polluted except by consent of the mind'; *Legenda Aurea*, 'De
Sancta Lucia virgine'). A woman who has been raped without her
consent has not given up anything of her chastity; she is not guilty of
lust. In C. 32 q. 5, Gratian calls together many Christian authorities to
support Lucy's assertion, as a few of the rubrics illustrate: 'Melior est
uirginitas mentis quam carnis' ('Virginity of the mind is better than
virginity of the flesh'; c. 1); 'In corpore pudicitia uiolari non potest, si
mens inuiolata seruetur' ('Chastity cannot be violated in the body if
the mind remains unviolated'; c. 7); 'Nec peccatum, nec iusticia opere
sine uoluntate perficitur' ('Neither sin nor works of justice are done

---

19   Friedberg, in his edition of the *Decretum*, ends the quotation of direct discourse from
     Lucy before the final sentence of this *dictum*. That line on 'de sensibus et voluntatibus'
     does not appear in the *Legenda aurea* or *Speculum historiale* but does show up in Ado
     of Vienne's *Martyrology* and other earlier sources available to Gratian. On Gratian's
     sources in composing C. 32 q. 5, see Atria Larson, 'A Note on a Hagiographical Source
     for Gratian's *Decretum*: The Quotation Attributed to St. Lucy in C. 32 q. 5', *Traditio*
     (2025, forthcoming).

without the will'; c. 10). It is not the status of the body (inflected by physical violence) that determines culpability, but the status of the mind (inflected by consent).

Later decretists and commentators would develop the scholastic distinctions of conditional and absolute will around this case, but those distinctions postdate Gratian.[20] And for Lucy, the distinctions do not matter, because she is an unambiguous example of absolute will by any interpretation: her will is so strong that she *is not raped* or indeed moved at all. She is famously immobile, fixed by the Holy Spirit. In her words, however, she asserts that even if her body *had* been moved — that is, if she *had actually been dragged off and raped* — the violation of her body would not matter theologically or eschatologically, for it is the consent of the will that guards the psychological threshold between blameless *vis* (experienced as object) and culpable *luxuria* (perpetrated as subject). Lucy verbally anticipates that a 'double crown' will await her in the afterlife even if the thousand men do succeed carrying her off. Her future indicative verb claims that eschatological honour not just for her hypothetical future self, but also implicitly for imagined women who will actually be raped in times to come: 'castitas michi *duplicabitur* ad coronam'.

Gratian's emphasis on consent in C. 32 q. 5 allows for the possibility that a woman can be physically violated and yet possess a 'virginity of the mind' or 'chastity of the mind', as well as the possibility that she may be physically *pudica* and yet be guilty of sinful mental concupiscence (*Dec.* C. 32 q. 5 c. 12). Dante takes a similar approach when treating lust in *Inferno* 5: he makes the atypical choice to focus on the mental ethics of desire rather than the physical torture of the lustful. This is a highly unusual move for vision literature, as Barolini has laid out in detail, but it is a more familiar move for canon law, where the legal analysis of lust is an exploration of will and consent.[21]

---

20   The decretists' focus on conditional and absolute will in their commentary on Gratian illustrates the importance of Lucy's case to the broader canonistic analysis of consent and the will. See Larson, 'Lucretia (and Lucia) and the Medieval Canonists'; Wolfgang P. Müller, 'Lucretia and the Medieval Canonists', *Bulletin of Medieval Canon Law*, 19 (1989), pp. 13–32.

21   Teodolinda Barolini, 'Dante and Cavalcanti', pp. 70–75; Barolini, 'Dante's Sympathy for the Other', in *Dante's Multitudes: History, Philosophy, Method* (Notre Dame, IN: Notre Dame University Press, 2022), pp. 22–34.

Canon law provides what I believe is the earliest known source for the verse that Dante uses to define lust in *Inferno* 5: 'i peccator carnali, | *che la ragion sommettono al talento*' ('the carnal sinners, | who subject reason to the rule of lust'; *Inf.* 5.38–39). The same expression appears in canon law, in Latin, in the ordinary gloss to the same question of the *Decretum* where St. Lucy expresses the power of her consent. A canon from Isidore states: 'Non potest corpus corrumpi, nisi prius animus corruptus fuerit. Munda namque a contagione animi caro non peccat' ('The body cannot be corrupted, unless the mind is corrupted first. The flesh does not sin when the mind is free of contamination'; *Dec. C.* 32 q 5 c 8). The ordinary gloss to this text anticipates Dante's 'la ragion sommettono al talento' ('they subject reason to the rule of lust'): 'Nam tunc homo peccat cum mens per delectationem subiugatur' ('man sins when the mind is made subject to desire'; Ordinary Gloss to *Dec. C.* 32 q. 5 c. 8).

This statement, while perhaps conventional in a Christian analysis of sin, is notable because it uses the same distinct syntax that would later worm its way into Italian vernacular poetry. Dante commentators have already assembled a collection of vernacular citations expressing the idea of 'subordinating reason to desire', which they use to gloss *Inferno* 5.39, but the addition of the canonistic gloss in Latin would be the earliest attestation of this formula:

> Folgore da San Gimignano (fl. 1260), *Quando la voglia segno-reggia tanto*, v. 10: 'chi sommette ragion a voluntade'
>
> *La tavola ritonda* 75 (preserved in a manuscript of 1446): 'io non voglio sottomettere la ragione alla volontà'
>
> Meo Abbracciavacca (d. 1313), sonetto 5.3: 'e qual sommette a voglia operazione'
>
> Guido Cavalcanti (d. 1300), *Donna me prega*, v. 33: 'ché la 'ntenzione per ragione vale'[22]

These verses all express the juxtaposition of a rational mental faculty (*ragione* and *operazione* in Italian, *mens* in Latin) with an appetite of desire (*volontà, intenzione*, and *talento* in Italian, *delectatio* in Latin), with the syntax hinging on a verb of submission. Sin occurs when a

---

22   I have assembled this list by referring to Barolini, 'Dante and Cavalcanti', pp. 77–79.

person uses free will to subordinate the rational mind to the drive of desire. Within that purely psychological arena, consent is the threshold between virtuous refusal and culpable subjugation to *delectatio*, regardless of what occurs with the body. Saint Lucy, in medieval canon law, hagiography, and theology, emblematizes that power of consent to exonerate a person from guilt or complicity in violence. And she is not merely representative of that power through allegory or synecdoche: Lucy speaks in direct discourse.

In Lucy's most famous words, she asserts that she would be rewarded for the merit of her will even if her body were forced to yield. Gratian quotes this line in the *Decretum* ('Si inuitam me feceris uiolari, castitas michi duplicabitur ad coronam'; *Dec.* C. 32 q. 5), as does Thomas Aquinas, twice, in the *Summa Theologiae* (*ST* 2 2ae q. 124 a. 4 obj. 2; *ST* Suppl. q. 96 a. 5 repl. to obj. 4). In these foundational texts of law and theology, a woman saint's voice rings out to state a crucial principle of consent. This role as authoritative speaker is something that the Lucy of canon law shares with the Beatrice of the *Commedia*, whom Barolini calls a 'Beatrix loquax': she is a woman who speaks with deep authority, delivering theological and ethical lessons.[23] Many of the features that Lucy possesses in the textual history of canon law are, in the *Commedia*, refracted across other women: there are glints of bold and saintly Lucia in Beatrice's authoritative character, and Dante addresses Lucia's signature issues of will and compulsion with the cases of Francesca and Piccarda.

A deeper exploration of *Inferno* 5 and *Paradiso* 3–4 as they intersect with *Decretum* C. 32 q. 5 remains to be written. I will limit myself here to emphasizing that Lucia's absence in *Paradiso* 3–4 is a very marked one. The canonistic and hagiographical Saint Lucy possesses the absolute will that Dante deems defective in Piccarda and Constance in *Paradiso* 3–4. Barolini writes that Dante's choice to focus on these two women 'casts doubt on the very category of blame-free involuntary action, by suggesting that it will always (at least when the external force is applied by human beings, with whom one can negoti-

23   Barolini, *Undivine Comedy*, p. 303 n. 36; Barolini, 'Notes toward a Gendered History of Italian Literature, with a Discussion of Dante's *Beatrix Loquax*', in *Dante and the Origins of Italian Literary Culture*, pp. 360–78.

ate) devolve into mixed action';[24] and suggests that Dante deliberately
chooses these examples to push his thinking to the extreme, so great
are the ethical stakes. Piccarda and Constance were victims of violence,
and their wills were also deficient in their subsequent response to that
violence, and they were also saved. Dante creates this series of facts in
order to isolate each conceptual element in his analysis of free will, an
analysis he develops at a theological and eschatological level. His philosophical rigor sits uncomfortably with readers who would prefer not
to associate victims of violence with blameworthiness in any context,
for such an association between rape and blame — when applied in a
human, practical, social context — has devastating consequences for
victims of sexual violence. Piccarda and Constance present a *problem*
in a way Lucy does not, because there is no room for human interpretation or doubt about Lucy's will. In the end her body was *not* moved by
the men who tried to take her in their power. Yet Dante pointedly does
not include her in *Paradiso* 4 with Saint Lawrence and Gaius Mucius
Scaevola, Beatrice's male examples to illustrate that 'così salda voglia
è troppo rada' ('but it is all | too seldom that a will is so intact'; *Par.*
4.87), though Lucy's heroic will is of the same order. Lucia's absence in
Paradiso 4 sharpens the gendered contrast between the two steadfast
men and the two fragile nuns.[25] Dante exploits that contrast to generate sympathy for those women, for they are flawed and humanized,
unlike the distant men whose exemplary status elicits little emotional
response in the reader.[26] Lucy is inextricably part of this canto, because
it is an exploration of precisely the issues that her story raises across
medieval law, hagiography, and theology, but Lucia herself is a silent
presence.

~

---

24   Barolini, 'Dante and Aristotle', p. 268.

25   Barolini, 'Dante and Aristotle', p. 271.

26   While it is beyond the scope of this essay to discuss in detail, I note that Gratian,
       too, used a flawed and humanized example to reinforce his treatment of consent. The
       second pillar of his argumentation is Lucretia, who appears in C. 32 q. 5 via canons
       extracted from Augustine's *City of God*. Lucretia is a necessary complement to Lucia,
       for she *was actually raped*. The status of her will is ambiguous and that ambiguity makes
       her a powerful, relatable example.

When Dante's Lucia appears in *Inferno* 2, *Purgatorio* 9, and *Paradiso* 32, she seems more a lady of lyric than a Christian saint or legal exemplum. Here is Lucia's appearance in *Inferno* 2 in full:

> 'Donna è gentil nel ciel che si compiange
> di questo 'mpedimento ov' io ti mando,
> sì che duro giudicio là sù frange.
>   Questa chiese Lucia in suo dimando
> e disse: — Or ha bisogno il tuo fedele
> di te, e io a te lo raccomando —.
>   Lucia, nimica di ciascun crudele,
> si mosse, e venne al loco dov' i' era,
> che mi sedea con l'antica Rachele.
>   Disse: — Beatrice, loda di Dio vera,
> ché non soccorri quei che t'amò tanto,
> ch'uscì per te de la volgare schiera?
>   Non odi tu la pieta del suo pianto,
> non vedi tu la morte che 'l combatte
> su la fiumana ove 'l mar non ha vanto?'
>
>   ('In Heaven there's a gentle lady — one
> who weeps for the distress toward which I send you,
> so that stern judgment up above is shattered.
>   And it was she who called upon Lucia,
> requesting of her: "Now your faithful one
> has need of you, and I commend him to you".
>   Lucia, enemy of every cruelty,
> arose and made her way to where I was,
> sitting beside the venerable Rachel.
>   She said: "You, Beatrice, true praise of God,
> why have you not helped him who loves you so
> that — for your sake — he's left the vulgar crowd?
>   Do you not hear the anguish in his cry?
> Do you not see the death he wars against
> upon that river ruthless as the sea?"')
> (*Inf.* 2.94–108)

Lucia intervenes in *Inferno* 2's dramatization of doubt, as the pilgrim expresses hesitation about his potentially transgressive voyage only to have those doubts assuaged by Virgil's reassurance that 'tre donne benedette' ('three blessed ladies') have sanctioned his voyage from on high. An unnamed 'donna gentile' (now generally recognized as the Virgin Mary) expresses to Lucia her concern about Dante; then Lucia moves and speaks to Beatrice; then Beatrice comes to Virgil to

commission him as Dante's guide; all of which Virgil relays to Dante in
the diegesis of *Inferno* 2. Lucia's actions and speech are reported within
Beatrice's extended speech to Virgil, which is in turn embedded within
Virgil's speech to Dante in *Inferno* 2 as an 'autobiographical pre-history'
constructed from the *Vita nuova* through the *Commedia*.[27]

Lucia, the early Christian virgin martyr who heroically resisted
gang rape at a brothel, becomes a conduit between the mother of
Christ and Dante's dead Florentine beloved. Maria and Lucia both
speak in the lexicon of Dante's *Vita nuova*. Lucia reprises the praise
paradigm by calling Beatrice 'loda di Dio vera', as many commentators
have noted by reference to *Vita nuova* 26.[28] The *Vita nuova* already
establishes an association between Beatrice and Maria in heaven: after
her death, Beatrice's residence in paradise is 'ove è Maria' ('where
Mary is').[29] And when Maria first speaks to Lucia in *Inferno* 2, she
calls Dante a *fedele* of Lucia ('Or ha bisogno il tuo fedele | di te'; *Inf.*
2.98–99), using a term that also has a history in the *Vita nuova*. In
Vita nuova 12.2, a weeping Dante secludes himself in his room after
Beatrice denies him her greeting, and there he defines himself as Love's
fedele in need of help: 'e quivi, chiamando misericordia a la donna de la
cortesia, e dicendo "Amore, aiuta lo tuo fedele", m'addormentai come
un pargoletto battuto lagrimando' ('and there, calling on the mercy of

---

27   I am following the *Commento Baroliniano* here: '*Inferno* 2 thus communicates the
      crucial autobiographical pre-history of the *Commedia*: the story of how Dante learned
      to find *consolatio* in dead Beatrice. At the same time that *Inferno* 2 communicates the
      protagonist's "true" pre-history, the canto also enacts a pre-history in its fiction, by
      telling of a meeting in Limbo between Beatrice and Virgilio that precedes the account
      of *Inferno* 1' (para. 49). Teodolinda Barolini, '*Inferno* 2: Beatrix Loquax and Con-
      solation', *Commento Baroliniano*, Digital Dante (Columbia University Libraries, 2018)
      <https://digitaldante.columbia.edu/dante/divine-comedy/inferno/inferno-2/> [ac-
      cessed 3 June 2025].

28   Anna Maria Chiavacci Leonardi, in her commentary to *Inf.* 2.103, states: 'Questa idea
      è fondamentale nella *Vita Nuova* (see 26.1–2), alla quale il richiamo, se si uniscono a
      questo i due versi successivi, non potrebbe essere più preciso.'

29   Beatrice's death is described through reference to Maria as well: 'lo segnore della giu-
      stizia chiamòe questa gentilissima a gloriare sotto la 'nsegna di quella regina benedetta
      virgo Maria' ('the Lord of Justice called his most gracious of women to glory under
      the banner of that blessed queen the Virgin Mary'; *Vn* 19). Quotations from the *Vita
      nuova* are from Dante Alighieri, *La Vita Nuova di Dante Alighieri. Edizione critica*, ed. by
      Michele Barbi (Florence: Bemporad e Figlio, 1932). English translation from Dante
      Alighieri, *Vita Nova*, trans. by Andrew Frisardi (Evanston: Northwestern University
      Press, 2012).

the lady of benevolence and grace, and saying "Love, help your faithful one!" I fell asleep crying like a little boy who'd been beaten'; *Vn* 12.2). The reference to Dante as Lucia's *fedele* in *Inferno* 2 has flummoxed readers because it seems to indicate a personal devotion to Lucia not attested anywhere else in Dante's works, including elsewhere in the *Commedia*.[30] The term *fedele* itself, though, links Lucia to both Love and Beatrice: Dante is 'lo tuo fedele' to Love in *Vita nuova* 12.2, 'il tuo fedele' to Lucia in *Inferno* 2.28, and '[i]l tuo fedele' to Beatrice in *Purgatorio* 31.134.[31] Fidelity to Lucia, patterned on the socially established convention of personal devotion to a dead saint, mirrors Dante's unconventional devotion to the dead Beatrice.[32]

Lucia's role in *Inferno* 2 is one of both blessed resistance and blessed motion: Beatrice introduces Lucia as 'nimica di ciascun crudele' ('enemy of every cruelty') and Lucia's first action is 'si mosse' ('[she] moved'; *Inf.* 2.100–01). The first descriptor derives directly from her legend while the second is an inversion of how she is depicted in Dante's sources. She is an enemy of all cruelty just as she is in the *Legenda aurea*, where she states that 'corruptores autem mentis

---

30   The closest thing to a reference to Saint Lucy in Dante's other works is a technical astro-
     nomical discourse in *Convivio* 3.5, where Dante will use the names 'Lucia' and 'Maria'
     to represent imaginary cities on the northern and southern poles of the Earth. Mary is
     north and Lucia is south. In the imagined geography of the *Commedia*, purgatory is on
     the south pole, and so there is a resonance between the city Lucia in the *Convivio* and
     Mount Purgatory in the *Commedia*; Lucia and Maria define the imagined geographical
     space of *Convivio* 3.5 as they define the imagined celestial space of heaven as recounted
     in *Inferno* 2. But the *Convivio* passage does not facilitate a confirmation of St. Lucy as
     Dante's particular patron saint. My thanks to Louis Moffa for his insights on Lucy's
     spatial function in the *Convivio*.

31   In *Purgatorio* 31, three ladies/nymphs/theological virtues exhort Beatrice to look at
     Dante: "'Volgi, Beatrice, volgi li occhi santi" | era la sua canzone "al tuo fedele | che,
     per vederti, ha mossi passi tanti!"' ("'Turn, Beatrice, o turn your holy eyes | upon your
     faithful one", their song beseeched, | "who, that he might see you, has come so far"';
     Purg. 31.133–35). Dante makes other references to the concept of being a *fedele* or one
     of a group of *fedeli* (in *Paradiso* 26.60, Dante designates himself *fedele* in the sense of
     Christian believer, and in the prose of *Vita nuova* 3.9 he describes *A ciascun'alma* as
     being addressed to 'tutti li fedeli d'Amore', 'all of Love's faithful') but the references to
     Dante's own *fedeltà* to a specific person, with a possessive adjective, are more restricted.

32   The idea that Dante must remain faithful to Beatrice even after her death and not
     transfer his will to a new love (an ethical conflict dramatized in the *Vita nuova*'s episode
     of the *donna gentile*) is not at all standard in the prior lyric tradition. See Teodolinda
     Barolini, 'Errancy: A Brief History of Dante's *Ferm voler*', in *The Oxford Handbook
     of Dante*, ed. by Manuele Gragnolati, Elena Lombardi, and Francesca Southerden
     (Oxford: Oxford University Press, 2021), pp. 568–69.

et corporis nunquam scivi' ('I have never known corrupters of mind or body', *Legenda aurea*, 'De Sancta Lucia virgine'). In her martyrdom, she is famously immoveable, as she states to Paschasius: 'aeque ut primum immobilem me videbis' ('you shall see me immoveable just as before', *Legenda aurea*, 'De Sancta Lucia virgine'). In *Inferno* 2, she is not immobile at all but *defined* by motion, and thus her very movement endorses the blessedness of her purpose in the afterlife, just as her immobility before Paschasius's men endorses her integrity of will in life.

Dante's challenge in *Inferno* 1–2 is precisely one of will. In *Inferno* 2.95, Beatrice describes the obstacle in Dante's journey as an *impedimento*. Dante glosses this concept at the beginning of the *Convivio*, where he writes that two types of internal impediment or defect can block a man from the pursuit of knowledge and spiritual perfection:

> Dentro da l'uomo possono essere due difetti e impedi[men]ti: l'uno da la parte del corpo, l'altro da la parte de l'anima. Da la parte del corpo è quando le parti sono indebitamente disposte, sì che nulla ricevere può, sì come sono sordi e muti e loro simili. Da la parte de l'anima è quando la malizia vince in essa, sì che si fa seguitatrice di viziose delettazioni, ne le quali riceve tanto inganno che per quelle ogni cosa tiene a vile.

> (Within man there can be two defects and impediments: one in the body and one in the soul. On the part of the body, when the members are improperly arranged, so that the body cannot receive anything, like deafs and mutes and others like them. On the part of the soul, when malice overcomes it, so that it makes itself a follower of vicious pleasures, in which it becomes so deceived that because of them it holds everything worthless.)
> (*Conv.* 1.1.3)

As defined in the *Convivio*, an impediment is a defect within a person which blocks that person from proceeding along the straight path. (In the only other use of the word *impedimento* in the *Commedia*, Beatrice will explain to Dante that he is 'privo | d'impedimento' in *Paradiso* 1.139–40.) In canon law, the term *impedimentum* is a technical term for an obstacle that prevents a sacrament from being performed: in the case of marriage, for instance, common impediments are nonage (being under the age of consent) or consanguinity (blood relation). In the *Convivio*, Dante defines impediments as a perversion of the will when malice overcomes the soul, which 'si fa seguitatrice di viziose delettazioni' ('makes itself a follower of vicious pleasures'). As Barolini has argued, this citation should be added to the catalogue of variants on the verse 'la ragion sommettono al talento' ('they subject reason to the rule of lust') from *Inferno* 5.39. In the Latin variant of the phrase attached to Gratian's quaestio on rape, the equivalent of *talento* is *delectatio*, just like Dante's *delettazione* here in *Convivio* 1.1.3: 'mens per delectationem subiugatur'.[33] The reflexive verb *si fa* ('makes itself') in the *Convivio* captures the same sense of voluntary self-subjugation to sin that is expressed through the verb *sommettono* ('they subject') in *Inferno* 5 and *subiugatur* ('is made subject') in the canonistic gloss.

After Lucia assists in the resolution of Dante's crisis in *Inferno* 1–2, she will intervene again at a moment of doubt in the poem's middle canticle. In *Purgatorio* 9, Dante sleeps and dreams that he is ravished by a golden eagle. Using the lexicon of *raptus*, he compares himself to Ganymede 'quando fu ratto al sommo consistoro' ('when he | was snatched up to the high consistory'; *Purg.* 9.24) and describes himself being carried off and burned together with the eagle: 'e me rapisse suso infino al foco. | Ivi parea che ella e io ardesse' ('it snatched me up to the fire's orbit. | And there it seemed that the eagle and I were burning'; *Purg.* 9.30–31).[34] *Raptus* is a term for visionary experience. It is also a crime in Roman and canon law, often classified by Christian thinkers as a type of illicit sex or *luxuria* along with crimes like fornication and incest.[35] Strictly speaking, the crime of *raptus* is abduction without consent: it is in this sense of 'involuntary motion' that the term *raptus* can signify both sexualized abduction for the purpose of marriage

---

33   See Barolini, "'Only Historicize'", pp. 5–8.

34   See Barolini, '*Purgatorio* 9: Raptus', *Commento Baroliniano*, Digital Dante <https://digitaldante.columbia.edu/dante/divine-comedy/purgatorio/purgatorio-9/> [accessed 3 June 2025].

35   Elizabeth Casteen argues: 'the rapt female saint also conceptually mirrored and overlapped the victim of rape, as hagiographers and mystical writers drew on legal and literary conventions of raptus to describe the experience and physical manifestation of mystical rapture. Both rapture and claims of sexual violence were often doubted, and the proving of both hinged on understandings of women's volition, physicality, and tendency to deceive and be deceived'. See Elizabeth Casteen, 'Rape and Rapture: Violence, Ambiguity, and Raptus in Medieval Thought', in *The Sacred and the Sinister: Studies in Medieval Religion and Magic*, ed. by David J. Collins (University Park: The Pennsylvania State University Press, 2019), pp. 91–116 (p. 96).

and mystical abduction for the purpose of vision. Even though *raptus* is the etymological source of the modern term 'rape', its definition in medieval law does not require sexual violation. However, in both practice and theory, *vis* and *raptus* frequently went together (Gratian uses what is indisputably a rape case to set up his treatment of *raptus* in the *Decretum*, for instance, even though he judges that case not to be an abduction and treats the crime of *vis* elsewhere).[36] Both *vis* and *raptus* contain sexualized violence: *raptus* is a movement of the body from location to location without consent and *vis* is a movement of the body in the same place — through forced sexual contact — without consent.

In *Purgatorio* 9, Dante recounts a dream of being moved by violence, a violence that acquires sexual undertones through the verb *rapere* and the comparison to Ganymede, whom Jupiter abducted because of his beauty. Dante wakes from his dream of *raptus* in fear: 'diventa' ismorto, | come fa l'uom che, spaventato, agghiaccia' ('and I went pale, as will | a man who, terrified, turns cold as ice'; *Purg.* 9.41–42). That fear is linked to the spectre of Ulyssean transgression when Dante compares himself to Achilles awakening on Skyros, 'là onde poi li Greci il dipartiro' ('the isle the Greeks would later make him leave'; *Purg.* 9.39). It was the fraudulent counsels of Ulysses that convinced Achilles to leave Skyros and join the Trojan war, and so that simile aligns Dante with an Achilles seduced by Ulysses. Into these layers of violence, abduction, and transgression, Dante introduces Lucia once more. Here is her second appearance in the text of the *Commedia*:

> 'Non aver tema', disse il mio segnore;
> 'fatti sicur, ché noi semo a buon punto;
> non stringer, ma rallarga ogne vigore.
>   Tu se' omai al purgatorio giunto:
> vedi là il balzo che 'l chiude dintorno;
> vedi l'entrata là 've par digiunto.
>   Dianzi, ne l'alba che procede al giorno,
> quando l'anima tua dentro dormia,
> sovra li fiori ond' è là giù addorno

---

36 Gratian treats *raptus* primarily in C. 36, where the case narrative describes a man who invites a woman to a banquet and then rapes her. The case narratives for C. 36 (on *raptus*) and C. 32 (on *vis*) both use the same verb, *opprimere*, to describe sexual violence. In *Decretum* C. 36: 'finito convivio juvenis virginem oppressit'; in *Decretum* C. 32 'quemdam rogavit, ut vi uxorem opprimeret suam.'

venne una donna, e disse: "I' son Lucia;
lasciatemi pigliar costui che dorme;
sì l'agevolerò per la sua via".
    Sordel rimase e l'altre genti forme;
ella ti tolse, e come 'l dì fu chiaro,
sen venne suso; e io per le sue orme.
    Qui ti posò, ma pria mi dimostraro
li occhi suoi belli quella intrata aperta;
poi ella e 'l sonno ad una se n'andaro'.

    (My lord said: 'Have no fear; be confident,
for we are well along our way; do not
restrain, but give free rein to, all your strength.
    You have already come to Purgatory:
see there the rampart wall enclosing it;
see, where that wall is breached, the point of entry.
    Before, at dawn that ushers in the day,
when soul was sleeping in your body, on
the flowers that adorn the ground below,
    a lady came; she said: "I am Lucia;
let me take hold of him who is asleep,
that I may help to speed him on his way".
    Sordello and the other noble spirits
stayed there; and she took you, and once the day
was bright, she climbed — I followed behind.
    And here she set you down, but first her lovely
eyes showed that open entryway to me;
then she and sleep together took their leave'.)
(*Purg.* 9.46–63)

As in *Inferno* 2, Lucia is mediated by Virgil's narration; and as in *Inferno* 2, when Lucia 'si mosse, e venne' and then 'disse' ('moved herself, and came', then 'said'; *Inf.* 2.101, 103), here too Virgil describes how a lady 'venne […] e disse' ('came […] and said'; *Purg.* 9.55). Lucia's presence and her blessed motion rewrite the visionary violence, desexualizing Dante's abduction by the eagle. At the same time, Lucia is identified with the dream of violence: 'poi ella e 'l sonno ad una se n'andaro' ('then she and sleep together took their leave'; *Purg.* 9.63). Like the eagle, Lucia picks Dante up and moves him, but she uses the lighter verb *pigliare*: like *rapire/rapere* this can mean 'to take', yet *pigliare* has no automatic connotation of violence. Lucia's function in this moment is typically read as the intervention of allegorized grace in Dante's journey. *Purgatorio* 9 — where Lucia insists on her own specific

identity: 'I' son Lucia' (*Purg.* 9.55) — is also the closest Dante comes
to including his Lucia directly within a treatment of violence and will.
The statement of her name is the only thing that allows identification
of this *donna* as St. Lucy, and that name is the only thing that secures
her movement of Dante as a benign transportation rather than perilous
abduction. Lucia's appearance in the ninth canto is followed by a
warning about deviation in the tenth:

> Poi fummo dentro al soglio de la porta
> che 'l mal amor de l'anime disusa,
> perché fa parer dritta la via torta,
>   sonando la senti' esser richiusa;
> e s'io avesse li occhi vòlti ad essa,
> qual fora stata al fallo degna scusa?
>
> (When I had crossed the threshold of the gate
> that — since the soul's aberrant love would make
> the crooked way seem straight — is seldom used,
>   I heard the gate resound and, hearing, knew
> that it had shut; and if I'd turned toward it,
> how could my fault have found a fit excuse?)
> (*Purg.* 10.1–6)

The 'mal amor [che] fa parer dritta la via torta' is a restatement of
the *Convivio*'s 'malizia [dell'anima] che si fa seguitatrice di viziose
delettazioni' (1.1.3). Both phrases articulate the will's consent to sinful
desire, the negative manifestation of the free-willed power of consent
which St. Lucy asserts in alignment with the Holy Spirit.

In Lucia's third and final appearance in *Paradiso* 32, she is the last
instance of the familiar formula in which Dante's guide points out the
various souls that reside in each neighbourhood of the afterlife. We
come back full circle to *Inferno* 2 with Bernard's gloss on Lucia as he
finishes describing the celestial rose to Dante:

> e contro al maggior padre di famiglia
> siede Lucia, che mosse la tua donna
> quando chinavi, a rovinar, le ciglia.
>   Ma perché 'l tempo fugge che t'assonna,
> qui farem punto, come buon sartore
> che com' elli ha del panno fa la gonna;
>   e drizzeremo li occhi al primo amore,
> sì che, guardando verso lui, penètri
> quant' è possibil per lo suo fulgore.

(And opposite
   the greatest father of a family,
Lucia sits, she who urged on your lady
when you bent your brows downward, to your ruin.
   But time, which brings you sleep, takes flight, and now
we shall stop here — even as a good tailor
who cuts the garment as his cloth allows —
   and turn our vision to the Primal Love,
that, gazing at Him, you may penetrate —
as far as that can be — His radiance.)
(*Par.* 32.136–44)

Lucia sits across from Adam and next to John the Baptist. Here, Lucia is defined by reference to the events recounted in *Inferno* 2: 'Lucia, che mosse la tua donna | quando chinavi, a rovinar, le ciglia' ('Lucia sits, she who moved your lady | when you bent your brows downward, to your ruin'; *Par.* 32.137–38). Dante does not write of Lucia's saintly and unbending will; he writes of Lucia's intervention to rescue Dante from the bending of his own will. In *Paradiso* 32 Lucia is marked by motion ('che mosse la tua donna'), now a transitive motion that moved Beatrice rather than the intransitive motion by which Lucia moved herself in *Inferno* 2 ('si mosse'). She is associated with visionary sleep, as she was in *Purgatorio* 9, where again her role was to move Dante along the path (*UDC*, pp. 144–47). And similarly to *Purgatorio* 9, the description of Lucia in *Paradiso* 32 comes shortly before an explicitly voiced possibility of Ulyssean transgression and deviation:

   'Veramente, *ne* forse tu t'arretri
movendo l'ali tue, credendo oltrarti,
orando grazia conven che s'impetri
   grazia da quella che puote aiutarti'

   ('But lest you now fall back when, even as
you move your wings, you think that you advance,
imploring grace, through prayer you must beseech
   grace from that one who has the power to help you.')
(*Par.* 32.145–48)[37]

In all three moments when Lucia appears in the poem, she anchors an episode where Dante rehearses and rejects a fear of transgression. She

---

37   Words like *ali* and *oltrarti* are integral to the *Commedia*'s Ulyssean lexicon and always inevitably evoke Ulysses, no matter where they appear in the poem. See *UDC*, p. 251.

exerts her will and sets herself in motion twice to propel Dante along his path in the *Commedia*. Only in *Paradiso* does she dwell in the holy immobility for which she was remembered as a martyr and a saint.

Beyond the world of the *Commedia*, Lucy is recognized in other medieval texts for her powerful words of defiance which assert the force of her consent — and claim a radical inheritance in the afterlife. As Gratian and Aquinas both quote in direct discourse, Lucy defies Paschasius to say that 'si inuitam me feceris uiolari, castitas michi duplicabitur ad coronam', and it is this citation that enshrines Lucy as a saint of unbending will in the *Decretum* (C. 32 q. 5). In the *Commedia*, Dante reorganizes the historically-attested Lucy by translating the ethical and conceptual issues of her *passio* to other women and adding a lyric and personal dimension to this established saint, associating her more with Beatrice than with Piccarda (a woman who serves a similar narrative purpose for Dante as Lucy serves for Gratian). Lucia in the *Commedia* is an outspoken woman saint translated into a lyric key, and her multifaceted presence in Dante's poem reinforces the authority of Beatrice, who is the inverse: a lyric lady who becomes a divine female authority. In trying to determine why Dante calls himself *fedele* of Lucia, readers have found only scant crumbs of evidence in Dante's biography for his personal devotion to her. In the *Commedia*, it is the other way around: Dante's active reworking of Lucy and her legend creates a Lucia — and a Beatrice — worthy of his poetic and theological devotion.

Prophetic Models and Structures in an Undivine *Comedy*

GIUSEPPE LEDDA

Barolini's *The Undivine Comedy* devotes chapter 7, 'Nonfalse Errors and the True Dreams of the Evangelist', to the final cantos of Dante's *Purgatorio* (specifically cantos 29, 32, and 33), whose importance to Dante's self-representation as poet-prophet is well known and occurs through a wealth of references to biblical prophets, apostles, evangelists, and visionaries.[1] Over the past fifteen years or so, I myself have been studying the perspective that this self-representation has cast over the poem as a whole.[2] Nowadays, such a perspective seems dangerous as it exposes scholars to the risk of being criticized as naïve catholic readers. Indeed, many colleagues, both in Italy and abroad, consider any study on the relationship between Dante and late-medieval religious culture to be a useless — if not harmful — reactionary repetition of old-fashioned

---

1   Teodolinda Barolini, *The Undivine Comedy: Detheologizing Dante* (Princeton: Princeton University Press, 1992), pp. 143–64 and 313–24, hereafter *UDC*. Subsequent references given in parentheses in the main text.

2   See for instance Giuseppe Ledda, 'Modelli biblici nella *Commedia*: Dante e san Paolo', in *La Bibbia di Dante. Esperienza mistica, profezia e teologia biblica in Dante*, ed. by Giuseppe Ledda (Ravenna: Centro Dantesco dei Frati Minori Conventuali, 2011), pp. 179–216; Ledda, 'La danza e il canto dell'"umile salmista": David nella *Commedia* di Dante', in *Les Figures de David à la Renaissance*, ed. by Elise Boillet, Sonia Cavicchioli, and Paul-Alexis Mellet (Geneva: Droz, 2015), pp. 225–46; Ledda, *La Bibbia di Dante* (Turin: EMI, 2015).

ideas, of no interest for twenty-first-century Dante readers. I shall add that such a criticism is often rooted in a banal and (in my opinion) misleading reading of Barolini's *Undivine Comedy*.[3]

To further discuss this point, I shall begin with another book by Teodolinda Barolini: *Dante's Poets*, the first of her books which I read on the recommendation of my maestro (Ezio Raimondi).[4] My first reading of this book dates back to the 1990s, and at the time I perceived it as a brilliant development of the seminal insight offered by Gianfranco Contini's 'Dante come personaggio-poeta'.[5] However, I soon realized that while Contini's essay develops within the boundaries of Dante's dialogue with medieval lyric traditions in the vernacular, Barolini's book expands the field by considering Dante's response to late-medieval poetry in the vernacular alongside his dialogue with classic epic poetry in Latin. Additionally, in *Dante's Poets* Barolini manages to develop this topic while paying constant attention to the religious dimension of Dante's poem in order to demonstrate that Dante eclipses Virgil and the Latin poets thanks to the theological superiority of his poem, which grants him the capability to express a truth denied to its classical forerunners.

What I believe is even more important in this project, however, is Barolini's (not yet fully developed) attempt to apply this perspective not only to pagan authors, but also to biblical texts. In fact, this latter insight allows Barolini to suggest that Dante took up biblical authors like David as models, according to which he manages to define a more precise idea of a poetics whose features lie at the crossroad of its divinely inspired contents and the humbleness of its author: in other words, the idea of the sacred poet. By assuming David as his model, Dante eventually moves beyond the models offered by the Latin poetic

---

3   For a survey of this attitude in the context of Italian Dante scholarship, see Giuseppe Ledda, 'Cultura religiosa: ricordi autobiografici di un lettore novecentesco di studi su Dante', in *Now Feed Yourself: Anglo-American and Italian Scholarship on Dante*, ed. by Zygmunt G. Barański, Theodore J. Cachey Jr., and Anna Pegoretti (Oxford: Legenda, 2024), pp. 201–27.

4   Teodolinda Barolini, *Dante's Poets: Textuality and Truth in the 'Comedy'* (Princeton: Princeton University Press, 1984), hereafter *DP*. Subsequent references given in parentheses in the main text.

5   Gianfranco Contini, 'Dante come personaggio-poeta della *Commedia*', in Contini, *Un'idea di Dante. Saggi danteschi* (Turin: Einaudi, 1976), pp. 33–62.

tradition (especially Virgil). My work as a *dantista* has been greatly influenced by my experience as student at the University of Bologna, where I attended Ezio Raimondi's classes. During his course on Italian literature, Raimondi quoted extensively from Barolini's *Dante's Poets* in order to develop a more comprehensive theory of Dante's figural appropriation of both biblical and classical models, with the aforementioned case of David as a starting point.[6]

In this regard, the most important chapter of Barolini's *Dante's Poets* is the last, entitled 'Dante: "ritornerò poeta"', where she traces the passage of 'the poetic mantle' from Vergil (i.e. a non-Christian poet) to Statius, and finally to Dante himself, 'the poet whose Christian faith is a *sine qua non* of his poetics' (*DP*, p. 269). Dante is able to surpass his poetic predecessors thanks to his assumption of the biblical model of David, 'l'umile salmista' ('humble psalmist'; *Purg.* 10.65):[7] 'as David's humility makes him more glorious, so the *comedìa's* lowly standing makes it more sublime' (*DP*, p. 276). Not by chance, as Barolini explains, 'all of the *Paradiso's* three references to David [...] seem designed to contribute to the identification of the inspired biblical poet with the inspired Italian poet' (*DP*, p. 277): like David, Dante is the author of a new 'tëodia' (i.e. his 'poema sacro' or 'sacred poem'; *Par.* 25.1, 73). It is thus fair to conclude (in Barolini's own words) that 'to go beyond a great model — to get past Vergil — Dante requires a humble model, on whose example he can forge his own humbly superior poetics' (*DP*, p. 278).

In the last chapter of *Dante's Poets*, Barolini focuses on another biblical author: John the Evangelist, evoked by Cacciaguida in his prophetic investiture: 'the emphasis on making truth manifest anticipates the description of the Gospel of John as "l'alto preconio che grida

---

6   For Ezio Raimondi's use of *Dante's Poets* during his classes at the University of Bologna, see Ezio Raimondi, *Intertestualità e storia letteraria. Da Dante a Montale* (Bologna: CUSL, 1991), pp. 410–11; and Giuseppe Ledda, 'Osservazioni sul contributo di Ezio Raimondi agli studi danteschi: bilanci e prospettive', in *Ezio Raimondi lettore inquieto*, ed. by Andrea Battistini (Bologna: Il Mulino, 2016), pp. 117–23.

7   Quotations from the *Commedia* are taken from Dante Alighieri: *La Commedia secondo l'antica vulgata*, ed. by Giorgio Petrocchi, Società Dantesca Italiana, Edizione Nazionale, 2nd rev. edn, 4 vols (Florence: Le Lettere, 1994). English translations come from Dante Alighieri, *The Divine Comedy*, trans. by Allen Mandelbaum, 3 vols (Berkeley: University of California Press, 1980–82).

l'arcano di qui là giù sovra ogne altro bando"' (*DP*, p. 283).[8] This said, Barolini adds a remark that anticipates a crucial theme of *The Undivine Comedy*: 'If Dante's poem is a vision, it is the same kind of vision afforded Saint John in the Apocalypse, the vision of one who is in a waking sleep, like the old man who personifies the Apocalypse in the allegorical procession and who comes forward "dormendo, con la faccia arguta"' (*DP*, pp. 284–85).[9] Following this line of reasoning, in a footnote Barolini discusses a hugely relevant passage from *Purgatorio* 29 (the description of the four animals), in which the mention of Saint John plays a key role in shaping Dante's poetic authority: 'Dante openly aligns himself with John earlier in this canto, where he cuts short the description of the four animals surrounding the chariot with the injunction to read Ezekiel; however, on the question of the number of their wings, "Giovanni è meco e da lui si diparte" ("John is with me, and departs from him," i.e. Ezekiel (*Purg.* 29.105)). Thus the poet is one of the prophets, who — although they may differ on details — share knowledge of the truth' (*DP*, p. 285 note 105).

This said, we shall now move to *The Undivine Comedy*. I took my first step into the field of Dante studies in the 1990s, aiming to bring together the legacy of Contini's scholarship and various rhetorical, structuralist, narratological, and broadly formalistic approaches. Although atheist and culturally secular, I soon realized the need to investigate more seriously the religious dimension of Dante's *Commedia*. This meant adopting a non-conformist approach in the context of Italian scholarship on Dante, as Italian scholars have regularly denied or marginalized this particular feature of Dante's poetry. While a superficial reading of Barolini's *Undivine Comedy* might lead us to consider the proposal to detheologize Dante as something like a negation of the religious dimension of Dante's poem, as I understand it, detheologizing does not mean denying the importance of religious culture or the relationship with the scriptural tradition for a better understanding of Dante's poetry. On the contrary, it takes seriously the illusion of theological truth construed by Dante, thanks to a study of the literary

---

8   Here Barolini references *Paradiso* 26.44–45: 'which more than any other proclamation | cries out to earth the mystery of Heaven'.

9   The quote references *Purgatorio* 29.144: 'his features keen, advanced, as if in sleep'.

and poetic strategies he uses in order to create this illusion. Conceived as such, Barolini's proposal to dethologize Dante reveals itself as perfectly consistent with the aim to study the ways in which Dante adapts and responds to a wealth of religious tradition and models. One could be even more precise by saying that such a perspective is necessary in order to dethologize Dante. Barolini's proposal thus is perfectly consistent with an approach to Dante's poem based on the study of religious cultural influences in his works, including textual and intertextual analysis, the examination of biblical and religious models present in the text, an exploration of the poem's relationship with the languages, doctrines and practices of medieval religious culture, and so on and so forth.

Not by chance, the biblical authors discussed in the last pages of *Dante's Poets* (David and John: the two models upon which Dante builds his own identity as author of a sacred poem capable of overcoming the classical model offered by Virgil) become an initial point of reference in the first pages of *The Undivine Comedy*. Here, Barolini evokes these two biblical models in relation to the *theologus-poeta* dichotomy — that is, the critical tendency that 'keeps resolutely apart' (*UDC*, p. 8) Dante's poetry and Dante's theology. However, as Barolini explains, 'the two coincide — in a poet who models himself on David, the "humble psalmist" [...], who like David composes a *tëodia* and speaks as *scriba Dei* [...], with what he considers a theologically-vested authority at least equal to that of the author of the Apocalypse' (*UDC*, p. 8).

Barolini's insights on David as a model for Dante have been developed by various scholars (I have written something myself on this topic), and recent scholarship has further demonstrated the fundamental importance of the author of the Psalms as a model for Dante's self-representation as the poet of the *Commedia*.[10] However, after this

---

10   See for instance Theresa Federici, 'Dante's Davidic Journey. From Sinner to God's Scribe', in *Dante's 'Commedia': Theology as Poetry*, ed. by Vittorio Montemaggi and Matthew Treherne (Notre Dame, IN: Notre Dame University Press, 2010), pp. 180–209; Ledda, 'La danza e il canto'; Marco Veglia, 'Una controfigura biblica', in Veglia, *Dante leggero. Dal priorato alla 'Commedia'* (Rome: Carocci, 2017), pp. 111–47; Nicolò Maldina, '"Per poenitentiam factum prophetam". Filigrane davidiche nel prologo della *Commedia*', in *Poesia e profezia nell'opera di Dante*, ed. by Giuseppe Ledda (Ravenna: Centro Dantesco dei Frati Minori Conventuali, 2019), pp. 163–78.

seminal reference in its first chapter, *The Undivine Comedy* devotes no great space to David. Nonetheless, while chapters 6–7 mention David (albeit not as a model for Dante self-representation),[11] the volume's final reference to David deals precisely with this point. Commenting on a famous passage from *Paradiso* 23, Barolini proposes a clever connection between the jumping of the 'sacrato poema' and David's humble dancing: 'the sacred poem must jump, just as the mountains bizarrely skip, and as David — the divinely inspired cantor of those mountains — shames his wife by humbly dancing and leaping before the sacred ark' (*UDC*, p. 227).[12]

The first chapter of *The Undivine Comedy* repeatedly alludes to two additional models for Dante's prophetic identity: St. John and St. Paul. Barolini underscores that 'we have not dealt with the implications of Dante's claims to be a second St. Paul, a second St. John' (*UDC*, p. 20). Then she explains that her book 'is an attempt to analyze the textual metaphysics that makes the *Commedia*'s truth claims credible and to show how the illusion is constructed, forged, made — by a man who is, precisely, after all, "only" a *fabbro*, a maker, ... a poet' (*UDC*, p. 20). This idea aligns precisely with my own work on Dante's use of biblical models (such as David, Paul, John and other biblical prophets) and on his use of hagiographical models in the *Commedia* (Boethius, Saint Francis, Saint Dominic, Peter Damianus, Benedict). Thanks to these models, Dante creates a sort of auto-hagiography with his *Commedia*.[13]

Focusing on chapter 7 of Barolini's *Undivine Comedy*, I would like to discuss how, over the last three decades, scholars have developed a critical perspective that aims at analysing the ways in which Dante builds his own authority, both as a poet and as a sacred author, i.e. as a poet inspired by God, but a poet nonetheless, or (to put it more precisely) a poet who, once in paradise, becomes the sacred poet of a sacred poem. To study Dante's relationships with religious culture

---

11 See *UDC*, pp. 123, 125, 129, 164.

12 Here the passage specifically references *Paradiso* 23.61–63, *Purgatorio* 10.55–69, and Psalms 113.4: 'montes exultaverunt ut arietes, | et colles sicut agni ovium'.

13 See note 2 of the current essay and, for a synthesis of my studies on this subject along with further bibliographical references, see Giuseppe Ledda, 'Poesia e agiografia nella *Commedia*', in *Dante poeta cristiano e la cultura religiosa medievale. In ricordo di Anna Maria Chiavacci Leonardi*, ed. by Giuseppe Ledda (Ravenna: Centro Dantesco dei Frati Minori Conventuali, 2018), pp. 215–58.

from a formalistic perspective, one must analyse the literary, rhetorical, narratological, and intertextual structures and strategies that Dante utilizes in order to construct the prophetic and theological authority of his text. Among these structures and strategies, truth-claims play a particularly special role, as Barolini masterfully notes, along with (and this is what I shall add to her own thoughts) the biblical intertextuality and references to characters as models for both Dante-character's visionary experience and for the literary mission that Dante-poet accomplishes in writing the poem.[14]

Barolini refers to Paul, mentioned in *Inferno* 2 as a model and guarantor of Dante's 'prophetic status' (*UDC*, p. 57): this biblical figure is mentioned repeatedly in chapter 7, as we shall see. John will also play a crucial role in chapter 7, but he is referenced in chapter 4 in its treatment of *Inferno* 19, a canto in which 'The Apocalypse is Dante's preferred source' (*UDC*, p. 78). Here 'the pilgrim specifically cites St. John as his authority when he accuses the popes in language taken directly from the Apocalypse: "Di voi pastor s'accorse il Vangelista"' (*UDC*, p. 78). At the end of this canto, Virgil listens with pleasure to the pilgrim's true words: 'lo suon de le parole vere espresse' (*Inf.* 19.123), and Barolini explains that the poet's words are true 'because what he recounts was revealed to him, as the contents of the Book of Revelations were revealed to St. John'; thus in this canto 'our poet's identity as a true prophet has been validated' (*UDC*, p. 79). Around the time of *The Undivine Comedy*'s publication, Rachel Jacoff, Mirko Tavoni, and Zygmunt Barański had further enriched the prophetic genealogy of *Inferno* 19 with the model of Jeremiah.[15] These scholars have argued that Dante's reference to the breaking of the 'battezzatoio' ('basin for baptizing'; l. 18) aims to confer the pilgrim, who has not yet received any prophetic investiture, the authority of a biblical prophet by activating the model of Jeremiah, whom the Lord ordered to break

---

14 For this distinction and for its relevance within the field, see Giuseppe Ledda, 'Dante Alighieri, Dante-poet, Dante-character', in *The Cambridge Companion to Dante's 'Commedia'*, ed. by Zygmunt G. Barański and Simon Gilson (Cambridge: Cambridge University Press, 2019), pp. 28–42.

15 See Rachel Jacoff, 'Dante, Geremia e la problematica profetica', in *Dante e la Bibbia*, ed. by Giovanni Barblan (Florence: Olschki, 1988), pp. 113–23; Mirko Tavoni, 'Effrazione battesimale tra i simoniaci (*If* XIX 13–21)', *Rivista di letteratura italiana*, 10 (1992), pp. 457–523; Zygmunt G. Barański, *Dante e i segni* (Naples: Liguori, 2000), pp. 147–72.

an amphora in front of the people as a sign of the prophetic authority
God had conferred to him.

As noted, Barolini studies how Dante's prophetism contributes to
the poem's theological credibility, as is especially the case in chapter 7
of *The Undivine Comedy*, devoted to the last cantos of *Purgatorio*. As
usual, the author pays great attention to the themes of truth and to the
poet's truth-claims. The chapter opens by recalling a very important
yet neglected topic in Dante studies: the broad medieval visionary
tradition that includes a great number of texts narrating journeys to the
otherworld. As Jacques Le Goff, quoted by Barolini, explains: 'these
journeys were considered "real" by the men of the Middle Age, even
if they depicted them as "dreams" (somnia)'.[16] As Barolini comments,
Dante likewise 'believed that his journey was, in some essential sense,
real' (*UDC*, p. 143).

As mentioned previously, here I shall focus on the problem of
prophetic authority rather than the problem of truth. In this regard,
it is crucial to remember that a fundamental feature of this visionary
tradition is the presence of prophetic investitures. Barolini investigated
this feature in an essay that dates back to 1993, later published as
a chapter in *Dante and the Origins of Italian Literary Culture* (2006)
with the title 'Why Did Dante Write the *Commedia*? Dante and the
Visionary Tradition'.[17] As Barolini explains here, in the first prophetic
investitures of *Purgatorio* 32 and 33, 'Beatrice echoes many visionary
texts, which commonly contain an obligation of *denuntiatio*'.[18] It is true
that protagonists of medieval visionary texts regularly receive from
their guide the order to show, reveal, make public (in some cases even
by preaching at mass) everything they saw and heard during their
journey through the afterlife. Therefore, it is fair to conclude that the
prophetic model, characterized by the order to disclose to men what

---

16   Jacques Le Goff, *The Birth of Purgatory*, trans. by Arthur Goldhammer (Chicago:
      University of Chicago Press, 1984), p. 177. Quoted in *UDC*, p. 143.

17   Teodolinda Barolini, 'Why Did Dante Write the *Commedia*? Dante and the Visionary
      Tradition', in Barolini, *Dante and the Origins of Italian Literary Culture* (New York:
      Fordham University Press, 2006), pp. 125–31 and 399 (originally published in *Dante
      Studies*, 111 (1993), pp. 1–8).

18   Barolini, *Dante and the Origins*, p. 125.

has been revealed to the visionary, is common to all texts belonging to the visionary tradition.

Taking up this model, Dante goes even further by inserting into the *Commedia* more prophetic investitures than his visionary predecessors. He refers directly back to biblical models in order to establish his authority as prophet and poet of the afterlife. Not by chance, Dante always shapes his own prophetic investitures in such a way that they are particularly faithful to the biblical model, starting from Beatrice's pronouncement in the Earthly Paradise. In fact, the very first prophetic investiture of the poem is a direct translation of the investiture of John at the beginning of the Apocalypse: 'Quod vides, scribe in libro' ('What you see, write in a book'), translated by Beatrice as 'quel che vedi, [...] fa che tu scrive' ('transcribe what you have seen'; *Purg.* 32.104–05). While the order to reveal what has been shown during an otherworldly journey is present in nearly all medieval texts about the afterlife, Dante shapes his own prophetic investitures upon the biblical model, neglecting other visionary precursors.[19]

Moreover, Dante places the model offered by Saint Paul at the very centre of his own prophetic identity as a traveller through the afterlife and a narrator of this experience. In fact, in the words spoken by St. James in *Paradiso* 25, 'sì che, veduto il ver di questa corte, | la spene, che là giù bene innamora, | in te e in altrui di ciò conforte' ('so that, when you have seen this court in truth, | hope – which, below, spurs love of the true good — | in you and others may be comforted'; *Par.* 25.43–45), resounds the echo of the Pauline model evoked in the Second canto of the *Inferno*: here Dante says that Paul was transported into Heaven 'per recarne conforto a quella fede | ch'è principio alla via di salvazione' ('to bring us back assurance of that faith | with which the way to our salvation starts'; *Inf.* 2.29–30). Dante's prophetic mission is redefined as similar to that of Saint Paul: they are both allowed to see Paradise so as to comfort, to strengthen in men the hope of the 'gloria futura' ('future glory'; *Par.* 25.68). Not by chance, in the very same canto, David is also evoked as a model for Dante's prophetic identity.[20]

---

19   See Giuseppe Ledda, 'Dante e la tradizione delle visioni medievali', *Letture Classensi*, 37 (2008), pp. 119–42.

20   In addition to the works already mentioned, see Giuseppe Ledda, 'L'esilio, la speranza, la poesia: modelli biblici e strutture autobiografiche nel canto 25 del *Paradiso*', *Studi e problemi di critica testuale*, 90 (2015), pp. 257–77.

As for the model of St. John, in chapter 7 of *The Undivine Comedy*, Barolini explicitly states that 'Dante considered himself [...] a new St. John' (*UDC*, p. 144). In considering Barolini's discussion of the visionary status of Dante's experience (which, in her thorough argumentation, she conceives as a 'waking sleep'), I shall limit myself to underscoring only one particular aspect. One of the strongest objections to the visionary interpretation of Dante's experience is that the allusions to sleep that appear at the beginning and end of the poem (*Inf.* 1.10–12, *Par.* 32.139–41) are weak and vague, while on the contrary, when Dante means to present an experience as visionary or oneiric he does so by clearly constructing a specific frame: he refers explicitly to the acts of falling asleep and waking up with clear verbal expressions for the epistemic modality of such experiences, such as 'in sogno di parea veder' ('in dream I seemed to see'; *Purg.* 9.19) or 'mi parve in una visione estatica [...] esser tratto, e vedere' ('I seemed, suddenly, to be caught up in an ecstatic vision and to see'; *Purg.* 15.85–87).[21]

Regarding the weakness and vagueness of the poet's liminal allusions to sleep, Barolini wisely observes: 'I take their elusive presence as part of Dante's Pauline strategy, stemming from his need to veil in mystery the ultimate mode of an experience that he himself — like St. Paul — was unable to explain [...]' (*UDC*, p. 144).[22] Moreover, Barolini links the Pauline model with Dante's ambiguous discussion of the corporeal status of his otherworldly experience (a problem equally apparent in the medieval visionary tradition) when noting this corporeality in the first canto of *Paradiso*: 'In maintaining an ambiguity that characterizes otherworld journeys of all periods, Dante is deliberately following his avowed and greatest model, St. Paul, whose ambiguity regarding the corporeality of his raptus' (*UDC*, p. 148) Dante imitates. Thus, Dante chooses Paul as a model for those experiences in which vision and voyage do not conflict: 'In choosing Paul as a model, Dante chooses a precursor that "went" as well as "saw"; further, he chooses a precursor who left his mode of going notoriously unexplained' (*UDC*, p. 148).[23]

---

21   See also *Purg.* 17.10–15, 21–25, 34, and 43; *Purg.* 19.10; *Purg.* 27.97–98.

22   Here Barolini refers to Paul in 2 Corinthians 12.2–4.

23   Here the reference is to 2 Corinthians 2.12–13: 'sive in corpore nescio, sive extra corpus nescio, Deus scit', echoed by Dante in *Par.* 1.73–75: 'S'i' era sol di me quel che creasti |

However, the model upon which Barolini bases her consideration of Dante's experience as a 'waking sleep' is instead St. John and his 'venir dormendo con la faccia arguta' (see *UDC*, p. 145), even while quoting a passage by Michele Barbi to remind us that St. Augustine also presented St. Paul as one who 'quasi dormiens vigilaret': 'Bernard's cryptic verse, "perché 'l tempo fugge che t'assonna" is thus to be understood with the help of Augustine on Paul: Dante is as though awake while sleeping, [...] just like St. John, the author of the Apocalypse' (*UDC*, p. 146).[24]

An extremely interesting passage is that in which Dante presents the four animals symbolizing the four Gospels (*Purg.* 29.94–105).[25] In this passage, as Barolini observes, Dante 'tells us, in unmistakable and emphatic terms, that his representational act is to be considered on a par with those of biblical prophets': 'The passage presents a visionary genealogy: Dante moves from Ovidian Argus, to an Old testament prophet, to a prophet of the new dispensation, the author of the text that will appear at canto's end in visionary posture, as the *senex* who approaches "dormendo con la faccia arguta"' (*UDC*, pp. 155–56).[26] I want to stress a point generally unnoticed by Dante scholars:

---

novellamente, amor che 'l ciel governi, | tu 'l sai, che col tuo lume mi levasti' ('Whether I only was the part of me | that You created last, You — governing | the heavens — know: it was Your light that raised me').

24   Here the reference is to *Par.* 32.139 ('But time, which brings you to sleep, takes flight [...]').

25   'vennero appresso lor quattro animali, | coronati ciascun di verde fronda. | Ognuno era pennuto di sei ali; | le penne piene d'occhi e li occhi d'Argo, | se fosser vivi sarebber cotali. | A descriver lor forme più non spargo | rime, lettor; ch'altra spesa mi strigne, | tanto ch'a questa non posso esser largo; | ma leggi Ezechïel, che li dipigne | come li vide da la fredda parte | venir con vento e con nube e con igne; | e quali i troverai ne le sue carte, | tali eran quivi, salvo ch'a le penne | Giovanni è meco e da lui si diparte' ('four animals came on; | and each of them had green leaves as his crown; | each had six wings as plumage, and those plumes | were full of eyes; they would be very like | the eyes of Argus, were his eyes alive. | Reader, I am not squandering more rhymes | in order to describe their forms; since I | must spend elsewhere, I can't be lavish here; | but read Ezekiel, for he has drawn | those animals approaching from the north; | with wings and cloud and fire, he painted them. | And just as you will find them in his pages, | such were they here, except that John's with me | as to their wings; with him, John disagrees'; *Purg.* 29.92–105).

26   For a more recent and extensive treatment of this passage by Barolini, see also Teodolinda Barolini, 'Arachne, Argus, and St. John', in Barolini, *Dante and the Origins of Italian Literary Culture* (New York: Fordham University Press, 2006), pp. 158–71 and 406–11.

the animals which Dante sees differ not only from the ones seen by
Ezechiel (because they have six wings and not four), but also from the
animals seen by John (because they have the same number of wings,
but different aspects). Only Dante saw the animals in that specific form,
and his authority comes both from his vision and from his prophetic
models. Nonetheless, Dante clearly underscores his status not only as
a prophet but also as a poet (i.e. someone who 'sparge rime') so as to
emphasize the poetic nature of his text.[27]

John is evoked three times in the final cantos of *Purgatorio*, and he
holds great importance as the main source of the *tableaux vivants* which
the pilgrim views in the garden of Eden.[28] However, John's importance
as a model for Dante, underscored by Barolini with special reference to
the modality of the visionary experience and to its contents, must be
considered with regard to the role of Saint John as a model for Dante's
own prophetic investiture as well: as already noted, the first of many
investitures he receives in the poem is perfectly modelled upon the first
given to John in the Book of Revelations (1.10): 'quod vides scribe in
libro', 'quel che vedi fa [...] che tu scrive' ('transcribe what you have
seen'; *Purg.* 32.104–105).[29] Thus Barolini concludes: 'The pilgrimage
of Dante's *mente peregrina* is a pilgrimage in the footsteps of St. Paul,
of St. John: the pilgrimage of a prophetic voyeur bent on recounting
in pellucid verse the nonfalse errors of his divine imaginings' (*UDC*,
p. 165).

---

27 For the biblical references, see Ezekiel 1.1–12, and Apocalypse 4.1–8. For my reading
    of Dante's passage, see Giuseppe Ledda, *La guerra della lingua. Ineffabilità, retorica e
    narrativa nella 'Commedia' di Dante* (Ravenna: Longo, 2002), pp. 131–35. See also
    Lucia Battaglia Ricci, 'Scrittura sacra e "sacrato poema"', in *Dante e la Bibbia*, ed. by
    Giovanni Barblan (Florence: Olschki, 1988), pp. 113–23. On the intertwining of
    prophetic and poetics claims in these cantos, see Zygmunt G. Barański, 'Lettura e
    interpretazione del canto XXXIII', in *Voci sul 'Purgatorio' di Dante. Una nuova lettura
    della seconda cantica*, ed. by Zygmunt G. Barański and Maria Antonietta Terzoli (Rome:
    Carocci, 2024), pp. 885–924; Pietro Ruggeri, 'Poesia e profezia nei canti del Paradiso
    terrestre', *L'Alighieri*, 65 (2025), pp. 53–75.

28 See for instance Sergio Cristaldi, 'Un ipotesto biblico: l'Apocalisse', *Letture Classensi*,
    37 (2008), pp. 83–117.

29 There will be other models too, such as Jeremiah for the last investiture in St. Peter's
    words: 'apri la bocca e non asconder quel ch'io non ascondo' ('speak plainly there,
    and do not hide that which I do not hide'; *Par.* 27.65–66), imitating 'Levate signum,
    praedicate et nolite celare' (Jeremiah 50.2).

Chapter 9 of *The Undivine Comedy*, devoted to the Heaven of Sun, is central to the topics I am discussing here. Barolini, among many other things, emphasizes once again the prophetic dimension that Dante claims: 'Dante's stress on prophecy in this heaven is related to the heaven's concern with narrative, his own narrative, for to write a text defined as true [...] is to write a prophetic text' (*UDC*, p. 214).

However, I shall conclude my paper here on the coattails of this suggestion, hoping to have shown that we can detheologize Dante through a discussion about theology, mystics, and religious culture, along with biblical, visionary, and prophetic models. Or, to put it in better terms: not only can we do so — we must.

Divining *The Undivine Comedy*
Reflections and Recollections
ZYGMUNT G. BARAŃSKI

> For Teo naturally, but also for all 'the won-
> derful Americans I've met on my journey' [1]

On the penultimate day of May 2024, Teo and I did something that
we had never done before. We met in the historic shadow of Windsor
Castle — ah Teo, the redoubtable Anglophile — , enjoyed an excellent meal, and, over several hours, never once mentioned matters even
vaguely academic. We were, if truth be told, in the company of Susanna,
her sister, and Maggie, my partner. However, I don't believe that we
were simply being considerate to our family members. We were behav-
ing in a manner that is not common in the academy. We had gone out
as friends and not as colleagues. And let's be honest, when was the last
time, dear reader, that you spent time with a fellow academic without
talking shop…? We had done so without artifice or calculation: our
friendship of over thirty years had eclipsed our professional identities
and concerns.

---

1   The quotation is taken from 'The Great American Novel' by Beans on Toast (aka
     Jay McAllister), a prolific English singer songwriter. The song is found on his album
     Rolling Up the Hill (Xtra Mile Recordings, 2015). It chronicles Jay's musings about
     the US and his doings while on tour, which I find strike a chord with my complicated
     feelings, impressions, and experiences born from my own many years of 'touring'
     North America.

Anyone present at our first meeting in October 1989 would never have imagined that Teo and I would become good friends. All I'm prepared to say about that evening in and around NYU's Casa Italiana is that both of us, in our different ways, can be a bit prickly. Yet, like the proverbial two negatives 'mysteriously' making a positive, the prickles lost their barbs. Irritation ceased. Scholarly respect is a great balm. And when did friendship begin to complement academic regard? To be honest, I'm not sure. I can be certain, however, that by 1992, the year of *The Undivine Comedy*'s publication, we were friends. My copy of the book affirms it: 'For Zyg — interlocutor and friend, with best wishes, Teo' is inscribed in black ink and slightly sloping script on the first page.

I was deeply impressed by Teo's new book.[2] Its boldness and originality, as well as its difficulty — difficulty as a virtue, of course, and not as a *vitium* —, were striking. This was sustained, serious scholarship. I immediately felt impelled to recognize publicly the importance of *The Undivine Comedy*, not least because I had started to hear murmurings — *murmur*, the pernicious whispering sin undermining medieval religious communities — murmurings, I repeat, about the book, which seemed to me seriously to misunderstand and to misrepresent it (on this, more anon). *Speculum* generously allowed me to write an extended review of Teo's monograph, which appeared in 1994.[3] This was followed a year later by an article in *Italian Studies* that attempted to assess the significance of *The Undivine Comedy* and of Giuseppe Mazzotta's *Dante's Vision and the Circle of Knowledge*, which had appeared a year after Teo's book. My review considered the works both in themselves and in light of their relationship to Singleton's scholarship, and more generally to the sway that Singleton still held over North American *dantismo* in the early 1990s.[4]

What was it, over thirty years ago, that had struck me about *The Undivine Comedy*? First and foremost, that it was so unexpected. 'Unex-

---

2   Teodolinda Barolini, *The Undivine Comedy: Detheologizing Dante* (Princeton: Princeton University Press, 1992), hereafter *UDC*. Subsequent references given in parentheses in the main text.

3   Zygmunt G. Barański, review of Teodolinda Barolini, *The Undivine Comedy* (1992), *Speculum*, 69 (1994), pp. 1106–09.

4   Zygmunt G. Barański, 'Dante, America, and the Limits of "Allegory"', *Italian Studies*, 50 (1995), pp. 139–53.

pected' is possibly the wrong term, since Teo had trailed (and trialled) some of her ideas in a series of provocatively innovative articles, of which 'Re-presenting What God Presented: The Arachnean Art of the Terrace of Pride', published in 1987, had swiftly become canonical.[5] Yet, reflecting further, 'unexpected' *is* the correct term. Although *The Undivine Comedy* is distinguished by its rigorous and rich engagement with the tradition of *dantismo* (and not exclusively in its notes, as several reviewers reductively observed), its methodological perspective, its tone, its concerns were vibrantly and excitingly outside the mainstream of international Dante scholarship of the early nineties. A limpidly honest voice willing — if on occasion a bit bluntly — to take to task how we had been and were continuing to read Dante. To put it a bit more concretely, Teo's book constituted a striking departure from and a challenging corrective to both North American Singletonian 'allegorizing' Dantism and the stylistic 'philologizing' approaches of Italian *dantologia*. As someone who, for a number of years, had also been working on questions that were not part of the established primary interests of the majority of Dantists — first the poet's relationship to medieval literary theory, criticism, and exegesis and, by 1992, the impact on Dante of symbolic, hermeneutic, and divinely inspired revealed traditions with their roots in Scripture and Neoplatonism, and more generally what has since become known as 'Dante's intellectual formation' —, I could not but be captivated by someone who was so obviously following her own scholarly interests and enthusiasms rather than timidly adhering to matters and approaches imposed externally by the academy and by the sanctioned norms of our subject. The inherent and continuing conservatism of *dantismo* has long been a bugbear of mine, although it is only fair to acknowledge that such conservatism has its institutional and professional causes and reasons. At the same time, I remain convinced, as does Teo — Zoom is a fantastic bridge for effortlessly spanning oceans, and I write these reflections with her voice in my head —, that an effective way of countering actual or perceived 'crises in the humanities' is to develop strong, independent

---

5   Teodolinda Barolini, 'Re-presenting What God Presented: The Arachnean Art of the Terrace of Pride', *Dante Studies*, 105 (1987), pp. 43–62.

intellectual voices rather than acquiesce and compromise to current fads and orthodoxies.

As I read *The Undivine Comedy* back then, I became increasingly persuaded that, despite some quite notable differences of temperament and manner, as well as of academic preference, I was communing with a kindred spirit. Teo had in fact intuited this before I had, as her dedication makes clear: 'friend and interlocutor' — thank you, Teo. Indeed, as I shall discuss, there were interesting points of convergence between our research projects which, at first sight, might seem very different: the neo-formalist close reader and the cultural historian and Continian neo-*filologo*. And yet, the signs of confluence had always been there. As I write, I am remembering a long conversation that we had one afternoon in Teo's NYU office soon after she had been appointed to her post at Columbia. We were both more than affably surprised to discover that among the Dantists who had had the greatest impact on our thinking were many of the same names. Moreover, these were not necessarily the names most frequently cited or whose influence was readily discernible in the writings of our peers. By the 1990s, how many Dantists in the English-speaking world had made significant recourse to Gianfranco Contini's ground-breaking, genuinely transformative essays on the poet? Indeed, and the same I would say holds true today, how many had actually read him?[6] I continue to think that there is something 'Continian' about the prose style of *The Undivine Comedy*: the lexical and syntactic density, the knowing allusiveness, the at times startling logical connections, and the accumulation of references to different parts of the poem within a single paragraph, within a single argumentative thread. What I'm referring to is, of course, that productive 'difficulty' which I mentioned earlier. And then there was Pat Boyde. Not the co-editor of Dante's lyric poetry, and most certainly not the author of the comfortably elegant but tepidly flat 1981 *Dante Philomythes and Philosopher*, but the Pat Boyde who, in *Dante's Style in his Lyric Poetry* (1971), had originally and suggestively fused medieval rhetoric and twentieth-century stylistics to offer

---

6   Nevertheless, for almost fifty years, Contini's essays have been conveniently collected in the *Piccola Biblioteca Einaudi*: Gianfranco Contini, *Un'idea di Dante* (Turin: Einaudi, 1976).

a description and analysis of the character and development of Dante's style in his *rime*. It is not hard to appreciate how Pat's work could have had a bearing on Teo's engagement with the *Commedia*'s form and on my interest in its poetics. Despite their arch-establishment status — the Scuola Normale and Cambridge — both Contini and Boyde were 'outsiders' in terms of the substance of their Dante scholarship. And that fact, too, is likely to have had an effect on the ways in which Teo and I had decided to pursue our research interests.

What I have conveyed in the preceding two paragraphs is largely written from the perspective of my seventy-three-year-old self. Nonetheless, my fundamental point of departure — *The Undivine Comedy*'s 'unexpectedness' — will always belong to my forty-year-old self. How did I articulate that sense of intellectual and professional surprise, or better, what aspects of the book had captured my attention? Furthermore, reflecting now on *The Undivine Comedy* and on Teo's scholarship more generally in light of what I wrote about both soon after the book's appearance, what did I miss about their significance with respect to the *dantismo* of the early 1990s?

'It is difficult to think of any other book that tells us as much and in such detail about the poet's manipulative formal genius and the ideological and emotional implications of his mimetic strategies'.[7] There is little doubt in my mind that this sentence pithily encapsulates what, at least for me, was crucial and determining about *The Undivine Comedy*. Indeed, I still hold to that view. The same claim regarding its exceptionality, and not simply in general terms, can still be made today. Given the forthright yet apposite manner in which, in *The Undivine Comedy*, Teo, as we all know, deals with the shortcomings of Singleton's essentially content-based approach to matters relating to the *Commedia*'s truth claims, matters which, as she vigorously determines, are also inescapably formal, it would be annoyingly redundant to rehearse them here. Her formalist challenge to Singleton's sway over what had become an accepted and recognizably 'American' allegorical approach to Dante was not just unexpected, given Singleton's persistent and forceful canonicity (in institutional terms too), but it also offered a liberating analytical framework for *The Undivine Comedy*, as

---

7   Barański, *Speculum* review, p. 1108.

well as compelling evidence that American Dantism was anything but a critical monolith. Things could never be the same again, — and they most certainly have not been — in the wake of *The Undivine Comedy*'s publication. The spell had been broken. It had become much more difficult, to quote Steven Botterill — always an acute reviewer of our field —, for a scholar to rely on 'the identification of allegorical meaning in the *Commedia*, when elevated into a principle, [...] to legitimate the creation of the critic's own narrative alongside — or rather beyond — that of the *Commedia* itself'.[8] Teo's rallying call could not have been more different: our responsibility as critics lies within the poem, within its textual weave.

Yet, for all its punchy originality, *The Undivine Comedy*, as I noted at the very start of my *Speculum* review, has some of its roots in Teo's previous monograph, *Dante's Poets: Textuality and Truth in the 'Comedy'*,[9] the implications of whose precisely indicative subtitle, and not just for her second book, have been rather too frequently and unjustifiably 'elided' — in more than one instance literally, by not citing it. The tendency has been to draw on *Dante's Poets* as a sort of 'manual' on the poet's attitude and recourse to several of his key *auctores* — Scriptural, classical, vernacular —, and, as a result, it has been consulted in a piecemeal fashion. At the same time, given the ties between Teo's two books, it is important to acknowledge that, in *Dante's Poets*, there is no explicit challenge to Singleton, although, equally, his presence and influence are significantly curtailed, especially when compared to the work of many American Dantists of the time. He is one among a large body of scholars, normally cited, like others, with respect for a critically useful observation. Only once is his contribution emphasized and distinguished:

> Without denying that Dante subscribes wholeheartedly to the notion that his poem is the instrument of a divine message, I would suggest that as a poetic strategy granting the poet absolute freedom and authority, the fiction of the *Comedy* is

---

8   Steven Botterill, '*Dante Studies* and the Study of Dante', in *Dante and Modern American Criticism*, ed. by Dino Cervigni, *Annali d'Italianistica*, 8 (1990), pp. 88–102 (p. 98).

9   Teodolinda Barolini, *Dante's Poets: Textuality and Truth in the 'Comedy'* (Princeton: Princeton University Press, 1984), hereafter *DP*. Subsequent references given in parentheses in the main text.

> unparalleled. If, in Singleton's formula, the fiction of the *Comedy* is that it is no fiction, then it follows that the strategy of the *Comedy* is that there is no strategy. (*DP*, p. 90)

I find the quotation striking and highly revelatory when considered in respect of the radical ways in which Teo deconstructs and reformulates Singleton's famous dictum in *The Undivine Comedy*. Rereading what she wrote in 1984 alongside what she would write in 1992 offers a telling insight into how boldly and independently her thinking developed over a relatively short period of time. In the article I published in *Italian Studies*, I highlighted both the nature and the consequences of her reaction to and rejection of Singleton. What I have only understood quite recently — inevitably there is something 'schizophrenic' about this presentation as I 'jump', a beloved Barolinian image, between two moments of my academic life now over thirty years apart — is that in its own quiet, understated manner, *Dante's Poets* likewise represents a noteworthy departure from Singleton and Singletonianism.

Especially since the late 1980s, North American Dante scholarship has become closely associated with the study of the ways in which, in his oeuvre, Dante adapted and revised his literary sources in order to highlight the literary and ideological *novitas* of his writings. This trend, of course, marks the principal means by which American Dantism slowly freed itself from the yoke of Singleton's deafness to poetry. This shift, in fact, is especially striking when it is remembered that, in the 1950s and 1960s, but also in the 1970s, American Italianists specializing in Dante showed little interest in the poet's debts to other writers. This situation may be striking, but it is hardly surprising. Singleton had defined, and hence delimited, American *dantismo* in terms of Scriptural allegory and medieval religious culture and theology. The fact that Dante was a consummate poet who would have been interested in other poets *qua* poets, and hence, to put it medievally, in the *lictera* of their poetry, is not contemplated in Singleton's understanding of the *Commedia*. Consequently, he left little to no space for the more strictly literary qualities of Dante's oeuvre, never mind, let's say, for secular pagan Latin poetry. Thus, in his first two books, Singleton never refers to a classical author. In *Journey to Beatrice*, Virgil and Ovid do put in an appearance: Virgil as a key character in the *Commedia*'s symbolic unfolding — 'Virgil is that natural light, being, in allegory, such a light

as was given to the "philosophers" before Christ';[10] Ovid as the poet of
the 'golden age' to which Matelda alludes. Singleton has no interest in
either poet outside the schema of his allegorical reading. When he mentions their texts — the opening of book 1 of the *Metamorphoses* and
Virgil's *Eclogue* 4 — they are subordinated to his ideas about 'justice,
original justice, and how that was lost'.[11] It should come as no surprise
that Singleton's 'allegorized' Virgil should be in close concord with the
Virgil of the allegorists: 'those scholiasts who came to be such great authorities for the interpreting of Virgil's works';[12] while, in Ovid's case,
Singleton embroils the ancient poet in an idiosyncratic and philologically untenable 'allegorical' elucidation, while shifting responsibility for
such an interpretation onto Dante: 'when Dante compares his experience to that of Glaucus who became "consort in the sea with the other
gods," he has more than human souls in mind. The "gods" must be the
angels, *first of all*, even though these do not appear here'.[13] Nothing
could be further from Teo's careful, philologically and textually based
reconstruction and analysis of Dante's attitudes to other poets.

Things had to change. And change they did: first, as a result of
Robert Hollander's work in the late 1960s on the *Commedia*'s debts
to the *Aeneid* and on the importance of the 'literal sense' for any
discussion of medieval allegory; then, and more substantially, with
the appearance of *Dante's Poets*. Teo, I believe, while establishing her
own critical voice, also showed others how to begin to find theirs,
even though it is sad to observe that, for a number of years, rather too
many did not acknowledge what they owed her. Most pointedly, Teo
definitively demonstrated that, to work on Dante, one did not need to
have Singleton at one's side. As its title suggests, the breadth of *Dante's
Poets* is noteworthy and unusual. Ancient epic poetry, the vernacular

---

10   Charles S. Singleton, *Journey to Beatrice*, 2nd edn (Baltimore and London: Johns
     Hopkins University Press, 1977), p. 263.

11   Ibid., p. 196.

12   Ibid., p. 195. Singleton is of course correct to highlight the significance of the com-
     mentary tradition; however, he does this in a largely anachronistic and self-serving
     manner. I have long been disquieted by Singleton's standing as a scholar and his impact
     on Dante studies, especially given his scholarly narrow-mindedness and his notorious
     reluctance to recognize his critical debts. I attempt to assess both Singleton and his
     legacy in Zygmunt G. Barański, 'Reflecting on Dante in America: 1949–1990', in *Dante
     and Modern American Criticism*, ed. by Cervigni, pp. 56–86; Barański, 'Dante, America'.

13   Singleton, *Journey to Beatrice*, pp. 28–29 (my italics).

lyric, and David, 'il cantor de lo Spirito Santo' (*Par.* 20.38), are assessed
in themselves but also in relation to each other so as to reveal Dante's
self-construction as an inspired Christian poet, the main concern of
her book, and, subsequently, a central pillar of *The Undivine Comedy*.
As I suggested earlier, Teo's second monograph grows out of the same
soil as *Dante's Poets*, as is also evident from her assessment of how
Dante draws on the writers of antiquity to 'raise fundamental questions
[...] regarding textuality in general: questions of belief and disbelief,
falsity and truth' (*DP*, p. 212), and from her acute appreciation of the
Commedia's idiosyncratic and revolutionary textuality: 'The *comedìa*
is [...] a genre that is devoted to the truth, rather than to the *parola
ornata*, it may exploit any register — high or low — but depends
entirely on none, since it must always be free to adopt the stylistic
register that most accurately reflects the truth of the situation at hand'
(*DP*, p. 280).

As one ponders, so the mind wanders.... I was supposed to be
concentrating on what I had found noteworthy about *The Undivine
Comedy* when I first read it. Instead, I have allowed present-day reflections to distract and ensnare me. My far-too-active historicist biases
have pushed aside soberly stated intentions of purpose, preferring to
sound trends in American Dante scholarship. If this had been a conventional academic article (never mind a student's piece of writing),
I would now have to rethink, redraft, reorganize. However, for me,
one of the pleasures of contributing to our volume is the possibility
and freedom to think and write in a relaxed, 'spontaneous', loosely
structured, dialogic manner — an extension of nearly forty years of
conversations with Teo, which, in recent years, have become more
frequent and engaged. I know she's going to read me, and so I want
her to hear my voice, to imagine that we're chatting.

Enough! Time to get back to 1994–95. The promise of the subtitle
to *Dante's Poets* had achieved full intellectual and critical flourishing. As
I wrote then (and I don't think I can say it better now),[14] the nub of
Teo's achievement, as I indicated above in passing, was to have established that '[t]he issue of the poem's "realism" (and "its concomitant
surrealism" [*UDC*, p. 60]) constitutes — as it still does today — one

---

14   Barański, *Speculum* review, p. 1107.

of its great interpretative dilemmas [...], a question that affects the poem's every fibre, since "the stylistic correlative to the *comedìa*'s truth claims" is "its manifoldness" [*UDC*, p. 76]'. This is a genuinely key insight — an insight that, more importantly, is given concrete textual endorsement on every page of *The Undivine Comedy*. As I read, I began to think almost immediately how Teo's stress on *stylistic manifoldness* might usefully converge with my research of the time on the *Commedia*'s plurilingual *comicità*, its radically disruptive poetics, especially as we were both endeavouring to account for the poem's uniqueness with respect to its formal inventiveness and its energetic striving for verisimilitude. We were asking the same central question albeit from different yet inter-related perspectives, our abutting aims, even if we didn't appreciate it then, 'to analyze the textual metaphysics that makes the *Commedia*'s truth claims credible, and to show how the illusion is constructed, forged, made — by a man who is precisely, after all, "only" a *fabbro*, a maker [...] a poet' (*UDC*, p. 20).

What I also found energizing and stimulating was the breadth of *The Undivine Comedy*'s vision. It was anything but common to read a boldly overarching investigation of the entire *Commedia*. Fragmentation, unsurprisingly, has always bedevilled the study of the 'sacrato poema' ('sacred poem'; *Par.* 23.62).[15] Yet, I must admit, it was Teo's consideration of one part of the *Commedia* that most appealed to me. What really struck a chord was her rigorous demonstration of the jaw-dropping reductiveness of deeming Dante's portrayal of Paradise as 'cloyingly serene' (*UDC*, p. 167) — both Teo and I see the advantage of a no-nonsense adverb —, of deeming the *Paradiso* a canticle that was disinterested in drama and narrative. Indeed, '[r]ather than content himself with merely saying that heaven is eternal, he [Dante] actively confronts the narrative implications of its timelessness, demonstrating the difference between asserting eternity and representing timelessness in his disparate treatments of hell and heaven'; and he does this by problematizing those indefatigable narrative stalwarts: 'space and time' (*UDC*, p. 170). *Paradiso*, for too long pushed into the background by

---

15   I cite the *Commedia* from Dante Alighieri, *La Commedia secondo l'antica vulgata*, ed. by Giorgio Petrocchi, 2nd edn, 4 vols (Florence: Le Lettere, 1994). English translations are from Dante Alighieri, *The Divine Comedy*, trans. by Allen Mandelbaum, 3 vols (Berkeley: University of California Press, 1980–82).

Inferno's representational vehemence and *Purgatorio's* chiaroscuro nostalgia and biographism, was being returned to the fore of our scholarly attention, as, concurrently, was also being done by Giuseppe Mazzotta and by Lino Pertile.[16] My own serious engagement with the *Paradiso* only begins after the intellectual jolt that I received from *The Undivine Comedy*. The three chapters on the third canticle that cannot but bring to mind, *mutatis mutandis*, Dante's poetic achievements in the third part of his poem, reveal Teo at the height of her critical and analytical powers. By privileging her discussion of the *Paradiso*, am I not in danger of reasserting that hermeneutic fragmentation I have just bemoaned? Possibly. I would prefer, however, to think that, dealing with a book that explicates well and at length the role of paradox in the *Commedia*, I'm simply finding myself caught in the trap of paradox that is an inherent feature of every text and of every act of reading.

Inextricably entwined with questions of form, narrative, and truth is Teo's insistence that Dante's and the *Commedia's* religious claims be taken seriously and approached with respect. Put so starkly, it might not unreasonably be assumed that, on this issue at least, she was following Singleton's lead. And indeed she was — at least to a point. Through his work on the impact of Scriptural exegesis on the *Vita nova* and the *Commedia*, Singleton, especially in contrast to critical trends in Italy, had restored Dante's standing as a religious writer. Yet, as we know, by focusing almost exclusively on the *Commedia's* theological and moral content, Singleton had swept away its poetry. The legacy he left Teo was twofold. On the one hand, and in clear opposition to Singleton's emphases, it spurred her commitment, as we have seen, to the *Commedia's* poetic fabric. On the other, and positively, Singleton's standpoint highlighted the critical need to acknowledge and assess the poem's religious ambitions. However, instead of imprisoning herself, like so many other contemporary American Dantists, within an 'allegorical' cage, Teo turned her attention to other modes of medieval religious writing and, more importantly, she gauged their literary, and not simply their ideological significance for Dante. Poetry

---

16   Giuseppe Mazzotta, *Dante's Vision and the Circle of Knowledge* (Princeton: Princeton University Press, 1993); Lino Pertile, *La punta del disio: semantica del desiderio nella 'Commedia'* (Fiesole: Cadmo, 2005), which collects essays mostly written in the 1980s and 1990s.

and religious belief could comfortably co-exist. Thus, her emphasis on 'visionary' literature and experience, whether in their aulic authoritative expressions — the 'enraptured' Paul of the Second Letter to the Corinthians, St John the recipient of apocalyptic *visiones*, Augustine's and Aquinas's exegesis of both events — or in their hugely successful 'popular' variant of adventurous and graphic accounts of the afterlife, was vital not only for her main argument but also for Dante scholarship more generally. At any rate, it should have been invigorating for Dante scholarship, but, alas, things didn't quite work out in that way, as I shall soon elucidate. In the last twenty or so years, Dante's predominant, wide-ranging, and deep-seated connections to Christian religious culture broadly understood have developed into a major and multifaceted area of research.[17] Yet, Teo's contributions to the field are rarely properly acknowledged or understood. However, I'm getting ahead of myself. More of that meandering reflection....

I'm pleased to note — and I hope that I don't sound too smug in saying this — that I did appreciate the significance of *The Undivine Comedy*'s religious turn. By the early to mid-90s, I was deep at work on the essays that, in 2000, would converge in *Dante e i segni*, which is often credited with opening a space — especially in Italy and in the United Kingdom — for the study of the poet's religious culture. As I grappled, largely in academic isolation, with the implications of Dante's fascination with divinely inspired forms of knowledge, to learn that Teo was taking his visionary and prophetic contentions not just seriously but also as the basis of her re-evaluation of the *Commedia* was invigorating and reassuring. Yet, although Teo is among the scholars I cite most frequently in *Dante e i segni*, I rarely do so with reference to the sacred. The ways in which we were approaching the matter of Dante's religious prerogatives were quite distinct. While I hope that, in examining the role of the *vestigia Dei* in the poet, I was able to keep matters of textuality and truth to the fore, never 'disengaging form from

---

17   See Giuseppe Ledda, 'Cultura religiosa: ricordi autobiografici di un lettore novecentesco di studi su Dante', in *Now Feed Yourself: Anglo-American and Italian Scholarship on Dante*, ed. by Zygmunt G. Barański, Theodore J. Cachey Jr., and Anna Pegoretti (Oxford: Legenda, 2024), pp. 201–27; Paola Nasti, 'Ri-teologizzare Dante? Percorsi e prospettive per Dante e la cultura del suo tempo', *Letture Classensi*, 50 (2022), pp. 63–121, and Nasti, 'Religion and the Religious in Dante Studies', in *Now Feed Yourself*, ed. by Barański, Cachey, and Pegoretti, pp. 167–200.

content' (*UDC*, p. 17, slightly adapted), my emphases were much more culturally historical than Teo's emphases. Indeed, in my review of *The Undivine Comedy*, I did observe that

> what does remain a bit in the shade is the extent to which the problem of the dichotomous relationship between truth and language — 'the gap that exists between what he [Dante] says and what he has actually wrought' [*UDC*, p. 19] — had, for centuries, been central to the symbolic-exegetical character of Christian epistemology. To put it simply, despite the supreme literary originality of the *Commedia*, the questions it raises remain deeply rooted in its own time.[18]

The comment is valid, but it was a tad unfair. Teo's primary interest was, as I have said before, the text and much less the context out of which the *Commedia* emerged.

We all know why *The Undivine Comedy*'s contribution to our estimation of Dante as a religious poet has not just remained substantially unrecognized but has, in fact, also been drastically, unfairly, and grotesquely distorted. That title and that subtitle. Even as insightful and appreciative a reader of *The Undivine Comedy: Detheologizing Dante* as Steven Botterill ends his review of 'this almost wholly admirable book' with a long paragraph that begins '"Almost", because there remains the question of that ill-chosen title'.[19]

I remember soon after *The Undivine Comedy* had appeared, either in an email or in person (this I don't remember), 'accusing' Teo of having 'plagiarized' her title: it was one of my silly remarks that often fall flat. Teo demanded an explanation. *Nie-Boska komedia* — *The Un-Divine Comedy* — is the title of one of the great works of Polish nineteenth-century literature; indeed, despite its recourse to antisemitic tropes, 'a masterpiece not only of Polish but also of world literature',[20] which, like many other works of that most Dantean of centuries, is profoundly indebted to the poet and the *Commedia*. The

---

18   Barański, *Speculum* review, p. 1108.
19   Steven Botterill, review of Teodolinda Barolini, *The Undivine Comedy* (1992), *Italica*, 71 (1994), pp. 404–05 (p. 405).
20   Czesław Miłosz, *The History of Polish Literature* (London: Macmillan, 1969), p. 244. The play has been regularly translated into English, most recently in Zygmunt Krasiński, *The Undivine Comedy*, trans. by Charles S. Kraszewski (Lehman, PA: Libella Veritatis, 1999).

play's author, Zygmunt Krasiński, was twenty — Dante, I like to imagine, would have felt a twinge of irritated envy — when, in 1833, he wrote the prose drama. Krasiński appears to have chosen the title to stress that the setting and action of his play are firmly in the here-and-now, thereby highlighting the stark contrast between the divine order of Dante's afterlife and the decidedly non-divine world that he was describing. For most of the work's four parts, the tenor is bleakly pessimistic: the degeneracy of the nobility, the failure of art, the grim violence of the class struggle, everywhere the pall of death, suicide, disease. And yet, (in)famously, the *Nie-Boska komedia* ends with the revolutionary leader Pankracy, after routing the forces of reaction, having a vision of a burning cross and of Christ. His last words just before he dies are 'Galilaee vicisti!' ('Galilean, you have won!'). The *Nie-Boska komedia* is astonishingly and unexpectedly transformed into the *Boska komedia*.

Something not entirely dissimilar might be said to occur with Teo's title. *The Undivine Comedy: Detheologizing Dante* leads one to expect a study — far from the first — whose aim is to challenge or even elide the *Commedia*'s religious character. And this, alas, is still how rather too many today deem its remit to be. Moreover, especially in Italy, this unfortunate misconception has been bolstered by the shudderingly unacceptable — at least as far as I am concerned — *La 'Commedia' senza Dio. Dante e la creazione di una realtà virtuale* that 'disfigures' the title page of the Italian translation of Teo's book.[21] Teo and I have often talked about her title and the unintended and unexpected effects it has engendered. It is for her to go into detail as to how the titles were finally arrived at. All I feel able to say is that, originally, Teo was considering a title along the lines of the soberly precise *Dante and Narrative*. We have jokingly mused that a book with such a title placed next to my blandly descriptive *Dante e i segni* would have made of them fine companion pieces, which, in many ways, they most certainly are.

Teo lucidly explains the exact meaning of her neologism 'detheologizing'; and her explanation bears repeating, especially given the years of misapprehension:

---

21 Teodolinda Barolini, *La 'Commedia' senza Dio. Dante e la creazione di una realtà virtuale*, trans. by Roberta Antognini (Milan: Feltrinelli, 2003).

> Detheologizing is not antitheological; it is not a call to abandon
> theology or to excise theological concerns from Dante criti-
> cism. Rather, detheologizing is a way of reading that attempts
> to break out of the hermeneutic guidelines that result in theolo-
> gized readings whose outcomes have been overdetermined by
> the author. Detheologizing, in other words, signifies releasing
> our reading of the *Commedia* from the author's grip, finding a
> way out of Dante's hall of mirrors. (*UDC*, p. 17)

In the remainder of her book, as we know, Teo undertakes the task of
'detheologizing' the *lictera* of the *Commedia*, which she accomplishes
with acumen, rigour, and commitment, revealing in detail the workings
of Dante's formal strategies and their repercussions both on the poem
and on its readership. She demonstrates the ever-changing ways in
which Dante's poetry accommodates his religious beliefs and ends —
what she terms his 'theology' —, and the myriad combinations into
which his religious beliefs and ends shape his poetry. *The Undivine
Comedy* leaves no doubt that Dante is both a poet and a man of faith
(I'm loathe to use the tag *poeta-theologus* or *theologus-poeta* given our
increasing understanding of their problematic status, as, for the same
reason, I am reluctant to employ 'theology' and 'theologian' — by the
late thirteenth and early fourteenth century, all these terms were con-
tested and semantically fluid and unstable). To put it simply, Teo fulfils
brilliantly the task she had set herself. Yet, and I can sense the frus-
tration of all of us who have read *The Undivine Comedy* 'tutta quanta'
(*Inf.* 20.114), it is also regrettably the case that her book has been
deemed to argue in favour of the very opposite of what it actually and
successfully proves. One of the problems with neologisms is that their
makers cannot control their reception, especially when one of their
constituent elements already has a deep-seated value in a linguistic
culture. This is the case with the prefix *de-* in English which, with its
origins in the Latin preposition 'de' — 'from', 'away from', 'out of' —,
has connotations implying 'moving away/from', 'reversing', 'removing'.
On glancing at the title of Teo's book, it must have seemed 'obvious'
to some that they had 'divined' its 'anti-theological' message and thus
did not need to investigate further. This is sad. Even more, it is an
indictment of a serious lapse in professional judgment and integrity
that, as academics, especially academics responsible for reading re-
liably, we should do everything to avoid. Yet, I cannot but wonder,

alongside my dear much-missed friend Steven Botterill, how things might have gone if, instead of 'detheologizing', Teo had alighted upon 'retheologizing'....[22]

The moment has come to bring these recollections and reflections to a close. There is no question that *The Undivine Comedy* has stood the test of scholarly time; and I hope that what I have penned begins to give some idea as to why this is so. And there is more. Particularly effective, especially in recent years, has been the influence of Teo's suggestions regarding the intricacies of the *Commedia*'s narrative structure. I must admit that, back in the mid-1990s, I didn't quite realize how significant this aspect of her book actually is. In my review, I refer to it but twice, and then rather blandly and only in the concluding paragraph. The first time I highlight how 'her various arguments are [...] brought back to the central concepts of realism, narrative, and truth' (I'll get to my second reference imminently).[23] I am now well aware of the consequence of Teo's 'narratological' promptings, including those in *Dante's Poets*, not least because they were of value to two of my former doctoral students. Both were interested in Dante's characterization techniques, specifically the formal and structural implications of the *varietas* of the poet's characters, what Teo synthesized as the 'greater textual resonance' and *seductiveness* of some of these.[24]

'She — naturally Teo — offers unambiguous evidence of the co-herence and unity of the *Commedia*'s organization by demonstrating that similar formal and narrative structures, and thus similar ideo-logical concerns, underpin the poem as a whole'[25] — this is of course my second allusion to narrative. I believe I was trying to bolster my first reference. However, while the point I made was not invalid — the continuity of interests and strategies across the *Commedia* — the manner in which I phrased it was potentially misleading. To speak

22   Botterill, review of *The Undivine Comedy*, p. 405.

23   Barański, *Speculum* review, p. 1109.

24   I am thinking of Laurence E. Hooper — who, like Steven Botterill, left us much, much too soon —, 'Characterization', in *The Cambridge Companion to Dante's 'Commedia'*, ed. by Zygmunt G. Barański and Simon Gilson (Cambridge: Cambridge University Press, 2019), pp. 43–60; and of Katie Sparrow, 'Dante's Dantes: Self-Characterization in the *Vita nova* and *Commedia*' (unpublished doctoral thesis, University of Notre Dame, 2023) <https://doi.org/10.7274/1j92g735d7f> [accessed 18 April 2025].

25   Barański, *Speculum* review, p. 1109.

of 'coherence and unity' casts into shadow what, for me today, is most important about Teo's proposals regarding the poem's narrative make up: the fact that 'Dante holds the aporias and contradictions of a prophetically inspired poem [...] within the rigorous embrace of paradox', and that this is especially so with respect to the 'contradictions inherent in the project of representing paradise' (*UDC*, pp. 13, 174). Unlike Teo, most Dantists tend to be blind to the *Commedia*'s structural complexity. Consequently, they do not feel the need to engage with the implications of its formal organization. The very strong impression that emerges from the critical tradition is that, in general, Dante scholars consider the structure of the *Commedia* to be a non-question, since, for all intents and purposes, it has been definitively resolved.[26] As far as they are concerned, at the macrostructural level, the *Commedia* is unproblematically dominated by notions of progress, success, fulfilment, orderliness, and perfection, notions that appear to be justified and regularly reaffirmed by the providential character both of the journey and of the writing. It thus goes without saying that, from this perspective, the *Commedia* is an elegant and harmonious text of concise and ineluctable homogeneity, in which each element functions effortlessly and faultlessly both in itself and in relation to all the other elements that constitute it. Time and again, mechanistically and monotonously, mention is made of a single and inviolate structure that succeeds in tidily circumscribing the development, the logic, the *narratio*, and the form of the poem. Among readers of the *Commedia*, the conviction has spread that, in the poem, and in particular in the *Paradiso*, where — 'sì com' io dovea' ('as I ought') — the *viator* inexorably moves towards God, the 'fine di tutt' i disii' ('the end of all desires'; *Par.* 33.46–47), everything holds and everything fits: 'l'opera

---

26   It is telling that the author of the most substantial book written in recent years on the poem's moral structure should have prefaced his excellent study by writing defensively: 'Even to myself, writing a book about the structure of the *Divine Comedy* seems a very old-fashioned, if not positively reactionary, thing to do. There was a time when books were written on this subject, for the most part in the early years of the [twentieth] century. Nowadays, if the subject is treated at all, it is as a brief note to those few places in the *Commedia* where the structure of the *cantica* is discussed explicitly. As a separate subject, the poem's structure seems to have been exhausted, or discredited': Marc Cogan, *The Design in the Wax: The Structure of the 'Divine Comedy' and its Meaning* (Notre Dame, IN: University of Notre Dame Press, 1999), p. xix.

più saldamente unitaria d'ogni tempo' ('the most solidly unified work of all time');[27] 'il [...] rapporto [di ogni passo] con il discorso generale sviluppato nel poema, la sua connessione con la fitta e complessa rete di messaggi che, intrecciandosi nelle sue varie parti, fanno dell'opera un mirabile monolite, un "Sistema" compatto in cui ogni particolare è in collegamento con il tutto e funzionale ad esso' ('the [...] relationship [of each passage] with the general discourse developed in the poem, its connection with the dense and complex network of messages which, intertwining in its various parts, make the work an incredible monolith, a compact "System" in which every detail is connected to the whole and functional to it');[28] 'Tutta l'invenzione del poema si fonda sull'armonioso ordine che regge l'universo e lo fa simile a Dio ([Par.] 1.103–05): dalla sua struttura primaria [...] alle secondarie, e sempre ragionate, suddivisioni, tutto l'aldilà dantesco resiste come invenzione — quasi un blocco di diamante — per la qualità dotata di ordine, vale a dire di intelligibilità' ('The whole invention of the poem is based on the harmonious order that governs the universe and makes it similar to God ([Par.] 1.103–05): from its primary structure [...] to the secondary, and always well-thought-out, subdivisions, the whole of Dante's afterlife endures as an invention — almost a block of diamond — thanks to the quality endowed with order, that is to say with intelligibility').[29]

From this perspective, throughout the many 'anni' ('years') that made Dante 'macro' ('thin') because of his dedication to the 'poema sacro' (*Par.* 25.1–3), he never deviated from handling and arranging his poetic material with the same measured and harmonizing dedication. As in the 'volume' that 'lega' 'ciò che per l'universo si squaderna' ('binds' 'what, in the universe, seems separate, scattered'; *Par.* 33.86–87) — creation constitutes the ultimate and most authoritative model of the *Commedia* —, each part comfortably finds its place in the totality

---

27   Aldo Vallone, *Strutture e modulazioni nella 'Divina Commedia'* (Florence: Olschki, 1990), p. 172.

28   Enrico Malato, 'Avvertenza del curatore', in Dante Alighieri, *La Divina Commedia*, ed. by Enrico Malato, 3 vols (Rome: Salerno Editrice, 2021–), I: *Inferno* (2021), pp. xix–xxix (p. xx).

29   Dante Alighieri, *Commedia*, ed. with commentary by Anna Maria Chiavacci Leonardi, 3 vols (Milan: Mondadori, 1991–97), III: *Paradiso* (1997), p. 875.

of the whole and in relation to all the other parts: 'The poem, in fine, declares everywhere, with its terza rima, that it is an analogue to God's "poem", to God's book of the created universe. And even as all things in that universe reveal among themselves an order, so the parts of Dante's poem in its symmetries'.[30] In short, the poem and the poet are perfect. Yet, with Singleton once more firmly in her sights, Teo impressively demonstrates, *documenti testuali alla mano*, that, despite its seeming 'diamantine' flawlessness, it is far from the case that, in the *Commedia*, and especially in the *Paradiso*, everything holds and everything fits.[31] We have again allowed ourselves to become confused and mesmerized by Dante's 'hall of mirrors' (*UDC*, p. 17), and have passively allowed the poet to lead us out of the maze. Instead, we should have recognized that '[e]ven the contradictions fundamental to this poem and its poetic authority are confronted analytically, through the syllogistic method' (*UDC*, pp. 230–31) in *Paradiso* 24; that in *Paradiso* 30.28–30 'Dante is constrained to demote his earlier failure in canto 23, which now turns out not to have existed, in order to claim priority for this, his newest failure' (*UDC*, p. 241); and that 'the difference God made cannot be in vain [...]. At the same time, this is an attitude with which Dante will struggle throughout the *Paradiso*, since it also accounts for the specter of disunity in the realm of unity' (*UDC*, p. 182), an insight which Teo has recently reiterated a bit more forcefully: 'il *Paradiso* delinea il conflitto che Dante prova nel cercare di venire a patti col fatto che nel regno dell'unità ci sia ineguaglianza' ('*Paradiso* outlines the conflict that Dante feels in trying to come to terms with the fact that in the realm of unity there is inequality').[32]

This should have been 'all about' Teo. Yet, other American friends have on occasion sneaked in. And that feels right. On the one hand, I

---

30 Charles S. Singleton, *Dante's 'Commedia': Elements of Structure* (Cambridge, MA: Harvard University Press, 1954), p. 58. Immediately after, Singleton refers to 'the unfolding of its [the *Commedia*'s] form as the fulfillment of a *necessary* pattern' (p. 59; my italics).

31 I borrow the image from Lino Pertile, 'Dimenticare Beatrice', in *La punta del disio*, pp. 235–46 (p. 245): 'La mia impressione è che qualcosa non quadri del tutto in quest'ultimo tratto della storia [namely the Empyrean]'.

32 Teodolinda Barolini, 'Il Limbo di Dante e l'equità di accesso: non-Cristiani, bambini, e i criteri di inclusione ed esclusione, da *If* 4 a *Pd* 32', *Italianistica*, 50 (2021), pp. 49–64 (p. 61).

have wanted to stress that Teo's achievements as a scholar and specifically in *The Undivine Comedy* can best be gauged by considering them in relation to the wider context of (American) Dante studies. On the other, as I wrote, I found myself thinking about the fifteen or so years that I have spent in North America since my first visit in the Spring of 1985. Teo is not only very much part of my nearly forty-year American 'journey', but she has also helped shape it, as is also true of the many other 'wonderful Americans' that I have had the privilege to meet. To put it slightly differently, I don't imagine that I would have written this piece, and certainly not in the form it has taken, if I hadn't become something of an 'American' myself. 'Cause I love the American culture, its music, books and poetry | And the wonderful Americans that I've met on my journey'.[33] Thanks to everyone, and with a special thanks to Teo.[34]

READING, JULY 2024

---

33   Beans on Toast, 'The Great American Novel'.
34   I should also like to thank Ed Barański, Ted Cachey, Simon Gilson, and Lino Pertile for their comments on an earlier version of this tribute. Much as I enjoyed writing it, it's a genre with which I'm unfamiliar. I was very much in need of your advice.

IV. DETHEOLOGIZE TO DRAMATIZE

Dante and 'visibile parlare'

LINA BOLZONI

My contribution takes inspiration from chapter 6 of *The Undivine Comedy*, 'Re-presenting What God Presented: The Arachnean Art of the Terrace of Pride'. In this chapter, Barolini provides a metapoetic reading of the terrace of pride, demonstrating in a highly convincing manner that its ekphrastic artwork constitutes 'an authorial meditation on the principles of mimesis as they apply to Dante and to his art',[1] a meditation that immediately violates traditional boundaries because art overcomes nature and because of the involvement of different senses. Moreover, the comparison with the caryatides, whose image 'fa del non ver vera rancura' ('makes the unreal give rise to real distress'; *Purg.* 10.133),[2] tells us that the unreal suffering of the sculpted images causes real distress in the pilgrim-observer. Here Dante describes reality using the experience of art and offers a synthesis of the canto that asks what is real and what is not: 'This line, "la qual fa del non ver vera rancura", epitomizes the theme at the heart of this canto, the question

---

1   See Teodolinda Barolini, *The Undivine Comedy: Detheologizing Dante* (Princeton: Princeton University Press, 1992), p. 122, hereafter *UDC*. Subsequent references given in parentheses in the main text.

2   All citations from the *Divina Commedia* are drawn from Dante Alighieri, *La Commedia secondo l'antica vulgata*, ed. by Giorgio Petrocchi (Milan: Mondadori, 1966–67). Translations into English, with modifications at times for clarity, are from Dante Alighieri, *The Divine Comedy*, trans. by Allen Mandelbaum, 3 vols (Berkeley: University of California Press, 1980–82).

the poet is posing throughout: what is reality, what is truth?' (*UDC*, p. 125). If God's art is real, Barolini argues, Dante's art wishes to represent reality: 'And so we find the programmatic use of a lexicon that blurs the boundary between the divine mimesis and the text that is charged with reproducing it' (*UDC*, p. 126). Similarly: 'the various techniques for blurring the boundary between art and life employed in the representation of the reliefs also serve to blur the distinction between God's representation and the representation that represents it' (*UDC*, p. 130). And: 'the "visibile parlare" of the engravings works to suggest the interchangeability of the two artists and to approximate on the page what God did in stone' (*UDC*, p. 130).

At the same time, Barolini notes — in what, in my view, is one of the most important contributions of the chapter — that Dante is fully conscious of the risks that such an operation entails: his reference to Arachne, who is 'mad' ('folle') like Ulysses, is also a reference to the significance that Ovid gives to this story, and to the risks human representation implies. In Ovid's telling, Arachne presumes to be the goddess Minerva's rival, her 'aemula' (*Metamorphoses*, 6.83): 'Arachne, *aemula* indeed, matches verisimilitude with greater verisimilitude' (*UDC*, p. 131). This is a risk that Dante, however, is determined to assume — all the way to the end.

In this essay I would like to focus on some of the ways that Dante seeks to realize this 'visibile parlare' (visible speech), employing a kind of mimesis that competes with its divine equivalent: 'these cantos speak of Dante's greatness and establish the poet as an Arachne, as *aemulus*; indeed, they constitute in themselves an Arachnean act of emulation' (*UDC*, p. 141). My viewpoint will be above all that of reception, or rather of how the pact that the poet creates with his own readers is realized.

I believe the recurrent use of a lexicon that implicates the visual senses, which picks up on that of the figurative arts — I limit myself to recalling here Beatrice 'col volto di riso dipinto' ('with a smile painted on her face'; *Par.* 29.7) — brings us back to a fundamental characteristic of the poem: that is, the attempt to reveal the afterlife by rendering it almost visible to one's physical eye, as well as to the eye of one's mind, with all that this entails in terms of universal consciousness, a prophetic vision of the present, and interior transformation. For this reason, the Dantean journey is also a progressive training of one's sight. The poet states in *Purgatorio* 26.58: 'Quinci sù vo per non esser più cieco' ('That I be blind no longer, through this place | I pass'). Throughout the poem his guides — first Virgil and then Beatrice — lead him gradually to see, to look fixedly, to forcefully turn his gaze, and to orient it in the correct direction.

The cantos of *Purgatorio* in which humility is exalted and pride is punished give us an extraordinary example of this phenomenon:

> 'Non tener pur ad un loco la mente'
> disse 'l dolce maestro, che m'avea
> da quella parte onde 'l cuore ha la gente.
> Per ch'i' mi mossi col viso, e vedea
> di retro da Maria, da quella costa
> onde m'era colui che mi movea,
> un'altra storia ne la roccia imposta;
> per ch'io varcai Virgilio, e fe'mi presso,
> acciò che fosse a li occhi miei disposta.
>
> ('Your mind must not attend to just one part',
> the gentle master said — he had me on
> the side of him where people have their heart.
> At this, I turned my face and saw beyond
> the form of Mary — on the side where stood
> the one who guided me — another story
> engraved upon the rock; therefore I moved
> past Virgil and drew close to it, so that
> the scene before my eyes was more distinct.)
> (*Purg.* 10.46–54)

Virgil is more than anything the director of Dante's gaze here: at the beginning, he is on the left, on the side of the heart, and following his words Dante moves so that he has the second scene right in front of his eyes. The view, or rather the description of the various sculptures, corresponds to the stopping points along a precise journey that we as reader-viewers must also follow and reconstruct with precision in our mind.

In this particular moment, Virgil's invitation to gaze assumes one of its most convincing, almost expressionist forms. It is an invitation to look at and to recognize the penitents, the prideful bent towards the ground due to the boulders they must carry, such that Virgil himself had trouble identifying them at first beyond their twisted figures.

Within the human figure resides, in fact, the image, or the divine correspondence, which sin corrodes and can even destroy:

> Ed elli a me: 'La grave condizione
> di lor tormento a terra li rannicchia
> sì che ' miei occhi pria n'ebber tencione.
>   *Ma guarda fiso là, e disviticchia*
> *col viso* quel che vien sotto a quei sassi'
>
> (And he to me: 'Whatever makes them suffer
> their heavy torment bends them to the ground;
> at first I was unsure of what they were.
>   *But look intently there, and let your eyes*
> *unravel* what's beneath those stones')
> (*Purg.* 10.115–19; emphasis mine)

The use of 'disviticchia' ('unravel'; v. 118) in these verses makes the reader almost feel the effort of distinguishing or disentangling something that is tightly bound, like a tendril on a plant, and brings back the phonic heaviness of the rhyme 'rannicchia' ('curls up'; v.116). It is again Virgil who signals to Dante the novel placement of the examples of pride:

> ed el mi disse: 'Volgi li occhi in giùe:
> buon ti sarà, per tranquillar la via,
> veder lo letto de le piante tue'.
>
> (He said to me: 'Look downward, for the way
> will offer you some solace if you pay
> attention to the pavement at your feet'.)
> (*Purg.* 12.13–15)

And it is Virgil who, at the end of the path, invites him to lift his gaze, to shift his perspective to see the angel:

> [...] 'Drizza la testa;
> non è più tempo di gir sì sospeso.
>   Vedi colà un angel che s'appresta
> per venir verso noi'
>
> ([...] 'Lift up your eyes;
> it's time to set these images aside.
>   See there an angel hurrying to meet us')
> (*Purg.* 12.77–80)

Let us turn now to how Dante describes the images carved into the wall and the floor of the terrace. His first remark relates to the extraordinary quality of the sculptures:

[...] io conobbi quella ripa intorno
che dritto di salita aveva manco,
          esser di marmo candido e addorno
d'intagli sì, che non pur Policleto,
ma la natura lì avrebbe scorno.

([...] I discovered that the bordering bank —
less sheer than banks of other terraces —
          was of white marble and adorned with carvings
so accurate — not only Polycletus
but even Nature, there, would feel defeated.)
(*Purg.* 10.29–33)

In an ideal competition, these images would be victorious both over nature and over the greatest works of antiquity, here represented by Polyclitus, for they directly convey divine art, of which nature and human art are mere imitations. But Dante tells us something more, and at the same time something less generic. He looks up close, with a fixed and attentive gaze, and communicates to us his reactions as a viewer:

L'angel che venne in terra col decreto
de la molt' anni lagrimata pace,
ch'aperse il ciel del suo lungo divieto,
          dinanzi a noi pareva sì verace
quivi intagliato in un *atto* soave,
che non sembiava imagine che tace.

          (The angel who reached earth with the decree
of that peace which, for many years, had been
invoked with tears, the peace that opened Heaven
          after long interdict, appeared before us,
his gracious action carved with such precision —
he did not seem to be a silent image.)
(*Purg.* 10.34–39; emphasis mine)

The image seems real, endowed with life and voice, thanks to the 'atto soave' (the 'gracious action') of verse 38, the posture and attitude as they are represented. If the 'imagine che tace' ('image that is silent') refers to the ancient tradition in which the visual arts do not possess the voice that characterizes poetry, the reference to the 'atto' — an act that will be reprised shortly, in reference to the Virgin Mary — places prominence on the instrument with which painting can overcome its limitations (as Leonardo da Vinci will observe in detail). Specifically, it impresses a voice and emotions on the images. But this is still not enough:

Giurato si saria ch'el dicesse '*Ave!*';
perché iv' era imaginata quella
ch'ad aprir l'alto amore volse la chiave;
     e avea in *atto* impressa esta favella
'*Ecce ancilla Dei*', propriamente
come figura in cera si suggella.

     (One would have sworn that he was saying, '*Ave*';
for in that scene there was the effigy
of one who turned the key that had unlocked
     the highest love; and in her stance there were
impressed these words, '*Ecce ancilla Dei*',
precisely like a figure stamped in wax.)
(*Purg.* 10.40–45; emphasis in v. 43 mine)

We are well beyond the traditional instruments of the visual arts: here we do not find the artist's inclusion of carved tablets on which one could read the citations that synthesized the evangelical account of the Annunciation. Here, instead, the 'act' is permeated by the word, just like a seal imprints a figure on wax. However, in this case the figure is not the issue, but rather the words that the observers seem to hear, so that the effect is to convey a very strong sense of reality.

This move toward illusionism is made even more complex in the second bas relief, which represents the transportation of the sacred ark along with the punishment of Uzzah, who arrogates to himself a task that is not reserved for him. It also represents the dance of David, the 'humble psalmist' ('umile salmista'):

Era intagliato lì nel marmo stesso
lo carro e ' buoi, traendo l'arca santa,
per che si teme officio non commesso.
     Dinanzi parea gente; e tutta quanta,
partita in sette cori, a' due mie' sensi
faceva dir l'un 'No', l'altro 'Sì, canta'.
     Similemente al fummo de li 'ncensi
che v'era imaginato, li occhi e 'l naso
e al sì e al no discordi fensi.

     (There, carved in that same marble, were the cart
and oxen as they drew the sacred ark,
which makes men now fear tasks not in their charge.
     People were shown in front; and all that group,
divided into seven choirs, made
two of my senses speak — one sense said, 'No',

the other said, 'Yes, they do sing'; just so,
about the incense smoke shown there, my nose
and eyes contended, too, with yes and no.)
(*Purg.* 10.55–63)

Dante is in front of the bas relief with his body, and therefore also with
his senses. What is enacted for us — who in our turn participate in
his experience — is the conflict that is created between the different
senses: between sight and hearing, in relation to the song being sung,
and between sight and smell, in relation to the smoke of the incense
that is imagined there ('imaginato' repeats the same verb used in verse
41 for the representation of the Virgin Mary). The illusionism and the
appearance of life that are properties of the images are here reprised
and reinforced, to the point of synaesthesia: the conflict between the
senses comes into play, and the featured senses widen to include smell.
There is also an example of incorrect reception within the scene being
represented. Michal, David's wife, is the example of someone who does
not know how to grasp the correct meaning, who does not properly
invert the message connected to appearance and to exteriority:

> Di contra, effigïata ad una vista
> d'un gran palazzo, Micòl ammirava
> sì come donna dispettosa e trista.
>
> (Facing that scene, and shown as at the window
> of a great palace, Michal watched as would
> a woman full of scorn and suffering.)
> (*Purg* 10.67–69)

The third bas relief with its example of humility, that of Trajan and
the widow, seems at first less invested in the illusionistic effect: the
widow is 'di lacrime *atteggiata* e di dolore' ('acting as one in tears and
sadness would'; v. 78, emphasis mine), while the splendid emblems,
the golden eagles, seem to move in the wind ('sovr'essi in vista al vento
si movieno' or 'above their heads [...] moving in the wind'; v. 81). But
then a rapid theatrical dialogue comes to life in front of us (the carvings
'pareva dir'; 'seemed to be saying'; v. 83). The exchange concludes
with a gloss or commentary of sorts, in the form of the magnificent
oxymoron 'visibile parlare' ('visible speech'), perhaps inspired by the
formula 'verba visibilia' (see *UDC*, p. 307 note 7) of Saint Augustine,

who uses it incidentally in reference to the corporeal language of actors in the theatre (*De doctrina christiana*, 2.3):

> Colui che mai non vide cosa nova
> produsse esto visibile parlare,
> novello a noi perché qui non si trova.
>
> (This was the speech made visible by One
> within whose sight no thing is new — but we,
> who lack its likeness here, find novelty.)
> (*Purg.* 10.94–96)

What Dante witnessed, we are reminded, is the work of God, who is evoked here with a periphrasis that positions him from the viewpoint of the spectator. The pleasure that the work induces in the observer is connected to the quality of the author, or rather of the 'fabbro' ('maker'):

> Mentr' io mi dilettava di guardare
> l'imagini di tante umilitadi,
> e per lo fabbro loro a veder care
>
> (While I took much delight in witnessing
> these effigies of true humility —
> dear, too, to see because He was their Maker)
> (*Purg.* 10.97–99)

It is also connected to the newness of the artifact, to its being a 'cosa nova':

> Li occhi miei, ch'a mirare eran contenti
> per veder novitadi ond' e' son vaghi
>
> (My eyes, which had been satisfied in seeking
> new sights — a thing for which they long)
> (*Purg.*10.103–05)

Dante thus gives us precise instructions for our reading: we must revive within ourselves the illusion of reality generated by the images, revive their capacity to engage our senses, to create a theatre in our mind. And we must appreciate the unique nature of their maker and their resulting newness, which in and of itself is a source of pleasure. But that is not enough. We are invited into an affective form of involvement, which draws sustenance from the evocation of a shared earthly experience that then is projected onto the places and the images that the poem offers us. This is the case of the evocation of the caryatids, which immediately follows Virgil's invitation to look fixedly and, using sight, *to unravel* the figures who advance oppressed by boulders:

> Come per sostentar solaio o tetto,
> per mensola talvolta una figura
> si vede giugner le ginocchia al petto,
>> la qual fa del non ver vera rancura
> nascere 'n chi la vede; così fatti
> *vid' io color, quando puosi ben cura.*
>> Vero è che più e meno eran contratti
> secondo ch'avien più e meno a dosso;
> e qual più pazïenza avea ne li *atti,*
>> piangendo parea dicer: 'Più non posso'.

> (Just as one sees at times — as corbel for
> support of ceiling or of roof — a figure
> with knees drawn up into its chest (and this
>> oppressiveness, unreal, gives rise to real
> distress in him who watches it): such was
> the state of those I saw when I looked hard.
>> They were indeed bent down — some less, some more —
> according to the weights their backs now bore;
> and even he whose aspect showed most patience,
>> in tears, appeared to say: 'I can no more'.)
> (*Purg.* 10.130–39; emphasis mine)

Here the reference to a visual memory, easily shared by his public, permits Dante to aid in the visualization of the penitents who are atoning for their pride. Analogous procedures to those we have observed in the description of the examples of humility carved into the wall are applied here to the distorted figures of the oppressed penitents: beyond an emphasis on the concentration of the gaze, we find again the thematic term 'atti' ('acts'),[3] which mediates between interiority and exteriority as well as suggesting the presence of language and with language the related emotion (unbearable suffering in this case). The poet's recall of caryatids is directed precisely at generating this affective involvement: the represented bodies and the comparison of them to unreal sculpted caryatids causes real distress in the observer ('del non ver vera rancura'; v. 133). Affective involvement breaks down

---

3   Translated above by Mandelbaum as 'aspect'.

the boundaries between real and artificial for the spectator, so that
one is made to participate empathically in the suffering represented.
The evocation of the caryatids becomes all the more effective in this
context if we recall, as critics have noted, that during Dante's lifetime
two caryatids could be found on one of the doors of the cathedral of
Civita Castellana. Below them we find the following inscription, which
communicates the dialogue between these two sculpted figures:[4]

> Teneas, gative, aiutame
> Non possum quia crepo.
>
> (Help me, you jerk
> I cannot because I'm dying.)

We don't know if Dante saw these figures, even if Civita Castellana is
cited in *De vulgari eloquentia* 1.13.2. Nevertheless, we can bear in mind
that similar inscriptions associated with caryatids could also be found
elsewhere. A reader of the poem could thus recall images that really did
speak, and who expressed, maybe in an efficient mix of Latin and the
vernacular, a suffering without remedy.

There is a functionally analogous reference to the visual experiences of Dante's contemporaries further along: it is the evocation of
'tombe terragne' ('pavement tombs'), or of tombs excavated into the
earth and closed by a slab on which the portrait of the dead person is
chiselled, represented in such a way to recall his or her social status:

> Come, perché di lor memoria sia,
> sovra i sepolti le tombe terragne
> portan segnato quel ch'elli eran pria,
>   onde lì molte volte si ripiagne
> per la puntura de la rimembranza,
> che solo a' pii dà de le calcagne,
>   sì vid' io lì, ma di miglior sembianza
> secondo l'artificio, figurato
> quanto per via di fuor del monte avanza.

---

4   Anna Maria Chiavacci Leonardi, in her commentary on *Purgatorio*, writes: 'in una
     porta della cattedrale di Civita Castellana si trovavano al tempo di Dante due cariatidi
     (ora nella chiesa di S. Antonio), sotto le quali si legge questa iscrizione: "Teneas, gative,
     aiutame | Non possum quia crepo" ("Aiutami, disgraziato; non posso perché crepo").
     L'indicazione è del Fallani (ad locum)'. See Dante Alighieri, *Commedia*, ed. with
     commentary by Anna Maria Chiavacci Leonardi, 3 vols (Milan: Mondadori, 1991–
     97), II: *Purgatorio* (1994), p. 313 note 139. The last reference is to the commentary of
     Giovanni Fallani.

> (As, on the lids of pavement tombs, there are
> stone effigies of what the buried were
> before, so that the dead may be remembered;
>   and there, when memory — inciting only
> the pious — has renewed their mourning, men
> are often led to shed their tears again;
>   so did I see, but carved more skillfully,
> with greater sense of likeness, effigies
> on all the path protruding from the mountain.)
> (*Purg.* 12.16–24)

The reminder of those 'tombe terragne' — pavement tombs that we can still see today in churches, cloisters, and cemeteries and that were a feature of shared common experience — serves to introduce the scenes of punished pride that are carved into the floor of this terrace.

Very striking here is the emotional charge that such a memory brings with it: 'la puntura de la rimembranza' ('the pain of recollection'; v. 20) characterizes an impassioned memory that goes far beyond this passage and involves the entire process of knowledge, of memory, and of transformation that the *Commedia* constructs.[5] There are selected recipients for this action of memory, one that incites only the pious — 'che solo a' pïi dà de le calcagne' ('which only kicks the heels of the pious'; v. 21) — and that is described in terms that reintroduce with effective realism the theme of the 'puntura', as Francesco da Buti noted: 'come si pugne lo cavallo co li sproni che sono a le calcagna' ('as one stings a horse with the spurs at one's heels').[6] The reader is invited to join this particularly sensitive and pious slice of the public: the stinging memory, full of renewed pain caused by the pavement tombs, constitutes the perspective one needs to prepare oneself to 'see' the images carved into the floor of this terrace. Such images, as we are reminded at the end of the description of exemplary scenes, are of a superior artistic quality to those of human art, evoked here with particular attention to the instruments, to the techniques (the brush of the painter, the stick used to draw), and to the 'ingegno

---

5   For further discussion of a 'memoria appassionata' within the text, see Lina Bolzoni, 'Dante o della memoria appassionata', *Lettere Italiane*, 60.2 (2008), pp. 169–93.

6   See Francesco da Buti, *Commento di Francesco da Buti sopra La Divina Commedia di Dante Allighieri*, ed. by Crescentino Giannini (Pisa: Fratelli Nistri, 1858–62), ad loc. The English has been supplied by the translator.

sottile' ('discerning mind'; v. 69) that is required of the artist and/or
their public. The whole culminates in an emphasis on the convincing
illusion created by the images, on their ability to give the impression
of reality:

> Qual di pennel fu maestro o di stile
> che ritraesse l'ombre e ' tratti ch'ivi
> mirar farieno uno ingegno sottile?
>   Morti li morti e i vivi parean vivi:
> non vide mei di me chi vide il vero,
> quant' io calcai, fin che chinato givi.
>
> (What master of the brush or of the stylus
> had there portrayed such masses, such outlines
> as would astonish all discerning minds?
>   The dead seemed dead and the alive, alive:
> I saw, head bent, treading those effigies,
> as well as those who'd seen those scenes directly.)
> (*Purg.* 12.64–69)

But there is something else that as readers we must know how to
see. We must see the acrostic VOM that takes shape on the space
of the page when, shattering the linearity of writing, we revisit the
initial letters of the twelve *terzine* that present exemplary descriptions
of pride: 'Vedea', 'O', and 'Mostrava', each repeated four times, with
the same words forming the beginning of each verse in the thirteenth
terzina that follows (*Purg.* 12.25–63). What we must know how to see,
therefore, is the word UOM or man (U and V were written with the
same symbol in inscriptions). That is, we must know how to recognize,
in the weft of language, the signs or the fragments that we must then
reconstruct into a word that in turn reinforces the apostrophes against
the pride of the 'figliuoli d'Eva' ('sons of Eve'; v. 71).

   Barolini has given a splendid analysis of the artistry of the acrostic,
the 'artificio' ('artifice'; v. 23) that Dante inscribes into his text: 'The
figured ground is imitated by the figured text, which now launches into
its own *artificio*, the acrostic whose *artificiosità*, frequently criticized, is
in fact intended to imitate divine *artificio*' (*UDC*, p. 127). She demonstrates how the acrostic revives, at the level of poetic writing, the
mimesis of the figured artifice: the figured ground of the terrace, she
writes, is imitated and in a certain sense reproduced by the 'figured' text
of the acrostic. For this reason, she notes, the acrostic is not an arbitrary

appendix but is fully inserted into the text. Very meaningful, too, is the comparison that she suggests with *Paradiso* 18–19 in the heaven of justice: *Paradiso* 19 is the other canto of the *Commedia* in which an acrostic appears (*Par.* 19.115–41), and this is the heaven where the souls eventually compose the shape of the eagle and initially compose the words 'Diligite iustitiam [...] qui iudicatis terram' (*Par.* 18.91–93), thus indicating that in God *signum* and *res* coincide.

We can observe, moreover, that the acrostic is a rhetorical artifice traceable to that 'parola dipinta' ('painted word') to which Giovanni Pozzi dedicated a remarkable book, identifying various expressions of the attempt to go beyond the boundary between visible and legible, between body and word.[7]

Here, from this clue, we can begin to interrogate ourselves with respect to the nature of Dante's task, and with respect to the sense of his 'visibile parlare'. Cantos 10–12 of *Purgatorio* seemingly propose no more than ekphrases of divine works of art, situated in the afterlife, which act as images of humility and pride. But we have seen how accurately the extraordinary nature of these works is described, and how little by little we are invited, almost compelled, to make them live again within us. And it is precisely Dante, the poet, who does this and here makes us see, with his words, a new and divine art. The cantos of 'visibile parlare' are a sort of *mise en abyme* of the entire poem — a poem that does not only seek to overcome the boundaries between the worldly and the otherworldly, and to measure itself according to divine excess and the ineffable, but also to show us the world of the afterlife.

It is in this key that the passages in which the language of painting is used to describe poetic writing acquire particular relief. I will present two examples. At the end of the list of the 'spiriti magni' ('great-hearted souls'; v.119) whom Dante sees in the noble castle of Limbo, we read the following:

> Io non posso *ritrar* di tutti a pieno,
> però che sì mi caccia il lungo tema,
> che molte volte al fatto il dir vien meno.

7   See Giovanni Pozzi, *La parola dipinta* (Milan: Adelphi, 1981).

(I cannot here describe them all in full;
my ample theme impels me onward so:
what's told is often less than the event.)
(*Inf.* 4.145–47; emphasis mine)

More elaborate is the implicit pictorial comparison found in the words
of Statius, who in purgatory explains how he became Christian thanks
to the poetry of Virgil:

Per te poeta fui, per te cristiano:
ma perché *veggi mei ciò ch'io disegno,*
a *colorare* stenderò la mano.

(Through you I was a poet and, through you,
a Christian; but that *you may see more plainly,*
I'll set my hand *to color* what I sketch.)
(*Purg.* 22.73–75; emphasis mine)

Drawing and, later, color come to represent various moments in the
poem's narration, which gradually make themselves more precise, and
in fact take on shape and life.

We can additionally see the signs of tension between visible and
legible as it steadily emerges in the poem and becomes an element of
Dante's rivalry with the classical poets, beginning with Virgil himself.
Upon the invitation of his guide in the forest of the suicides, Dante
breaks off a branch from which spill both the blood and the laments of
Pier della Vigna. Virgil will apologize to Piero, explaining that Dante
does not have sufficient faith in what he read in the *Aeneid* (3.22–68)
on the topic of Polydorus:

'S'elli avesse potuto creder prima'
rispuose 'l savio mio, 'anima lesa,
ciò c'ha veduto pur con la mia rima,

non averebbe in te la man distesa;
ma la cosa incredibile mi fece
indurlo ad ovra ch'a me stesso pesa'.

(My sage said: 'Wounded soul, if, earlier,
he had been able to believe what he
had only glimpsed within my poetry,

then he would not have set his hand against you;
but its incredibility made me
urge him to do a deed that grieves me deeply'.)
(*Inf.* 13.44–51)

At the same moment in which Dante shows off his recall of the *Aeneid*, he also underlines the superiority of visibility, of the perceptible experience that creates a credibility much superior to that of words alone ('ciò c'ha veduto pur con la mia rima'; v. 48). It is precisely this eloquent visuality that Dante believes he transmits. We read, for example, at the beginning of canto 14 in *Inferno*:

> Indi venimmo al fine ove si parte
> lo secondo giron dal terzo, e dove
> *si vede di giustizia orribil arte.*
>   A ben manifestar le cose *nove,*
> dico che arrivammo ad una landa
>
> (From there we reached the boundary that divides
> the second from the third ring — and the sight
> of a dread work that justice had devised.
>   To make these strange things clear, I must explain
> that we had come upon an open plain)
> (*Inf.* 14.4–8; emphasis mine)

And shortly after we find the exclamation that demands our attention as readers:

> O vendetta di Dio, quanto tu dei
> esser temuta da ciascun che legge
> ciò che fu manifesto a li occhi miei!
>
> (O vengeance of the Lord, how you should be
> dreaded by everyone who now can read
> whatever was made manifest to me!)
> (*Inf.* 14.16–18)

We may only *read*, but the text attempts to make us participants in the vision that Dante experienced, to make it 'manifest' before our eyes.

As Teodolinda Barolini has shown, Dante is the new Ulysses, and also the new Arachne. Knowing well the risks that his mimesis of the divine entails, the risks of what is effectively a sort of Arachnean competition with the divine, he nevertheless arrives safely in port. At least, that is what he tells us.

TRANSLATED BY LAURA DINARDO

Ovidio senza Dio
Ovidian Myth and Sexual Violence in the *Commedia*
JULIE VAN PETEGHEM

In *The Undivine Comedy*, Teodolinda Barolini defined 'detheologizing' as 'a way of reading that attempts to break out of the hermeneutic guide-lines that result in theologized readings whose outcomes have been overdetermined by the author'.[1] In this essay I will explore how Dante's own treatment of the Latin poet Ovid's *Metamorphoses* may feature aspects of such a reading approach. At the time that Dante wrote the *Commedia*, the interpretation of Ovid's epic poem had been shaped by centuries of readers and commentators.[2] While Ovid wrote the *Meta-morphoses* in a world without God, medieval Christian writers often

---

1   Teodolinda Barolini, *The Undivine Comedy: Detheologizing Dante* (Princeton: Prince-ton University Press, 1992), p. 17, hereafter *UDC*. Subsequent references given in parentheses in the main text. The first half of my essay's title alludes to *The Undivine Comedy*'s title in its Italian translation: *La 'Commedia' senza Dio: Dante e la creazione di una realtà virtuale*, trans. by Roberta Antognini (Milan: Feltrinelli, 2003).

2   On the medieval commentary tradition surrounding Ovid's *Metamorphoses*, see Ralph J. Hexter, 'Medieval Articulations of Ovid's *Metamorphoses*: From Lactantian Seg-mentation to Arnulfian Allegory', *Mediaevalia*, 13 (1998), pp. 63–82; Jamie C. Fumo, 'Commentary and Collaboration in the Medieval Allegorical Tradition', in *A Handbook to the Reception of Ovid*, ed. by John F. Miller and Carole E. Newlands (Hoboken, NJ: Wiley, 2014), pp. 114–28; Amanda J. Gerber, 'Rethinking Ovid: The Commentary Tradition', in Gerber, *Medieval Ovid: Frame Narrative and Political Allegory* (New York: Palgrave Macmillan, 2014), pp. 11–50; Julie Van Peteghem, *Italian Readers of Ovid from the Origins to Petrarch: Responding to a Versatile Muse* (Leiden: Brill, 2020), pp. 18–26.

turned his myths into vehicles that conveyed moral, allegorical, and Christianized meanings. Medieval commentators in particular overde-termined such readings of the *Metamorphoses*, and their interpretations continue to inform the scholarship on Dante's Ovid.[3] Even though in the *Commedia* Dante at times presents moral readings of the *Metamor-phoses* in the vein of the medieval commentary tradition on Ovid's works, featuring *in bono/in malo* readings of the myths of the *Meta-morphoses*, he also frequently engages directly with Ovid's Latin verses, focusing on their literal meaning and paying particular attention to the Latin poet's narrative strategies. As I will illustrate in this essay, Dante's detheologized readings of Ovid vis-à-vis the commentary tradition are particularly prevalent in the *Commedia*'s moments of sexual violence, modelled after stories of rape in the *Metamorphoses*. About half of the stories in the *Metamorphoses* feature some form of coercion or sexual assault, and, like Ovid, Dante likewise does not always make this the focal point when featuring these myths.[4] But while medieval commen-tators diminished or altogether erased sex and force from Ovid's myths of rape, instead making the stories about something else (mainly faith and morality or natural phenomena), Dante at various points in the *Commedia* breaks out of the commentators' allegorical interpretative frame and instead directly confronts the sexual violence and power abuse at the core of Ovid's myths.

In her recent study on Dante and violence, Brenda Deen Schildgen placed violence against women within the domestic and familial sphere, analysing the coercion and violence inflicted upon historical fe-male characters in the *Commedia* such as Francesca, Pia, and Piccarda.[5] Focusing on Dante's readings of Ovid's myths of rape underscores that sexual violence in the *Commedia* extends well beyond the realm of

3   For an entry point into the vast bibliography on Dante and Ovid, see Van Peteghem, *Italian Readers of Ovid*, p. 169 note 1; and Luca Marcozzi, 'Ovidius "regulatus poeta": Dante e lo stile delle *Metamorfosi*', in *I classici di Dante*, ed. by Paola Allegretti and Marcello Ciccuto (Florence: Le Lettere, 2017), pp. 135–55, with a brief overview of the main critical approaches at pp. 135–44.

4   Amy Richlin counts over fifty stories in 'Reading Ovid's Rapes', in *Pornography and Representation in Greece and Rome*, ed. by Amy Richlin (New York: Oxford University Press, 1992), pp. 158–79 (p. 158).

5   Brenda Deen Schildgen, 'Violence in the Domestic Sphere in the *Commedia*', in Schildgen, *Dante and Violence: Domestic, Civic, Cosmic* (Notre Dame, IN: University of Notre Dame Press, 2021), pp. 55–98 <https://doi.org/10.2307/j.ctv19m63z2.8>.

the domestic and targets both women and men. It is too simple to reduce Dante's engagement with Ovid's poetry — especially in passages
where the Latin poet's presence is more elusive — to mere intertextual
flourishes. Violence, as classicist Carole E. Newlands notes, is 'central [...] to the themes and verbal texture of Ovid's *Metamorphoses*'.[6]
Through comparisons with other medieval reader responses to Ovid's
accounts of sexual violence, it will become clear that Dante did not shy
away from this crucial thematic aspect of Ovid's poetry.

THE LANGUAGE OF SEXUAL VIOLENCE

In the *Commedia,* instances of sexual violence do not occur where one
might most expect them: in the circle of lust (*Inferno* 5) and among
the sodomites (*Inferno* 15) in hell. In Dante's poem, the punishments
of the lustful 'peccator carnali' (those who 'sinned within the flesh'; *Inf.*
5.38) and sodomites are not explicitly connected with sexual violence
— a remarkable contrast, as Teodolinda Barolini has often pointed
out, with earlier vision literature and artistic representations of the
Christian afterlife, which featured graphic depictions in word or image
of the sexual punishments of these sinners.[7] The most violent presence
in *Inferno* 5 comes from the force of the 'bufera infernal', the infernal
whirlwind (*Inf.* 5.31) that without any pause 'mena li spirti con la sua
rapina; | voltando e percotendo li molesta' ('drives on the spirits with
its violence: | wheeling and pounding, it harasses them'; *Inf.* 5.32–
33).[8] *Molestare* in Dante's verse — here in *Inferno* 5.33 and in its other
attestations in the poem (*Inf.* 13.108, *Inf.* 28.130, *Par.* 17.130) — does
not have the sexual connotation that the verb contains in modern

6   Carole E. Newlands, 'Violence and Resistance in Ovid's *Metamorphoses*', in *Texts and
    Violence in the Roman World*, ed. by Monica Gale and J. H. D. Scourfield (Cambridge:
    Cambridge University Press, 2018), pp. 140–78 (p. 140).

7   See for instance Teodolinda Barolini, 'Dante's Sympathy for the Other, or the Non-
    Stereotyping Imagination: Sexual and Racialized Others in the *Commedia*', *Critica del
    testo*, 14 (2011), pp. 177–204 (pp. 178–82).

8   The text is quoted from Dante Alighieri: *'La Commedia' secondo l'antica vulgata*, ed.
    by Giorgio Petrocchi, Società Dantesca Italiana, Edizione Nazionale, 2nd rev. edn, 4
    vols (Florence: Le Lettere, 1994). English translations come from Dante Alighieri, *The
    Divine Comedy*, trans. by Allen Mandelbaum, 3 vols (Berkeley: University of California
    Press, 1980–82).

Italian and its English cognate 'to molest'. Similarly, the violent force
of *rapina* is, at least in the poetry of Dante, physical but not sexual.[9]

Rapina's Latin root, *rapere*, however, lays bare the difficulty in adequately rendering in English what this Latin verb and the cluster of
words derived from it, both in Latin (e.g., *raptus, raptio*) and in Italian
(e.g., *rapina, rapinare, rapire, ratto*), precisely indicated in the Middle
Ages. Literally meaning 'to violently carry off', *rapere* already in classical Latin expanded its meaning over time from the forceful seizure
of material goods to include the abduction of women. In Roman law,
raptus was 'the abduction of a woman against the will of the person
under whose authority she lived',[10] but, as Mariah L. Cooper notes, it
'did not necessarily include coitus'. During the Middle Ages, however,
raptus 'became synonymous with abduction and/or sexual violence'.[11]
In Gratian's *Decretum*, *raptus* is one of five different kinds of 'illegal
coitus'.[12] Not every illicit coitus should be called *raptus*, we read in
Gratian; it refers to when a girl is 'violently ('uiolenter') taken away
from her father's house, in order to have her, after she has been corrupted ('corrupta'), as his wife, whether the force ('uis') be carried
out only on the girl, or only on her relatives, or on both' (*Dec. C. 36*

---

9   The word *rapina* was attested with sexual connotations during Dante's time: we find
    'rapina di lussuria', perhaps not surprisingly so, in the Tuscan translations of Ovid's
    Ars Amatoria (late thirteenth–early fourteenth century). On these translations see
    Publius Ovidius Naso, *I volgarizzamenti trecenteschi dell'"Ars amandi' e dei 'Remedia
    amoris'*, ed. by Vanna Lippi Bigazzi, 2 vols (Florence: Accademia della Crusca, 1987).
    'Veneris [...] rapina' in Ovid's verses 'quaecumque est Veneris subita uiolata rapina, |
    gaudet' (*Ars am.* 1.675–76) in Italian translation became 'Qualunque rapina di lussuria
    è isforzata, si gode' (p. 255), and the less accurate 'qualunque cosa le sia fatta per subita
    rapina di lussuria, ella se ne rallegrerà' (p. 428). The original text of Ovid's amatory
    works is quoted from Publius Ovidius Naso, *Amores; Medicamina Faciei Femineae;
    Ars Amatoria; Remedia Amoris*, ed. by Edward J. Kenney, rev. edn (Oxford: Oxford
    University Press, 1994).

10 James A. Brundage, 'Rape and Seduction in the Medieval Canon Law', in *Sexual
    Practices and the Medieval Church*, ed. by Vern L. Bullough and James A. Brundage
    (Amherst, NY: Prometheus Books, 1982), pp. 141–48 (p. 141).

11 Mariah L. Cooper, *Representations of Rape and Consent in Medieval English Laws and
    Literature* (Leeds: Arc Humanities Press, 2024), p. 6.

12 See the brief discussion in Elena Lombardi, '"Che libito fe' licito in sua legge": Lust
    and Law, Reason and Passion in Dante', in *Dantean Dialogues: Engaging with the
    Legacy of Amilcare Iannucci*, ed. by Maggie Kilgour and Elena Lombardi (Toronto:
    University of Toronto Press, 2013), pp. 125–54 (p. 130) <https://doi.org/10.3138/
    9781442663213-008>. See also Schildgen, 'Violence in the Domestic Sphere', p. 61.

q. 1 c. 2).[13] Not every *raptus* was rape as it is understood today, but force was always part of it. Thus, when Dante's Piccarda in the heaven of the moon tells the pilgrim that her brother's men 'fuor mi rapiron de la dolce chiostra' ('took me — violently — from my sweet cloister'; *Par.* 3.107), she is not talking about sexual assault; rather, she means that they forced her by violent means to abandon monastic life for a politically advantageous marriage arranged by her brother.[14]

Within the realms of medieval Christian mysticism, *raptus* took on a different meaning. As Dyan Elliott describes, in that context the term *raptus* (rapture in English) denoted 'a trance-like state of abstraction induced by proximity to the Godhead', the 'idea of being physically overpowered by the divine presence', an experience which for some, like Thomas of Aquinas, took on violent connotations.[15] This concept is also featured in Dante's *Commedia*, most notably in the references to Saint Paul's rapture into the third heaven (2 Corinthians 12.2–4). '"Io non Enëa, io non Paulo sono"' ('"For I am not Aeneas, am not Paul"'; *Inf.* 2.32), a doubtful pilgrim told his newly minted guide Virgilio in the dark wood after learning of his upcoming journey from hell to heaven — Paul's *raptus* and Aeneas's descent into Hades (*Aeneid* 6) served as notable precedents of living men visiting the afterworld. At the opening of *Paradiso*, Paul's rapture is again evoked when the pilgrim, together with his guide Beatrice, moves from earthly paradise on top of mount purgatory to the first heaven of paradise (*Paradiso* 1). Dante does not call this ascent a rapture — he coins the phrase 'trasumanar' (*Par.* 1.70) and illustrates the concept with the transformation of Ovid's Glaucus (*Par.* 1.67–72) — but Pauline language permeates the passage.[16]

---

13   For the relevant Latin text of the *Decretum* see Lombardi, '"Che libito fe' licito"', pp. 146–47 note 12. Translation mine.

14   See the Piccarda episode in Schildgen, 'Violence in the Domestic Sphere', pp. 72–90.

15   Dyan Elliott, 'Raptus/Rapture', in *The Cambridge Companion to Christian Mysticism*, ed. by Amy Hollywood and Patricia Z. Beckman (Cambridge: Cambridge University Press, 2012), pp. 189–99 (p. 189) <https://doi.org/10.1017/CCO9781139020886.013>.

16   See Kevin Brownlee, 'Pauline Vision and Ovidian Speech in *Paradiso* I', in *The Poetry of Allusion: Virgil and Ovid in Dante's 'Commedia'*, ed. by Rachel Jacoff and Jeffrey T. Schnapp (Stanford: Stanford University Press, 1991), pp. 202–13 <https://doi.org/10.1515/9781503623422-017>.

At a previous moment of transition in the poem, Dante does explicitly recall the concept of mystical rapture through the use of the verb *rapire*. In *Purgatorio*, the poet marks the transition from ante-purgatory to the gate of purgatory with a dream experienced by the pilgrim, in which an eagle 'terribil come folgor discendesse' ('terrible as lightning, it | swooped') seemed to have snatched him up ('me rapisse suso') to the flames (*Purg.* 9.29–30). In this passage Dante exploits the multiple meanings of *rapire*: it is the mystical experience to be transported closer to (a pagan or Christian) god, the abduction of a person, and the sexual violence that accompanies that act. The earlier reference to the Ovidian myth of Ganymede (*Purg.* 9.19–24) makes clear that Dante indeed intended *rapire* also to evoke rape as we understand it today.[17] The eagle is the bird of Jupiter, king of Roman gods who, as we read in Ovid, burned with love ('amore | arsit') for Ganymede (*Met.* 10.155–56)[18] and took on the shape of an eagle, the only bird who could also carry his characteristic lightning bolts (*Met.* 10.158), spreading his wings up into the air in order to snatch ('abripit') Ganymede away (10.159–60). Ovid's *abripere* (an intensified *rapere*) becomes 'fu ratto' in Dante's account of the myth:

> in sogno mi parea veder sospesa
> un'aguglia nel ciel con penne d'oro,
> con l'ali aperte e a calare intesa;
>   ed esser mi parea là dove fuoro
> abbandonati i suoi da Ganimede,
> quando fu ratto al sommo consistoro.
>
>   (in dream I seemed to see an eagle poised,
> with golden pinions, in the sky: its wings
> were open; it was ready to swoop down.
>   And I seemed to be there where Ganymede
> deserted his own family when he
> was snatched up for the high consistory.)
> (*Purg.* 9.19–24)

---

17   On this episode see especially Bruce W. Holsinger, 'Sodomy and Resurrection: The Homoerotic Subject of the *Divine Comedy*', in *Premodern Sexualities*, ed. by Louise Fradenburg and Carla Freccero (New York: Routledge, 1996), pp. 243–74 (pp. 252–59); Leyla M. G. Livraghi, '*Raptus* e *deificatio* ovidiani nel sistema della *Commedia*', in *Ortodossia ed eterodossia in Dante Alighieri: atti del convegno di Madrid (5–7 novembre 2012)*, ed. by Carlota Cattermole, Celia de Aldama, and Chiara Giordano (Alpedrete: Ediciones de la Discreta, 2014), pp. 691–709.

18   The text is quoted from Ovid, *Metamorphoses*, ed. by Richard J. Tarrant (Oxford: Oxford University Press, 2004).

Ovid well documents Jupiter's predatory behaviour toward boys and girls, often in animal disguise, in the *Metamorphoses*.[19] If there would be any doubt about the sexual nature of these *raptus*, the pregnancies that often follow effectively underscore it. Dante tempers the violence of the Ganymede myth in his purgatorial dream by mentioning next the Greek hero Achilles who woke up, confused, in an unknown location — his mother had secretly carried him away while asleep to avoid the Trojan War draft (*Purg.* 9.34–42). While still done without Achilles's consent, this abduction was not violent and was motivated by maternal love — quite the contrast with Jupiter's *raptus* of Ganymede in the shape of an eagle, the majestic bird of prey. It is precisely this combination of animal imagery and Ovidian myth that defines the passages in Dante's poem where sexual assault is most clearly depicted: canto 25 of the *Inferno*.

In the seventh ditch of Dante's *Malebolge* (*Inferno* 24–25), the fraudulent thieves are punished. Those who stole in life have their human shape taken from them in the afterlife, as they are transformed into snakes and other hybrid creatures. The descriptions of these transformations are some of the most graphic and violent scenes in Dante's poem. After first seeing a giant heap of slithering snakes (the souls of thieves who had already turned into serpents), the pilgrim and Virgilio witness three transformations: the thief Vanni Fucci, bitten by a snake, bursts into flames and immediately rises from his ashes like a phoenix, taking on his former shape once again (*Inf.* 24.97–118); a snake-shaped thief violently attacks a human-shaped thief, morphing into a single creature that is half-man, half-snake (*Inf.* 25.49–78); and a snake-shaped thief attacks a human-shaped thief, with the two exchanging forms (*Inf.* 25.79–141).

As scholars have long noted, these Dantean transformations are modelled after stories in Ovid's *Metamorphoses*: Vanni Fucci's transformation should be read alongside Pythagoras's description of the phoenix (*Met.* 15.391–407), the hybrid man-snake transformation alongside the story of Salmacis and Hermaphroditus (*Met.* 4.274–

---

19   See James Robson, 'Bestiality and Bestial Rape in Greek Myth', in *Rape in Antiquity: Sexual Violence in the Greek and Roman Worlds*, ed. by Susan Deacy and Karen F. Pierce (London: Duckworth, 1997), pp. 65–96 (pp. 83–88).

388), and the man-snake shape-swap alongside the myth of Cadmus and Harmonia (*Met.* 3.95–114 and 4.563–603).[20] Dante is not coy about the Latin poet's relevance: right before the final transformation in *Inferno* 25, he calls out Ovid together with Lucan, who went deep into snake lore in book 9 of his epic poem *Pharsalia*. Dante boasts: 'Taccia Lucano [...] del misero Sabello e di Nasidio', 'Taccia di Cadmo e d'Aretusa Ovidio' ('Let Lucan now be silent, where he sings | of sad Sabellus and Nasidius', 'Let Ovid now be silent, where he tells | of Cadmus, Arethusa'; *Inf.* 25.94–97). In other words, be silent now, classical poets, on the transformations of your characters; Ovid 'due nature mai a fronte a fronte | non trasmutò' ('never did | transmute two natures, face to face'; *Inf.* 25.100–01), as Dante was about to do. Dante's numerous literary borrowings from these two singled-out Latin poets, in a *bolgia* of hell meant to punish theft, bring to the foreground questions about poetic authority and influence, as well as Dante's positioning of his Christian poetry in the vernacular against pagan Latin verses.[21] My focus here is on Dante's poetic choice to adopt Ovid's imagery of sexual assault through his reading of the Salmacis and Hermaphroditus story.[22] Especially when comparing Dante's rendition of Salmacis's

---

20   To explore Ovid's and Dante's parallel passages side by side, see *Intertextual Dante*, ed. by Julie Van Peteghem, *Digital Dante* (Columbia University Libraries, 2017) <https://digitaldante.columbia.edu/intertexual-dante-vanpeteghem/>.

21   See in particular Robert J. Ellrich, 'Envy, Identity, and Creativity: *Inferno* 24–25', *Dante Studies*, 102 (1984), pp. 61–80; Caron Ann Cioffi, 'The Anxieties of Ovidian Influence: Theft in *Inferno* 24 and 25', *Dante Studies*, 112 (1994), pp. 77–100; Leyla M. G. Livraghi, 'Esemplarità del mito e agone con gli antichi in *Inferno* 24– 25', in *I classici di Dante*, ed. by Paola Allegretti and Marcello Ciccuto (Florence: Le Lettere, 2017), pp. 59–90; and Leyla M. G. Livraghi, 'Sabello e Nasidio, Cadmo e Aretusa: strategie dell'*aemulatio* dantesca nelle metamorfosi di *Inferno* 25', *Dante: Rivista internazionale di studi su Dante Alighieri*, 14 (2017), pp. 55–66.

22   I briefly mention two less prominent Ovidian myths that further inform Dante's descriptions of sexual violence in this canto. Dante's mention of the nymph Arethusa in 'Taccia di Cadmo e d'Aretusa Ovidio' (*Inf.* 25.97) has long puzzled Dante scholars, since this Ovidian character (*Met.* 5.572–641) seemingly plays no role in *Inferno* 25. The entry point to Arethusa's relevance, as Teodolinda Barolini rightly signaled, is the rape occurring in Ovid's account. See Teodolinda Barolini, '*Inferno* 25: Shape, Substance, Sex, Self', in *Commento Baroliniano*, *Digital Dante* (Columbia University Libraries, 2018), pars. 49–50 <https://digitaldante.columbia.edu/dante/divine-comedy/inferno/inferno-25/> [accessed 29 May 2025]. The Theban prophet Tiresias (*Met.* 3.316–38) appears among the diviners punished in the fourth ditch of the *Malebolge*, where Dante recounts his transformation from man to woman and back to man (*Inf.* 20.40–45). Both these transformations occurred when Tiresias disturbed

sexual aggression in the *Commedia* with the interpretations in medieval commentaries on the *Metamorphoses*, Dante's distinct reading
practices are on full display.

READING OVID'S STORY OF SALMACIS AND HERMAPHRODITUS IN THE MIDDLE AGES

Today rape is no longer 'the dirty little secret of Ovidian scholarship', as
the classicist Leo C. Curran wrote in 1978,[23] even though until Stephanie McCarter's 2022 translation of the *Metamorphoses*, Ovid's Latin
accounts of sexual assault had largely remained 'lost in translation'.[24] At
the time, Curran criticized his field's refusal to take rape seriously and
the 'commentators' arabesques of euphemism' around this prevalent
topic in Ovid's poem.[25] In 'Reading Ovid's Rapes' (1992), Amy Richlin further unpacked her fellow classicists' treatment of sexual assault in
the *Metamorphoses*, noting that critics 'have ignored [Ovid's stories of
rape], or traced their literary origins, or said they stood for something
else or evidenced the poet's sympathy with women'.[26] Richlin likely
did not intend her observation to have such a long reach, but with the
exception of Ovid's presumed sympathy for the violated women (of no
interest to medieval commentators), these different critical responses
to Ovid's rapes are also found in the medieval commentaries on the
Metamorphoses, as will become clear from their interpretations of the
Salmacis and Hermaphroditus story. These commentators rarely speak
in one voice,[27] but they all do, to use Curran's phrase, 'arabesques'

---

mating serpents, as Ovid writes (*Met.* 3.325), which Dante repeats ('li duo serpenti
avvolti', 'the two entwining serpents'; *Inf.* 20.44) and then evokes again in the violent
copulation scenes in *Inferno* 25.

23   Leo C. Curran, 'Rape and Rape Victims in the *Metamorphoses*', *Arethusa*, 11.1–2
     (1978), pp. 213–41 (p. 214). For a short overview of the current scholarship, see Ovid,
     Change Me: Stories of Sexual Transformation from Ovid, trans. by Jane Alison (Oxford:
     Oxford University Press, 2014), p. 137.

24   Stephanie McCarter has written extensively about the reticence around rape in the
     poem's modern English translations. See, for instance, Ovid, *Metamorphoses*, trans. by
     Stephanie McCarter (New York: Penguin Books, 2022), pp. xxi–xxx, xxxiv–xxxv.

25   Curran, 'Rape and Rape Victims', p. 215.

26   Richlin, 'Reading Ovid's Rapes', p. 158.

27   As I summarized in Van Peteghem, *Italian Readers of Ovid*, p. 19: 'The medieval
     Ovidian commentary tradition is not a monolith, but a diverse, varied, and changing
     corpus of texts'. See also the works cited in note 3.

around Salmacis's sexual assault.[28] And while their conclusions about the story's meaning may at times baffle us readers today, they had clearly read their Ovid and engaged with specific passages in this myth. So let us start with a summary of the story.

In the *Metamorphoses*, we find the story of Salmacis and Hermaphroditus in book 4 (vv. 274–388), as part of the stories the daughters of the Boethian king Minyas tell each other while abstaining from the festivities for the god Bacchus. The narrator Alcithoë announces she will tell how the spring Salmacis, which makes the limbs of anyone who entered its waters soft, got its bad reputation (vv. 285–87). The young boy, Hermaphroditus, son of Mercury (Hermes) and Venus (Aphrodite) with traits of both in his face and his name (vv. 290–91), had left his native mountains to travel the world and one day ended up in Caria near this Salmacis spring (vv. 288–301) — the territory of the namesake nymph Salmacis. Unlike other followers of the virgin goddess Diana, Salmacis showed no interest in hunting, but instead enjoyed doing her hair, lounging by the spring, and picking flowers (vv. 302–15). Salmacis is immediately taken by Hermaphroditus: the moment she saw him, she had to have him (vv. 316–19). The nymph does not turn to force right away; she first flatters Hermaphroditus with words, which makes the boy, who did not know what love was, blush and become even more attractive to her (vv. 320–33). Unable to contain herself, Salmacis then tries to steal a kiss, but Hermaphroditus threatens to go away if she does not leave him alone. Salmacis ostensibly complies, but hides nearby the spring to keep gazing at the boy, who, thinking he is finally alone, undresses and gets into the water (vv. 334–55). At the sight of his naked body, Salmacis can no longer contain herself. She jumps into the spring and triumphantly forces her-

---

28   On the medieval reception of Ovid's stories of rape, see Mark Amsler, 'Rape and Silence: Ovid's Mythography and Medieval Readers', in *Representing Rape in Medieval and Early Modern Literature*, ed. by Elizabeth Robertson and Christine M. Rose (New York: Palgrave Macmillan, 2001), pp. 61–96, which focuses on the commentary tradition and the literary works of Chaucer, Gower, and Christine de Pizan. Enenkel studied the early modern reception of the myth of Salmacis and Hermaphroditus in the commentaries (from the fourteenth century on) and in the visual arts in Karl Enenkel, 'Salmacis, Hermaphrodite, and the Inversion of Gender: Allegorical Interpretations and Pictorial Representations of an Ovidian Myth, ca. 1300–1770', in *The Figure of the Nymph in Early Modern Culture*, ed. by Karl Enenkel and Anita Traninger (Leiden: Brill, 2018), pp. 53–148 <https://doi.org/10.1163/9789004364356_004>.

self on Hermaphroditus, who fails to push off her aggressive advances (vv. 356–70). Two transformations occur in the conclusion of the story — the prayers of both Salmacis and Hermaphroditus are heard. Before jumping in the water, Salmacis prays to the gods that they may be together forever (vv. 370–72). Salmacis's rape of Hermaphroditus leads to the two fusing together; Hermaphroditus becomes a half-man ('semimarem', v. 381, 'semiuir', v. 386), a child of two forms ('biformis', v. 387). The violated and transformed Hermaphroditus requests his divine parents that from now on anyone entering the spring be altered the same way he was, thus transforming the waters of the Salmacis spring (vv. 380–88).

The commentary on the *Metamorphoses* by the French schoolmaster Arnulf of Orléans (second half of the twelfth century) offers a good entry point into the medieval reader responses to this Ovidian story. Arnulf divided his commentary into three parts: philological glosses, lists of all the *mutationes* pertaining to each book, and allegorical explanations of those 'mutations'.[29] On Arnulf's list of transformations featured in book 4, we find 'Salmacis in fontem. Ermofroditus in semivirum' ('Salmacis [transformed] into a spring. Hermaphroditus [transformed] into a half-man').[30] In his two-sentence note, Arnulf first traces Hermaphroditus's genealogy, and then explains the meaning of Salmacis and Hermaphroditus: 'coniuncti fuerunt, id est se compassibili et indissolubili amore dilexerunt. De fonte nihil aliud est

---

29   Arnulf's allegorical readings differ from the oldest surviving commentary on the *Metamorphoses*, the *Metamorphoseon narrationes* (probably fifth or sixth century). The *Narrationes*, short prose summaries inserted in between Ovid's stories, survived in seven medieval manuscripts, including three written in Italy (Van Peteghem, *Italian Readers of Ovid*, pp. 20–21). Even though the *narratio* on Salmacis and Hermaphroditus is on the longer side, it still packs the story's main events into just fourteen lines (Publius Ovidius Naso, *Metamorphoseon Libri xv, Lactanti Placidi Qui Dicitur Narrationes Fabularum Ovidianarum*, ed. by Hugo Magnus (Weidmann, 1914; repr. New York: Arno Press, 1979), pp. 648–49).

30   The text is cited from *Ovide moralisés latins: Arnoul d'Orléans, 'Allegoriae'; Jean de Garlande, 'Integumenta'; Giovanni del Virgilio, 'Allegoriae'*, ed. by Jean-Marie Fritz with the collaboration of Cristina Noacco (Paris: Classiques Garnier, 2022), pp. 132–33. Translation mine. Adding *tituli* to Ovid's myths was common practice in commentaries, and is still custom in many translations. Stephanie McCarter's different translation approach is clear in her title for this story: 'Salmacis rapes Hermaphroditus' (Ovid, *Metamorphoses*, p. 105). As Jean-Marie Fritz noted, this *allegoria* of the story is absent from many manuscripts, even though Salmacis and Hermaphroditus are consistently featured among the book 4 *mutationes* (p. 133 note 95).

quam locus ille deliciosus erat, et ex nimiis deliciis sequitur luxus et effeminatio quoniam loca placentia invitant nos ad pausandum' ('they were joined together, that is, they held each other dear in a passionate and indissoluble love. The spring is nothing else than a lovely place, and from excessive delights follow debauchery and feminine softness because pleasant places invite us to pause'). As we see here for the first time, Arnulf cancelled Salmacis's aggression and Hermaphroditus's firm refusal from Ovid's story: it was love ('amore dilexerunt') and the two literally became inseparable (Arnulf's adjective 'indissoluble' was clearly chosen with the location of their 'love' encounter, the spring, in mind). In his moralizing reading, Arnulf did not point the finger at Salmacis, the aggressor in Ovid's tale, but at anyone who, like Hermaphroditus, stops to enjoy a pleasant place. And enjoying such pleasantries in excess leads to *luxus* and *effeminatio*.

The English schoolmaster John of Garland followed Arnulf's example in his *Integumenta Ovidii*, a 520-verse long commentary on select Ovidian myths (ca. 1230), and also read the *Metamorphoses* through an allegorical lens, setting out to reveal the 'sermo [...] uerus' ('true account') of Ovid's stories, hidden under the cover ('integumentum') of history (vv. 57–62).[31] John does not shy away from the sex featured in the myth of Salmacis and Hermaphroditus, but interprets it in purely biological terms (vv. 193–94): 'Cellula matricis fons fertur Salmacis in qua | infans conceptus hermofroditus erit' ('The spring Salmacis is said to be the chamber of the womb in which the hermaphrodite child is conceived'). This reference to the *cellulae* of the womb in a literary commentary illustrates how concepts from medieval embryology had become widespread during the thirteenth century. Medieval naturalists, as Leah DeVun has most recently analysed, designated a place for intersex individuals, referred to as hermaphrodites, within biological reproduction.[32] In their view, the womb consisted of multiple chambers (ranging from three to seven), and the sperm's location, together with the quality and the quantity

---

31   The text is quoted from John of Garland, *Integumenta Ovidii*, ed. and trans. with commentary by Kyle Gervais (Kalamazoo, MI: Medieval Institute Publications, Western Michigan University, 2022). English translations mine.

32   Leah DeVun, *The Shape of Sex: Nonbinary Gender from Genesis to the Renaissance* (New York: Columbia University Press, 2021), pp. 102–33 (especially pp. 113–15).

of the male and female sperm, were defining factors to the sex of the foetus — presenting an understanding of biological sex not as a binary but along a spectrum where men and women could be more or less masculine or feminine. The hermaphrodite, however, conceived in the middle chamber of the womb, was equally both.

John of Garland's compact verse interpretations of Ovid's myths were influential and often quoted in later commentaries. The anonymous commentator of the so-called 'Vulgate Commentary' on the *Metamorphoses*, created around 1260 in central France and circulating widely in France and Italy, cites John's couplet about Salmacis twice (without attribution) in his extended glosses on the story.[33] As Frank Coulson has noted, the Vulgate commentator pays close attention to the literary qualities of Ovid's poem, often signalled through references to other Ovidian, classical, or contemporary works.[34] For instance, the Vulgate commentator clarifies Ovid's grafting simile used to explain how the nymph and the boy became one in their union with technical botanical language from Vergil's *Georgics* (note at v. 375). After explaining Ovid's statement that the merged Salmacis and Hermaphroditus seemed 'neutrumque et utrumque' ('both neither and either') in simple biological terms — the transformed Hermaphroditus is now 'partim uir partim femina' ('part man, part woman') — the commentator mentions 'magister Galterus' (the twelfth-century French poet Walter of Châtillon), and cites verses, without attribution, from his Latin poem the *Alexandreis* describing the fading light at dusk with the same adjectives 'neutrum' and 'utrum' (note at v. 379). While mainly presenting a literary connection, in comparing this Ovidian transformation with a natural phenomenon, the Vulgate commentator is hinting at different meanings behind Ovid's literal words. He did this more explicitly in his gloss on Salmacis's 'loca [...] haec tibi libera trado, | hospes' ('I freely leave you this place, guest'), in response to Hermaphroditus, who, desperate about her harassment, threatened to

---

33 The text is cited from *Commentaire Vulgate des 'Métamorphoses' d'Ovide. Livres I–V*, ed. by Frank T. Coulson and Piero Andrea Martina, trans. by Piero Andrea Martina and Clara Wille (Paris: Classiques Garnier, 2021), pp. 597–613. English translations mine.

34 Frank T. Coulson, 'Literary Criticism in the Vulgate Commentary on Ovid's *Metamorphoses*', in *Medieval Textual Cultures: Agents of Transmission, Translation and Transformation*, ed. by Faith Wallis and Robert Wisnovsky (Berlin: De Gruyter, 2016), pp. 121–32.

leave. The commentator explained 'this place' not as the literal spring, but through citing, without attribution, John of Garland's distich interpreting the spring as the womb's chamber where hermaphrodites were conceived (note to vv. 337–38).

The Vulgate commentator fully embraces this allegorical approach in his final interpretation of the story (note to v. 388). 'Moralis est ista mutatio' ('This transformation is moral'), he opens the note, and the author Ovid teaches us how to explain it. The explanation is simple: What else can the spring (Salmacis) mean than lust ('luxuriam')? And what else is the half-man (Hermaphroditus) than someone who is 'mollem' ('soft') and 'effeminatum' ('effeminate')? Arnulf's *luxus* that followed from excessively enjoying lovely places here becomes *luxuria*, even though its source — in men or in women? — is unknown.[35] But then the commentator offers a second way to understand the story: Hermaphroditus's transformation refers to 'carnalem copulam' ('copulation'), when a man and a woman are mixed together (his verb 'ammiscetur' recalls Ovid's 'mixta duorum | corpora' at *Met.* 4.373–74) and seem 'neutrum et utrumque' ('neither and either'). The Vulgate commentator focuses on the man, not the woman, in the act, noting that during sex he is considered a half-man. Or, option number three: the spring refers to Christ, because Christ is 'fons […] uiuus' ('the living source') from which all true rivers flow, and Christ ordered marriage to our ancestors, according to the biblical verse 'Et erunt duo in carne una' ('and they will be two in one flesh'), found in Genesis 2.24 (the creation of Adam and Eve), and Mark 10.8 (Jesus's discussion on the lawfulness of divorce). Here again, the commentator does not shy away from the sex featured in the Ovidian story, but even more explicitly replaces the rape scene in Ovid's story with sexual intercourse within the bounds of marriage. And, as if three different readings do not suffice, the commentator offers a final interpretation 'secundum aliam allegoriam' ('according to another allegory'), citing again without attribution John of Garland's verses on the hermaphrodite's creation within a certain chamber of the womb.

---

35   Ovid indeed explicitly stated that 'causa latet', the cause is unknown (*Met.* 4.287). The Vulgate commentator expresses this doubt through a (unattributed) verse from the *Amores* (1.9.29): 'Mars dubius, nec certa Venus' ('Mars is doubtful and neither Venus is certain').

Giovanni del Virgilio, Dante's correspondent in the *Eclogues*, is another commentator who embraces the biological interpretation of this Ovidian story. Giovanni was the first to teach the classical Latin poets Virgil, Ovid, Lucan, and Statius at the University of Bologna in 1321. His *Expositio* and *Allegorie librorum Ovidii* (1322–23), which combine interpretations in prose and poetry, are connected to these teachings.[36] First interpreting Salmacis 'naturaliter', in the natural sense in the *Allegorie*, Giovanni's short verses on the conception of hermaphrodites are similar but not identical to John of Garland's distich.[37] Giovanni's moral reading ('ad mores'), on the other hand, offers new interpretations of Ovid's myth. While Salmacis is *voluptas* or lust (so far, nothing too new), Hermaphroditus is what happens when lust is joined ('unitur') with *sermo* or speech: lustful speech pervades the thoughts and words of humans and renders them 'libidinosus' ('lustful'). This interpretation addresses Salmacis's (failed) attempts to seduce Hermaphroditus with words — she was indeed very direct in communicating her desire (*Met.* 4.320–28).[38] Giovanni also integrates Hermaphroditus's request that others be made the same (*Met.* 4.383–86). The literal union of Salmacis and Hermaphroditus becomes lustful speech, which, in Giovanni's view, could spread.[39]

The 1322–23 dating of Giovanni's *Expositio* and *Allegorie*, right after Dante's death, excludes these works from Dante's possible Ovidian reading list. Two other commentaries on Ovid's *Metamorphoses*

---

36 The text is cited from *Ovide moralisés latins*, pp. 344–47. On Giovanni del Virgilio's teachings, see pp. 38–39.

37 'Cellula matricis que concipit Hermofroditum | Salmacis est medio cum fuit usa Venus'. His prose interpretation reads: 'Salmacis est quedam cellula in matrice in qua, si mulier recipiat sperma hominis, nascitur hermofroditus, id est homo habens utrumque sexum'.

38 As Jean-Marie noted in *Ovide moralisé latins*, p. 347 note 93, Giovanni del Virgilio may be elaborating on the work of the so-called Third Vatican Mythographer, also counted among Arnulf of Orléans's sources (Arnulf of Orléans, *Ovide moralisés latins*, pp. 23–27) and dated to the eleventh century (*The Vatican Mythographers*, ed. and trans. by Ronald E. Pepin (New York: Fordham University Press, 2008), pp. 8–10). The Third Vatican Mythographer does not systematically provide allegorical interpretations of Ovid's myths, focusing instead on select classical divinities. Mercury's son Hermaphroditus, he explains, signifies a 'certain wantonness of speech' (p. 284), using 'lascitavitem', while Giovanni has 'voluptatem'.

39 Instead of *Inferno* 25, Giovanni's interpretation rather brings to mind *Inferno* 18, where pimps, seducers, and flatterers are punished.

from first half of the fourteenth century — the anonymous *Ovide moralisé* (composed between 1316 and 1328) and Pierre Bersuire's *Ovidius moralizatus* (first version started in 1340) — similarly cannot be considered possible sources for Dante's engagement with Ovid's *Metamorphoses*, but nevertheless are, like Giovanni's writings, valuable reference points in understanding Ovid criticism during that time. Often confused for their similar titles, the *Ovide moralisé* and the *Ovidius moralizatus* both place God and Christianity front and central in their interpretations, but otherwise take very different approaches to Ovid's poem. The anonymous author of the *Ovide moralisé*, a loose French translation and extensive explanation of the *Metamorphoses* five times as long as Ovid's poem, first explains Salmacis and Hermaphroditus according to 'the art of physical science', repeating the hermaphrodite's conception within the woman's womb (vv. 2224–49).[40] He then explains Salmacis is a woman wasting her life in vain delight (vv. 2250–81), a 'whore' who corrupts the 'perfect' and 'manly' Hermaphroditus (vv. 2326–32). The myth's real meaning, the author concludes, is God's condemnation of religious men who, when abandoning monastic life, try to both live religiously and pursue the delights of the world (vv. 2333–54). The Benedictine monk Pierre Bersuire (ca. 1290–1362), who interpreted the same myth in the *Ovidius moralizatus*, a series of mythological *exempla* for preachers, reaches a different, positive conclusion.[41] Bersuire interpreted the union of Salmacis ('human nature given to leisure') and Hermaphroditus (Christ), who descended upon the fountain (the 'glorious Virgin, clear, limpid, and pure'), as the dual nature of Christ, part divine (Hermaphroditus) and human (Salmacis). Bersuire had to alter Ovid's account to make his line of interpretation work: Ovid's Salmacis drips with desire and pursued Hermaphroditus aggressively with words, but Bersuire's Salmacis loved Hermaphroditus 'through charity' and 'humbly asked for him at the Incarnation through the prophets'

---

40   The text is quoted from Cornelis de Boer, *Ovide moralisé; poème du commencement du quatorzième siècle* (Amsterdam: Müller, 1915), vv. 2224–2389, and the translation from *The Medieval French Ovide Moralisé: An English Translation*, ed. and trans. by K. Sarah-Jane Murray and Matthieu Boyd, 3 vols (Woodbridge, Suffolk: Brewer, 2023).

41   The text and translation are cited from Pierre Bersuire, *The Moralized Ovid*, ed. and trans. by Frank T. Coulson and Justin Haynes (Cambridge, MA: Harvard University Press, 2023), pp. 296–99.

(par. 27–28). The transformed Hermaphroditus's softness ('mollis') is benign: the Virgin made him feminine ('effeminavit') in changing his hardness into piety, the Christian *pietas* (par. 28).

SALMACIS AND HERMAPHRODITUS IN THE *COMMEDIA*

Dante's reading of the Ovidian myth of Salmacis and Hermaphroditus in the *Commedia* significantly differs from the medieval commentators writing before, during, and slightly after his time. No guidance of a commentary is needed to understand the role of erotic desire — or *luxus* (Arnulf of Orléans), *luxuria* (the Vulgate commentator), *voluptas* (Giovanni del Virgilio) — in Ovid's myth, but when reading only the medieval commentators' interpretations, one would never realize this story features rape. While none of them ignored the 'union' of Salmacis and Hermaphroditus, they all glossed over Salmacis's sexually aggressive behaviour. According to Arnulf of Orléans, the two were joined in love. The Vulgate commentator mentioned their 'carnal copulation', but sanitized Salmacis's rape, interpreting it as sexual intercourse within the bounds of Christian marriage. Pierre Bersuire reframed her erotic desire for 'coupling' as the humble longing to be one with God. The others skipped over the sex, only focusing on Hermaphroditus's resulting transformation, explaining it in moral or natural terms.

Seemingly uninterested in any hidden meanings, Dante focuses directly on Ovid's verses and translates several features of Salmacis's sexual assault into the text of the *Commedia*: like Ovid's Salmacis gripped Hermaphroditus, Dante's serpent-shaped soul clung ('implicat', *Met.* 4.362; 's'appiglia', *Inf.* 25.51) to another soul. Salmacis's hands grabbed Hermaphroditus's body ('subiectat', *Met.* 4.359), while Dante's serpentine attacker grips ('avvinse', *Inf.* 25.52) the other soul's belly, and after attacking his victim's arms and face, moves his tail in between his thighs and straightens it behind his loins (*Inf.* 25.52–57). And like Ovid, Dante uses natural similes to underscore the violence of the attack. Ovid's first comparison features a snake, caught in an eagle's beak and aggressively coiling its body around the bird's talons and wings (*Met.* 4.362–64). Dante directly copies Ovid's next image of ivy gripping a tree: Ovid's simile 'utue solent hederae longos intexere

truncos' ('or as ivy twines around large trunks'; *Met.* 4.365) becomes
'Ellera abbarbicata mai non fue | ad alber sì, come l'orribil fiera | per
l'altrui membra avviticchiò le sue' ('No ivy ever gripped a tree so
fast | as when that horrifying monster clasped | and intertwined the
other's limbs with its'; *Inf.* 25.58–60). While Ovid tempers the language of violent assault by reducing in the following simile Salmacis
and Hermaphroditus's union to the horticultural technique of grafting
a branch into a tree (*Met.* 4.375–76), Dante is in this particular instance
more explicit than Ovid in describing sexual assault. Ovid describes
Salmacis's assault with the language of military battle,[42] but 'subiectat
[...] manus' ('Salmacis moves down her hands'; *Met.* 4.359), with
the verb communicating her downward movement through the prefix
sub-, is the closest Ovid's text comes to approaching Hermaphroditus's
groin. Dante's serpent-shaped thief aggressively attacks with his tail (a
stand-in for the male sexual organ) the human-shaped thief between
his legs. In Dante's final metamorphosis, modeled after Ovid's Cadmus and Harmonia story, the poet again mentions the male sexual
organ without naming it: the snake-shaped soul's hind feet became 'lo
membro che l'uom cela' ('the member that man hides'; *Inf.* 25.116),
while the opposite happened to 'del suo' ('that of') the human-shaped
soul (*Inf.* 25.117). Like Ovid did for Cadmus (*Met.* 4.576–89), Dante
points out how various human body parts took on serpentine forms,
but only Dante included genitals in that list. Medieval commentators
on the *Metamorphoses* did not address the sexual violence in Ovid's
story of Salmacis and Hermaphroditus, but even Dante's more explicit scenes are rarely described for what they are: 'sexualized Ovidian
transformations', 'rape'.[43]

Inversion marks both Ovid's and Dante's accounts of sexual assault.
At first, Ovid's Salmacis displays gender-conforming behaviour: the
nymph took pleasure in distinctively feminine activities, like doing

---

42 See Ovidio, *Metamorfosi*, ed. by Alessandro Barchiesi and Gianpiero Rosati, trans.
    by Ludovica Koch and Gioachino Chiarini, 6 vols (Milan: Mondadori, 2005–15), II
    (2007): *Libri III–IV*, p. 291, for several examples, including 'pugnantem [...] tenet',
    'hostem', 'pugnes'.

43 Gary P. Cestaro, 'Sodomite, Homosexual, Queer: Teaching Dante LGBTQ', in *Ap-
    proaches to Teaching Dante's 'Divine Comedy'*, ed. by Christopher Kleinhenz and
    Kristina Olson, 2nd edn (New York: Modern Language Association of America, 2020),
    pp. 103–09 (p. 107); Barolini, '*Inferno 25*', pars 23–25.

her hair and picking flowers on the meadow — an activity that often
gets girls (arguably most famously Persephone) noticed by predatory
men.[44] But from the moment Hermaphroditus shows up, he is subject
to her 'male gaze'.[45] As Ovid noted from the beginning, Hermaphroditus's father and mother appear in his face and name, and throughout
the story the boy presents as sexually ambiguous: manly in his desire to
explore the world, blushing like a virgin girl at Salmacis's flattery. This
is not the sole instance in Ovid's poem where a woman pursues a man,
but only in this story does Ovid recount a woman's sexual aggression in
such great detail.[46] Salmacis's *modus operandi* is similar to that of many
male predators: her initial reaction to Hermaphroditus (*Met.* 4.316)
— 'puerum uidit uisumque optauit habere' ('She saw the boy, and
once she saw him, wanted to have him') — is not much different, for
instance, from Pluto's response when he first saw Persephone (*Met.*
5.395–96): 'paene simul uisa est dilectaque raptaque Diti; | usque adeo
est properatus amor' ('almost all at once Dis saw her, loved her, and
seized her away; that was how fast his love was'). Ovid also infuses
this role-reversing in the story's similes. As Alessandro Barchiesi and
Gianpiero Rosati noted, the aggressor Salmacis is 'ut serpens' ('like a
snake') attacking an eagle (*Met.* 4.362) — turning raptor into prey.[47]

In Dante's canto, too, the prey become the predators. As Teodolinda Barolini writes, 'When the thieves are in their human shapes,
they are victims of their comrades in their serpent shapes. When they
are in their serpent shapes, the previous victims are now perpetrators,
intent upon victimizing their fellow thieves'.[48] In this shape-shifting
cycle of victims changing into victimizers, Dante transforms Ovid's

---

44   See for instance Ovidio, *Metamorfosi*, III: *Libri V–VI* (2009), pp. 203–04.

45   Salzman-Mitchell analysed the gender instability in this episode in Patricia B. Salzman-
      Mitchell, *A Web of Fantasies: Gaze, Image, and Gender in Ovid's Metamorphoses*
      (Columbus: Ohio State University Press, 2005), pp. 160–66: Salmacis is 'a sexually
      ambiguous character who wavers between being an object of the gaze [...] and having
      an intrusive gaze' (p. 162).

46   Ovid dedicated eighteen verses to Salmacis's unwanted verbal advances and twenty-
      three verses to the actual assault. In contrast, he captures the story of another raped
      man in only a half-verse: Cephalus mentions that Aurora 'took him away against his
      will' ('inuitumque rapit', *Met.* 7.704). On the few female predators in Ovid's poem, see
      Curran, 'Rape and Rape Victims in the *Metamorphoses*', p. 216.

47   Ovidio, *Metamorfosi*, II: *Libri III–IV*, p. 291.

48   Barolini, '*Inferno* 25', par 19.

female aggressor Salmacis (only 'ut serpens' in the *Metamorphoses*) into an actual male serpent attacking a human man.[49] Like female perpetrators, male-on-male sexual aggression is rare in Ovid's poem — there are only a few passages on male same-sex desire and force is only present in Jupiter's *raptus* of Ganymede, the Ovidian myth Dante featured in *Purgatorio* 9.[50] Salmacis's fixed gaze on the young boy (*Met.* 4.316) becomes in Dante's ditch of theft a pattern of intense stares: first, the pilgrim's sustained focus on the three thieves, right before one of them is attacked by a snake ('Com' io tenea levate in lor le ciglia' ('As I kept my eyes fixed upon those sinners'; *Inf.* 25.49)); then, the other two human-shaped souls (and, by extension, the pilgrim, Virgil, and the reader) are looking at the incredible joining of snake and man ('Li altri due 'l riguardavano' or 'The other two souls stared'; *Inf.* 25.67); and finally, in the canto's last metamorphosis, the intense stare-off between a small serpent and one of those remaining human souls: 'Elli 'l serpente e quei lui riguardava' ('The serpent stared at him, he at the serpent'; *Inf.* 25.91).[51] But while Salmacis's eyes fixate on Hermaphroditus's beautiful face and body, it is not the beauty of their human and serpentine bodily shapes that drives Dante's fraudulent thieves to eye and then sexually assault each other.

Dante's reading of the 'biformis' Hermaphroditus (*Met.* 4.387) draws on the ambiguity and instability inherent in Ovid's myth. His language to describe the snake-man hybrid is rooted in Ovid's verses: when Salmacis and Hermaphroditus's limbs were joined in a 'complexu [...] tenaci' ('tight embrace'), they were 'nec duo [...] sed forma duplex' ('not two but a double form') and seemed 'neutrumque et utrumque' ('both neither and either'; *Met.* 4.377–79). 'Vedi che già non se' né due né uno' ('Just see, | you are already neither two nor one!'; *Inf.* 25.69), both witnessing thieves on the sideline yelled when

---

49   On the presence of reptiles in representations of hell, see Giuseppe Ledda, *Il bestiario dell'aldilà: gli animali nella 'Commedia' di Dante* (Ravenna: Longo, 2019), pp. 22–27, 29.

50   For instance, Apollo 'loved' Hyacinthus 'above all others' (*Met.* 10.167); after Eurydice's death Orpheus 'transferred his love to young boys' (*Met.* 10.83–84).

51   Staring also features in Ovid's story of Cadmus. After killing a giant serpent, Cadmus learned about his future transformation (*Met.* 3.97–98): 'quid, Agenore nate, peremptum | serpentem spectas? et tu spectabere serpens' ('Why are you looking at the snake that you have killed, son of Agenor? You too will become a snake and be looked at').

the serpent-shaped and human-shaped soul were mid-transformation, and, once joined together, 'Ogne primaio aspetto ivi era casso: | due e nessun l'imagine perversa | parea' ('And every former shape was canceled there: | that perverse image seemed to share in both | and none'; *Inf.* 25.76–78). In their avoidance of rape, medieval commentators did not make much of 'forma duplex', the two-in-one-ness of the transformed Hermaphroditus, but focused instead on the biology of intersex hermaphrodites (John of Garland, the Vulgate commentator, Giovanni del Virgilio) or the literary quality of the 'both neither and either' phrase (the Vulgate commentator). Only Pierre Bersuire, writing after Dante, interpreted it — in line with his overall positive reading of the myth — as Christ's dual nature. Dante instead applies the concept of inversion prevalent in Ovid's myth: after replacing the female nymph with a male serpent and intensifying the sexual violence in the attack, he presents the resulting 'forma duplex' as an 'imagine perversa' ('perverse image'; *Inf.* 25.77), perhaps with a tinge of the Ovidian phrase 'obscenae Salmacis undae' ('the filthy waters of Salmacis') used in a later reprise of the myth (*Met.* 15.319).[52] It reads as a crude inversion of Christ's human and divine nature.[53] Nothing truly generative can come from their union: like Ovid's Hermaphroditus who presented sexually ambiguous from the beginning and through his transformation only became more explicitly what he already was, the transformed souls shift shape but ultimately remain forever fraudulent thieves punished in hell.

Dante features the Salmacis and Hermaphroditus story in purgatory as well. In hell, sexualized punishments are not inflicted on the lustful and sodomites but featured, through Ovid's myth, as violent male-on-male sexual intercourse in the ditch of theft. On purgatory's terrace of lust, two groups of souls appear; Guido Guinizzelli identifies his group's sin as 'ermafrodito' (*Purg.* 26.82), distinguishing it from the others who yell 'Soddoma' ('Sodom'; *Purg.* 26.79) — to be understood, using our contemporary terms, as excessive heterosexual

---

52 I follow Stephanie McCarter's translation of 'obscenae' as 'filthy', capturing how the word, as McCarter noted, suggests 'both "polluted" or "unclean" and sexually "obscene"' (Ovid, *Metamorphoses*, p. 564 note 17).

53 Especially in contrast with the Christ-like 'biforme' griffin (*Purg.* 32.96) in earthy paradise (Barolini, 'Inferno 25', par. 34).

and homosexual desire, respectively.[54] With the term 'hermaphrodite', Dante captures again the sexual violence and deviance he recognized in Ovid's myth; that the Latin poet was on his mind becomes clear from the subsequent reference to Pasiphaë who, aided by a wooden frame, had sex with a bull and got pregnant with the hybrid Minotaur (*Met.* 8.131–37).[55] As in *Inferno* 25, Dante features a half-human, half-animal creature resulting from sexual intercourse, but here in purgatory Dante is even more forceful in framing excessive desire as bestial: the lustful souls, Guinizzelli states, followed their appetite 'come bestie' ('like beasts'; *Purg.* 26.84), calling out the name of Pasiphaë, she who 's'imbestiò ne le 'mbestiate schegge' ('in | the bestial planks, became herself a beast'; *Purg.* 26.87). Ovid's poem offers again the language and imagery to poetically formulate these views.

Several scholars have connected Dante's readings of Ovid with certain medieval commentaries or even specific manuscripts of the *Metamorphoses*. While that could in some cases explain Dante's word choice at certain points in the *Commedia*, none of these medieval 'editions' of the *Metamorphoses* can be considered as Dante's only and

---

54   While I read Dante's 'peccato [...] ermafrodito' here in purgatory alongside his reading
     of the Salmacis and Hermaphroditus myth in *Inferno* 25, I recognize the various mean-
     ings of the hermaphrodite beyond the interpretations of medieval commentators on
     the *Metamorphoses*. The figure was perhaps most frequently associated with sodomy,
     but, as Holsinger notes, 'the association of hermaphroditism with both heterosexual
     and homosexual practice is ubiquitous in high medieval treatments of the subject'
     (Holsinger, 'Sodomy and Resurrection', p. 261; and more examples in John E. Boswell,
     'Dante and the Sodomites', *Dante Studies*, 112 (1994), pp. 63–76 (p. 71)). For a
     positive reading of 'Jesus the Hermaphrodite' in alchemical literature, see DeVun, *The
     Shape of Sex*, pp. 163–99. Some medieval commentators picked up on Ovid's language
     about Hermaphroditus's 'softening' — 'remolliat' (*Met.* 4.286); 'mollita' (*Met.* 4.381);
     'mollescat' (*Met.* 4.386) — and referred to Hermaphroditus's 'soft' side by calling him
     'mollis', or even mentioning his 'effeminatio', which were terms also associated (but
     not exclusively) with sodomy (see, for instance, Erin V. Abraham, *Anticipating Sin in
     Medieval Society: Childhood, Sexuality, and Violence in the Early Penitentials* (Amster-
     dam: Amsterdam University Press, 2017), pp. 140–42). No medieval commentator on
     the *Metamorphoses*, though, directly associates Hermaphroditus with sodomy, while
     they do mention male same-sex desire in their glosses on the Ganymede myth. For
     a short overview on Ganymede in the commentaries, see Holsinger, 'Sodomy and
     Resurrection', p. 258.

55   Ovid described the Minotaur with the same phrase 'semiuir' used for Hermaphroditus
     (*Met.* 4.386) in the *Ars amatoria* (2.24: 'semibouemque uirum semiuirumque bouem'
     ('the man who was half-bull, the bull who was half-man')).

unquestionable Ovidian text.[56] The comparison of Dante's treatment
of sexual violence, such a prevalent topic in Ovid's poem, with the interpretations in medieval commentaries on the *Metamorphoses* especially
underscores Dante's different reading practice. I am not suggesting
to remove these commentaries from Dante's radar, but perhaps he
may have found that its commentators' 'hermeneutic guidelines' —
everything in the *Metamorphoses* is about something else, mainly faith
and morality — 'overdetermined' the readings of Ovid's poem, to return to Barolini's definition of 'detheologizing'. In contrast to these
medieval commentators, Dante did not gloss over the sexual assault in
Ovid's story of Salmacis and Hermaphroditus, but instead recognized
the ambiguity and instability Ovid explored in this myth. A 'reader
against the grain' of Ovid during his own time,[57] Dante ultimately
aligns more with the view prevalent in modern Ovid criticism that the
Metamorphoses 'portrays human identity as something unstable and
uncertain'.[58]

---

56   See my discussion on the search for Dante's (copy of) Ovid in Van Peteghem, *Italian*
     Readers of Ovid, pp. 172–80.
57   On 'Reading Against the Grain', see the introduction to Teodolinda Barolini, *Dante and*
     the Origins of Italian Literary Culture (New York: Fordham University Press, 2006), pp.
     1–20.
58   Charles Segal, 'Il corpo e l'io nelle *Metamorfosi* di Ovidio', in Ovidio, *Metamorfosi*, I:
     Libri I–II (2005), pp. xv–ci (p. xviii and note 2). Translation mine.

In Praise of Detheologizing

ELENA LOMBARDI

The *Commedia* makes narrative believers of us all. By this I mean that we accept the possible world (as logicians call it) that Dante has invented; we do not question its premises or assumptions except on its own terms. *We read the Commedia as Fundamentalists read the Bible,* as though it were true, and the fact that we do this is not connected to our religious beliefs, for on a narrative level, we believe the *Commedia* without knowing that we do so.[1]

In 1992, Barolini's statement was prophetic. And for us, young graduate students in New York City in the 1990s, it was an extraordinary breath of fresh air. We became, at once, narrative believers, excited readers of that narrative, and delighted critics of our reading. This was liberating, especially for those of us who came from Italy and from a rather rigid and yet rigorous philological training, enlivened, if anything, by an ever-waning Marxist critique.

The *Commedia* was no longer the revered national poem, so much so that I received a degree in 'Letters' at university without needing

---

1   Teodolinda Barolini, *The Undivine Comedy: Detheologizing Dante* (Princeton: Princeton University Press, 1992), p. 16, emphasis mine, hereafter *UDC*. Subsequent references given in parentheses in the main text.

to study it properly (following Contini's *diktat*, our courses comprised 'Dante senza la *Commedia*')[2]; in graduate school in New York, it became a playground. The swings and slides for our reading were revolutionary ideas that were unknown to traditional Italian education and were experiencing their heyday in American universities then: feminism, gender studies, cultural studies, deconstructionism — a trust, in other words, in the text's capacity for endless experimentation, and the production of meaning and counter-meaning. We felt we were going under the surface of a text that we had all along accepted as canonical and undiscussed. The more we dug into the various meanings it produced, the more its lies were eerily looking like the truth.

We gave the 'poetic assent' — as T. S. Eliot required — and off we went on the most exciting literary ride of all.[3] There were new poetics, and Never-Before-Travelled-Paths, nonfalse errors and true dreams, problems, oh so many delightful problems, mimeses and paradoxes, closures and incipits, jumps and fits and starts to mark a beautiful, impalpable, lyric textuality; and an ornate, chic, monster, 'maravigliosa ad ogne cor sicuro' ('amazing to the surest heart; *Inf.* 16.132),[4] who 'serves as an outrageously paradoxical authenticating device' (*UDC*, p. 59) for the poem's truth claims. To me, and, I am sure to many Dante scholars, 'Ulysses, Geryon and the Aeronautics of Narrative Transition' is an essay-wonder. It is the moment when we discover how deeply entangled are fraud and fiction within the body of the monster, and how cleverly Dante, in the most absurdly fictional moment of his poem, both embraces and eschews the peril of invention by dragging us, the readers, into becoming witnesses to an oath: an oath upon a

---

2   The entry on 'Dante Alighieri' in our university textbook, Contini's *Letteratura Italiana delle origini*, began like this: 'Poiché ovviamente nei lettori dell'antologia si presume familiarità con la *Divina Commedia*, le pagine qui offerte valgono come una presentazione delle opere dette minori (e minori di fatto, ma unicamente rispetto al livello supremo della *Commedia*), e in qualche misura consentono di giudicare quello che Dante sarebbe nella nostra storia letteraria se non avesse scritto il poema' (Gianfranco Contini, *Letteratura Italiana delle origini* (Florence: Sansoni, 1985), p. 297).

3   T. S. Eliot, 'Dante' [1929], in Eliot, *Selected Essays* (London: Faber and Faber, 1972), pp. 237–77.

4   Quotations from the *Commedia* are from Dante Alighieri, '*La Commedia*' secondo *l'antica vulgata*, ed. by Giorgio Petrocchi, Società Dantesca Italiana, Edizione Nazionale, 2nd rev. edn, 4 vols (Florence: Le Lettere, 1994). The English translations are from Dante Alighieri, *The Divine Comedy*, trans. with commentary by Charles S. Singleton, 6 vols (Princeton: Princeton University Press, 1970–75).

text, one that is normally placed upon a sacred book as we are invited to think. The text, however, is not a written and bound book but simply the sounds ('note') of a *comedìa*. And yet, after avowing our oath and accepting the bet, we the readers are ready to fly (sail?) on Geryon's opulent back, so involved are we in the making of this non-fraudulent fiction.

With its array of chapters on all the pressing issues of the *Commedia*, with its firm but not hierarchical point of view, with the finest and yet most piercing style a critic could wish for (in itself, I believe, part of a 'form' that 'is not abstractable as a surface value'; *UDC*, p. 17), and a strong and rigorous voice that still manages to speak directly to each of its readers, *The Undivine Comedy* has revolutionized Dante studies in so many ways, many of them surely unpredictable then, and many more in the process of evolving. It has created a 'school' in the truest sense of the term, an equal conversation of thinking minds across time and space. Its biggest achievement, to me, is to put at the centre of its grand enquiry, again and for the first time, '"only" a *fabbro*, a maker ... a poet' (*UDC*, p. 20).

Barolini's 'prophecy', however, had an ominous streak that we failed to appreciate back then. There is indeed a 'fundamentalism' in Dante studies which appears to be dictated by the text itself but is, in fact, the consequence of a strange connivance between two *logoi* — philo-logy and theo-logy — that turns Dante studies into a perfect logo-logy.[5] In it, excitingly, the author is coextensive to his main text, thanks to the pliable and stretchable avatar Dante-*agens*, and yet the text is ultimately controlled by a divinity (sometimes strangely similar to a post-tridentine or even protestant God). Eden is a manuscript, an 'original' not yet stained by the 'sin' of variation, error, or, god forbid, desire. Instead of pondering on the reasons for this rather extraordinary phenomenon and how it occurred in and around a sophisticated and fragile piece of literature, as Barolini invited us to do, we have often relied on the two combined *logoi* as the bottom-line explanation for nearly every doubt raised by Dante's work (and/as life). In other words,

---

5   I adapt here a term from Kenneth Burke, *The Rhetoric of Religion: Studies in Logology* (Berkeley: University of California Press, 1970), bracketing it, however, with Dantean irony.

we have constructed a much more Christian Dante, a more prophetic
writer, more of a preacher and a moralist than he probably was. We have
constructed a Dante who himself believes the narrative produced by
his own work. A self-believer, an auto-prophet, a converter of reading
souls, the leader and sole follower of a cult centred around the conviction that a young unknown Florentine woman is no less than Faith
herself, the writer of a 'sacred poem', and yet, strangely, this madman
is also a slick Thomist and the defender of an unspecified Christian
orthodoxy.

One could object that the logology on Dante is not new, and that
the notion of the consistency of Dante's life, work and — for lack of a
better word — religiosity, solidified as soon as his strange poem started
circulating, no doubt due to the puzzlement of the first readers faced
with this extraordinary piece of literature that was similar to nothing
they had read before, or after. What strikes me is the fact that such conviction, which had settled for centuries into a bland 'literary history'
kind of narrative, has not budged, unlike countless others have done
under the pressure of the late-modern and postmodern concerted attack on authority and on textual consistency. Indeed, if anything, this
narrative has become stronger. While other authors were proclaimed
dead, and revered texts were flayed open to expose the monsters of the
unconscious or flattened to fit more or less congruous contemporary
discourses, Dante became an Ur-author, and the *Commedia*'s consistency has become ever tighter. The only ghost text that the *Commedia*
seems able to produce is its own justification, either that of the controlling, moralist, Christian author or that of 'God' himself. I do not
advocate impaling the *Commedia* on the stake of psychoanalytical or
cultural studies that are becoming at once more exhausted and more
zealous. Personally, I would rather bring the *Commedia* back into literary studies, mild as they may be, the gentler the better, actually:
like Statius and Virgil, I am still convinced that Eden is Parnassus
(*Purg.* 28.139–48). I am simply wondering how all of this came to be.
Why such endurance on the part not of a rude text — the scroll of a
preacher, the rustic vernacular adaptation of the umpteenth epigone of
the Homeric tales (we read those because, remember, 'Dante did not
read Homer'), or the lacklustre treatise on deadly sins claiming that
even sweating too much is a form of lust (I read that one, understood

why there were so many saunas in NYC, and started frequenting the
Tenth Street Baths) — but of a precious, sophisticated, delicate piece
of literature: one so adventurous, so visionary (in a stylistic sense),
so thin-skinned or no-skinned that it could (and does, and wants to)
burst open at every metaphor, at every daring simile; a work suffused
with mourning and melancholia, open to the subversive laughter of the
comic, to the manic neologism of the finest theo-logy, and to the error,
wandering, and variance of real philo-logy.

Dante begs his readers to understand this much at the beginning
of the *Paradiso*, in a proem that always leaves me wondering about
the poet's lack of skin and desire for passivity with respect to literary
stimulus:

> O buono Appollo, a l'ultimo lavoro
> fammi del tuo valor sì fatto vaso,
> come dimandi a dar l'amato alloro.
>   Infino a qui l'un giogo di Parnaso
> assai mi fu; ma or con amendue
> m'è uopo intrar ne l'aringo rimaso.
>   Entra nel petto mio, e spira tue
> sì come quando Marsïa traesti
> de la vagina de le membra sue.

> (O good Apollo, for this last labor make me such a vessel of
> your worth as you require for granting your beloved laurel.
> Thus far the one peak of Parnassus has sufficed me, but now I
> have need of both, as I enter the arena that remains. Enter into
> my breast and breathe there as when you drew Marsyas from
> the sheath of his limbs.) (*Par.* 1.13–21)

This is a perfect reverse-Ovidian moment: while Ovid's Marsyas,
undergoing the 'classic' punishment for artistic hubris, asks Apollo
'why do you tear me from myself?' ('quid me mihi detrahis?', *Metamorphoses* 6.385), Dante begs the god to tear him from himself —
embracing his openness, fragility and excitement as he approaches the
last feat.

Still, an insensitive artistic hubris — mostly if not fully condoned
by the fact that we are dealing with a Christian writer penning a Christian poem — is what we normally attribute to Dante. Take Dante's
life for instance. Unlike any other writer, medieval or modern, we

take bits of information from his works to be factual truth, and we construct a fairly linear biography without acknowledging that this is, actually, a very well curated autobiography.[6] And yet, since his work is in turn strangely linked to divine narrative, we excise from it any hints of anxiety, misgivings, shortcuts, indecision, and fear, not to mention error. Even his exile — whose tragic effects Dante never tires of telling his readers — becomes some sort of Augustinian moment that makes Dante Dante, that turns his gaze from earth to heaven and, after a short moment of lapse into belligerent politics, wrong loves, heterodoxy, and textual failures sets him on the way to prophecy, global political vision, *caritas*, preaching, salvation, and textual completion.

Brave and determined like his writing, serious and yet comically virile like the statue that was placed in Piazza Santa Croce for the sixth centenary of his birth, the first in the newly united Italy, Dante becomes a jack-of-all-trades for moral life-writing and for various degrees of Italianness (in Italy) and everyman-liness (abroad).

The sacred poem is a case in point: 'The sacred poem to which heaven and earth have so set hand' is so powerful a construct that we fail to notice the hesitation, the fatigue, the illogical optative, the mixed hypothetical clause, ('se mai continga […] ritornerò'), the tragic sense of the passing of time, the melancholia for lost Florence, the strange overlapping of politician and poet, the absurd image of the lamb enemy to the wolves, and the violence of the cruelty that bans him. At most, Dante's *magrezza* becomes a symptom of his increased, 'divine' authority. The fact that we know that Dante never came back to Florence, but that his poem did soon after his death, instead of making paranoids of all Dantisti, seems to reassure us even more of the prophetic power of our author.[7]

> Se mai continga che 'l poema sacro
> al quale ha posto mano e cielo e terra,
> sì che m'ha fatto per molti anni macro,

---

6   See Manuele Gragnolati and Elena Lombardi, 'Autobiografia d'autore', *Dante Studies*, 136 (2018), pp. 143–60; and Elisa Brilli and Giuliano Milani, *Dante's Lives: Biography and Autobiography* (London: Reaktion, 2023).

7   See the reading by Nicolò Crisafi, *Dante's Masterplot and Alternative Narratives in the 'Commedia'* (Oxford: Oxford University Press, 2022), pp. 163–67.

vinca la crudeltà che fuor mi serra
del bello ovile ov' io dormi' agnello,
nimico ai lupi che li danno guerra;
    con altra voce omai, con altro vello
ritornerò poeta, e in sul fonte
del mio battesmo prenderò 'l cappello.

(If ever it comes to pass that the sacred poem to which heaven
and earth have so set hand that it has made me lean for many
years should overcome the cruelty which bars me from the fair
sheephold where I slept as a lamb, an enemy to the wolves
which war on it, with changed voice now and with changed
fleece a poet will I return, and at the font of my baptism will
I take the crown.) (*Par.* 25.1–9)

Had it not been for Barolini, we also would have failed to notice that
the 'sacred poem is forced to jump' at the sight of his dead beloved's
beautiful smile. The chapter 'The Sacred Poem is forced to Jump: Closure and the Poetics of Enjambment' shows the emergence, toward the
end of the vision, of a 'lyrical' — that is 'nondiscursive, nonlinear or
circular, "dechronologized" and affective' (*UDC*, p. 221) — textuality
that runs counter to but also inextricably merges with the 'narrative'
aspect of the poem, that is 'discursive, logical, linear, "chronologised,"
and [...] intellective' (*UDC*, p. 221). Moreover, this chapter invites us
to experience

the end of this poem as being stranded in an eternal present, on
a very high peak that was attained by dint of following behind
the voice, the all-making voice, that suddenly is no more. The 'I'
that has led us for so long does not return; it leaves us there, in
that vast emptiness, without it. And not all this canto's fearful
symmetry can compensate for that loss, for the fact that this
poem too must die. (*UDC*, p. 256)

And yet, despite Barolini's warning against 'hegemonic laws of reading'
that 'divide and conquer' (*UDC*, p. 224), we still tend to read not only
the *Commedia* but all Dante's work as solely a linear progression, a
watertight and coherent story of loving, writing, and being saved that
merges in the grand avenue of the *Commedia*. The parts that do not fit
into this narrative are labelled as failures, vagrants, or, at best, objects
of palinode. Bad love, heterodoxy, and rubbish writing are one and

the same, it seems (one is tempted to agree insofar as the *Convivio* is concerned).

The author's propensity for controlling his work does the rest, as shown for instance in Dante's first great trompe-l'œil, the *Vita nuova*. Manuele Gragnolati has uncovered the strategies of author-ial performance in the *Vita nuova*, showing how the prose bends the lyric (and tames desire) into a coherent narrative of loving and writing.[8] Gragnolati's stance on the *Vita nuova* ties in with Barolini's ground-breaking edition of the *Rime*, which re-establishes the freedom, equality, and fragmentary nature of Dante's lyric corpus.[9] And yet, so powerful is our reception of Dante's narrative on his own writing that it still sends philology off track to hunt for nonexistent texts and clunky hypotheses.[10] See, for instance, what happens with the 'cosette per rima' ('trifles [...] in rhyme') of *Vita nuova* 5.4, occasional poems that Dante claims he wrote for the first screen lady and decided not to include in the *libello*.[11] As Gragnolati has shown, critics still debate which poems among Dante's *Rime* could be identified as these 'trifles'. Trusting the existence of the 'cosette per rima', though, we end up believing in the reality of the screen ladies, or at least in the fiction of 'other loves' challenging without success the main track that from Beatrice (already) leads to God.

The same goes for other texts that are mentioned but not included in the *Vita nuova*: the Latin letter to some powerful rulers at the end of the *libello* (*Vita nuova* 30.1), and the letter in poetic form bearing the names of the sixty most beautiful women in Florence (*Vita nuova* 6.2). The only reason I mention it, says Dante, is because

---

8   Manuele Gragnolati, 'Authorship and Performance in Dante's *Vita nova*', in *Aspects of the Performative in Medieval Culture*, ed. by Manuele Gragnolati and Almut Suerbaum (Berlin: de Gruyter, 2010), pp. 123–40, and *Amor che move. Linguaggio del corpo e forma del desiderio in Dante, Pasolini e Morante* (Milan: Il Saggiatore, 2013).

9   Dante Alighieri, *Rime giovanili e della 'Vita Nuova'*, ed. by Teodolinda Barolini, with notes by Manuele Gragnolati (Milan: Rizzoli, 2009).

10   See for instance the strange hypothesis of the 'double ending' of the *Vita nuova*, as retold by Barolini in 'The Case of the Lost Original Ending of Dante's *Vita Nuova*: More Notes Toward a Critical Philology', *Medioevo letterario d'Italia*, 11 (2014), pp. 37–43.

11   Text from Dante Alighieri, *Vita Nuova*, ed. by Michele Barbi (Florence: Società Dantesca Italiana, 1960). English translation from Dante Alighieri, *Vita Nuova*, trans. by Mark Musa, Oxford World Classics (Oxford: Oxford University Press, 2008).

'maravigliosamente addivenne, cioè che in alcuno altro numero non soffense lo nome de la mia donna stare se non in su lo nove, tra li nomi di queste donne' ('miraculously it happened that the name of my lady appeared as the ninth among the names of those ladies, as if refusing to appear under any other number'; *Vita nuova* 6.2). So, which is the lady who goes on the boat trip with Guido, Lapo, Vanna, and Lagia? 'She who is number thirty'? And why would you hang out (at sea, of all places) with Number Thirty if you have secured the salvific love of Number Nine, some of us wonder? Luckily, famous as it might be for a certain facility of rhythm, *Guido i' vorrei* is an 'excluded', 'extravagant' poem, not so great now that I think of it, with all that Arthurian plush: so not Dante; a *divertissement* at best. And so we go about ironing away contradictions and inconsistencies in Dante's work, with a twofold moral and aesthetic press, to the point of excluding or ignoring the *Fiore* from Dante's canon, because 'he' would not write something so morally crude (and, therefore, stylistically unrefined). The letter to Cangrande della Scala, though, whose mediocre Latin and utter lack of irony strike me as truly un-Dantean — that one we take as 'most probably Dante's' because it tells the story we want to hear: that of the four levels of reading, of letter and allegory and how well they fit together; of the normalisation of the Ovidian proem; of punishment and reward, and of more reading souls to be saved.

The simplification that occurs in the classroom is even more evident. As we toy with Dante's truth claims — it is easy, and fun, and rewarding to expose them in class — we do fall sometimes into the trap of the moralist. I still remember fondly the first time I listened to John Freccero's graduate lecture on canto 10. Raised in Auerbach's awe for the kind and broken Cavalcante de' Cavalcanti — so consumed with love and concern for his son that he forgets about himself and the Hell that surrounds him, a figure so compassionately drawn by the masterful hand of the poet — I had never contemplated the biting sting of infernal irony; I had never noticed the comic side of the story, drawn by the cruel hand of a bitter poet, in which the old man no longer understands basic grammar ('dicesti elli ebbe?' ('did you say "he had"?'), he exclaims in *Inf.* 10.68, failing to see that the use of the past tense does not automatically mean one is dead) and is unable to appreciate the difference between physical death and salvation (when he asks about Guido, his question is not 'is he saved?', but 'is he alive?'; l. 68). And indeed, his son is not even a great poet after all, as his slightly imperfect rhyme ('lume', 'come', 'nome', ll. 65–69) plastered all over the end of the canto shows.[12]

Downstream from that magisterial lecture, however, there is the moralist simplification of considering everything and everyone that Dante places in Hell as inherently bad, corrupt, flawed (yes, they are in Hell), and, worse than that: uncomplicated, uninteresting. Downstream there is the Dantist who, when asked how they would explain to undergraduates the beauty, complexity, and fragility of infernal characters, answered plainly that there was not much to explain and then added, with their eyes going slightly blank: 'after all, Dante was a just man. If he put Brunetto in Hell, he did so for a reason'. A cruder version of this is a half-jocular response I received during the chit-chat over drinks after a talk on *Inferno* 5 that 'dopo tutto, Francesca era una puttana' ('Francesca was a whore, after all'). After all.

Hosts of young people — open, modern, gender-savvy, secular, hopefully sexually active young people, that is — chant hymns to the poet's 'pure' love for Beatrice as opposed to Francesca's lust. 'What is pure love, pray?' you ask. 'Spiritual love'. 'Which is?' 'Chaste'. 'Mmm?' 'Not of the body'. And you are tempted to say: 'have you ever felt it? A, any, form of love — or friendship or emotion or intellectual excitement or spirituality for God's sake! — that does not imply a flutter of the gentle heart, pleasure, sweet sighs and doubtful desires, getting pale, looking into each other's eyes, and feeling utterly overcome?' But, you are the Dante teacher, and you eventually take the high road of comedy and say, just before leaving the classroom: 'Guys, do you know that medieval monks had visions about kissing Jesus with their tongue?'

The fundamentalism of Dante studies reaches its acme when, instead of a logology, it turns into a philo-theology, finding that the text's incontrovertible message is such-and-such because 'God' says so.

---

12   See Erich Auerbach, 'Farinata and Cavalcante', in Auerbach, *Mimesis: The Representation of Reality in Western Literature* (Princeton: Princeton University Press, 2013), pp. 174–202. Traces of Freccero's lesson on canto 10 can still be found in John Freccero, 'Infernal Irony: The Gates of Hell', in Freccero, *Dante: The Poetics of Conversion* (Cambridge, MA: Harvard University Press, 1986), pp. 93–109, but they are in no way equal to the enchantment of his lectures.

One example brings me to yet another area of Dante studies that has greatly benefited from Barolini's contributions: the canto of Francesca da Rimini. Very much like the lustful lovers battered by contrary gales, so too the canto is always at a turbulent cross-wind, with various interpretations pushing it 'di qua, di là, di giù, di sù'. Barolini's late-1990s diptych on Francesca manages what centuries of exegesis failed to do: it both historicizes and poeticizes Francesca.[13] 'Realpolitik, Romance, Gender' brings to us the scant pieces of information on the historical and gendered Francesca, while 'Inferno V in Its Lyric Context' helpfully desexualizes Francesca (and the whole canto) and places it (again, gently and intelligently) within aspects of the poetic background from which she originates. The fragments come together, though not seamlessly; the fissures expose the wreckage, pain, and bias that surround the silenced real life and the faltering yet passionate fictional voice of a medieval woman. Thus, Barolini successfully separates Francesca from the future readings of Francesca and leaves it to history and literature to illuminate the fine fragments of a life-turned-poetry.

I would like to add a very small bit of detheologising on this much studied canto. During her opening speech, Francesca agrees to speak to Dante through a series of courteous statement. This courtly conversation, however, is not taking place on a sofa, but in a rough and wild environment: in the midst of a storm. And yet, the characters manage to converse.

> Di quel che udire e che parlar vi piace,
> noi udiremo e parleremo a voi,
> mentre che 'l vento, come fa, *si/ci* tace.

(Of that which it pleases you to hear and to speak, we will hear and speak with you, while the wind, as now, is silent for us.) (*Inf.* 5.94–96, italics mine)

Line 96 is famous for carrying a textual crux: 'ci tace' or 'si tace'? This ambiguity, in turn, allows for several interpretations: 'the wind is silent'

---

13   Teodolinda Barolini, 'Dante and Cavalcanti (On Making Distinctions in Matters of Love): *Inferno* 5 in its Lyric Context', *Dante Studies*, 116 (1998), pp. 31–63, and 'Dante and Francesca da Rimini: Realpolitik, Romance, Gender', *Speculum*, 75 (2000), pp. 1–28.

(reflexive si), 'the wind is silent here' (ci = 'qui', 'here'), 'the wind is silent for us' (ci = 'for us'), 'the wind silences us' (ci = 'us'). Depending on the choice of variant and its interpretation, this controversial line either suggests that the infernal storm might potentially rest for a moment, or confirms the impossibility of any sort of relief.

Let us embed the various interpretations into the canto. We have just left Limbo, a dimly lit, quietly sorrowful place, where the only sound, creepy as it might be, is that of sighs, and we are now thrown into a place stripped — literally 'muted' — of any kind of light: 'loco d'ogne luce muto | che mugghia come fa mar per tempesta, | se da contrari venti è combattuto' ('mute of all light, which bellows like the sea in tempest when it is assailed by warring winds'; *Inf.* 5.28–30). 'Dolenti note' ('doleful notes', l. 25) are heard, and 'molto pianto [...] percuote' ('much wailing smites'; l. 27) the traveller. The unrelenting storm savages the spirits with its 'rapina' ('rapine'; l. 32) and 'voltando e percotendo li molesta' ('whirling and smiting, it torments them'; l. 33). Unlike an earthly storm, which does eventually settle, the infernal storm never pauses and there is no hope of even a slight remission of pain ('non che di posa, ma di minor pena', 'no hope of less pain, not to say of rest'; l. 45).

And yet, they manage to speak. But what happens to the wind? *Aguzza le orecchie, lettor.* Does it:

1. die down every once in a while, like in a normal storm, and then pick up again? This is interesting, because it puts pressure and uncertainty on Francesca's speech. Will she manage to say all she wants to say before the next gust comes in? We can imagine her rushing her lines, trying to get to the fateful end, looking nervously at the next incoming vortex, sounding almost mechanical and ever more frightened.

2. never stop, and the poor souls have to shout to be heard, their beautiful lines butchered and broken by the roaring wind? This is a properly tragic but also 'romantic', Wuthering-Heightsy view of the episode.[14]

---

14 Intriguingly, I cannot find any trace of this interpretation (the wind silences us) — which seems to me very plain both in terms of grammar and logic — in the main

Or

3. have the four actors stopped in a special corner of the circle, less
windy than the rest, perhaps near the mysterious ruin or away
from the worst of the storm, or actually right at its eye, where
they say it is quiet? Is this a 'corner of paradise' as one reader put
it, where the two souls can momentarily replay their love; or,
with less exaggeration, is it a mini-limbo, a mournful but quiet
place that allows at least some kind of respite and reflection?

In line with my work on the canto, I see these as possible scenarios
with which the text presents us.[15] Only a dramatic performance of
canto 5 can pin this and many other lines (importantly, the anaphoric
lines) to one particular interpretation. Each reader, however, is invited
to contemplate and inhabit the various possibilities.

Canto 5, I contend, is a powerful lesson on reading: the *Commedia*
requires present, acute readers, and therefore we are trained, especially
at the beginning, to be open, inventive, intelligent readers, but also
to notice that we are bound to our time and inclinations and age

---

list of commentaries from the Dartmouth Dante Project or in dedicated essays. I may
have read it or heard it somewhere and then forgot (in which case, apologies), but my
impression is that I've 'always' read it like this. In the Italian education system, at least
when and where I attended school, pupils started to read and sometimes memorize
episodes from the *Commedia* in primary school at age eight or nine, and then again a
more extended reading in middle school at twelve or thirteen, and eventually would
read the whole *Commedia*: one cantica per year would be read in the last three years
of high school, in dedicated weekly 'Dante' sessions. Therefore, this might be the way
little Elena, without much sense of history, language, or poetics (or self, for that matter)
read the line for the first time and understood, without doubt or hesitation, that the
roaring wind was interrupting the lover's delicate speech, their voices becoming hoarse
and helpless, their precious words mangled by the cruel noise. 'Amore [...] amore [...]
amore': maybe this is all one could hear. A misreading? Even better: little Elena would
have had a great teacher in misreading in this very canto, the heroine herself. Too young
to comprehend at the age of nine? Dante begs to disagree. But before you lean towards
accepting the prophetic powers of little Elena's reading, I must tell you how, around
that time, I read the beginning of Alessandro Manzoni's ode to Napoleon, *Il cinque
maggio*. The ode begins with the announcement of Napoleon's death — 'Ei fu.' ('He
died.') — and then moves to a complex simile between the leader's dead body and
the shock that paralyses the entire planet at the news of his death ('Siccome immobile
[...] così percossa e attonita | la terra'). Too long a simile for my powers of recitation,
I rearranged the lines as follows: 'Ei fu, siccome immobile': he was dead, because he
no longer moved.

15 See, in particular, Elena Lombardi, *The Wings of the Doves: Love and Desire in Dante
and Medieval Culture* (Montreal: McGill Queens University Press, 2012).

(not always midlife); to our life and its eventfulness, to our present concerns, to the way our teachers taught us and how we dissented (*'Siete ancora qui, Ser Brunetto?'*); to our understanding of textual authority and the pleasure we take in language's hall of mirrors, to the amount of knowledge we have on one specific topic (never enough and yet always presumptuous), and more.

Unless, of course, God comes in to nail down our interpretation. In this case, God is also in a conundrum, though. Do they

4. allow the wind to be silent in that specific place and time in order for Dante to have a conversation with the souls and see for himself what kind of disgusting and deceitful lechers (she, the little whore, in particular) they are, so that this journey, willed from above, ends up converting more readers?

Or do they

5. not allow the wind to be silent because we shouldn't at any time believe that God has any mercy for the damned? *La pietà per i dannati,* the most unhelpful concept of all!

Although in this example they are, themselves, perplexed, this is not the sole time in which 'God' weighs heavily in the interpretation of the *Commedia*: that is, an entirely fictional, textualized God, the creation of their own creation, their ontology bound to a minute textual variant, which most likely slipped out of the pen of a yawning scribe.

This is why *The Undivine Comedy* is as timely and important today as it was thirty years ago, not only as one of the greatest scholarly books on Dante, but also as a continuing source of inspiration, pleasure, and resistance.

Heavenly Paradoxes and Their Pleasures

MANUELE GRAGNOLATI

I began graduate school at Columbia University in 1994, when *The Undivine Comedy* was still hot off the press. Teodolinda Barolini's book had marked my intellectual life more than any other. I was coming from a degree in Classical Philology with a specialization in Greek and Latin grammar from the University of Pavia, and my encounter with the concept of 'detheologizing' as 'releasing our reading of the *Commedia* of the author's grip, finding a way out of Dante's hall of mirrors'[1] had been both revolutionary and empowering. I could recognize in it the importance given to the rigorous handling of the text, which was at the core of my previous formation, while I could also finally find an inspiration, and a justification, for interpreting literature and appreciating its beauty and power.

In this essay I will not linger on the personal details of my encounter with *The Undivine Comedy* and with Barolini as a teacher and an academic mentor. I will simply mention that I came to graduate

---

1 Teodolinda Barolini, *The Undivine Comedy: Detheologizing Dante* (Princeton: Princeton University Press, 1992), p. 17, hereafter *UDC*. Subsequent references given in parentheses in the main text. Just prior, Barolini explains that 'Detheologizing is not antitheological; it is not a call to abandon theology or to excise theological concerns from Dante criticism. Rather, detheologizing is a way of reading that attempts to break out of the hermeneutic guidelines that Dante has structured into his poem, hermeneutic guidelines that result in theologized readings whose outcomes have been overdetermined by the author.' *UDC*, p. 17.

school at Columbia University to write a dissertation on twentieth-century literature, but it only took a few of Barolini's classes on Dante's *Commedia* for me to switch to Dante, and indeed I ended up writing a dissertation on the relationship between body and soul in medieval eschatology.[2] In these pages I share some reflections on the chapters that *The Undivine Comedy* dedicates to *Paradiso*, in particular chapters 8 and 10, focusing on three questions: what does it mean to be in heaven, how can a poet describe the encounter in words, and how does a reader experience that description. I will begin with chapter 8, entitled 'Problems in Paradise: The Mimesis of Time and the Paradox of *più e meno*', which opens by pointing to the impossible task that Dante as a poet faces when writing the *Paradiso*. What is it that makes the writing of *Paradiso* more difficult than *Inferno* and *Purgatorio*, and ultimately impossible?

As Barolini explains, this difficulty has to do with time and with the incompatibility between the rootedness of language and narrative in time on the one hand and, on the other, the fact that heaven is outside of time. Remembering, with Paul Ricoeur, that 'The world unfolded by every narrative work is always a temporal world', Barolini asks: 'What happens when the world unfolded in narrative is supposed to be a world outside of time? What happens if the author of such a world is fully aware of the temporality of language and takes steps to counter it? What are the steps an author can take to counter what is finally not counterable?' (*UDC*, pp. 166–67).

Through Aristotle, Dante knows that time 'comports otherness, difference, non-identity, nonsimultaneity' (*UDC*, p. 167), and he also knows, with Augustine, that language is bound to time, is a function of time. Language is therefore a differential medium, unable to express simultaneity. However, God is precisely sameness and simultaneity. He is by definition eternal and, like heaven, outside of time. With Boethius, Barolini explains that God's eternity is not simple endless-ness, perpetual addition of time, never-ending duration, which is the

---

2   Manuele Gragnolati, *Identity, Pain and Resurrection: Body and Soul in Bonvesin da la Riva's 'Book of the Three Scriptures' and Dante's 'Commedia'* (doctoral thesis, Columbia University, 1999). After being substantially reworked, the dissertation became the monograph *Experiencing the Afterlife: Soul and Body in Dante and Medieval Culture* (Notre Dame, IN: Notre Dame University Press, 2005).

temporality of hell.[3] Rather, the dimension of God and heaven is that of the *totum simul*, a contemporaneous simultaneity that, unlike time, consists not of a linear addition of before and after but, we could say, is like a single thick point, an instant where everything is simultaneously co-present, where everything is the same at the same time. Dante's problem with writing *Paradiso* is that of rendering 'a condition defined as beyond space and time in a medium [language] that is intractably of space and time' (*UDC*, p. 169).

After setting out the formal problem of the *Paradiso*, which will be treated mainly in the following chapters and to which I will return later, chapter 8 turns to exploring its thematic correlative, namely the philo-sophical paradox of the one and the many, which is already present in the first tercet of the canticle: 'La gloria di colui che tutto move | per l'universo penetra, e risplende | in una parte più e meno altrove' ('The glory of the One who moves all things | permeates the universe and glows | in one part more and in another less'; *Par.* 1.1–3).[4] The obsessive question of the *Paradiso*, which is constantly reformulated throughout the canticle, is 'how can the universe be one and yet receive God's light in different degrees?' (*UDC*, p. 172). In other words, how can God's heaven accommodate difference while remaining one? In fact, what is striking in Dante's concept of heaven is the paradoxical way in which it combines what cannot logically be combined: a sense of unity, whereby everything is merged with God in a state of sameness and undifferentiation, and an appreciation of multiplicity, difference and singularity. Barolini writes (and shows) that Dante, in his under-standing of heaven, is less of a monist than commonly assumed and actually reveals an enormous — and striking — 'dedication to the cause of difference and pluralism: to the individual, the specific, the many' (*UDC*, p. 173).[5] According to Barolini, paradox, and particu-

---

3   One can think of infernal endlessness also in terms of useless repetition: see the section 'Ripetizioni infernali' in my book *Amor che move. Linguaggio del corpo e forma del desiderio in Dante, Pasolini e Morante* (Milan: Il Saggiatore, 2013), pp. 79–83.

4   Quotations from the *Commedia* are from Dante Alighieri: *La Commedia secondo l'antica vulgata*, ed. by Giorgio Petrocchi, Società Dantesca Italiana, Edizione Nazio-nale, 2nd rev. edn, 4 vols (Florence: Le Lettere, 1994). English translations come from Dante Alighieri, *The Divine Comedy*, trans. by Allen Mandelbaum, 3 vols (Berkeley: University of California Press, 1980–82).

5   Barolini has devoted much of her subsequent scholarship to exploring Dante's commit-ment to multiplicity and difference: see her recent volume *Dante's Multitudes: History, Philosophy, Method* (Notre Dame, IN: Notre Dame University Press, 2022).

larly the paradoxical coexistence of unity and multiplicity, is the cipher of Dante's heaven, and the *Paradiso* will repeatedly articulate this paradox, striving to 'create a text that encompasses the illusion of the one and the many as coexistent and simultaneous' (*UDC*, p. 174).

The rest of the chapter brilliantly analyses the first nine cantos of *Paradiso* and shows that the main strategy which Dante deploys to render heaven's paradoxical coexistence of unity and multiplicity is that of alternation. For instance, in canto 1 the poet stresses unity, while in canto 2 he stresses difference, 'and so on from one to the other, in the hope that the diachronic package he offers us will convey some idea of the synchronic reality he experienced' (*UDC*, p. 176). The chapter is full of many insightful and genius points, as for instance the analysis of *Paradiso* IV, where Barolini shows that the souls' 'condescension' — their showing themselves to the pilgrim in the different Heavens while actually all being in the Empyrean — occurs not only for the sake of the pilgrim, who wouldn't otherwise understand how the blessed can all be perfectly happy and yet enjoy different degrees of happiness, but also the poet, who is to compose not a 'mystical haiku' but a third canticle that, like the previous ones, is composed of thirty-three cantos (*UDC*, p. 188).

Rather than reviewing the chapter point by point, I will engage with it from the perspective of my research on the concepts of 'experiencing the afterlife' and 'eschatological anthropology', namely what it means to live in the otherworld and what it tells us about Dante's understanding of the human being.[6] In particular, I will take a cue from Barolini's observation that Dante's dedication to the notions of difference and pluralism causes him to repudiate, in canto 25 of *Purgatorio*, Averroes's doctrine of the common intellect insofar as it denies the immortality of the individual soul.

The passage to which Barolini refers is part of Statius's embryological elucidation in *Purgatorio* 25, where he aims to explain how the individual separated soul can continue to have an experience of the afterlife, and in particular to feel the physical pains of hell and purga-

---

6   See Gragnolati, *Experiencing the Afterlife*, and Manuele Gragnolati, 'Eschatological Anthropology', in *The Oxford Handbook of Dante*, ed. by Manuele Gragnolati, Elena Lombardi, and Francesca Southerden (Oxford: Oxford University Press, 2021), pp. 447–63.

tory, while being separated from its body in the eschatological time before the resurrection. Dante imagines that when the soul separates from its body at physical death and proceeds to the afterlife, it contains the structure of the body as a sort of DNA and can unfold itself into a body of air that is endowed with all the senses and has an individual form. As I have shown in my dissertation and first book, Dante's theory combines the principles of different and logically incompatible scholastic doctrines on the relationship between body and soul in a way that allows the aerial body to 'function' as a paradox in the *Commedia*.[7] In what sense as a paradox? In the sense that the aerial body stands at once for the fullness of experience of the separated soul and the need for the resurrection of the body; in other words, the aerial body symbolizes both the intensity of the separated soul's experience and its imperfection.

In the following part of this essay, I will look at experience in the afterlife from the perspective of the paradox between the one and the many, sameness and difference, which *The Undivine Comedy* posits as the cipher of Dante's heaven. First, I will return to purgatory, whose function would seem to solve the paradox in favour of sameness and detachment from particularity.[8] I will begin with a scene on the shores of Mount Purgatory — the pilgrim's encounter with the shade of his old friend Casella — which rewrites the Virgilian motif of the failed embrace between a living person and a dead one. When Casella leaves his group of shades and moves forward to embrace Dante, words such as 'abbracciarmi' and 'affetto' charge the scene with a sense of intimacy and affection: 'Io vidi una di lor trarresi avante | per abbracciarmi, con sì grande affetto, | che mosse me a far lo simigliante' ('I saw one of those spirits moving forward | in order to embrace me — his affection | so great that I was moved to mime his welcome'; *Purg.* 2.76–78). Dante-pilgrim attempts to embrace the shade in front of him, but fails three times because, as the poet laments, shades in the otherworld are 'vane' or empty, insofar as they have an appearance but no substantiality:

---

7   See especially Gragnolati, *Experiencing the Afterlife*, pp. 139–60.

8   I have explored this topic over the course of many years. Here I am drawing on Gragnolati, 'Eschatological Anthropology'. See also Manuele Gragnolati, 'Ombre a abbracci. Riflessioni sull'inconsistenza nella *Commedia Dante*', *Chroniques italiennes web*, 39 (2020), pp. 30–43.

'Ohi ombre vane, fuor che ne l'aspetto! | tre volte dietro a lei le mani avvinsi, | e tante mi tornai con esse al petto' ('I saw one of those spirits moving forward | in order to embrace me — his affection | so great that I was moved to mime his welcome'; *Purg.* 2.79–81). The two friends have both just arrived in purgatory, and it is important to note that, as Casella indicates, they are still attached to their past desires as represented by their mortal bodies: 'Così com'io t'amai | nel mortal corpo, così t'amo sciolta' ('As I loved you when I was | within my mortal flesh, so, freed, I love you'; *Purg.* 2.88–89). The same affection is shown by Dante, who relapses into nostalgia for earthly pursuits, asking his friend to sing as he often used to do in their youth (*Purg.* 2.106–11). Casella performs Dante's *canzone Amor che ne la mente mi ragiona* so beautifully that all the souls are completely enchanted by the sweetness of the performance and forget that they are in purgatory to embark on a journey of purification which will eventually lead them to heaven (*Purg.* 2.112–17).

The remainder of the episode (*Purg.* 2.118–33), which revolves around Cato's return and rebuke of the lingering souls, shows that the mutual affection that the two friends still feel for each other is wrong and that attachment to the body, affection for friends and loved ones, and nostalgia for the past are also deemed improper and must be remediated in purgatory. Indeed, the moral structure of Dante's understanding of purgatory prescribes that the souls in this realm learn to detach themselves from anything transient and re-direct all their desires towards God. According to what Barolini has identified as Dante's Augustinian paradigm of desire, attachments to one's mortal body and its symbolic expression of nostalgia for earthly affections are considered distractions that the soul must abandon in purgatory if it wants to attain the complete love for God necessary to reach heaven.[9]

This Augustinian discourse of desire, introduced with the pilgrim's arrival at the shores of Mount Purgatory, is reiterated with Beatrice's reproach in the garden of Eden at the mountain's summit. Beatrice confirms that, albeit beautiful, the earthly body is mortal, and one should neither be too attached to it nor replace it with some other

---

9   See especially chapter 5 of *UDC*: 'Purgatory as Paradigm: Travelling the New and Never-Before-Traveled Path of This Life/Poem', pp. 99–121.

mortal good, as the pilgrim did after her own death (*Purg.* 30.127–32 and 31.49–57). Like the episode of Casella, Beatrice's words frame Dante's concept of purgatory with the idea that, in order to redirect their desire towards God and gain heavenly bliss, the purging souls must relinquish their nostalgic attachment to the mortal body and the earthly affections it represents. The temporal, linear process of purgatory is an experience of what I have called 'productive pain' that transforms the souls' desires and teaches them to love in the same selfless and gratuitous way in which Christ did on the cross, allowing them to recuperate their original similitude with Christ that sin had erased, and thereby making them ready to ascend to heaven.[10]

Once in heaven, the souls need not wait for the resurrection of the body in order to enjoy the full vision of God, and the *Paradiso* is filled with passages indicating that upon arrival in heaven, the blessed have immediate access to the beatific vision and are granted perfect bliss — a state that the poem calls 'pace' and which corresponds to having all one's desires satisfied: 'Lume è là sù che visibile face | lo creatore a quella creatura | che solo in lui vedere ha la sua pace' ('Above, on high, there is a light that makes | apparent the Creator to the creature | whose only peace lies in his seeing Him'; *Par.* 30.100–02).

The sign of the souls' happiness in heaven is the light surrounding them, which is proportional to the degree of their *visio Dei*:

> Luce divina sopra me s'appunta,
> penetrando per questa in ch'io m'inventro,
>   la cui virtù, col mio veder congiunta,
> mi leva sopra me tanto, ch'i' veggio
> la somma essenza de la quale è munta.
>   Quinci vien l'allegrezza onde fiammeggio;
> per ch'a la vista mia, quant' ella è chiara,
> la chiarità de la fiamma pareggio.

> (Light from the Deity descends on me;
> it penetrates the light that enwombs me;
>   its power, as it joins my power of sight,
> lifts me so far beyond myself that I
> see the High Source from which that light derives.

---

10   Gragnolati, *Experiencing the Afterlife*, pp. 89–137. See also Manuele Gragnolati, 'Gluttony and the Anthropology of Pain in Dante's *Inferno* and *Purgatorio*', in *History in the Comic Mode: Medieval Communities and the Matter of Person*, ed. by Rachel Fulton and Bruce W. Holsinger (New York: Columbia University Press, 2007), pp. 238–50.

From this there comes the joy with which I am;
I match the clearness of my light
with equal measure of my clear insight.)
(*Par.* 21.83–90)

Beginning in the Heaven of Mercury, shades disappear from the poem
and the pilgrim can only see featureless lights, which can be taken as a
sign of the extent to which, in line with the Augustinian and Christo-
logical paradigm of purgatory, heavenly souls have indeed learned to
detach from their past and to transform personal and individual attachments into *caritas*, i.e. absolute and unconditional love for God that
opens the self and is also gratuitous love for everyone else.

This condition achieved and manifested by heavenly souls corresponds to a merging with God which radically opens the self. Thus, for
instance, Lino Pertile and Steven Botterill have indicated that Beatrice,
who can be considered the symbol of the pilgrim's personal and individual attachments, must eventually depart to be replaced by Bernard
of Clairvaux before the pilgrim can reach ultimate union with God.
Robin Kirkpatrick likewise has spoken of a 'spirit of dispossession' that
characterizes the condition of being in heaven, while Christian Moevs
has indicated that the redirection of desire from mortal to immortal
goods can be understood as a 'spontaneous crucifixion of the self' and
that 'love is selflessness, and self is lovelessness'.[11] Regarding Barolini's
analysis of unity and multiplicity, one could say that the luminosity
surrounding the souls in heaven and hiding the features of their aerial
bodies represents the side of oneness, whereby the soul has dissolved
the boundaries of the ego and merged with God.

However, if we move to *Paradiso* 14, we can also appreciate the
other side of the paradox: that of singularity, difference, multiplicity.
The pilgrim and Beatrice are in the Heaven of the Sun when, read-

---

11 Lino Pertile, *La punta del disio: semantica del desiderio nella 'Commedia'* (Fiesole:
    Cadmo 2005), pp. 235–46; Steven Botterill, *Dante and the Mystical Tradition: Bernard
    of Clairvaux in the 'Commedia'* (Cambridge: Cambridge University Press, 1994), pp.
    64–86; Robin Kirkpatrick, 'Polemics of Praise: Theology as Text, Narrative and Rhet-
    oric in Dante's *Commedia*', in *Dante's 'Commedia': Theology as Poetry*, ed. by Vittorio
    Montemaggi and Matthew Treherne (Notre Dame, IN: University of Notre Dame
    Press, 2010), pp. 14–35 (p. 23); and Christian Moevs, *The Metaphysics of Dante's
    'Comedy'* (New York: Oxford University Press 2005), pp. 89–90. See also Heather
    Webb, *Dante's Persons: An Ethics of the Transhuman* (Oxford: Oxford University Press,
    2016).

ing the pilgrim's mind, Beatrice asks what will happen to the blessed
souls' luminosity when the fleshly body resurrects at the end of time.
Solomon explains that the resurrection of the flesh and the material
reconstitution of the person will allow for an increase of beatific vision,
happiness, and luminosity:

> Come la carne glorïosa e santa
> fia rivestita, la nostra persona
> più grata fia per esser tutta quanta:
>   per che s'accrescerà ciò che ne dona
> di gratüito lume il sommo bene
> lume ch'a lui veder ne condiziona;
>   onde la visïon crescer convene,
> crescer l'ardor che di quella s'accende,
> crescer lo raggio che da esso vene.
>
>   (When, glorified and sanctified, the flesh
> is once again our dress, our persons shall,
> in being all complete, please all the more;
>   therefore, whatever light gratuitous
> the Highest Good gives us will be enhanced —
> the light that will allow us to see Him;
>   that light will cause our vision to increase,
> the ardor vision kindles to increase,
> the brightness born of ardor to increase.)
> (*Par.* 14.43–51)

Solomon then adds that the luminosity of the resurrected body will be
stronger than that of the soul:

> Ma sì come carbon che fiamma rende,
> e per vivo candor quella soverchia,
> sì che la sua parvenza si difende;
>   così questo folgór che già ne cerchia
> fia vinto in apparenza da la carne
> che tutto dì la terra ricoperchia.
>
>   (Yet even as a coal engenders flame,
> but with intenser glow outshines it, so
> that in that flame the coal persists, it shows,
>   so will the brightness that envelops us
> be then surpassed in visibility
> by reborn flesh, which earth now covers up.)
> (*Par.* 14.52–57)

By suggesting that in heaven the person's features will be visible again
when the earthly body resurrects, the poem points to that element of

singularity, plurality, and difference that seemed to have been put aside
by the soul's merging with God but that, nevertheless, continues to be
a crucial component of the experience in/of heaven.

This idea is confirmed in the following verses describing the joy
and enthusiasm with which souls react to the prospect of reuniting
with their fleshly bodies — the same mortal bodies that have remained
on Earth as corpses — thus revealing an intense nostalgia for what has
been left behind ('disio d'i corpi morti'):

> Tanto mi parver sùbiti e accorti
> e l'uno e l'altro coro a dicer 'Amme!',
> che ben mostrar disio d'i corpi morti:
>
> forse non pur per lor, ma per le mamme,
> per li padri e per li altri che fuor cari
> anzi che fosser sempiterne fiamme.
>
> (One and the other choir seemed to me
> so quick and keen to say 'Amen' that they
> showed clearly how they longed for their dead bodies —
>
> not only for themselves, perhaps, but for
> their mothers, fathers, and for others dear
> to them before they were eternal flames.)
> (*Par.* 14.61–66)

Unlike many other passages in *Paradiso* that highlight the souls' current
state of happiness, contentment, and 'pace', here the poem emphasizes
the intensity with which these souls long to recuperate their bodies and
increase their happiness. As Kirkpatrick notices, the presence of words
belonging to the 'low' register like 'amme' (the vernacular form for the
Latin *amen*) and 'mamme' is striking in such a highly theological passage.[12] If these words are typical of that *sermo humilis* modelled upon
the Bible that the *Commedia*, according to Auerbach's well known interpretation, takes as the model for its linguistic variety, the specific use
of the word 'mamma' is, as Barolini writes, the passionate 'expression
of their desire to love fully in heaven what they loved on earth'.[13] This

---

12   In Dante Alighieri, *The Divine Comedy*, ed. and trans. by Robin Kirkpatrick, 3 vols
     (London: Penguin, 2006–07), III: *Paradiso* (2007), p. 389.

13   *UDC*, p. 138; Erich Auerbach, 'Sermo humilis', in Auerbach, *Literary Language and its
     Public in Late Latin Antiquity and in the Middle Ages*, trans. by Ralph Manheim (New
     York: Pantheon Books, 1965), pp. 25–66. See also Jennifer Rushworth, *Discourses of
     Mourning in Dante, Petrarch, and Proust* (Oxford: Oxford University Press, 2016), pp.
     47–53.

aspect exemplifies the singularity that the souls continue to express in heaven as well as Dante's particular and striking appreciation of difference. It is indeed significant that the souls' desire for the return of their dead body thus expresses a relational sense of the self, moving beyond the concerns of contemporary theologians who focused on the exclusive relation of the individual to God and who were less interested in the idea that personal attachments continue among the blessed.

Thus, there seems to be an unresolved tension, or a paradox, between the blessed souls' desire for their dead bodies and the Augustinian paradigm of detachment that characterizes the process of purgatory as an education in selflessness and dispossession. Dante's poem underscores that, no matter how luminous and happy in their union with God, even in heaven the fleshless souls are but incomplete fragments lacking something tightly connected to their intimate affections, and that ultimate happiness is only possible with the final return of their fleshly body and the recovery of their full singularity.

Paradise as imagined by Dante is thus marked by the paradoxical co-existence of a desire to lose oneself in God (unity) and of a desire to regain one's own history carried in the materiality of one's own body (difference/singularity). In recent years my interests have leaned toward the connections between the persistence of the souls' individuality and historicity in heaven, Auerbach's concept of the *figura* as that which maintains both an allegorical and historical meaning, and most importantly his notion that the *Commedia*'s mixing of styles and use of *sermo humilis* invert the movement of the figural interpretation so that, ultimately, the earthly pole prevails over the eschatological one.[14] Before I conclude by returning to the final chapter of *The Undivine Comedy*, I would like to suggest that the paradox between unity and plurality also informs Dante's much-debated relationship with Beatrice. As we have seen, several critics have argued that at a certain point in the narrative Beatrice must withdraw so that the pilgrim — with the help of Bernard of Clairvaux and Mary — can unite with God, and this withdrawal is understood as a sign that there is no place for eros or the

---

14   Manuele Gragnolati, 'Insegnare con un classico. La complessità di Dante e lo spirito critico', in *In cattedra. Il docente universitario in otto autoritratti*, ed. by Chiara Cappelletto (Milan: Cortina, 2019), pp. 177–214.

lyric mode in Dante's heaven. However, while Beatrice's withdrawal indicates that even in heaven she continues to convey something not fully compatible with God and connected instead with eros, her lyric past, and embodiment, the *Commedia* also suggests that even after the souls have attained the beatific vision, their desire for their earthly bodies carries the trace of their individual memory and history, which in Dante's case will arguably continue to include his love for Beatrice.[15]

I will now move to the last chapter of *The Undivine Comedy*, entitled 'The Sacred Poem is Forced to Jump: Closure and the Poetics of Enjambment'. This extraordinary chapter is perhaps the one that has most profoundly marked me, insofar it has shown me what textuality is and how it can be read. The chapter returns to the formal problem introduced in chapter 8, which is Dante's impossible task of representing the *totum simul* of paradise through the medium of language, which is necessarily bound to temporality and multiplicity. In particular, the chapter focuses on 'high paradise' and shows that, towards the end of the canticle, Dante deploys the strategy of alternating two different textual modes: on the one hand, a properly 'narrative' mode based on the Aristotelian sense of time as duration and continuum that is 'discursive, logical, linear, "chronologized" and [...] intellective' and that corresponds to the traditional way in which narrative operates; and, on the other, a 'lyrical' mode based on the Augustinian sense of time as an indivisible instant that is 'the opposite, i.e., nondiscursive, nonlinear circular, "dechronologized", and affective' (*UDC*, p. 221). As Barolini exemplifies through her astounding reading of cantos 23, 30, and 33, the lyrical mode resists subdivision and logical explanation and is instead characterized by 'apostrophes, exclamations, heavily metaphoric language, and intensely affective similes' (*UDC*, p. 221). It 'represents nothing less than Dante's attempt to forge an oxymoron, an adynaton, a paradox: namely linguistic/diagetic *uguaglianza*, "equalized" language' (*UDC*, p. 221). Referring to the metapoetic tercet 'e così, figurando il paradiso, | qui convene saltare lo sacrato poema, | come chi trova suo cammin riciso' ('And thus, in representing Paradise, | the sacred poem has to leap across, | as does a man who finds his

---

15   See Manuele Gragnolati, '*Paradiso* xiv e il desiderio del corpo', *Studi Danteschi*, 78 (2013), pp. 285–309.

path cut off'; *Par.* 23.61–63), Barolini calls it a 'jumping' textuality and
shows that through its fragmented and fractured nature it bends the
linear temporality of narrative and logical intellection, while through
the insistent use of affective images and metaphors it approximates
circularity and thereby the equalized condition of heaven. Let us think
for instance of the concluding canto of *Paradiso* and, in particular, of
the portion that follows Bernard's prayer to Mary and describes the pilgrim's final ascent towards the beatific vision and unity with the Divine
(*Par.* 30.46–145). As Barolini shows, the poet weaves this story into
three circular movements (*Par.* 30.46–75, 76–105, and 106–45) and
arranges the three 'textual building blocks' of which they are composed
— brief moments of plot describing what happened to the pilgrim or
what he saw; metapoetic statements on the impossibility of describing
what the poet has experienced or seen; and apostrophes to the Divine
asking for help in doing so — in such a way that the text prevents the
emergence of any narrative line and keeps jumping like a firework. And
if the jumping style of canto 33 represents 'Dante's supreme attempt to
engage the fractured, circular, equalized mode of *eguaglianza*', it is not
anti-mimetic insofar as it 'seeks to approximate the circling, surging,
orgasmic approach of the soul to the fulfilment of its heart's desire'
(*UDC*, p. 252).

In the book *Amor che move*, where I have provided a 'diffractive
reading' of Dante's works with those of twentieth-century authors Pier
Paolo Pasolini and Elsa Morante, I have further developed Barolini's
intuition that the *Paradiso*'s jumping textuality conveys the desire of
the blessed souls in the Empyrean. In particular, I have read Dante's
text through the lens of two twentieth-century aesthetic theories arguing that in its fragmentariness and resistance to linearity, poetic
textuality is imbued with desire.[16] First, Julia Kristeva's concept of the

---

16 Gragnolati, *Amor che move*, and 'Diffracting Dante's *Paradiso*: Transformation, Iden-
    tity, and the Form of Desire', in *Cultural Reception, Translation, and Transformation
    of Italian Literature: Essays in Honour of Martin McLaughlin*, ed. by Guido Bonsaver,
    Brian Richardson, and Giuseppe Stellardi (Oxford: Legenda, 2017), pp. 352–66.
    My reading of Dante and Morante relies on collaborations with Sara Fortuna, espe-
    cially: 'Between Affection and Discipline: Exploring Linguistic Tensions from Dante
    to *Aracoeli*', in *The Power of Disturbance: Elsa Morante's 'Aracoeli'*, ed. by Manuele
    Gragnolati and Sara Fortuna (Oxford: Legenda, 2009), pp. 8–19; 'Allattamento e
    origine del linguaggio tra la *Commedia* dantesca e *Aracoeli* di Elsa Morante', in *Par-*

'revolution of poetic language' links a corporeal and desirous mode of
signification to the experience of suckling at the mother's breast and
claims that this pre- or proto-linguistic mode, which is subsequently
lost in the fully symbolic language of the adult subject, can be reacti-
vated through a poetry that subverts the ordinary order of language at
all levels (morpho-syntactic, semantic, and phonologic), as in the case
of the nineteenth- and twentieth-century vanguard works that Kristeva considers in her essay.[17] Second, Leo Bersani's reformulation of
the concept of 'artistic sublimation', understood as a form of sexuality
within the movement of the text, which — in the case of fragmented
texts that frustrate comprehension, progress, and closure — expresses,
enacts, and invokes the reader to experience the paradoxical and indeed masochistic pleasure of what Bersani argues to be sexuality in
its ontological state, before its domestication and sanitization by the
teleology of reproductive sexuality.[18]

While in *Experiencing the Afterlife* I had focused on the unexpected
and paradoxical conflation of incompatible eschatological emphases
that takes place in the Empyrean, where the pilgrim is allowed to see
the blessed with features that will only become visible after their bodily
return,[19] in *Amor che move* I argued that Dante's poem not only stages
the resurrection of the body before the end of time but also conveys
this experience in its textuality. Drawing on Gary Cestaro's book on
the 'nursing' and maternal texture of the vernacular,[20] I proposed the
concept of 'forma del desiderio' ('the form of desire') and suggested
that in the cantos devoted to the description of the Empyrean, the
jumping textuality identified by Barolini can be understood in terms of
a complex combination of a 'revolution of poetic language' à la Kristeva

---

ole di donne, ed. by Francesca Maria Dovetto (Ariccia: Aracne, 2009), pp. 271–303;
'*Attaccando al suo capezzolo le mie labbra ingorde*: corpo, linguaggio e soggettività da
Dante ad *Aracoeli* di Elsa Morante', *Nuova Corrente*, 55 (2008), pp. 85–123.

17   Julia Kristeva, *La Révolution du langage poétique: l'avant-garde à la fin du xixe siècle.
     Lautréamont et Mallarmé* (Paris: Seuil 1974); in English: *The Revolution of Poetic
     Language*, ed. by Leon S. Roudiez, trans. by Marguerite Waller (New York: Columbia
     University Press, 1984).

18   Leo Bersani, *The Freudian Body: Psychoanalysis and Art* (New York: Columbia Univer-
     sity Press, 1986).

19   Gragnolati, *Experiencing the Afterlife*, pp. 139–78.

20   Gary Cestaro, *Dante and the Grammar of the Nursing Body* (Notre Dame, IN: Notre
     Dame University Press, 2003).

that reactivates the corporeal and affective dimension of the vernacular, and an 'artistic sublimation' à la Bersani that replicates the paradoxical pleasure of being in heaven: a pleasure that, as we have seen, consists of both losing and finding oneself.[21]

I will conclude this essay with one additional proposition that moves from looking at the content and the form of *Paradiso* to considering the experience of reading it. In fact, while rereading *The Undivine Comedy* for the preparation of this chapter, I was intrigued by the attention it devotes to the affective experience of reading and writing. For instance, Barolini notes that humans enjoy linear narratives made of *disugguaglianza* and 'stories with beginnings, middles, and ends', and when readers are confronted not with a sustained narrative that they can grasp but with the disruptions of the jumping textuality, as for instance in canto 23 of *Paradiso*, they feel challenged and experience a setback, frustrated that the canto resists their 'attempts to make sense of it, to conquer it', as though they were plunged in a textual ocean which they are unequipped to navigate (*UDC*, p. 224). Similarly, from the perspective of the poet, the final cantos of *Paradiso* are said to be informed by an anxiety: 'the anxiety of the impending end, the anxiety of having to end without delivering the satisfaction that only God could deliver' (*UDC*, p. 240). The chapter seems to imply that the pleasure of reading the text consists in the progression that the poem achieves despite its fragmented, non-linear, jumping textuality. Indeed, as I have mentioned before, the chapter indicates an orgasmic movement in the final canto, approaching and backing off, approaching and backing off again, then finally arriving, to the extent that the void in which the readers find themselves at the end of the poem seems to correspond to the little death following orgasmic arrival and its jouissance. However, I wonder whether one could also consider with Bersani and with much of queer theory that pleasure is not necessarily linear or teleological but can also be masochistic as an enjoyment, for instance, of the meandering of errancy and deferral, the intensity of suspension and repetition, or the bewilderment of confusion.[22] Allowing for such paradoxical

---

21   See Gragnolati, *Amor che move*, pp. 149–61.

22   Bersani, *The Freudian Body*. See also Jack Halberstam, *The Queer Art of Failure* (Durham, NC and London: Duke University Press, 2011); and Teresa de Lauretis, 'Queer

pleasure, which for Bersani is at the core and nexus of sexuality and aesthetics, suggests that through its mobilization the text succeeds in conveying to the reader what is logically impossible — the *totum simul* of unity and plurality, mystical abandonment and retained identity. Supporting this paradox through an equally paradoxical enjoyment may not measure up to 'the satisfaction that only God could deliver', but it does provide a properly literary, undivine pleasure.[23]

Texts, Bad Habits, and the Issue of a Future', *GLQ: A Journal of Lesbian and Gay Studies*, 17.2–3 (2011), pp. 243–63.

23   For another reading that emphasizes the nonnormative pleasure characterizing the poem's ending, see Bruce W. Holsinger, 'Sodomy and Resurrection: The Homoerotic Subject of the *Divine Comedy*', in *Premodern Sexualities*, ed. by Louise Fradenburg and Carla Freccero (New York: Routledge, 1996), pp. 243–74.

V. DETHEOLOGIZE TO MODERNIZE

The Role of the Reader in Actualizing the *Commedia*

F. REGINA PSAKI

In academia, we rarely take or have the time to revisit major works of scholarship to examine how they have lasted and unfolded, how they have influenced and changed the fields they touch.[1] Fast fashion may be the closest parallel to the 'production' model of academic writing that has prevailed of late, in North America at least. Academics must regularly disseminate a given number of scholarly products which display sufficient innovation, heft, and influence to make them 'leaders' in their field (though for all academics to be leaders is a mathematical and logical impossibility). The unintended consequences of the reward (and penalty) structure of humanities research have included overproduction, saturation, and waste (work left unread); ever more minute and aggressive differentiation (once called balkanization); and a great deal of work coming out before it is ready. The result of making academics work at a conveyor belt rather than an artisanal workbench has been an academic treadmill moving too fast to pause and recognize the actual giants among us, and the works which truly merit revisiting with the advantage of hindsight.

---

1   Portions of this essay were presented at the symposium entitled '*The Undivine Comedy Thirty Years Later*' (October 21, 2022) and at the International Congress of Medieval Studies in Kalamazoo, MI (May 9–11, 2024). The result is greatly indebted to the organizers, interlocutors, and presiders on both occasions.

I can't think of a game-changing book in Dante Studies more
deserving of such re-examination than Teodolinda Barolini's *The Undivine Comedy: Detheologizing Dante*.[2] The present essay collection
offers the reconsideration, re-appreciation, and reframing that important works deserve, and which we need for perspective, for inspiration,
and for a reminder of what excellent scholarship really looks like. I am
honoured to have this opportunity to revisit Barolini's achievement in
The Undivine Comedy. I owe a great deal to the book: it has influenced
my engagement with the *Commedia* for decades, in ways I've been too
fully steeped in to see with perfect clarity. As an assistant professor
I was invited to review it; the assignment made me read the book in
granular, even maniacal detail, and I imprinted on it early. Imprinted
not only metaphorically, either: my marginal notes in *The Undivine
Comedy* rival those I've scrawled in the *Divine Comedy*. I came to the
book from a wide diversity of Dante mentors, from Giuseppe Mazzotta
to Antonio Mastrobuono, Winthrop Wetherbee, Rachel Jacoff, and
Marilyn Migiel. Barolini has been a mentor to the world at large, and
I come from that world: not her student, yet still very much formed
by her long-distance instruction. My understanding of the *Paradiso* in
particular owes an immense debt to her book.

Chapter 8 of *The Undivine Comedy*, 'Problems in Paradise: The
Mimesis of Time and the Paradox of *più e meno*', focuses on *Paradiso* 1–
9 (*UDC*, pp. 166–93). It articulates the nature and necessity of Dante's
juggling act in the celestial paradise between unity and multiplicity,
between identity and difference, between time and eternity, between
place and non-spatiality. The first third of the chapter surveys the back-
story of the Platonic/Aristotelian binary in Dante's philosophical and
theological background, and details how the first tercet of *Paradiso*
maps out the poles of unity and multiplicity, identity and diversity, in
the celestial paradise. Barolini shows that the poem is indeed fractal,
self-similar at every level of magnification: the canticle's first two lines
correspond to the first two cantos, and the third line to the third canto,
as just one example among many. The middle third of the chapter

---

2   Teodolinda Barolini, *The Undivine Comedy: Detheologizing Dante* (Princeton: Prince-
     ton University Press, 1992), hereafter *UDC*. Subsequent references given in paren-
     theses in the main text.

probes *Paradiso* 1 and 2; the last third tracks how the poet alternates between privileging unity/identity as the paradisal mode of being, and privileging multiplicity/diversity as the necessary condition of creation, of individuality in humanity, and of the poetic *representation* of the immaterial and non-linguistic condition she calls 'heavenly homology' (*UDC*, p. 185). With her signature energy and deft precision, Barolini examines Dante's play with the contrasts and contradictions he deploys, diffuses, and most importantly defuses. She highlights his 'active pursuit of a new kind of discourse; [...] the concerted attempt to abandon straightforward narrativity for a more fractured, less discursive, less linear, ultimately more "equalized" or "unified" textuality' (*UDC*, p. 226).

The first part of this essay will examine one dimension of Barolini's detheologizing analysis of not only the *Paradiso*'s content, but also its making and its poet's self-fashioning in this culminating stage of the *Commedia* as a whole. In taking in this legendarily challenging canticle, we as readers can remain enmeshed in the dimension of the plot and track the strategies and innovations that Dante the poet deploys in representing that storyline. To circumvent the limitations of human intellect, ensnared as it is in the existential and perceptual grid of time and space, the poet sets up so many devices and premises: neologism, celestial telepathy, semiotic play, analogy, metaphor in every sense, chiasmus, deep allusion and intertextuality, rhyming play *ad infinitum*. We could spend our entire working lives analysing and interpreting these representational solutions. Or, following Barolini's lead, we can also step back and foreground Dante the historical author who creates a narrator, Dante the poet, who both engages and circumvents the conundrum of reconciling the material and immaterial dimensions of being. The second half of the essay takes, as an example of this dynamic, a recent translation of the *Commedia* by American poet Mary Jo Bang, who addresses this same conundrum with and through the added filters of modernization — of technique, voicing, and frames of reference and intertext.

This historical author Barolini spotlights, and about whose compositional practice and working conditions we know so little, has given us a third mode of understanding his challenge of representing the immaterial within the material (if not concrete) medium of language.

This third mode differs from the way taken by the pilgrim in his historically unique journey through the realms of the afterlife and represented
by the poet in his mighty wrestling act, more like Jacob and the angel
than like the spontaneous and immediate 'Fiat lux', let alone the serene
and simultaneous 'In principio erat verbo'. I would describe the third
mode of understanding as the assimilation of the poem into the very
fibre of readers' minds, our neural pathways (we have different terms
than Dante did), where the linear sequentiality to which the poem
and its readers are confined in the reading journey, can dissolve into
immediacy *and* simultaneity. For some twenty years I've been reading
the *Commedia* in full a couple of times per year; the repetition has
made each line and passage resound more and more within an acoustic
and conceptual *copresence* in my mind of the poem as a whole.[3] With
repetition, over time the poem shapes its addressee into a soundbox
within which every reading resonates more immediately, deeply, and
fully.

Can I legitimately infer that Dante the historical author intended
this? No, and yes. I'm quite certain Dante never posited a world where
books were cheap, literacy levels high, memories enfeebled, and education open to all and sundry — even women — and in the vernacular,
at that, whether ours or his. A time of Dante Societies and seventh
centenaries and Digital Dantes and instantaneous access to relevant
primary and secondary sources and hundreds of translations in dozens
of languages — a time when, somewhere in the world, the poem is
always in active dialogue with someone. But I'm equally certain that
Dante did posit a future in which the *Commedia* would not just be read
but reread, obsessively studied and parsed, and if not memorized then
at least committed to a devoted recollection, however partial and shifting. I think he foresaw readers bringing to bear on the multisensorial
poem our own embodied senses — especially the aural sense — so
that each renewed contact with each moment of the *Commedia* would
call to mind dozens of related textual moments, telescoping across the
expanse of the poem and across the time it takes to read it — to make

---

3   I don't claim to know the poem as intimately as I wish, but only to know it more
     intimately than I used to, because of the two or three annual circumnavigations which
     bring me back each time to the starting point.

a resonant unity of the poem's differential components. If this sounds a bit like Joseph Frank's venerable model of spatial form, it both is and isn't.[4] The juxtaposed moments that structure the poem in the reader's mind are intentional and universal on the one hand, like the political canto sixes, and aleatory and individual on the other — specific to the single reader whose mind and memory link them for idiosyncratic reasons. Here I will concentrate on the former, the poet's patent constellations of textual loci. These constellations are comprised by marked parallels within various categories such as addressee; theme; imagery; rhetorical strategy; frame of reference; and characters, among others.

Among the recurrent strands that organize the poem for us is Dante's explicit invocation of its readers. Direct address to us punctuates the *Commedia*, from the first re-orienting 'Pensa, lettor, s'io mi sconfortai' ('Consider, reader, my dismay'; *Inf.* 8.94) to the last integrative 's'io torni mai, lettore, a quel divoto trïunfo' ('So, reader, may I once again return | to those triumphant ranks'; *Par.* 22.106–11), breaking the frame of the plot to shake the reader into looking at the mechanisms and pretexts of its construction.[5] Dante does not of course restrict apostrophe to interpellating the reader. Apostrophized throughout the poem are abstract concepts and allegorical personae; historical figures past or recent; mythological characters; God (by name or by periphrasis); and many more. Nor does Dante restrict his invocations of the reader to apostrophe: we see ourselves strongly implicated in phrases like 'nel mezzo del cammin di *nostra* vita' ('When I had journeyed half of *our life's* way'; *Inf.* 1.1, italics mine); 'possa lasciare *a la futura gente*' ('that I may leave to people of the future'; *Par.* 33.72, italics mine); and '*coloro* che questo tempo chiameranno antico' ('those who will call this present, ancient times'; *Par.* 17.119–20, italics mine).

---

4   Joseph Frank, 'Spatial Form in Modern Literature: An Essay in Two Parts', *The Sewanee Review*, 53.2 (Spring 1945), pp. 221–40.

5   Unless otherwise noted, I quote the Petrocchi edition of the *Commedia* and the Mandelbaum translation: Dante Alighieri, *La Commedia secondo l'antica vulgata*, ed. by Giorgio Petrocchi (Milan: Mondadori, 1966–67); Allen Mandelbaum, Dante Alighieri, *The Divine Comedy*, trans. by Allen Mandelbaum, 3 vols (Berkeley: University of California Press, 1980–82). Both are available on the Digital Dante site: <https://digitaldante.columbia.edu/dante/divine-comedy/>.

But I maintain that the poet's addresses to the reader *as* reader do organize the poem in memory more pointedly and actively even than those the narrating voice makes to larger groups — such as 'superbi cristian, miseri lassi' ('O Christians, arrogant, exhausted, wretched'; *Purg.* 10.121) or 'miseri seguaci' ('sad disciples'; *Inf.* 19.1) — groups to which the reader might conceivably belong or have belonged. Naming the reader as addressee in the very act of our reading recentres our presence as foundational to the acts of poetizing and prophesying that constitute the *Commedia*. Narrating the journey is not enough: Dante must narrate it to an *us*, if he is to make it the utterly unique truth-bearing composition it claims to be.

In countless ways Dante has put us into the poem, as he's put the poem into us. And what an undertaking that is: he has made the poem teach us how to read it, how to reread it. The first canticle is a preparatory lesson in reading: *Inferno* initiates us into a cornucopia of knowledge, patterns, and procedures we need for this reading journey. In narration and dialogue Dante lays out for us not only the figures of rhetoric but their use and misuse, and their function for different residents of hell. *Inferno* teaches us to evaluate an utterance in light of its source, and to find the unmarked relations between speakers — whether sinner, demon, or guide — and their utterances. It makes us see the consequences of deception and self-deception in damned souls, while dissociating the truth-value of the poem (and the veracity of the poet) from its factuality or fictionality. Barolini expounded this unforgettably, revealing the function of Ulysses as a lightning-rod for the condemnation of deceptive speech, mendacity, hubris, and boundary violation.[6] The very accusations that not only could be but were levelled against Dante in his own time, by Cecco d'Ascoli for example, he diverts onto a character who, unlike himself, was not divinely authorized to make his unprecedented journey.

As a self-teaching artifact, *Purgatorio* hovers in the overlap between this life and the next. The second canticle begins to delineate what in the afterlife is unlike earth, preparing the ground for the celestial paradise where earthly calculus is inadequate and misleading. It

---

6   Barolini, 'Ulysses, Geryon, and the Aeronautics of Narrative Transition', UDC, pp. 48–73.

continues the *Inferno*'s practice of having the poem's protagonist be an inset figure for its readers: his perplexity and curiosity are our own, as his learning and satisfaction are ours. But while the pilgrim has to start afresh in purgatory, discarding some lessons he's picked up in hell, we readers build on what the first canticle has taught us *about* reading. The central cantos of *Purgatorio* (and thus of the entire poem) are both an adult's map to the workings of love in mortal life, and a neophyte's introduction to the workings of love in eternity — to the experience of heaven. The whole canticle abounds in such novel revelations for the pilgrim; for the reader, the poet has announced that he must up his game so that his art may be sufficient to his matter:

> Lettor, tu vedi ben com' io innalzo
> la mia matera, e però con più arte
> non ti maravigliar s'io la rincalzo.
>
> (Reader, you can see clearly how I lift
> my matter; do not wonder, therefore, if
> I have to call on more art to sustain it.)
> (*Purg.* 9.70–72)

What the reader will see in the poetry goes beyond the content the pilgrim must master, to include the original and audacious poetic inventions which will multiply dramatically in the earthly paradise cantos.

The third canticle is the culmination of the author's practice of teaching the poem's protagonist truth and doctrine, as a pretext for teaching them to its readers, along with the way that poetry can vehicle them (or almost). *Paradiso* is cumulative, not supersessive, in the way it relies on every teaching and every technique purveyed in *Inferno* and *Purgatorio* while raising them to another level altogether: a mighty organ pulling out every stop, not indiscriminately but sapiently, for maximum beauty and efficacy. It requires no small mastery for Dante to train us through language to the prospect of bliss, a bliss to be gained through grace freely given — though mysteriously assisted by rectitude, humility, and love.

In other words, we readers were always on his mind. His poem is not solely a work of self-fashioning, but also a fundamentally outward-facing one. We are the receptacles into which the poem is poured: the beneficiaries of its food and drink, of the 'pan de li angeli' ('bread of angels'; *Par.* 2.11) which we crave. That is, so long as we are those happy few, not those ill-prepared 'in piccioletta barca' ('within [a] little bark'; *Par.* 2.1), however 'desiderosi d'ascoltar' ('eager to listen'; *Par.* 2.2). Despite the cantus firmus of the metaphor of nourishment fed to us or laid out for us — 'Messo t'ho innanzi; omai per te ti ciba' ('I have prepared your fare; now feed yourself'; *Par.* 10.25) — Dante is not merely filling his readers but forming us.

Beyond metaphors of navigation and nourishment, it would be lengthy and superfluous to detail even the most prominent thematic threads that guide readers across the great sea of the poem. But the paths Barolini tracks become master threads, likely foregrounded in every essay in this book, along which to follow the *undivine* dimension of Dante the author's undertaking: the path and its interruptions, where protagonists or poem are forced to jump; mad flights of arrogance and their calamitous failures, like that of Ulysses; acts of artistic hubris brought low, related to us in one such act which is decidedly not brought low. The process, both concrete and conceptual, of representing *to us* nothing less than everything in the physical and metaphysical world, occurs in a poem that purports to be not merely like God's grandchild but God's co-creation.[7]

The didactic purpose of so many of Dante's strategies and rhetorical figures matches and depends on (is served by) their beauty. For example, chiasmus intensifies and multiplies, from the compact — '"ingiusto fece me contra me giusto"' ('"made me unjust against my own just self"'); *Inf.* 13.72) — to the overflowing and manifold (*Par.* 14.28–60). The canny use of exact lexical repetition, which Barolini calls 'a technique that the poet will use frequently in the third canticle, as a way of signifying the paradox of the thing that both is itself and is the other' (*UDC*, p. 178), creates patterns that are fractal, similar at every level. She examines how this paradox works in the foundational passage where the pilgrim enters the sphere of the moon:

> S'io era *corpo*, e qui non si concepe
> com'una dimensione altra patio,
> ch'esser convien se *corpo* in *corpo* repe,

---

7   Dante has Virgil say that human art is almost like God's grandchild ('[...] a Dio quasi è nepote'; *Inf.* 11.105); the poet describes the co-creation by heaven and earth of this sacred poem ('l poema sacro | al quale ha posto mano e cielo e terra'; *Par.* 25.1–2).

accender ne dovria più il disio
di veder quella essenza in che si vede
come nostra natura e Dio *s'unio*.

(If I was *body* (and on earth we can
not see how things material can share
one space — the case, when *body* enters *body*),
then should our longing be still more inflamed
to see that Essence in which we discern
how God and human nature were made one.)
(*Par.* 2.37–42, italics mine)

Barolini neatly glosses the bookending strategy by which Dante establishes both a synchronic parallel (body into celestial body, both integration and integrity) and a diachronic structure with a telos:

> How the pilgrim can cease to be 'other' and become 'one' with
> the moon while both he and it remain themselves is a question
> that [...] adumbrates a greater mystery, namely that of the
> coexistence of human nature with God's divine nature in one
> united being, the mystery that Dante will try to render at his
> poem's end. (*UDC*, pp. 177–78)

This trinity of *corpo* (body) creates a memory-hoard in the reader, a hoard that decidedly will return to us when we reach the supreme vision where the final mystery is unveiled — the mystery not in fact of the nature of the trinity, but of the incarnation and the interpenetration of independent and unlike beings. 'How can one body, one "corpo," copenetrate with another and yet remain unperturbedly itself?' (*UDC*, p. 177). While the canto explains the joining of the pilgrim and the moon, and points to a later illumination of the joining of humanity and God, it also enacts both semantically and formally the entrance of the poem into the reader, 'while both he and it remain themselves' (*UDC*, p. 177). The poem does not change for entering us, and although we are changed, we do not become other than ourselves for its entry.[8]

In addition to mnemonic repetitions of forms (figures and etyma), Dante also strategically revisits various themes and frames of reference. To recall another Barolini book, *Dante's Poets*, the *dolce stil novo* as well as the larger corpus of medieval Italian lyric is imported into the

---

8   Plainly the poem does change when we adapt it, or translate it, or both, as in Mary Jo
     Bang's project, discussed below.

Commedia beginning with Francesca's quotations in *Inferno* 5.[9] It is recalled in the self-citations that punctuate *Purgatorio*. It suffuses the final dispositive interactions (often described as gallantry, dalliance) with Beatrice, the subject of his love lyrics in that sweet new style.[10] Or the poet thematizes God's 'other book', the created world: the recurring, elegiac evocations of this bright world glimmer against the black backdrop of hell like those June fireflies of *Inferno* 26.25–33. Likewise, the poet returns over and over to the tension of Church and State, obsessively probing the paradox that, although baptism into the Christian faith is humanity's only portal to the Church, and the Church its only certain way to God, nevertheless the Church can also be led badly, whether by men timorous and ineffectual or men evil and overreaching. Such leaders, though steeped in what Dante considers sin and error, are nonetheless God's anointed representatives on earth, so they must not be harmed or toppled.[11] Dante's themes and frames of reference are often shorthanded by characters historical (Constantine, Frederick II), mythological (Arachne, Jason), biblical (Saul, King David), and contemporary (Boniface VIII, Corso Donati). Their return carries with them into the forefront of the reader's memory both earlier occurrences and, after many readings, references yet pending in the poem. Through such deliberately repeated invocation and patterning, the historical author can create, locate, and preserve *within* the very reader whom he thematizes so insistently throughout the poem that 'more fractured, less discursive, less linear, ultimately more "equalized" or "unified" textuality' (*UDC*, p. 226) which Barolini talked about as Dante's aim.

To prepare ourselves to absorb Dante's poem is a formidable undertaking. We can faithfully do the mental training necessary to begin, but our era and context have drifted far from those of Dante, and we are far from the parameters of his original audience. We are the 'futura gente' ('future people'; *Par.* 33.72), by definition not medieval,

---

9   Teodolinda Barolini, *Dante's Poets: Textuality and Truth in the 'Comedy'* (Princeton: Princeton University Press, 1984).

10   The lively verb 'donnear' ('to long for'; *Par.* 24.118 and 27.88), for example, is a provocative repurposing of the register of love-lyric.

11   On destructive Church leadership see, for example, *Inf.* 4.59–60; *Inf.* 19.1–123; *Inf.* 27.85–132; *Purg.* 16.82–129; *Par.* 27.10–66.

and often neither Italian, nor Catholic, nor in many cases Christian at all. We struggle to master his language (and for most, including Italophones, it *is* a struggle). We painstakingly recreate a partial familiarity with the Christian doctrine and controversies that were Dante's daily bread. What we start off knowing of mediaeval science and technology you could put in a thimble and shake, and much of that understanding isn't even accurate as it rattles around in there. Most of us come to Dante's poem with not a tenth of his knowledge of classical myth, or literature, or philosophy, or history; nor have we a thousandth of his knowledge of his own times. All of these are load-bearing supports of the *Commedia*, and our distance from them makes it a challenge to meet the poem and absorb it, in its multiplicity and majesty. General readers and generalist students will not try to mediaevalize themselves by reading the poem dozens of times — and even for specialists who do, that process is very incomplete. What are they to do, then, those modern readers who *want* to know the *Commedia* but find it so effortful? Especially the third canticle, which for devotees is the summit and the payoff of the entire poem?

They can invite the poem into their present. The poem can come to them through a set of translations, adaptations, and 'tradaptations' that refer to what modern readers do know to teach them what they don't.[12] And while the slew of new Dantes can be inconsistent in usefulness, students sometimes arrive at the best of them through a fascination with the worst; and the best among them can be powerful conduits to the *Commedia* itself.[13] In 'the best' I include new translations by poets such as Mary Jo Bang, who tries paradoxically to preserve the *Commedia* by departing from it, rather than rendering its increasingly archaic distance from us. In what follows, I offer an overview of the ways that Bang's translation enacts Barolini's focus on the visible interface between the historical author and the reader, Dante's 'futura gente', in our time and place.

~

---

12   For the coinage *tradaptation* see Katherine Gillen and Kathryn Vomero Santos, 'Shakespeare and the Politics of Tradaptation', *PMLA*, 138.3 (May 2023), pp. 715–20.

13   For a rich overview of Dante invited into our world, see Giuseppe Antonelli, *Il Dante di tutti: un'icona pop* (Turin: Einaudi, 2022).

'Classics are perennial, but translations age and must be replaced': I first heard this from Giuseppe Mazzotta forty-two years ago, and the adage has held up. Consulting the translations of Cary (1814), Longfellow (1867), Sayers (1949–57), even Ciardi (1954–70), it's easy to see how thick the lens can be in places, how warped, and especially how dusty. A poem that we know well in Italian takes on overlays that blur and freeze a fluid verbal surface, and distance a narrative thrust that in its time had more immediacy and drive.

The past fifty years have seen an abundance of new English translations of the *Commedia*, and the digital revolution has enabled the circulation of many more translations than previous technologies and distribution networks had done. Scholarly translations, creative adaptations, graphic novels, adaptations in film, ballet, and opera, and — around the 2021 centenary — a plethora of impermanent revisitations of the *Commedia* have generated new analytical categories for interacting with new versions of the poem. No typology of translation has given Dante scholars a greater intellectual challenge than that of modern poets such as W. S. Merwin and Seamus Heaney, Ciaran Carson and Robert Pinsky, Lorna Goodison and Mary Jo Bang.[14] Dante scholars translating the original poem are typically more committed to reproducing its content and context in translation than to capturing its early ethical and aesthetic novelty. We often struggle to value properly the poetic translations that dust off the poem for the very audiences we most want to read it: students and non-specialists, for whom the most scholarly renditions in English leave the *Commedia* remote and, if not inert, at least tightly corseted in a stately register and specialized commentary.

This remains true, I think, despite the refined work scholars have done on the Dante translations done by poets.[15] Such work focuses on the window glass of new poetic translations or tradaptations, rather

---

14   Many translators of Dante who are also poets hew to the more scholarly side of their
      undertaking than the poetic side (one might think of Steve Ellis and Stanley Lombardo,
      for example).

15   *Dante's Inferno: Translations by Twenty Contemporary Poets*, ed. by Daniel Halpern
      (Hopewell, NJ: Ecco Press, 1993); *The Poet's Dante*, ed. by Peter S. Hawkins and
      Rachel Jacoff (New York: Farrar, Straus and Giroux, 2002); *Divine Comedies for the
      New Millennium: Recent Dante Translations in America and the Netherlands*, ed. by
      Ronald de Rooy (Amsterdam: Amsterdam University Press, 2003); *After Dante: Poets*

than on the Dantean landscape to be seen through it. But this approach certainly remains an alcove of Dante studies, not the main hall; and in the context of Barolini's *Undivine Comedy* I'm looking to privilege neither the original nor the translations, neither the historical author nor his future reader, but where these converge. I visualise a Venn diagram that is not static but dynamic, one that shows the *Commedia* in motion across a great sea of being that is equally multiplex and shifting: the great poem morphing not only through its many re-envisionings, but also within horizons both collective and individual. No one has access to some notionally 'real' or even 'complete' *Commedia*; readers access facets of it through the necessarily contingent lenses of our collective cultural horizon on the one hand, and our individual experiences, minds, bodies, languages, on the other.[16]

American poet Mary Jo Bang's translations of the *Commedia* are superlative examples of this dynamic. Her *Inferno* appeared in print in 2012, her *Purgatorio* in 2021, and her *Paradiso* in 2025.[17] I first encountered Bang's *Inferno* in a National Public Radio interview, with her musical, serious reading of the first tercet:

> Nel mezzo del cammin di nostra vita
> mi ritrovai in una selva oscura
> ché la diritta via era smarrita.
>
> (Stopped mid-motion in the middle
> Of what we call a life, I looked up and saw no sky —
> Only a dense cage of leaf, tree, and twig. I was lost.)
> (*Inf.* 1.1–3; *MJB*)

I, too, was lost. Mesmerized. At that point I'd been in love with the poem for well over half my life, had read it through fifty-four times in Italian, countless times for some sections, in Italian and in translation.

---

in *Purgatory: Translations by Contemporary Poets*, ed. by Nick R. Havely and Bernard O'Donoghue (Todmorden: Arc Publications, 2021).

16   A corollary of the *Commedia*'s multiplicity and mutability is that, while no translation is uniformly the best one, each gets some things uniquely and irreplaceably right (this is also true *in malo*).

17   Dante Alighieri, *Inferno*, trans. by Mary Jo Bang (Minneapolis: Graywolf Press, 2012); Dante Alighieri, *Purgatorio*, trans. by Mary Jo Bang (Minneapolis: Graywolf Press, 2021); Dante Alighieri, *Paradiso*, trans. by Mary Jo Bang (Minneapolis: Graywolf Press, 2025), hereafter *MJB* for Bang's translations. Subsequent references given in parentheses in the main text.

I'd never heard anything like what Bang was doing with my Dante —
because she was doing something with her Dante, not mine. She aimed
at a Dante for our time, in our language, through the filter of her own
poetry:

> How might the lines sound if I were to put them into collo-
> quial English? What if I were to go further and add elements
> of my own poetic style? Would it sound like a cover song, the
> words of the original unmistakably there, but made unfamiliar
> by the fact that someone else's voice has its own characteristics?
> Could it be, like covers sometimes are, a tribute that pays hom-
> age to the original, while at the same time radically departing
> from it? (*MJB Inf.*, p.7)

While my first reading pinged between reservation and awe, my second
and third not only integrated her Dante into mine, but rewired and
galvanized my understanding both of what Dante was doing in his time,
and what and how his poem can mean in ours.

Bang is careful in her translation principles and practice, and describes them in a 'Note on the Translation' in each of the first two
canticles.[18] Since Dante quotes and cites authors who are no longer
vivid to moderns, Bang imports more recent ones we might recognize;
the canto notes assiduously document her invocations of the corpus of
English lyric, or of modern song lyrics (another poetic corpus).[19] She
crafts punchy modernizations of some of Dante's phrasings, which jolt
the reader into our own time and our own lives.[20] Similarly, to balance
the events of Dante's present, Bang invokes events and aspects of our
own time 'to allow the poem to speak with intimacy about the world
we live in: the postmodern, post-9/11, Internet-ubiquitous present'
(*MJB Inf.*, p. 8). Bang doesn't replace Dante's cast of characters with

---

18   MJB, 'A Note on the Translation', in Dante, *Inferno*, pp. 7–12, and 'A Note on the
     Translation', in Dante, *Purgatorio*, pp. xvii–xxiv.

19   'There are lines from [...] Shakespeare, Emily Dickinson, Gertrude Stein, Allen Gins-
     berg, Alice Dunbar-Nelson, and Oscar Wilde, among others. There are snippets of
     songs from contemporary musicians, meant to echo the singers and songs Dante
     weaves into the poem: Bob Dylan, Cyndi Lauper, Led Zeppelin, Amy Winehouse, John
     Coltrane, Marvin Gaye, Talking Heads, Richie Havens, and others' (*MJB Purg.*, pp.
     xxi–ii).

20   'I wanted to [...] create an English-language version of the *Inferno* that would adhere
     to the original but would seem neither remote in time nor elevated in diction' (*MJB
     Inf.*, p. 8).

contemporary ones, as Sandow Birk does in his film and translation:[21] as she says, 'The characters had to remain as they were in the original but I would toy with the poem's rhetorical surface, as well as with the allusions and similes' (*MJB Inf.*, p. 9).

> [Dante] creates a tapestry of verisimilitude, a detailed world filled with everyday objects and recognizable people, architecture, and landscapes. I extended that gesture into the present by including references to such figures and objects as klieg lights and cameras, Susan Sontag and Sigmund Freud, Stephen Colbert and Eric Cartman. They all belong in any mirror that reflects this era. (*MJB Inf.*, p. 10)

She describes the sound-play she favours in place of rhyme and metre: the *sprezzatura* of her alliteration and assonance, in particular, conceals great care.[22]

These various features of her approach would offer one way to organize a reflection on Bang's translations, but I wanted readers of this essay to meet at least a few sustained lines of climactic passages of her *Commedia*. The closing lines from each canticle can encapsulate her specific revelation to me of how the poem perpetuates itself ('s'etterna'; *Inf.* 15.85) in new generations of readers. The culminations of each canticle resound in repeat readers so richly as to give us a 'cammino ascoso' ('hidden road') to 'ritornar nel chiaro mondo' ('to make our way back into the bright world') as *Inferno* closes:

> Luogo è là giù da Belzebù remoto
> tanto quanto la tomba si distende,
> che non per vista, ma per suono è noto
>   d'un ruscelletto che quivi discende
> per la buca d'un sasso, ch'elli ha roso,
> col corso ch'elli avvolge, e poco pende.
>   Lo duca e io per quel cammino ascoso
> intrammo a ritornar nel chiaro mondo;
> e sanza cura aver d'alcun riposo,
>   salimmo sù, el primo e io secondo,
> tanto ch'i' vidi de le cose belle

---

21 Sandow Birk, *Dante's Divine Comedy* (San Francisco: Chronicle Books, 2005), and *Dante's Inferno*, dir. by Sean Meredith (Ricochet Releasing, 2008).

22 'I've relied on the less regimented phonic echoes common to contemporary English poetry: internal, slant, and sign rhyme, alliteration and assonance' (*MJB Purg.*, p. xxi).

che porta 'l ciel, per un pertugio tondo.
    E quindi uscimmo a riveder le stelle.

(Down there, in a remote corner —
The distance of Beelzebub's tomb times two —
Is an area one can't find by sight in that low light
    But only by the sound of a stream that,
As it trickles down a slight incline,
Has carved a winding canyon through the rock.
    My teacher and I entered that secluded passage
That would lead us back to the lit world,
Not wanting to waste time resting, we climbed —
    Him first, then me — until we came to a round opening
Through which I saw some of the beautiful things
That come with Heaven. And there we walked out
    To once again catch sight of the stars.)
(*Inf.* 34.127–39; *MJB*)

At first sight, the verbal surface Bang gives to Dante's subdued transition doesn't draw attention to itself. It is sober and straightforward,
unrhymed and unmetered; as she notes, 'For his terza rima, I substi-
tuted the dominant music of contemporary poetry — assonant echoes,
internal rhyme, alliteration. At times I fell into accentual patterns,
mainly iambs and anapests' (*MJB Inf.*, p. 8). Its artfulness is best appre-
ciated read aloud. The sound play can be sly ('tanto quanto' becomes
'tomb times two'; *Inf.* 34.128; *MJB*) or overt: assonance is an audibly
binding element, as in long -I (*times, find, sight, light, slight, incline,
winding, climbed, time, sight*). Alliteration too has a cohesive effect, as
in initial w- (*one, winding, would, world, wanting, waste, we, which, with,
walked*) and s- (*sight, sound, stream, slight, secluded, saw, some, sight,
stars*). Bang is attentive to nuance: Dante's noun 'ruscelletto' is diminutive, her 'stream' is not, but she postposes a diminutive into the next
line's verb 'trickles' (l. 131). She discards the important reiterative
prefix *ri-*, diffusing it into longer phrases ('lead us back' for 'ritornar',
and 'once again to catch sight of' for 'riveder'); thus she preserves both
its reiterative freight, and its vital function of retrieving the opening of
Inferno 1 ('ritrovai', 'rinova', 'ridir', 'rimirar', 'ripresi', 'ritornar'). With
the verbs 'intrammo' ('entered'; l. 134), 'salimmo' ('climbed'; l. 136),
'uscimmo' ('walked out'; l. 139), Dante gives us — and Bang faithfully
echoes — the very iter of the *Purgatorio* to come, and the inverse of
the descent (l. 130) to the core of *Inferno*.

I have of course occasionally demurred. Bang renders 'quindi' as 'there' rather than 'thence' or 'from there' (*Inf.* 34.139; *MJB*), but so do many or even most English translations (and Bang does keep the sense properly locative, not temporal). 'Not wanting to waste time resting' (l. 135): 'waste time' is inserted, if plausible. Are disparities distracting? Not at all: they appear, only to illuminate and enrich the poem as it subsists in me, as it is part of me.

The end of *Purgatorio* is a more energetic and exhilarated, a more subjective and solitary transition than the anticlimactic close of *Inferno*.

> S'io avessi, lettor, più lungo spazio
> da scrivere, i' pur cantere' in parte
> lo dolce ber che mai non m'avria sazio;
>   ma perché piene son tutte le carte
> ordite a questa cantica seconda,
> non mi lascia più ir lo fren de l'arte.
>   Io ritornai da la santissima onda
> rifatto sì come piante novelle
> rinovellate di novella fronda,
>   puro e disposto a salire a le stelle.
>
> (If I had, Reader, a longer time to write, I would
> As far as possible sing of the sweet drink
> That never would've satisfied me,
>   But because all the cards
> Of the second canticle have been laid out,
> The limits of art won't let me go further.
>   I came back from those most holy waters
> Remade, no longer past repair,
> A new plant, renewed with new leaves —
>   Pure and ready to climb the stairway to the stars.)
> (*Purg.* 33.136–145; *MJB*)

Here, too, I admire the traces of the potter's hand. Bang modernises the image of the 'carte' ('pages') of 'questa cantica seconda' ('this second canticle'), shifting them into cards in a deck that have all 'been laid out' (l. 140; *MJB*): cards in a solitaire or a Tarot display, index cards or post-its (physical or digital) in a modern writer's practise.[23] At the

---

23   'As I went forward, these were the kind of substitutions I allowed myself — worker for peasant, car for cart, Aero for arrow — ones where the medieval original is embodied in the modern' (*MJB Inf.*, p. 9).

same time, in making this shift she has suppressed some significant content: 'piene' ('full') and 'ordite' ('disposed'; l. 139–40) are suppressed altogether; the specific 'lo fren' — in equitation it is 'the bit'; in a mechanism, 'the brake' — is made generic, 'the limits of art' (l. 141; *MJB*). Here as well, Bang carefully renders Dante's retrievals of *Inferno*'s reiterations: 'ritornai' ('I came back'; l. 142); 'rifatto' ('remade'; l. 143); '*ri*novellate' ('renewed'; l. 144, italics mine). Similarly, in 'I came back [...] to climb' she preserves Dante's echo of *Inferno*'s ending ('ritornar', 'salimmo', 'uscimmo'), as well as that of the abortive climb of *Inferno* 1. Dante's polyptoton with 'novelle' is compressed neatly from two lines into one: 'A *new* plant, re*new*ed with *new* leaves' (l. 144, italics mine), but loses the elegant chiasmus of 'piante novelle | rinovellate di novella fronda' (ll. 143–44). Given the novelty of the upcoming celestial paradise, and the centrality of the chiasmus in *Paradiso*, I regret this change that de-emphasizes them.

I described the culminating moment of the second canticle as solitary, due to Virgil's pointed absence; though Beatrice and Statius are present and accompany the pilgrim 'to the stars', they disappear in the last ten lines of *Purgatorio* 33 in favour of an unexpected companion: ourselves. The poet interpellates us, imbricating us almost shockingly in the present of composition: 's'io avessi, lettor, più lungo spazio [...] non mi lascia più ir lo fren de l'arte' ('If I had, Reader, a longer time to write [...] the limits of art won't let me go further'; *Purg.* 33.136–41; *MJB*). The historical author Dante places us at the elbow of the composing poet Dante as he narrates the pilgrim Dante rising from the water renewed and ready to climb to the stars. Again, from the poem's first address to the reader to the last, these moments have functioned to shift us from our world into his, but also from his world into ours. 'Whoa whoa whoa, what's this "no longer past repair" bit', I mutter, but Bang's note clarifies that a Mark Strand poem is being invoked (*MJB Purg.*, p. 356). I invariably hear in 'stairway to the stars' the Led Zeppelin song 'Stairway to Heaven', but that may be idiosyncratic: Bang doesn't specify an allusion, as she always does when one is intended.

Comparing Bang's notes on the third canticle to those of the first two reveals a heightened intention to render the depths and specificities and multiplicities of the *Paradiso*, particularly its dense weave of poetry, theology, philosophy, and history thematized in Barolini's chapter 8. Reading along as she translated and annotated the *Paradiso* has been one of my most vivid joys of recent years. It's a privilege to have been her consultant, attended to with far more solicitude than I would have imagined. The *Commedia*'s closing lines once again offer a microcosm of how the translator handles the challenges specific to this canticle.

> Qual è 'l geomètra che tutto s'affige
> per misurar lo cerchio, e non ritrova,
> pensando, quel principio ond' elli indige,
>   tal era io a quella vista nova:
> veder voleva come si convenne
> l'imago al cerchio e come vi s'indova;
>   ma non eran da ciò le proprie penne:
> se non che la mia mente fu percossa
> da un fulgore in che sua voglia venne.
>   A l'alta fantasia qui mancò possa;
> ma già volgeva il mio disio e 'l *velle*,
> sì come rota ch'igualmente è mossa
>   l'amor che move il sole e l'altre stelle.

> (Like the geometer who gives their all
> To squaring the circle, and still can't uncover,
> Through reasoning, the principle they need —
>   That's how I was at that new sight:
> Wanting to see how the image fit the circle
> And how it in-wheres itself there.
>   But my own wings weren't up to that,
> Had it not been that my mind was suddenly
> Struck by a bolt from the blue and I got my wish.
>   At that, the plug was pulled on my lofty fantasy:
> But my desire and will were already being turned,
> Just like the wheel that is equally moved,
>   By the love that moves the sun and the other stars.)
> (*Par.* 33.133–45; *MJB*)

There may be no locus in the poem where the stakes are higher, and Bang is both meticulous and a gambler. As always, a cohesive sound-scape is created by the alliterative wash, for example, of initial -w (*was, wanting, in-wheres, wings, was, wish, was, will, were, wheel*). But unlike the endings of *Inferno* and *Purgatorio*, at this culmination Bang clusters modern colloquial idioms, some alliterative at that: 'a bolt out of the blue'; 'the plug was pulled'; 'I got my wish'. At the poem's climax, she keeps the earthly and the contemporary side by side with the transcendent and the timeless, so that they re-enact the convergence of contradictory verities in which the whole canticle trades. With the serenity of Dante himself, Bang slips into her version these simultaneously coexisting impossibilia: the simile of squaring the circle; the balked craving which effort fails but revelation succeeds in satisfying; the absorption of the individual into the love that moves the entire universe. The component parts of the experiencing and the writing self — *mente, voglia, fantasia, disio, velle* — are integrated into the whole, bringing the whole of the reading self along, every time.

There is too much to say about this excerpt, but I'll conclude with the neologism 'vi s'indova' (*Par.* 33.138). The neologisms of the *Paradiso* have their detractors and their devotees, and I've fulminated against the habit of diluting or erasing them in translation, as Mandelbaum for example routinely does. At least in the notes, I've moaned, *explain* 's'io mi'intuassi, come tu t'inmii' (*Par.* 9.81, which in Mandelbaum's wretchedly pallid rendering is 'if I could enter you as you do me'). I know of no translator who has taken them in such a beautiful direction as Bang does, for example in her initial solution 'where-within-it it fit' for 'vi s'indova', and her subsequent choice 'in-wheres itself there'. She has found a way to highlight these coinages that express an otherwise inexpressible, inconceivable dynamic, neither flattening them (as in Mandelbaum's bland 'found place in it') nor letting them clank awkwardly along as I would do, marking them with an unlovely literalism. Because Dante presumably coined his neologisms to confront us with novelty and complexity, to make us wrestle for meaning, and to make that awareness — of something new to us — suffuse us, concretely and not only conceptually.

~

In her concluding remarks to the October 2022 symposium, Barolini said that Dante's 'narrative micro-strategies burrow into the reader's mind' and create suspension of disbelief, 'never more so than in the case of a poem that creates a virtual reality based on a revealed religion'. For 'in such a case the response to the work of art is conflated in the minds of many readers with their belief in their religion'. I could not agree more, and I maintain that Bang's translation, by bringing our present into the poem and the poem into our 'postmodern, post-9/11, Internet-ubiquitous present', exemplifies the permeability of the work of art and its reader's own worldview, with or without faith. By steeping us in his poetic creation, Dante makes of us not an audience, but an instrument; not an ear, but a soundbox; not a solitary reader bound on a single journey, but a communal and virtual incarnation of the poem. A kind of church of the *Commedia*, as communitarian and contentious as most churches seem to be. We are the volume in which the poem's leaves are bound up; we are the manuscript copies littered with marginal notes, corrections, manicules, our remembered or imagined illustrations, our errors of recollection or understanding, our palimpsested interpretations which we articulate and then over-write. The poem is multiplied infinitely in its readers, who embody and vehicle it in flesh and blood, as powerfully as written copies do (if more intangibly, sporadically, and unreliably). We are the locus where the sequence of single sounds converges into polyphony, where the diachrony of the 'dolci note' ('sweet notes') becomes the synchrony of 'dolce armonia' ('sweet harmony'; *Par.* 6.124–26).

It is within our minds that the poem's diachrony and synchrony enact their tidal pull between the binaries Barolini examines in chapter 8 of *The Undivine Comedy*: unity and multiplicity; identity and difference; time and eternity; place and non-spatiality; permanence and contingency. That the actualization of the poem lies in the locus of reader memory is one of the gifts of *The Undivine Comedy* I've honestly grasped from no other writing. I'm grateful to Barolini for being the extraordinary expositor of Dante that she continues to be, both in her recent, current and future work, and in the lasting reverb of her earlier writing. *The Undivine Comedy* has authorised us — the 'futura gente' whose world Dante did not foresee, but whose hunger and thirst he certainly did — to be full participants in, and incarnations of, this 'lapsing, unsoilable, | whispering sea'.[24]

---

24   'Ringsend', lines 21–22, in Oliver St John Gogarty, *The Poems and Plays of Oliver St John Gogarty* (Gerrards Cross, Bucks: Colin Smythe Limited, 2002), pp. 110–11 (p. 111).

From Detheologizing to Decolonizing
Toward a Reading of Dante and Alterity
AKASH KUMAR

Detheologizing as a method of reading Dante remains as vital now as it did when *The Undivine Comedy* was published in 1992. Barolini's fundamental insight that we must 'break out of the hermeneutic guidelines that Dante has structured into his poem, hermeneutic guidelines that result in theologized readings whose outcome has been overdetermined by the author'[1] provides the clearest path forward for new research and possibility in the ossified field that is Dante studies. In my view, this is applicable not only to theologizing as a praxis rooted in religious orientation, but also in the positioning of Dante as the father of Italian language and culture, the defining figure of Italian national identity. In other words, I view decolonizing Dante as a method of reading that is derived from Barolini's detheologizing, with the purpose of opening our reading of the poem out to global and cross-cultural currents as a way of moving beyond the overdetermined readings that stem from a nationalist and Eurocentric reception history.

This essay will draw inspiration from chapter 2, 'Infernal Incipits: The Poetics of the New', to dwell on how Barolini's meditation on

---

1   Teodolinda Barolini, *The Undivine Comedy: Detheologizing Dante* (Princeton: Princeton University Press, 1992), p. 17, hereafter *UDC*. Subsequent references given in parentheses in the main text.

narrative difference has much to offer with regard to Dante's interest in cultural difference. I argue that attention to Dante's postcolonial readers, especially Caribbean poets Derek Walcott and Lorna Goodison, may serve as a way to bring us back to the *Commedia* itself and attune ourselves to Dante's love of difference with a decolonizing sensibility. As a way of framing that approach, I would like first to consider one of the epigraphs from that chapter of *The Undivine Comedy*: a citation from the 1949 P. G. Wodehouse novel *The Mating Season*. As one can appreciate after many readings, there is a whole world in the epigraphs of Barolini's book. In this case, a citation from the comic mid-century English novel brilliantly introduces the narratological problem of beginnings and the dynamic between author and audience:

> But half a jiffy. I'm forgetting that you haven't the foggiest what all this is about. It so often pans out that way when you begin a story. You whizz off the mark all pep and ginger, like a mettlesome charger going into its routine, and the next thing you know, the customers are up on their hind legs, yelling for footnotes. (Wodehouse, quoted in *UDC*, p. 21)

I had never heard of P. G. Wodehouse when I first read *The Undivine Comedy*, and it would be a few years before I read my first Jeeves and Wooster novel (the 1934 *Right Ho, Jeeves*). Now, many years later, I can place this novel as occupying (quite aptly) a middle position in the complex of Jeeves and Wooster short stories and novels, ranging from the 1915 short story that marks the first appearance of Jeeves to the 1974 novel, *Aunts Aren't Gentlemen*, published shortly before the author's death. It now seems to me that this epigraph has more to it than the droll evocation of a narrator who realizes that he has forgotten to clue in his audience to the background of the story that he tells.

The Jeeves and Wooster dynamic is one that relies upon difference: Bertie is the bumbling London gentleman who goes to his club, visits family and friends in the country, and always manages to find himself in awkward situations as a result of well-intentioned meddling; Jeeves is his Spinoza-reading, poetry-quoting, unflappable gentleman's gentleman who always manages to save the day. The mere fact of their social difference — Bertie the gentleman, Jeeves his valet — is made far more apparent by the study in contrasts that they provide: we can feel assured that Jeeves would not find himself in the predicaments that

Bertie does, for he would be far too prudent for that. We might also imagine how Jeeves as narrator would fail utterly: his version of the story would be clinical and dry, matter-of-fact to the point of boredom. All of this, of course, resonates with a Dantean contention that nobility cannot possibly be conferred by birth alone ('Rade volte risurge per li rami | l'umana probitate'; 'How seldom human worth ascends from branch | to branch', as we read in *Purgatorio* 7.121–22).[2]

In this light, the link between narrative difference, the poetics of the new, and issues of identity evoked in the social difference between Bertie and Jeeves makes of this epigraph a lens through which we might consider Dante's difference-making in a broader sense. Jay Ruud draws attention to Wodehouse's use of chivalry as a kind of medievalism that creates an otherworld not dissimilar from that of the *Commedia*: 'Wodehouse is fully aware that his chivalry is an anachronism, practiced by his more idealistic characters against the modern, realistic, and mercantile interests of the powerful older women in his stories. But then, so is his Edwardian world: his characters adopt an outmoded sense of nobility, filtered through a by this time outdated Victorian sense that perfectly fits Wodehouse's Victorian society which is also an imagined, idealized place no longer existing in reality.'[3] This sense of Wodehouse's medievalism extends not only to gender and social class, but can even move in the direction of cultural difference. The end of *The Mating Season* finds Bertie Wooster, as is very often the case, having operated in a way that has undoubtedly enraged his aunt. Contrary to the usual paradigm, Bertie decides not to make a quick escape but instead to stay and confront the aged relative. The very last line of the novel frames this encounter as a medieval one: 'I squared the shoulders and strode to the door, like Childe Roland about to fight the paynim.'[4] Wodehouse at once evokes a Crusades paradigm, pitting

---

2   Quotations from the *Commedia* are from Dante Alighieri: *La Commedia secondo l'antica vulgata*, ed. by Giorgio Petrocchi, Società Dantesca Italiana, Edizione Nazionale, 2nd rev. edn, 4 vols (Florence: Le Lettere, 1994). English translations come from Dante Alighieri, *The Divine Comedy*, trans. by Allen Mandelbaum, 3 vols (Berkeley: University of California Press, 1980–82).

3   Jay Ruud, '"Never Built at All, and Therefore Built Forever": Camelot and the World of P. G. Wodehouse', *Connotations*, 24.1 (2014–15), pp. 105–21 (p. 106).

4   P. G. (Pelham Grenville) Wodehouse, *The Mating Season* (Woodstock: Overlook Press, 2001), p. 272. The Robert Browning poem 'Childe Roland to the Dark Tower Came'

Christian knight against 'paynim', and complicates the binary by making it a comic encounter between a bumbling nephew and peevish aunt,
thus making familial conflict out of what might otherwise be framed as
a clash of civilizations.

I will come back to this complicating of cultural difference, but
first I want to dwell on what it is that Barolini establishes about difference and newness as lying at the very heart of Dante's poetry. She
characterizes the *Commedia* as being more self-conscious than most
narratives in its embrace of the poetics of the new, and insists on this
as a profoundly human quality that is linked to difference. In dwelling
on the difference between angelic and human forms of knowledge as
evoked in *Paradiso* 29, she connects these two qualities. Angels do
not have their sight interrupted by new objects and so do not need
memory to distinguish between the old and new, unlike the human
need to create narratives bound in time for ourselves: 'The new ("novo
obietto") comports difference ("concetto diviso"), and both are essentially human' (*UDC*, p. 23). Barolini tellingly finds this idea of newness
and difference to be part of the very rhyme scheme of the *Commedia*
and draws attention to its insistent music: 'This process, whereby an
alterity, the new rhyme, becomes the identity of the subsequent tercet,
imitates the genealogical flow of human history, in which the creation
of each new identity requires the grafting of alterity onto a previous
identity' (*UDC*, p. 25). This connection between *terza rima*, alterity,
and identity is powerful on its own. Finding that it imitates the genealogical flow of human history is something far more powerful, in
that we can see in the very flow and movement of the poem a constant reminder of Dante's devotion to difference, his awareness of the
non-fixity of human identity in time and, indeed, in cultural crossings.

In this regard, it is perhaps of greater importance still that Derek
Walcott adopts and adapts *terza rima* for his 1990 epic novel *Omeros*.
In a work that dwells upon the creation of St. Lucia's identity through
the grafting of alterity in language, commerce, and culture by colonial
violence, it is Dante's meter — or rather, Walcott's version of *terza*

(first published in 1855) is certainly part of the reference here, but the antiquated word
'paynim' never appears in that poem and seems to be part of Wodehouse's expanded
approach to satirizing this Crusades dynamic at the conclusion of his novel.

rima — that persists and pervades throughout the various evocations of Homeric and Virgilian epic.[5] To dwell on what Walcott does with respect to the grafting of alterity onto a previous identity, we might look to a moment early on in *Omeros*, where the poet narrator (here, too, a telling use of the Dantean *personaggio-poeta* device) dwells on the relationship between the modern and ancient with a beloved who is soon to leave him:

> 'O-meros', she laughed. 'That's what we call him in Greek',
> stroking the small bust with its boxer's broken nose,
> and I thought of Seven Seas sitting near the reek
>   of drying fishnets, listening to the shallows' noise.
> I said: 'Homer and Virg are New England farmers,
> and the winged horse guards their gas station, you're right'.[6]

The name Homer is revealed to be a translation, a domestication that robs the original of its identity. Yet, that 'original' Greek form of the name and the marble bust of the long-dead poet are connected to the blind fisherman Seven Seas and the reek of drying fishnets, and to a living oral tradition of St. Lucia. In a broader sense, the anglicized forms of Homer and Virg (instead of Omeros and Vergilius) as New England farmers, along with a reference to Pegasus having long been used by Mobil Oil in its logo, ask us to think about the constant grafting of alterity onto previous identities, to interrogate the absorption of such alterity to the point of hiding the difference that lies beneath. As the encounter continues, the name 'Omeros' is made creole, a combination of different languages and of nature itself.

> [...] I said, 'Omeros',
>   and *O* was the conch-shell's invocation, *mer* was
> both mother and sea in our Antillean patois,
>   *os*, a grey bone, and the white surf as it crashes
> and spreads its sibilant collar on a lace shore.
> Omeros was the crunch of dry leaves, and the washes
> that echoed from a cave-mouth when the tide has ebbed.[7]

---

5   On Dante and Walcott, see especially Maria Cristina Fumagalli, *The Flight of the Vernacular: Seamus Heaney, Derek Walcott, and the Impress of Dante* (Amsterdam: Rodopi, 2001).

6   Derek Walcott, *Omeros* (New York: Noonday, 1990), p. 14.

7   Ibid.

By so parsing the name, fusing the elemental language of conch-shell and surf with Latin and patois, Walcott orients us not only to the incantatory possibilities of such cultural and linguistic fusion, but also to the inherent alterities in places such as his island of St. Lucia.

This embrace of difference, revealed by the unraveling and creoliz-ing of a seeming cultural monolith such as the name of Homer, might ask us to turn to issues of language with respect to Dante as well. I would like to do so by way of Jamaican poet Lorna Goodison, who has adapted select canti of the *Commedia* for some decades now. In the essay 'Some poems that made me', Goodison evocatively looks back at her poetic influences from childhood and beyond. Toward the end of this short piece, she writes the following about Dante: 'I would say that the poem that has had the greatest impact on my adult life is *The Divine Comedy*. My engagement with it began when I was one of several poets invited by the Southbank Centre in London to rewrite one of the Cantos from Dante's masterpiece. To date I have rewritten seven cantos, setting them all in Jamaica and employing Jamaican dialect in tribute to the great Italian poet who wrote in the local language of his people'.[8] Goodison's attention to issues of language and setting in her telling adaptations asks us to look at the language of the *Commedia* with perhaps a different sensibility. In her 2013 collection *Oracabessa*, Goodison rewrites *Inferno* 1 to stunning effect. Here is her version of the first simile:

> Like a swimmer who is out of her depth in big sea,
> > who battle the waves until she reach to shore
> and as she blow for breath she marvel at how
>
> she managed to escape from grave watery death.
> > Just like that, I turned back to study with awe
> the dark pass that no one before me had left alive.[9]

We can note how Goodison makes the extended simile her own, shift-ing the gender of the poetic subject (as she maintains throughout the canto) and subtly infusing the moment with a Jamaican vernacular

---

8   Lorna Goodison, *Redemption Ground: Essays and Adventures* (Brighton and Hove: Myriad Editions, 2018), p. 29.

9   I cite from the version collected in Lorna Goodison, *Collected Poems* (Manchester: Carcanet, 2017), p. 558.

sensibility. As Jason Allen-Paisant puts it, 'We witness Goodison ar-
ticulating a sense of personal identity, putting herself, instead of Dante,
at the centre of the poem'.[10] This is no wholesale transformation with
patois at every turn, but we nonetheless register shifts such as 'in big
sea' lacking a definite article and expressions like 'reach to shore' and
'blow for breath'. This is neither 'pure' English nor 'pure' Jamaican
creole; rather, it is a mix of languages, a blending that might, in fact,
ask us to reconsider Goodison's own characterization of Dante as a
great Italian poet who wrote in the local language of his people. Instead,
through this hybrid poetics, we might extend Dante's love of difference
to the poetic verve that insistently blends languages together throughout the *Commedia*. Through this insistent mixing of languages and
poetic registers in the work of Caribbean poets such as Derek Walcott
and Lorna Goodison, we might think of Virgil's apparent use of dialect
in *Inferno* 27, Arnaut Daniel's Occitan in *Purgatorio* 26, and telling
hybrids of Latin and vernacular throughout the poem as important
ways of combating the nationalist ideology of Dante as the father of
Italian.[11]

Goodison dedicates this published version of her *Inferno* 1 to
Derek Walcott and, indeed, goes on to transform the figure of the guide
into someone who seems to be none other than Walcott himself.[12]
When we come to the end of the canto and Virgilio's reveal of the
journey that will follow, we find that Goodison most tellingly expands
upon the terms of the guide's outsider status. Virgilio's statement of
difference that marks the terms of his exclusion 'perch'i' fu' ribellante
a la sua legge' ('since I have been rebellious to His law'; *Inf.* 1.125)
is expanded and transformed into a far greater rebellion: '[...] I who

---

10   See Jason Allen-Paisant, 'Dante in Caribbean Poetics: Language, Power, Race', in *The
      Oxford Handbook of Dante*, ed. by Manuele Gragnolati, Elena Lombardi, and Francesca
      Southerden (Oxford: Oxford University Press, 2021), pp. 668–85 (p. 680).

11   For more on this line of reading, see Akash Kumar, 'Authentically Speaking: Dante and
      the Politics of Language in Meloni's Italy', *Dante Notes*, November 21, 2022 <https://
      www.dantesociety.org/node/176> [accessed 28 May 2025].

12   Goodison has just published a full version of *Inferno* in which she has made the
      decision to move away from Walcott as the Virgil figure, instead choosing Jamaican
      poet Louise Bennett. We can certainly think further about the gender implications of
      this transformation. My thanks to Lorna Goodison for our inspirational exchanges and
      to Elizabeth Coggeshall for our discussions about Goodison's work over these past few
      years.

rebelled | against all forms of hierarchy and divisions of class and race'.[13] Heaven is depicted as a corrupt political regime in which straw bosses make biased decisions about who is permitted entry and who is excluded. Goodison thus relates the exclusion of Virgilio on religious and temporal grounds to a form of rebellion that rails against excluding alterity, particularly the sort of alterity based in class and race. This poignant adaptation might take us back to what Barolini observes as Dante's 'institutionalizing of difference' that causes critical overreach and his 'love of difference' (*UDC*, p. 33) that challenges all of us as readers. Goodison as a reader of Dante is perhaps picking up on the drama of Virgilio as one that implicates and elides the temporal, cultural, and geographical. As Barolini points out in her treatment of *Inferno* 4 and its seeming lack of excitement, 'its drama unfolds as the story of Vergil and the virtuous pagans unfolds and culminates in *Paradiso* 19's agonized questioning of the justice that condemns those deprived of the knowledge of God through no fault of their own' (*UDC*, pp. 37–38). Taken in this way, the rebellion is indeed oriented to more far-reaching hierarchies and forms of division, ones that include the man born on the banks of the Indus river who seems to be unjustly condemned through no other fault than a lack of access.

I would like to conclude this essay with one more postcolonial reader of Dante who, in a sense, combines a decolonizing and detheologizing approach to the *Commedia*: Salman Rushdie. Rushdie, by his very name, asks us to look with eyes more attuned to Dante's love of difference at the last name in the catalogue of non-Christian excellence that dominates *Inferno* 4: 'Averoìs, che 'l gran comento feo' ('Averroes, of the great Commentary'; *Inf.* 4.144). In his 2012 autobiography about his time under police protection in the wake of the Khomeini fatwa, Rushdie writes the following about his late discovery of the origin of his name:

> Anis renamed himself 'Rushdie' because of his admiration for Ibn Rushd, 'Averroës' to the West, the twelfth-century Spanish-Arab philosopher of Córdoba who rose to become the *qadi* or judge of Seville, the translator of and acclaimed commentator upon the works of Aristotle. His son bore the name for two

---

13   Goodison, *Collected Poems*, pp. 561–62.

decades before he understood that his father, a true scholar
of Islam who was also entirely lacking in religious belief, had
chosen it because he respected Ibn Rushd for being at the
forefront of the rationalist argument against Islamic literalism
in his time; and twenty more years elapsed before the battle
over *The Satanic Verses* provided a twentieth-century echo of
that eight-hundred-year-old argument.[14]

Rushdie's dwelling on his father's choice, his framing of Ibn Rushd as
embodying rationalism that opposed dogma and literalism, highlights
the radical nature of Dante's choice in his own time and in ours. This is
something made all the more apparent in the wake of the horrific attack
on Rushdie in 2022. On a more direct front, we might look to Rushdie's
essay 'Proteus', in which he frames his relationship to Shakespeare with
a look to Dante.[15] He contrasts his relationship to Ben Jonson and
Shakespeare in the following way:

> I acted in Jonson but he hasn't remained useful to me, whereas
> Shakespeare is both my door knocker and the owner of the
> domains to which the knock admits me, at once my Virgil
> opening the gates of hell and heaven, and the devil, and God,
> and I say this as a person who believes in neither God nor the
> devil, I believe only in Virgil, but I understand the nature of the
> contract of fiction, so I can agree to suspend disbelief in what I
> know is not to be believed in the hope of finding, by doing so,
> some truth on which I can rely, in which I can have faith.[16]

Rushdie is a detheologized reader of Dante. He also serves important
decolonizing purposes. Indeed, what it means to believe in Virgil is
nothing short of understanding the slow burn of the poem's drama that
stretches from first to last, that asks us to see, as Goodison does, what it
is to expand Virgil's rebellion to encompass a rebellion against all forms
of hierarchy and division. By so embracing Dante's love of difference,
we might continue to hope, as Rushdie does, to find some truth on
which we can rely.

---

14   Salman Rushdie, *Joseph Anton: A Memoir* (New York: Random House, 2012), pp.
     22–23.

15   For more on Rushdie's own reflections on the attack and his recovery, see Salman
     Rushdie, *Knife: Meditations After an Attempted Murder* (New York: Random House,
     2024).

16   I cite from the version collected in Salman Rushdie, *Languages of Truth: Essays,
     2003–2020* (New York: Random House, 2022), p. 34.

Translating *The Undivine Comedy*

ROBERTA ANTOGNINI

ATTENZIONE
La traduzione è ragnatela,
Cioè strapiombi e cornicioni,
Ma pure vincoli e cordoni.
Usare comunque cautela.

(ATTENTION
Translation is a cobweb,
Precipices and cornices,
But also, restrictions and ropes.
Use caution, nevertheless.)

Nicola Gardini[1]

My first true and mindful encounter with Dante took place in 1986. At the time, I was a student at NYU starting a PhD in Italian after completing my *laurea* in Milan. Before our first class, Teo Barolini, our young Dante professor, provided us with a bibliography, syllabus, and a meagre course description that read:

> This course consists of a guided tour through the *selva oscura* of the first half of the *Divina Commedia*: *Inferno* I through *Purgatorio* XVI. We will discuss interpretative issues, regarding — for instance — the allegorical question, the poem's intertextual currents, its relation to the other texts in Dante's canon, et al., but all such discussion will be grounded in our object of primary focus: namely, a thorough knowledge of the text.

---

1   Nicola Gardini, *Tradurre è un bacio* (Borgomanero: Giuliano Landolfi, 2015), p. 17, translation mine.

Knowledge of the text! Paradoxical as it seems, for an Italian university student in the eighties who had prepared her exams mostly relying on secondary sources, or at most reading texts on her own, it was a dream come true.

Little did I know then that in 1999, thirteen years later, Teo Barolini would ask me to translate her second book, *The Undivine Comedy*, into Italian. It was my first experience as a translator (and the beginning of a love affair with translation that never faded — even though it was my last stab at a non-fiction work). I learned, so to speak, to translate in the field, like most professional translators do. Although I knew nothing of translation theory or the history of translation, and therefore had no particular critical awareness of it, I had a background in the history of Italian language: this allowed me to engage in a translation strategy that involved a simple, careful, and almost maniacal reading of the original text (after all, in their day-to-day work, translators follow a strategy rather than a theory).[2] I regret not having kept a translation diary such as the one which, in imitation of the great American translator of Italian fiction, William Weaver, I would ask my students to keep years later when, as a result of my experience and subsequent fascination with the translation of *The Undivine Comedy*, I developed a course on literary translation at Vassar College.[3] A translation diary is a reflection on the translation process and its strategies, on problems encountered and decisions made, in an autobiographical key based on one's individual experience: something halfway between theory and practice.[4]

---

2   See Giancarlo Marchesini, 'Teorie della traduzione e strategie traduttive', in *I saperi del tradurre. Analogie, affinità, confronti*, ed. by Clara Montella (Milan: Franco Angeli, 2007), pp. 45–69 (p. 45).

3   See William Weaver's various publications of and about his translation diaries: 'In Other Words: A Translator's Journal', *The New York Times*, 19 November 1995, Sec. 7, p. 16; Weaver, 'Pendulum Diary', *Southwest Review*, 75.2 (Spring 1990), pp. 150–78; Weaver, 'The Process of Translation', in *The Craft of Translation*, ed. by John Biguenet and Rainer Schulte (Chicago: Chicago University Press, 1989), pp. 117–24 <https://www.gadda.ed.ac.uk/Pages/resources/babelgadda/babeng/weavertranslation.php> [accessed 23 April 2025].

4   Bruna Di Sabato, 'Tradurre il testo non letterario', in *I confini della traduzione*, ed. by Bruna Di Sabato and Antonio Perri (Limena: Libreriauniversitaria.it, 2014), pp. 47–69 (pp. 47–8). Once very rare — translators contented themselves with writing reflections in the form of essays in journals —, books written by translators on the translation process are becoming increasingly frequent. Both have enormous pedagogical value.

Though I wasn't a Dante scholar, I nevertheless considered myself a specialist in the field. After taking Teo's classes at NYU, I felt assured of my knowledge of the *Commedia*, and, instinctively, I felt that the intertext generated by translations is an essential part of the reading of a work and that mine, too, would contribute, in its own small way, to ensure the survival of Teo's book.[5] It took more than two years to complete my translation. Throughout that entire and memorable time, Teo and I — both strong believers, like Calvino, in the collaboration between author and translator — remained in close contact.[6] In 2003, the translated edition was published by Feltrinelli Editore in Milan.

One more element is necessary to complete this picture. The year 1999 was also my first as a visiting assistant professor at Vassar College, and I trusted that translating a book on Dante would greatly improve my academic English. I also trusted that such a close reading would help me enormously in writing my own book when the time came. Again, in Calvino's words, 'tradurre è il vero modo di leggere un testo'; 'si *legge* veramente un autore solo quando lo si traduce' ('translating is the true way to read a text; you really *read* an author only when

---

5   As Walter Benjamin claims in his 1923 famous essay, 'The Task of the Translator': 'Just as the manifestations of life are intimately connected with the phenomenon of life without being of importance to it, a translation issues from the original — not so much from its life as from its afterlife. For a translation comes later than the original, and since the important works of world literature never find their chosen translators at the time of their origin, their translation marks their stage of continued life'. Walter Benjamin, 'The Task of the Translator: An Introduction to the Translation of Baudelaire's *Tableaux Parisiens*', in *The Translation Studies Reader*, ed. by Lawrence Venuti (New York and London: Routledge, 2004), pp. 75–85 (p. 76). Many scholars have since appropriated the idea of translation as the 'continued life' of the original. As Susan Bassnett states: 'For, as Benjamin also reminds us, it is the translator who ultimately assures the survival of the text. By translating, a text reaches a wider pool of readers than the original author can ever have imagined'. Susan Bassnett, 'Intricate Pathways: Observations on Translation and Literature', in *Translating Literature*, ed. by Susan Bassnett (London: Boydell & Brewer, 1997), pp. 1–13 (p. 13). Likewise, as Cattani and others state in the introduction to their edited issue of *Ticontre*: 'Le traduzioni generano un intertesto e si inscrivono nella storia delle letture di un'opera, che contribuiscono a creare; esse assicurano il ciclo di nascita e rinascita continuo dei testi' ('Translations generate an intertext and are part of the reading of a work, which they contribute to creating; they ensure the continuous cycle of birth and rebirth of a text'; translation mine). Paola Cattani, Matteo Fadini, and Federico Saviotti, 'In principio fuit interpres', *Ticontre. Teoria Testo Traduzione*, 3 (2015), pp. 3–12 (pp. 10–11) <https://teseo.unitn.it/ticontre/article/view/957/957> [accessed 23 April 2025].

6   This collaboration, writes Calvino, first arises 'from the translator's questions to the author'. Italo Calvino, 'Tradurre è il vero modo di leggere un testo', in Calvino, *Mondo scritto e mondo parlato* (Milan: Mondadori, 2002), pp. 85–91 (p. 88).

you translate them).[7] Unfortunately, as a demonstration of how little consideration is given to translation, Vassar never considered my work as an academic publication. Many years have passed since then, but regrettably, in terms of the *visibility* of the translator, not a lot of progress has been made — though some publishers in Italy, notably smaller presses, have started to add the translator's name to the book cover.[8] The notion of *invisibility* is quite prominent in recent translation studies. It was employed rather polemically by Lawrence Venuti in his 1995 volume *The Translator's Invisibility*. This idea derives from a conception of translation as a 'second-order representation' vis-à-vis the original, 'whereas the translation is derivative, fake, potentially a false copy'.[9] In order to make the original stand out, translation must become invisible, 'producing the illusion of authorial presence whereby the translated text can be taken as the original',[10] an idiomatic translation that favours readers of the target text by adapting it to their expectations. The difficulty seems to be that translation is halfway between art and craft, and as a result, its standing among the intellectual professions seems to be the most abused.[11]

---

7   Italo Calvino, 'Tradurre è il vero modo', p. 87, and 'Sul tradurre', in Calvino, *Mondo scritto e mondo parlato*, pp. 47–59 (p. 51, italics in the original). Calvino was probably not the first and definitely not the last to say so, as it has become a common motto in translation studies.

8   Not Feltrinelli, the Italian publisher of *The Undivine Comedy*, or not yet at least. Edith Grossman, the celebrated literary translator who recently passed, 'was among the first to insist that on any book she translated, her name appear on the cover along with that of the author, a practice that publishers had traditionally resisted for both financial and marketing reasons. They liked to think that they could wave "a magic wand" and turn a book from one language into another, she joked in the interview. "And no human is involved. No human who needs to be paid?"' (Rebecca Chace, 'Edith Grossman, Who Elevated the Art of Translation, Dies at 87', Obituary, *The New York Times*, 4 September 2023 <https://www.nytimes.com/2023/09/04/books/edith-grossman-dead.html> [accessed 24 April 2025]). In her essay on translation, Grossman wrote: 'Putting to the side for a moment the dire state of publishing today or the lamentable tendency of too many publishers to treat translators cavalierly or dismiss them as irrelevant, the fact is that many readers tend to take translation so much for granted that it is no wonder translators are so frequently ignored. We seem to be a familiar part of the natural landscape — so customary and commonplace that we run the risk of becoming invisible'. See Edith Grossman, *Why Translation Matters* (New Haven: Yale University Press, 2010), pp. 26–27.

9   Lawrence Venuti, *The Translator's Invisibility* (New York: Routledge, 2008), p. 6.

10 Ibid.

11 See Laura Bocci, *Di seconda mano* (Milan: Rizzoli, 2004), p. 49.

In their introduction to one of the few collections of essays devoted to the translation of non-fiction works, authors Bramati and
Regattin complain that even though the linguistic problems one encounters are not very different from those of literary translation, unlike
literary works, the translation of texts belonging to humanistic or scien-
tific disciplines has so far not attracted much attention from scholars.[12]
And yet, Western thought on translation in the modern age begins with
the great humanist Leonardo Bruni and his brief unfinished treatise *De
interpretatione recta*, which describes his translation from Greek into
Latin of Aristotle's *Ethics*. Broadly speaking, a scholarly work could be
considered an ultimate form of intralingual (or endolinguistic) translation that is, according to the seminal definition by Roman Jakobson
in his 1959 essay on translation, an interpretation of verbal signs by
means of other signs in the same language.[13] Translating a scholarly
work is in some respects more complex than translating a literary work.
In fact, it entails not only analytical competence with regard to the
source text and reproductive competence with regard to the target text,
but also knowledge of many different fields and authors, which makes
it very close to scholarly research itself.[14] Furthermore, like a literary
work, it's a creative act, it demands aesthetic attention, the ability to
hear the true voice of the author. In Leonardo Bruni's words:

> [A translator] must possess a sound ear so that his translation
> does not disturb and destroy the fullness and rhythmical qual-
> ities of the original. For since in every good writer [...] there
> is both learning and literary style, he and he only will be a
> satisfactory translator [*interpres*] who is able to preserve both.[15]

12   Alberto Bramati and Fabio Regattin, 'Tradurre saggistica divulgativa: un'introduzione',
     Lingue Culture Mediazioni/Languages Cultures Mediation, 6.2 (2019), pp. 5–10 (pp.
     5–6) <https://doi.org/10.7358/lcm-2019-002-brre>.

13   Roman Jakobson, 'On Linguistic Aspects of Translation', in *The Translation Studies
     Reader*, ed. by Lawrence Venuti (New York: Routledge, 2004), pp. 138–43 (p. 139;
     italics in the original). The other two kind of translations are: 'interlingual translation
     or *translation proper* [...] an interpretation of verbal signs by means of some other
     language', and 'intersemiotic translation or *transmutation* [...] an interpretation of
     verbal signs by means of signs of nonverbal sign systems' (Ibid., p. 139).

14   See Johanna Monti, 'Alla ricerca della conoscenza. Quali strumenti per la traduzione
     saggistica?', in *Tradurre saggistica. Traduttori, traduttologi ed esperti a confronto*, ed. by
     Clara Montella (Milan: Franco Angeli, 2010), pp. 143–61 (pp. 144–46).

15   Leonardo Bruni, *The Humanism of Leonardo Bruni. Selected Texts*, trans. by James
     Hankins (Binghamton, NY: Medieval & Renaissance Texts & Studies in conjunction
     with the Renaissance Society of America, 1987), p. 220.

Even though Teo Barolini's voice was loud and clear, I had to listen
carefully to give Italian readers the same immersion in the text she was
able to provide, echoing her authority, passion, and fierceness. Sadly,
none of the correspondence between the two of us during that time
survives — Vassar changed its e-mail software in 2003, and I was not
able to retrieve any of the old messages. However, Teo had kept hard
copies of some of it. One comment I made while working on the first
two chapters stands out:

> Your writing is as dense as the concepts you express. But the
> fact that I understand every single word because it is as if I were
> listening to you while you're teaching is of great advantage. The
> problem is that I want to respect your 'density', your choice of
> words and composition, without rendering the Italian syntax
> less fluid than English, too heavy.

So, as I moved bag and baggage[16] into Teo's text, slowly and meticu-
lously translating the dense, cohesive pages of *The Undivine Comedy*, it
occurred to me that, in a way, I was repeating my student experience.
As I quickly discovered, the biggest challenge was that Teo's writing
is so deep and intense, so concentrated that while studying her book,
a student would be likely to underline almost everything; similarly, I
struggled to keep up during class because I wanted to write down her
every word. And still, everything is so wonderfully clear, so perfectly
'densely clear'. In another email, I would define her style as 'cumulative':
that is, repetitively accumulating new encounters with the 'new'. It is
almost as if she, by commenting on Dante, had become Dante himself,
adopting his own style in which everything counts, nothing is superfluous, and the writer's understanding of the subject runs incredibly
deep. In rereading my translation nineteen years later, I find myself in
the exact situation of 'finding the new within the old', repeating the
spiral-like structure of the transitional cantos described in *The Undivine
Comedy* at the end of chapter 3, 'Ulysses, Geryon, and the Aeronautics
of Narrative Transition':

> [...] transition, history, life itself are spiral-like, *ever going
> backward in order to go forward* (as the pilgrim goes anom-

---

16   'Armi e bagagli': this very appropriate idiomatic expression belongs to Bocci, *Di
      seconda mano*, p. 28.

alously backward in order to go forward from the usurers to Geryon, and Geryon backs into the spiral), ever finding the new within the old.[17]

([...] la transizione, la storia, la vita stessa sono a forma di spirale: indietreggiando sempre per poter andare avanti (nello stesso modo in cui il pellegrino deve, in modo anomalo, tornare indietro dagli usurai per andare verso Gerione, e Gerione deve indietreggiare prima di intraprendere il suo volo a spirale) trovando sempre il nuovo nel vecchio.)[18]

Inspired by these words that so beautifully describe 'transition', with my 'student eye' I retraced Geryon's steps — as Barolini observes, Geryon must recoil in order to start his spiralling journey down the ravine: 'Come la navicella esce di loco | in dietro in dietro, sì quindi si tolse' ('Just like a boat that, starting from its moorings, | moves backward, backward, so that beast took off"; *Inf.* 17.100–01)[19] — and was totally and newly engrossed by his function as a means of transportation, a tool of transition, a 'ferryman', a 'translator', if you wish, of the old into the new: the English *translate/translation/translator* originates from *translatum*, the past participle of Latin *transferre*, to bring from one place to another. Geryon embodies transition, the rite of passage Dante must overcome in order to go from one part of hell to another and, in this particular episode, from one canto to another.[20] Geryon literally carries Dante, the pilgrim and the poet, on his 'groppa'

---

17   Teodolinda Barolini, *The Undivine Comedy: Detheologizing Dante* (Princeton: Princeton University Press, 1992), p. 73, hereafter *UDC*. Subsequent references given in parentheses in the main text.

18   Teodolinda Barolini, *La 'Commedia' senza Dio. Dante e la creazione di una realtà virtuale*, trans. by Roberta Antognini (Milan: Feltrinelli, 2003; repr. 2013), p. 109.

19   Unless otherwise stated, quotations from the *Commedia* are from Dante Alighieri: *'La Commedia' secondo l'antica vulgata*, ed. by Giorgio Petrocchi, Società Dantesca Italiana, Edizione Nazionale, 2nd rev. edn, 4 vols (Florence: Le Lettere, 1994). English translations are from Dante Alighieri, *The Divine Comedy*, trans. by Allen Mandelbaum, 3 vols (Berkeley: University of California Press, 1980–82).

20   '[...] il volo di Gerione [...] assume quasi i caratteri di un rito di passaggio, configurandosi come una *mise en abîme* dell'intero percorso oltremondano dantesco' ('Geryon's flight [...] almost takes on the characteristics of a rite of passage, configuring itself as a *mise en abîme* of Dante's entire otherworldly journey'). Massimiliano Corrado, 'Omai si scende per sì fatte scale. Il volo di Gerione e di Dante', in *Lectura Dantis romana. Cento canti per cento anni*, ed. by Enrico Malato and Andrea Mazzucchi, 3 vols (Rome: Salerno, 2013–15), I.1: *Inferno. Canti I–XVI* (2013), pp. 526–72 (p. 526), translation mine.

('rump'; *Inf.* 17.80) from the shore to the bottom of the 'burrato' (*Inf.* 16.114), the ravine that divides the seventh and eighth circles.

Furthermore, Geryon's definition of 'ver ch'ha faccia di menzogna' ('truth that has the face of falsehood'; *Inf.* 16.124)[21] makes him essential from a textual perspective, reminding us once again of the translation process, the progression that sees the new text sprouting from the original, always on the verge of being *menzognero*. The idea that translation is untrue, unfaithful, is part of its history. According to David Bellos in his book *Is that A Fish in Your Ear*, the origin of this mistrust lies in oral translation during the Ottoman Empire, between the fifteenth and the twentieth centuries. The sultans and members of their court had 'a paranoid suspicion of forgery, and as a result writing was not used for all purposes of state'.[22] Particularly problematic were communications with Western Europe. Initially, the task was handled by the Republic of Venice, which recruited young apprentices, *giovani di lingua*, from across the Venetian and Ottoman territories and turned them into trusted translators of Ottoman Turkish and Arabic into Italian. Called *tercüman* in Turkish, and *dragomanno* in Italian, *dragoman* in English (from the Arabic *targuman*, 'interpreter'; targam, 'to translate'), they eventually became a hereditary caste. Because of their inevitable loyalty to the sultan (they were essentially enslaved), Europeans diplomats never trusted them. Thus, they were associated with deceitfulness and fraudulence, which led to the likely origin of the famous Italian proverb 'traduttore, traditore'.[23]

In *The Undivine Comedy*, Barolini uses the expression 'Geryon principle' to define Dante's strategy when describing something the reader will find difficult to believe. This principle stems from the depiction of the pilgrim's first encounter with the monstrous Geryon:

> Sempre a quel *ver* c'ha faccia di *menzogna*
> de' l'uom chiuder le labbra fin ch'el puote,
> però che sanza colpa fa vergogna;

---

21 Here the English translation is from Dante Alighieri, *The Divine Comedy of Dante Alighieri*, trans. by Henry Wadsworth Longfellow, 3 vols (Boston: Osgood, 1875).

22 David Bellos, *Is That a Fish in your Ear? Translation and the Meaning of Everything* (London: Penguin Books, 2012), pp. 124–30 (p. 123).

23 Maxim from Giuseppe Giusti, *Proverbi toscani*, ed. by Gino Capponi (Florence: Capponi, 1873), p. 268.

> ma qui tacer nol posso; e per le note
> di questa comedìa, lettor, ti giuro,
> s'elle non sien di lunga grazia vòte,
>   ch'i' *vidi* [...]

> (Faced with that *truth* which seems a *lie*, a man
> should always close his lips as long as he can —
> to tell it shames him, even though he's blameless;
>   but here I can't be still; and by the lines
> of this my Comedy, reader, I swear —
> and may my verse find favor for long years —
>   that through the dense and darkened air *I saw* [...])
> (*Inf.* 16.124–30, italics mine)

Dante uses the 'Geryon principle', for instance, when in *Inferno* 28.112–19 he writes that he *saw* Bertran de Born holding his head in his hand *just like a lantern* (note that in both cases, Dante employs the verb *to see*). As Barolini explains:

> By underlining what is apparently least verisimilar in his representation, and by letting us know that he fully shares our assessment regarding this material's lack of verisimilitude, which he does by posing as reluctant to represent it lest we lose confidence in him, the narrator secures our confidence for the rest of his story. [...] By urging us to identify heightened drama with decreased verisimilitude and credibility, Dante is subtly encouraging us to accept his text's basic fictions and assumptions: sodomites dancing in a circle under a pouring rain of fire or usurers sitting on the edge of an abyss with purses around their necks [...] are acceptable, but flying monsters are not and therefore require the author's direct intervention. In this way the poet becomes the arbiter of our skepticism, allowing it to blossom forth only in authorially-sanctioned moments of high drama. [...] these passages are the most exposed weapons in a massive and unrelenting campaign to coerce our suspension of disbelief, a campaign that the history of the *Commedia*'s reception shows to have been remarkably successful. The Geryon episode, however, constitutes an even more profound poetic gamble [...] for its emblematic verse is a double-edged sword and may be approached from the perspective of its last word, 'menzogna', as well as from the perspective of its first word, 'ver'. Rather than emphasize the poet's claim that his poem is a *ver* and remains such no matter what marvels it is forced to recount, we could ask: Why does this truth, this *comedìa*, have a *faccia di menzogna*? The answer is that even a *comedìa*, in order to

come into existence as text, must to some extent accommodate
that human and thus ultimately fraudulent construct, language.
(*UDC*, p. 61)

Even a *comedìa*, then, must 'translate' and rely on its audience's suspension of disbelief. The passage, the transition between what Dante
sees and what Dante writes, implies a pact of truth between him and
his readers. The same awareness with respect to writing occurs when
translating. Too much adherence to the original text can be detrimental
to its content while, on the other hand, excessive interpretation betrays
the original text. Finding the right balance is never easy. Precisely for
this reason, Geryon's episode is one of the richest and most significant of the entire *Commedia:* Geryon is suspended/balanced between
cantos, between the seventh and eighth circles of hell, between the
violent and the fraudulent. Geryon, Barolini argues, 'serves as an outrageously paradoxical authenticating device', so much so that he also
'serves as the poem's very baptismal font' (*UDC*, p. 59).[24] In Dante's
own words: 'per le note | di questa comedìa lettor, ti giuro' ('by the
lines | of this my Comedy, reader, I swear'; *Inf.* 16.127–28).

Applying Barolini's observation about Ulysses to Geryon, the
guardian of the eighth circle is 'textually privileged' as well.[25] His
presence extends over two cantos — *Inferno* 16 and 17 — and 128
verses, the length of an entire canto. Equally important is Geryon's
textual position on the border of the first half of the first canticle. Paolo
Cherchi describes canto 17 as 'a busy railroad station, where a number
of tracks end and new ones originate',[26] while Massimiliano Corrado
depicts it as a sophisticated narrative *matryoshka*.[27] In trying to grasp

---

24   I will take the opportunity to provide an *errata corrige*: my translation, I realize now,
     'betrays' the original, since I rendered 'outrageously paradoxical authenticating device'
     with 'paradossale dispositivo di autenticazione' (Barolini, *La 'Commedia' senza Dio*,
     p. 90), thus forgetting *outrageously*, which implies the very idea of a violation on Dante's
     part: in other words, playing God. I probably felt the accumulation awkward in Italian,
     but I could have easily solved the impasse by simply transforming the adverb into an
     adjective: 'paradossale *e oltraggioso* dispositivo di autenticazione'.

25   'The many readers who have glorified Ulysses (like those who have glorified Francesca,
     Farinata, Brunetto, and Ugolino) were privileging a figure who is indeed privileged by
     the poet, not morally or eschatologically but textually and poetically' (*UDC*, p. 51).

26   Paolo Cherchi, 'Geryon's Downward Flight; the Usurers', in *Lectura Dantis. Inferno.
     A Canto-by-Canto Commentary*, ed. by Allen Mandelbaum, Anthony Oldcorn, and
     Charles Ross (Berkeley: University of California Press, 1998), pp. 225–37 (p. 225).

27   Massimiliano Corrado, 'Omai si scende', p. 547.

these many layers, Dante scholars have produced dozens of varying interpretations. Reading them is almost as compelling as reading the two
cantos themselves.[28] My personal take — influenced by a 'translation'
strategy, which, between the two fundamental and eternal directions
(free or literal), leans towards the literal, in the sense of an extreme attention to the original — compels me toward a rational reading rather
than a symbolic one. This may be anachronistic with respect to Dante's
mindset, but it seems to me that in the end what Dante does is attempt
to translate what he *sees* as literally as possible.

As we begin canto 16, Dante and Virgil are in the third section of
the seventh circle where the violent against God, nature and art are
punished. They have just left Brunetto Latini and they are now close to
the Flegetonte waterfall that flows into the deep ravine (l'alto *burrato*)
that divides the seventh from the eighth circle, Malebolge, where the
sin of fraud is punished, the third and final subdivision of hell. Canto
16 opens with "l rimbombo' ('a murmur') of water falling into the next
circle. This projection towards the future is immediately interrupted by
the arrival of the three Florentine sodomites, and it resumes once again
with the sound of water that is now much closer. Indeed, it has become
so loud that it is hard hear. After the long simile comparing the waterfall
of Phlegethon to that of the Acquacheta river in the Tuscan-Emilian
Apennines, Geryon then takes over the scene from the moment he

---

28   In addition to the commentaries of Anna Maria Chiavacci Leonardi (Dante Alighieri,
      Commedia, ed. with commentary by Anna Maria Chiavacci Leonardi, 3 vols (Milan:
      Mondadori, 1991-97), I: Inferno (1991)) and Enrico Malato (Dante Alighieri, *La
      Divina Commedia*, ed. by Enrico Malato, 3 vols (Rome: Salerno Editrice, 2021-), I:
      Inferno (2021)), among the endless bibliography on the subject I have read: Enrico
      Proto, 'Gerione (*La corda – La sozza immagine di froda*)', *Giornale dantesco*, 8 (1900),
      pp. 65–105; Glauco Cambon, 'Examples of Movement in the *Divine Comedy*', *Italica*,
      40.2 (June 1963), pp. 108–31; Vittorio Sermonti's commentary on cantos 16 and 17
      in *L'Inferno di Dante* (Milan: Rizzoli, 1993), pp. 233–42 and 247–56; Emilio Pasquini,
      'Il canto di Gerione', *Atti e memorie*, 3rd ser., 4.4 (1967), pp. 346–68; Franco Ferrucci,
      'The Meeting with Geryon', in Ferrucci, *The Poetics of Disguise. The Autobiography
      of the Work in Homer, Dante, and Shakespeare*, trans. by Ann Dunnigan (Ithaca and
      London: Cornell University Press, 1980), pp. 66–102; Roberto Mercuri, *Semantica
      di Gerione. Il motivo del viaggio nella 'Commedia' di Dante* (Rome: Bulzoni, 1984);
      Paolo Cherchi, 'Geryon's Downward Flight'; Susan Noakes, 'From Other Sodomites to
      Fraud', in *Lectura Dantis. Inferno*, pp. 213–24; Massimiliano Corrado, 'Omai si scende';
      Luca Marcozzi, 'Dante vince la guerra della pietà', in *Lectura Dantis romana. Cento canti
      per cento anni*, ed. by Malato and Mazzucchi, I.1, pp. 484–525; Gennaro Ferrante, 'Il
      paradosso di Gerione', *Rivista di studi danteschi*, 20 (2020), pp. 113–33.

is first evoked by a mysterious rope, one of the *Commedia*'s puzzles
about which scholars have gone to great lengths trying to explicate
its meaning (definitely a 'translation' problem). Dante tells us (*Inf.*
16.106–08) that he had this rope wrapped around his waist and with it
he had once thought to capture the 'lonza a la pelle dipinta' ('the leop-
ard with the painted hide'; l. 108), which we remember from the first
canto as one of the three *fiere*. Rather than the monster itself, it is the
expectation of Geryon that occupies the stage. Virgil attracts Geryon
to the bank of the *burrato* by throwing Dante's knotted and coiled rope
into the chasm. This is all the letter of the text tells us.[29] Dante expects
something to happen after the tossing of the rope: '"convien che novità
risponda"' ('"and surely something strange must here reply"'; l. 115).
From this simple observation and temporal slowdown begins Dante's
textual reflection, which, in its extraordinary conciseness, links 'il ver
ch'ha faccia di menzogna' with the 'note | di questa comedìa'. Only
later will we finally *see* Geryon:

> ch'i' *vidi* per quell'aere grosso e scuro
> venir notando una figura in suso,
> maravigliosa ad ogne cor sicuro,
>> sì come torna colui che va giuso
> talora a solver l'àncora ch'aggrappa
> o scoglio o altro che nel mare è chiuso,
>> che 'n sù si stende, e da piè si rattrappa.
>
> (that through the dense and darkened air I *saw*
> a figure swimming, rising up, enough
> to bring amazement to the firmest heart,
>> like one returning from the waves where he
> went down to loose an anchor snagged upon
> a reef or something else hid in the sea,
>> who stretches upward and draws in his feet.)
> (*Inf.* 16.130–36, italics mine)

---

29   As Vittorio Sermonti observes, this is a very simple passage from a literal point of
      view ('Brano semplicissimo, sotto il profilo letterale'; *L'Inferno di Dante*, p. 240). The
      literal reading — the throwing of the rope as the only way for Virgil to make the
      monster aware of their presence, a reading that has had its supporters — as opposed
      to the allegorical interpretation is interestingly reminiscent of the dualism of literal
      translation vs. free translation. Barolini favours a 'metapoetic interpretation, based
      on the traditional interpretation of the cord as a symbol of fraud' (*UDC*, p. 63 note
      45). For a quick review of the most recent interpretations, Enrico Malato (*La Divina
      Commedia*, I: *Inferno*, p. 435) refers to Marcozzi, 'Dante vince la guerra', p. 524 note
      50.

Geryon materializes by swimming upwards, as if emerging from the water like a diver returning to the surface after having released the anchor. He is truly swimming in the air, with his body stretching and shrinking. But once at the bank, he will not emerge completely: in the following canto, Dante tells us that Geryon had pulled his head and torso out of the *burrato*, but not his tail that flickered in the air like that of a scorpion: he describes Geryon as standing like a rowboat pulled ashore, partly in the water and partly on land, in transition. Geryon's description continues at the beginning of canto 17, first introduced by Virgil (who is the only one to speak for the remainder of the canto; for differing reasons, neither Geryon nor Dante will say a word): "'Ecco la fiera con la coda aguzza'" ("'Behold the beast who bears the pointed tail'"; *Inf.* 17.1). From this point forward, Geryon is always described in animalesque terms: 'fiera pessima' ('squalid beast'; l. 23), 'bestia malvagia' ('malicious beast'; l. 30), 'fiero animale' ('brute animal'; l. 80). Geryon is a filthy image of fraud — the sin punished in the next circle — with its sharp tail infecting the world.

In classical mythology, Geryon was king of the island Erytheia in the Balearic Islands, a giant with three heads, six arms and six legs: that is, with three bodies united on a single torso. He possessed immense herds of red oxen guarded by the monstrous dog Orto. He was defeated and killed by Hercules (the tenth and last labour), who then placed the boundaries of the world right there, in Erytheia.[30] But Dante's Geryon is only slightly inspired by classical tradition — the monstrous king appears in the *Aeneid*, but he doesn't play much of a part. The figurative elements of Dante's monster derive from biblical and vernacular sources, demonstrating the breadth of his semantic and metaphorical importance. Not only the pilgrim's rope but Geryon himself is a *crux* in Dante studies, and interpretations of this figure are far from univocal.[31] In Dante's vision, Geryon is still *tergeminus*, triple, but within one body. Interestingly, this is consistent with the rest

---

30   Marcozzi, 'Dante vince la guerra', p. 518. I perceive here a possible connection between Geryon's indirect allusion to Hercules's pillars and Ulysses's words in *Inf.* 26.108–09: "'dov'Ercule segnò li suoi riguardi | acciò che l'uom più oltre non si metta'" ("'the narrows | where Hercules set up his boundary stones | that men might heed and never reach beyond'").

31   Mercuri, *Semantica di Gerione*, p. 13.

of his vision, inspired by the Christian doctrine of the trinity, one-in-three or three-in-one: 'era faccia d'uom giusto' along with the trunk of a snake, two hairy arms of a lion (but no wings!), a body painted with variegated embroidery and the poisonous tail of a scorpion.

The encounter with the usurers, the last sinners of the seventh circle, interrupts the sequence of tercets dedicated to Geryon. Dante meets the usurers while Virgil goes to ask Geryon '"che ne conceda i suoi omeri forti"' ('"if he can lend us his strong shoulders"'; *Inf.* 17.42). It is only at this point that pilgrim and readers are finally aware of Geryon's role as a means of transportation for the pilgrims' descent into the eighth circle, Dante's extraordinary nocturnal flight. It is again Virgil who, invoking Geryon's name for the first time in this canto with '"Gerïon, moviti omai"' ('"Now, Geryon, move on"'; *Inf.* 17.97), begins the flight by commanding the monster to move slowly, descending in wide spiralling turns:

> Come la navicella esce di loco
> in dietro in dietro, sì quindi si tolse;
> e poi ch'al tutto si sentì a gioco,
>   là 'v' era 'l petto, la coda rivolse,
> e quella tesa, come anguilla, mosse,
> e con le branche l'aere a sé raccolse.
>   *Maggior paura* non credo che fosse
> quando Fetonte abbandonò li freni,
> per che 'l ciel, come pare ancor, si cosse;
>   né quando Icaro misero le reni
> sentì spennar per la scaldata cera,
> gridando il padre a lui "Mala via tieni!",
>   che fu la mia, quando vidi ch'i' era
> ne l'aere d'ogne parte, e vidi spenta
> ogne veduta fuor che de la fera.
>   Ella sen va notando lenta lenta:
> rota e discende, ma non me n'accorgo
> se non che al viso e di sotto mi venta.
>   Io sentia già da la man destra il gorgo
> far sotto noi un *orribile scroscio*,
> per che con li occhi 'n giù la testa sporgo.
>   Allor fu' io più *timido* a lo stoscio,
> però ch'i' vidi fuochi e senti' pianti;
> ond'io *tremando tutto mi raccoscio*.
>   E vidi poi, ché nol vedea davanti,
> lo scendere e 'l girar per li gran mali
> che s'appressavan da diversi canti.

> (Just like a boat that, starting from its moorings,
> moves backward, backward, so that beast took off;
> and when he felt himself completely clear,
>
> he turned his tail to where his chest had been
> and, having stretched it, moved it like an eel,
> and with his paws he gathered in the air.
>
> I do not think that there was *greater fear*
> in Phaethon when he let his reins go free —
> for which the sky, as one still sees, was scorched —
>
> nor in poor Icarus when he could feel
> his sides unwinged because the wax was melting,
> his father shouting to him, "That way's wrong!"
>
> than was in me when, on all sides, I saw
> that I was in the air, and everything
> had faded from my sight — except the beast.
>
> Slowly, slowly, swimming, he moves on;
> he wheels and he descends, but I feel only
> the wind upon my face and the wind rising.
>
> Already, on our right, I heard the torrent
> *resounding*, there beneath us, *horribly*,
> so that I stretched my neck and looked below.
>
> Then I was *more afraid* of falling off,
> for I saw fires and I heard laments,
> at which *I tremble, crouching, and hold fast.*
>
> And now I saw what I had missed before:
> his wheeling and descent — because great torments
> were drawing closer to us on all sides.)
> (*Inf.* 17.100–26, italics mine)

Vittorio Sermonti beautifully describes the terrified Dante's spiral-like flight through the darkness on the back of a monster; the pilgrim attempts to ask Virgil to embrace him but cannot utter a word:

> Boat, then spatial eel, then glider, falcon, arrow from a bow. [...] Ovid tells us stories of fantastic flights and vertiginous heroics: Dante, the emotion of a night flight flown in flesh and blood. And scrupulously registers the perception of the blind descent in the swirling mists from below, and in the intensification of noises coming from the ground [...] in the fires of the city that unfold gradually [...] in the compulsion to lean out, in the fear of impact: in his curling up in the void. [...] To the reader of the twentieth century, all that remains is

> to notice how according to the documents in the spring of year
> 1300 Dante actually flew at night [...][32]

Dante's initial wonder at the sight of Geryon emerging from the ravine
at the end of canto 16 becomes, by the end of canto 17, a sheer physical
fear of flying — and not only because he is on the back of a monster
(anyone with a fear of flying can certainly relate!) — but also a sense
of dread that, like Ulysses, he has embarked on a 'folle volo', a foolish
endeavour destined for failure. He is but a Dante-translator who is
afraid of not being believed by his readers as he faithfully 'translates'
what he has seen.

   As suddenly as he had appeared, Geryon disappears. If we retrace
the steps, we'll notice that the first time Virgil mentions the monster in
canto 16, he uses the word 'tosto': fast, speedy, repeated twice: "'Tosto
verrà di sovra | ciò ch'io attendo e che il tuo pensier sogna [...] |
tosto convien ch'al tuo viso si scovra'" ("'Now there will soon emerge
| what I await and what your thought has conjured [...] | it soon must
be discovered to your sight'"; *Inf.* 16.121–22). Having completed his
function as a transitional vehicle, Geryon vanishes like an arrow let
loose from the string of a bow: 'discarcate le nostre persone | si dileguò
come da corda cocca' ('and once our weight was lifted from his back,
| he vanished like an arrow from a bow'; *Inf.* 17.135–36). Again, it is
noteworthy how the image of the rope — though, of course, a different
kind of rope — ends Geryon's narrative much as it had begun. It is
a magnificent double simile: in these last tercets of canto 17, Geryon
the arrow is also a falcon who, outraged at not being able to catch its
prey ('disdegnoso e fello'), disobeys the falconer by going ashore with
empty beak.

   With a Geryon-like spiral movement, let us then conclude these
brief considerations by returning to the beginning with an observation
on the Italian title of *The Undivine Comedy*. For better or worse, the title
is usually not the translator's responsibility but rather the decision of
the publisher. The problem was not simple: how to render in Italian

---

32   Sermonti, *L'Inferno di Dante*, p. 256, translation mine. According to Glauco Cambon,
     'Dante's aeronautical imagination proves every bit as lively and exact as Leonardo's; he
     has overlooked no detail of the concrete experience to be evoked, from the visual to
     the tactile kinetic and aural impact' (Cambon, 'Examples of Movement in the *Divine
     Comedy*', p. 113).

the perfection of the adjective *undivine*? There is no way to translate this term into Italian using a single word, which seems to confirm that translation is sometimes impossible. It is one of those typical examples to which Giusti's proverb 'traduttore-traditore' would apply and, as a matter of fact, Roman Jakobson used it as an example for untranslatability in other languages:

> If we were to translate into English the traditional formula *Traduttore, traditore* as 'the translator is a betrayer', we would deprive the Italian rhyming epigram of all its paronomastic value. Hence, a cognitive attitude would compel us to change this aphorism into a more explicit statement and to answer the questions: translator of what messages? betrayer of what values?[33]

Of course, translation is always possible, for as Umberto Eco said, it's only a matter of negotiation.[34] Gabriella D'Ina, who for many years was Feltrinelli's editorial director and our main interlocutor, came up with two possible solutions: *Dante senza Dio* and *La 'Commedia' senza Dio*, eventually choosing the second title. Translating the original subtitle, *Detheologizing Dante*, was also challenging: whereas a literal translation of the English 'detheologizing' was certainly possible, the absence in the Italian title of the adjective 'undivine' would have made it quite ineffective. So, Barolini opted instead for something radically different: *Dante e la creazione di una realtà virtuale* ('Dante and the creation of a virtual reality').

---

33   Jakobson, 'On Linguistic Aspects of Translation', p. 143. And see Gianfranco Folena, *Volgarizzare e tradurre* (Turin: Einaudi, 1991), p. 3.

34   Umberto Eco, *Dire quasi la stessa cosa. Esperienze di traduzione* (Milan: Bompiani, 2003), p. 18: 'la negoziazione essendo appunto un processo in base al quale, per ottenere qualcosa, si rinuncia a qualcosa d'altro — e alla fine le parti in gioco dovrebbero uscirne con un senso di ragionevole e reciproca soddisfazione alla luce dell'aureo principio per cui non si può avere tutto' ('negotiation being precisely a process according to which, in order to obtain something, something else is given up — and in the end the parties involved should come out of it with a sense of reasonable and mutual satisfaction in light of the golden principle according to which you can't have everything'; translation mine). Umberto Eco's 2003 book on translation, *Dire quasi la stessa cosa* ('saying almost the same thing') has never been translated into English, but in 1998 Eco was invited by Toronto University for a series of Goggio conferences, whose proceedings were published under the title *Experiences in Translation* (Toronto: Toronto University Press, 2001). A few years later Eco was invited by Oxford University to give eight Weidenfeld lectures. These, too, were published under the title *Mouse or Rat? Translation as Negotiation* (London: Phoenix, 2002).

La 'Commedia' senza Dio: in the end, we had to sacrifice the pun *undivine* in the title of the *Commedia,* making the witticism not immediately apparent in Italian since it requires an extra step on the part of the reader to grasp it (and, as in Jakobson's remark, it poses at least one question: why without God?), but the euphony created by the alliterations of *e* and *a* and the diphthongs *ia* and *io* preceded by the *d* sound is still quite beautiful.

EPILOGUE

On Reading *The Undivine Comedy* Thirty Years Later

JOAN FERRANTE

Thirty years ago, I was stunned by the brilliance of this book, a brilliance that was based on the simple but startling approach of focusing
not on what Dante says he is doing, but on what he actually does, on
how he manipulates us, forcing us to respond in his terms. Rereading
the book thirty years later, I am once again overwhelmed by the striking effectiveness of looking so closely at the tools Dante uses to do this,
creating tension and suspense where none should exist, using difference to enable a narrative that claims to describe unity. I am still struck
by how obvious some of Barolini's points seem once she has pointed
them out, not to say by how readers wrapped up in larger concepts had
failed to see the most basic tools with which Dante creates his universe.

It is now impossible to read the *Commedia* without being aware
of those tools. Once Barolini points them out, their importance is
obvious, but without her guidance one might easily have overlooked
the function of words like 'più' and 'meno', or 'l'un' and 'l'altro', to
create the sense of difference within the philosophic unity of Dante's
universe, difference without which there could be no narrative. As
without paradox there could be no narrative: on the terrace of pride,
though humility requires self-effacement, the text requires names and
cannot help but celebrate them; in the heaven of the Moon, Piccarda

tells us both that divine charity cancels out difference ('vuol simile a sé tutta sua corte', 'that would have all Its court be like itself'; *Par.* 3.45) and that difference exists ('beata son in la spera più tarda', 'blessed within the slowest of the spheres'; v. 51); in the heaven of the Sun, Thomas claims that the two saints (Francis and Dominic) are equal, that to speak of one is to speak of the other, but the text belies him, for the two lives are very different.[1]

The basic paradox inherent in Dante's claiming unity through diversity is sustained by structural techniques like *terza rima* and enjambement. *Terza rima*, a rhyme form that at once looks back and moves forward throughout the poem, also moves towards unity in the four triple 'Cristo' rhymes that occur in *Paradiso*. Various forms of enjambement also move towards unity: in *Paradiso* 23, which Barolini notes has no narrative thread but must jump from simile to simile, enjambement is 'a rupture that unifies' creating a 'circulata melodia';[2] if in canto 24, the break in the middle of a word ('differente — | mente'; vv. 16–17) emphasizes the rupture, the jump from canto 32 to canto 33 in the middle of a sentence brings the structural divisions together.

These are but a small sample of the brilliant insights that still strike me. *The Undivine Comedy* remains the most impressive work on the artistry of a great poet.

---

1   Quotations from the *Commedia* are from Dante Alighieri: *La Commedia secondo l'antica vulgata*, ed. by Giorgio Petrocchi, Società Dantesca Italiana, Edizione Nazionale, 2nd rev. edn, 4 vols (Florence: Le Lettere, 1994). English translations come from Dante Alighieri, *The Divine Comedy*, trans. by Allen Mandelbaum, 3 vols (Berkeley: University of California Press, 1980–82).

2   Teodolinda Barolini, *The Undivine Comedy: Detheologizing Dante* (Princeton: Princeton University Press, 1992), p. 228.

References

Abelard, *Dialectica*, ed. by Lambertus M. De Rijk, rev. 2nd edn (Assen, Netherlands: Van Gorcum & Comp., 1970)

Abraham, Erin V., *Anticipating Sin in Medieval Society: Childhood, Sexuality, and Violence in the Early Penitentials* (Amsterdam: Amsterdam University Press, 2017) <https://doi.org/10.1515/9789048534081>

Alighieri, Dante, *Commedia*, ed. with commentary by Anna Maria Chiavacci Leonardi, 3 vols (Milan: Mondadori, 1991–97)

—— *La Commedia secondo l'antica vulgata*, ed. by Giorgio Petrocchi, Società Dantesca Italiana, Edizione Nazionale, 2nd rev. edn, 4 vols (Florence: Le Lettere, 1994)

—— *Convivio*, ed. by Franca Brambilla Ageno (Florence: Le Lettere, 1995)

—— *Dante's Lyric Poetry: Poems of Youth and of the 'Vita Nuova'* (1283–1292), ed. by Teodolinda Barolini (Toronto: University of Toronto Press, 2014)

—— *Dante to Cangrande: English Version*, trans. by James Marchand <https://faculty.georgetown.edu/jod/cangrande.english.html> [accessed 21 May 2025]

—— *De vulgari eloquentia*, ed. and trans. by Mirko Tavoni, in *Opere*, dir. by Marco Santagata, 3 vols (Milan: Mondadori, 2011–), I: *Rime, Vita nova, De vulgari eloquentia* (2011), pp. 1067–1547

—— *De vulgari eloquentia*, trans. by Steven Botterill (Cambridge: Cambridge University Press, 1996) <https://doi.org/10.1017/CBO9780511519444>

—— *La Divina Commedia*, ed. by Enrico Malato, 3 vols (Rome: Salerno Editrice, 2021–)

—— *La Divina Commedia. Testo critico della Società Dantesca Italiana*, ed. by Giuseppe Vandelli with revised commentary by Giovanni Scartazzini (Milan: Hoepli, 1928)

—— *The Divine Comedy*, ed. and trans. by Robin Kirkpatrick, 3 vols (London: Penguin, 2006–07)

—— *The Divine Comedy of Dante Alighieri*, trans. by Henry Wadsworth Longfellow, 3 vols (Boston: Osgood, 1875)

—— *The Divine Comedy*, trans. by Allen Mandelbaum, 3 vols (Berkeley: University of California Press, 1980–82)

—— *The Divine Comedy*, trans. with commentary by Charles S. Singleton, 6 vols (Princeton: Princeton University Press, 1970–75)

—— *Epistola XIII*, in Dante, *Opere minori*, ed. by Giorgio Brugnoli, 2 vols (Milan and Naples: Ricciardi, 1979–88), II (1988), pp. 598–643

—— *Inferno*, trans. by Mary Jo Bang (Minneapolis: Graywolf Press, 2012)

—— *Opere di Dante*, ed. by Franca Brambilla Ageno and others (Florence: Polistampa, 2012)

—— *Le opere di Dante. Testo critico della Società Dantesca Italiana*, ed. by Giuseppe Vandelli (Florence: R. Bemporad & Figlio, 1921)

—— *Paradiso*, trans. by Mary Jo Bang (Minneapolis: Graywolf Press, 2025)

—— *Purgatorio*, trans. by Mary Jo Bang (Minneapolis: Graywolf Press, 2021)

—— *Rime giovanili e della 'Vita Nuova'*, ed. by Teodolinda Barolini, with notes by Manuele Gragnolati (Milan: Rizzoli, 2009)

—— *Vita Nova*, trans. by Andrew Frisardi (Evanston: Northwestern University Press, 2012

—— *La Vita Nuova di Dante Alighieri. Edizione critica*, ed. by Michele Barbi (Florence: Bemporad e Figlio, 1932)

—— *Vita Nuova*, ed. by Michele Barbi (Florence: Società Dantesca Italiana, 1960)

—— *Vita Nuova*, trans. by Mark Musa, Oxford World Classics (Oxford: Oxford University Press, 2008)

Allen-Paisant, Jason, 'Dante in Caribbean Poetics: Language, Power, Race', in *The Oxford Handbook of Dante*, ed. by Manuele Gragnolati, Elena Lombardi, and Francesca Southerden (Oxford: Oxford University Press, 2021), pp. 668–85 <https://doi.org/10.1093/oxfordhb/9780198820741.013.42>

Amore, Agostino, 'Lucia, santa', in *Enciclopedia Dantesca*, ed. by Umberto Bosco (Rome: Istituto della Enciclopedia Italiana fondata da Giovanni Treccani, 1970) <https://www.treccani.it/enciclopedia/santa-lucia_(Enciclopedia-Dantesca)/> [accessed 2 June 2025]

Amsler, Mark, 'Rape and Silence: Ovid's Mythography and Medieval Readers', in *Representing Rape in Medieval and Early Modern Literature*, ed. by Elizabeth Robertson and Christine M. Rose (New York: Palgrave Macmillan, 2001), pp. 61–96 <https://doi.org/10.1007/978-1-137-10448-9_3>

Antonelli, Roberto, 'In limine, tra *auctor* e *agens*: Francesca da Rimini', in *Dante poeta-giudice del mondo terreno* (Rome: Viella, 2021), pp. 85–103

—— 'L'intertestualità contesa: intertestuale, interdiscorsivo, intermemoriale', in *Mélanges en l'honneur de Mariella Di Maio*, ed. by Valentina Fortunato (Soveria Mannelli: Rubbettino, 2019), pp. 15–24

—— 'La morte di Beatrice e la struttura della storia', in *Beatrice nell'opera di Dante e nella memoria europea (1290–1990)*, Atti del Convegno internazionale, Napoli 10–14 dicembre 1990, ed. by Maria Picchio Simonelli, Amalia Cecere, and Mariarosaria Spinetti (Florence: Cadmo, 1994), pp. 34–56

—— 'Rima equivoca e tradizione rimica nella poesia di Giacomo da Lentini, I. Le canzoni', in *Bollettino del Centro di studi filologici e linguistici siciliani*, 13 (1977), pp. 20–126

—— 'Tempo testuale tempo rimico. Costruzione del testo e critica nella poesia rimata', *Critica del testo*, 1 (1998), pp. 177–201

—— 'Tra Farinata e Guido Cavalcanti', in Antonelli, *Dante poeta-giudice del mondo terreno* (Rome: Viella, 2021), pp. 93–96

Aquinas, Thomas, *The Summa Theologiae of St. Thomas Aquinas*, trans. by the Fathers of the English Dominican Province, 2nd rev. edn (London: Washbourne, 1920)

Auerbach, Erich, 'Farinata and Cavalcante', in Auerbach, *Mimesis: The Representation of Reality in Western Literature* (Princeton: Princeton University Press, 2013), pp. 174–202 <https://doi.org/10.2307/j.ctt3fgz26.11>

—— 'Sermo humilis', in Auerbach, *Literary Language and its Public in Late Latin Antiquity and in the Middle Ages*, trans. by Ralph Manheim (New York: Pantheon Books, 1965), pp. 25–66

Bang, Mary Jo, 'A Note on the Translation', in Dante Alighieri, *Inferno*, trans. by Mary Jo Bang (Minneapolis: Graywolf Press, 2012), pp. 7–12

—— 'A Note on the Translation', in Dante Alighieri, *Purgatorio*, trans. by Mary Jo Bang (Minneapolis: Graywolf Press, 2021), pp. xvii–xxiv

Barański, Zygmunt G., 'Dante, America, and the Limits of "Allegory"', *Italian Studies*, 50 (1995), pp. 139–53

—— *Dante e i segni* (Naples: Liguori, 2000)

—— 'Lettura e interpretazione del canto XXXIII', in *Voci sul 'Purgatorio' di Dante. Una nuova lettura della seconda cantica*, ed. by Zygmunt G. Barański and Maria Antonietta Terzoli (Rome: Carocci, 2024), pp. 885–924

—— 'Magister satiricus: Preliminary Notes on Dante, Horace and the Middle Ages', in *Language and Style in Dante*, ed. by John C. Barnes and Michelangelo Zaccarello (Dublin: Four Courts Press, 2013), pp. 13–61

—— 'Reflecting on Dante in America: 1949–1990', in *Dante and Modern American Criticism*, ed. by Dino Cervigni, special issue of *Annali d'Italianistica*, 8 (1990), pp. 56–86

—— review of Teodolinda Barolini, *The Undivine Comedy* (1992), *Speculum*, 69 (1994), pp. 1106–09

Barański, Zygmunt G., and Lino Pertile, 'Chronology', in *Dante in Context*, ed. by Zygmunt G. Barański and Lino Pertile (Cambridge: Cambridge University Press, 2015), pp. xx–xxiii <https://doi.org/10.1017/CBO9781139519373>

Barbi, Michele, 'Per il testo della *Divina Commedia*', in Barbi, *La nuova filologia e l'edizione dei nostri scrittori da Dante al Manzoni* (Florence: Sansoni, 1938; facsimile repr. Florence: Le Lettere, 1993), pp. 1–34

—— *L'ufficio di Dante per i lavori di via S. Procolo* (Florence: Sansoni, 1921)

Barolini, Teodolinda, 'Arachne, Argus, and St. John', in Barolini, *Dante and the Origins of Italian Literary Culture* (New York: Fordham University Press, 2006), pp. 158–71 and 406–11 <https://doi.org/10.5422/fordham/9780823227037.003.0009>

——'Archeology of the *Donna Gentile*', in Barolini, *Dante's Multitudes: History, Philosophy, Method* (Notre Dame, IN: Notre Dame University Press, 2022), pp. 225–42 <https://doi.org/10.2307/jj.21996052.17>

——'Bertran de Born and Sordello: The Poetry of Politics in Dante's *Comedy*', *PMLA*, 94.3 (1979), pp. 395–405

——'The Case of the Lost Original Ending of Dante's *Vita Nuova*: More Notes Toward a Critical Philology', *Medioevo letterario d'Italia*, 11 (2014), pp. 27–44; repr. in revised form in Barolini, *Dante's Multitudes: History, Philosophy, Method* (Notre Dame, IN: Notre Dame University Press, 2022), pp. 287–97 <https://doi.org/10.2307/jj.21996052.20>

——*La 'Commedia' senza Dio. Dante e la creazione di una realtà virtuale*, trans. by Roberta Antognini (Milan: Feltrinelli, 2003)

——'Contemporaries Who Found Heterodoxy in Dante: Cecco d'Ascoli, Boccaccio, and Benvenuto da Imola on Fortuna and *Inferno* 7.89', in Barolini, *Dante's Multitudes: History, Philosophy, Method* (Notre Dame, IN: Notre Dame University Press, 2022), pp. 45–57 <https://doi.org/10.2307/jj.21996052.8>

——'Critical Philology and Dante's Rime', *Philology*, 1.1 (2015), pp. 91–114

——'Dante and Aristotle on Voluntary and Involuntary Action: *Nicomachean Ethics* 3.1 in *Inferno* 5 and *Paradiso* 3–5', *Textual Cultures*, 16.2 (2023), pp. 247–74 <https://doi.org/10.14434/tc.v16i2.36773>

——'Dante and Cavalcanti (On Making Distinctions in Matters of Love): *Inferno* 5 in its Lyric Context', *Dante Studies*, 116 (1998), pp. 31–63; repr. in Barolini, *Dante and the Origins of Literary Culture* (New York: Fordham University Press, 2006), pp. 70–101

——'Dante and Cecco d'Ascoli on Love and Compulsion: The Epistle to Cino, *Io sono stato*, the Third Heaven', in Barolini, *Dante's Multitudes: History, Philosophy, Method* (Notre Dame, IN: Notre Dame University Press, 2022), pp. 243–65 <https://doi.org/10.2307/jj.21996052.18>

——'Dante and Francesca da Rimini: Realpolitik, Romance, Gender', *Speculum*, 75 (2000), pp. 1–28; repr. in Barolini, *Dante and the Origins of Italian Literary Culture* (New York: Fordham University Press, 2006), pp. 304–32

——*Dante and the Origins of Italian Literary Culture* (New York: Fordham University Press, 2006) <https://doi.org/10.5422/fordham/9780823227037.001.0001>

——*The Dante Course*, Digital Dante, 2015–2016 <https://digitaldante.columbia.edu/the-dante-course> [accessed 2 June 2025]

——'Dante's Limbo and Equity of Access: Non-Christians, Children, and Criteria of Inclusion and Exclusion, from *Inferno* 4 to *Paradiso* 32', in Barolini, *Dante's Multitudes: History, Philosophy, Method* (Notre Dame, IN: Notre Dame University Press, 2022), pp. 58–81 <https://doi.org/10.2307/jj.21996052.9>

—— *Dante's Multitudes: History, Philosophy, Method* (Notre Dame, IN: Notre Dame University Press, 2022)<https://doi.org/10.2307/jj.21996052>

—— *Dante's Poets: Textuality and Truth in the 'Comedy'* (Princeton: Princeton University Press, 1984) <https://doi.org/10.1515/9781400853212>

—— 'Dante's Sympathy for the Other, or the Non-Stereotyping Imagination: Sexual and Racialized Others in the *Commedia*', *Critica del testo*, 14 (2011), pp. 177–204; repr. in revised form in Barolini, *Dante's Multitudes: History, Philosophy, Method* (Notre Dame, IN: Notre Dame University Press, 2022), pp. 22–44 <https://doi.org/10.2307/jj.21996052.7>

—— 'Divine Comedy', in *The Palgrave Encyclopedia of the Possible*, ed. by Vlad P. Glăveanu (Cham: Palgrave MacMillan, 2022), pp. 437–44 <https://doi.org/10.1007/978-3-030-90913-0_254>

—— 'Errancy: A Brief History of Dante's *Ferm voler*', in *The Oxford Handbook of Dante*, ed. by Manuele Gragnolati, Elena Lombardi, and Francesca Southerden (Oxford: Oxford University Press, 2021), pp. 568–69 <https://doi.org/10.1093/oxfordhb/9780198820741.013.39>

—— 'Filologia critica e le Rime di Dante', in Barolini, *Il vento di Aristotele. Saggi danteschi* (Milan: La nave di Teseo, 2024), pp. 361–83

—— '*Inferno* 25: Shape, Substance, Sex, Self', in *Commento Baroliniano*, Digital Dante (Columbia University Libraries, 2018) <https://digitaldante.columbia.edu/dante/divine-comedy/inferno/inferno-25/> [accessed 29 May 2025]

—— '*Inferno* 2: Beatrix Loquax and Consolation', *Commento Baroliniano*, Digital Dante (Columbia University Libraries, 2018) <https://digitaldante.columbia.edu/dante/divine-comedy/inferno/inferno-2/> [accessed 3 June 2025]

—— 'Il Limbo di Dante e l'equità di accesso: non-Cristiani, bambini, e i criteri di inclusione ed esclusione, da *If* 4 a *Pd* 32', *Italianistica*, 50.1 (2021), pp. 49–64

—— 'Non-Christians in the Christian Afterlife', Digital Dante (Columbia University Libraries, 2018) <https://digitaldante.columbia.edu/dante/divine-comedy/inferno/inferno-4/> [accessed 5 June 2025]

—— 'Notes toward a Gendered History of Italian Literature, with a Discussion of Dante's *Beatrix Loquax*', in *Dante and the Origins of Italian Literary Culture* (New York: Fordham University Press, 2009), pp. 360–78 <https://doi.org/10.2307/j.ctt14bs01r.19>

—— 'The One and the Many as Philosophical and Narratological Key to *Paradiso*', in *Letteratura permanente. Poeti, scrittori, critici per Giorgio Ficara*, ed. by Igor Candido, Chiara Fenoglio, Raffaello Palumbo Mosca, Giulia Ricca, and Daniele Santero (Milan: La nave di Teseo, 2022), pp. 127–51

—— '"Only Historicize": History, Material Culture (Food, Clothes, Books), and the Future of Dante Studies', *Dante Studies*, 127 (2009), pp. 37–54;

repr. in Barolini, *Dante's Multitudes: History, Philosophy, Method* (Notre Dame, IN: Notre Dame University Press, 2022), pp. 3–21 <https://doi.org/10.2307/jj.21996052.6>

—— '*Paradiso* and the Mimesis of Ideas: Realism versus Reality', *SpazioFilosofico*, 8 (2013), pp. 199–208, repr. in Barolini, *Dante's Multitudes: History, Philosophy, Method* (Notre Dame, IN: Notre Dame University Press, 2022), pp. 121–36 <https://doi.org/10.2307/jj.21996052.12>

—— 'The Possible *Divine Comedy*', in *The Palgrave Encyclopedia of the Possible*, ed. by Vlad P. Glăveanu (Cham: Palgrave Macmillan, 2022), pp. 437–44 <https://doi.org/10.1007/978-3-030-90913-0_254>

—— '*Purgatorio* 9: Raptus', *Commento Baroliniano*, Digital Dante <https://digitaldante.columbia.edu/dante/divine-comedy/purgatorio/purgatorio-9/> [accessed 3 June 2025]

—— 'Re-presenting What God Presented: The Arachnean Art of the Terrace of Pride', *Dante Studies*, 105 (1987), pp. 43–62

—— '*Sotto benda*: The Women of Dante's Canzone *Doglia mi reca* in the Light of Cecco d'Ascoli', *Dante Studies*, 123 (2005), pp. 83–88

—— *The Undivine Comedy: Detheologizing Dante* (Princeton: Princeton University Press, 1992) <https://doi.org/10.1515/9781400820764>

—— 'L'Uno e i Molti quale chiave filosofica e narratologica alla lettura del *Paradiso*', in Barolini, *Il vento di Aristotele. Saggi danteschi* (Milan: La nave di Teseo, 2024), pp. 103–26

—— *Il vento di Aristotele. Saggi danteschi* (Milan: La nave di Teseo, 2024)

—— 'La *Vita nuova* e il caso del finale originario perduto. Verso una filologia critica', in Barolini, *Il vento di Aristotele. Saggi danteschi* (Milan: La nave di Teseo, 2024), pp. 349–59

—— 'Why Did Dante Write the *Commedia*? Or, The Vision Thing', *Dante Studies*, 111 (1993), pp. 1–8; repr. as 'Why Did Dante Write the *Commedia*? Dante and the Visionary Tradition', in Barolini, *Dante and the Origins of Italian Literary Culture* (New York: Fordham University Press, 2006), pp. 125–31

Barthes, Roland, 'L'Effet de Réel', *Communications*, 11 (1968), pp. 84–89

Bassnett, Susan, 'Intricate Pathways: Observations on Translation and Literature', in *Translating Literature*, ed. by Susan Bassnett (London: Boydell & Brewer, 1997), pp. 1–13

Battaglia Ricci, Lucia, 'Scrittura sacra e "sacrato poema"', in *Dante e la Bibbia*, ed. by Giovanni Barblan (Florence: Olschki, 1988), pp. 113–23

Bellos, David, *Is That a Fish in your Ear? Translation and the Meaning of Everything* (London: Penguin Books, 2012)

Benjamin, Walter, 'The Task of the Translator: An Introduction to the Translation of Baudelaire's *Tableaux Parisiens*', in *The Translation Studies Reader*, ed. by Lawrence Venuti (New York and London: Routledge, 2004), pp. 75–85

Bersani, Leo, *The Freudian Body: Psychoanalysis and Art* (New York: Columbia University Press, 1986)

Bersuire, Pierre, *The Moralized Ovid*, ed. and trans. by Frank T. Coulson and Justin Haynes (Cambridge, MA: Harvard University Press, 2023)

Birk, Sandow, *Dante's Divine Comedy* (San Francisco: Chronicle Books, 2005)

Bocci, Laura, *Di seconda mano* (Milan: Rizzoli, 2004)

Boethius, *De hypotheticis syllogismis*, ed. and trans. into Italian by Luca Obertello (Brescia: Paideia, 1969)

Bolzoni, Lina, 'Dante o della memoria appassionata', *Lettere Italiane*, 60.2 (2008), pp. 169–93

Bosco, Umberto, ed., *Enciclopedia Dantesca*, 6 vols (Rome: Istituto dell'Enciclopedia Italiana, 1970–1978)

Boswell, John E., 'Dante and the Sodomites', *Dante Studies*, 112 (1994), pp. 63–76

Botterill, Steven, *Dante and the Mystical Tradition: Bernard of Clairvaux in the 'Commedia'* (Cambridge: Cambridge University Press, 1994) <https://doi.org/10.1017/CBO9780511611735>

—— '*Dante Studies* and the Study of Dante', in *Dante and Modern American Criticism*, ed. by Dino Cervigni, special issue of *Annali d'Italianistica*, 8 (1990), pp. 88–102

—— review of Teodolinda Barolini, *The Undivine Comedy* (1992), *Italica*, 71 (1994), pp. 404–05

Bowsky, William M., *A Medieval Italian Commune: Siena under the Nine, 1287-1355* (Berkeley: University of California Press, 1981) <https://doi.org/10.1525/9780520328556>

Bramati, Alberto, and Fabio Regattin, 'Tradurre saggistica divulgativa: un'introduzione', *Lingue Culture Mediazioni/Languages Cultures Mediation*, 6.2 (2019), pp. 5–10 <https://doi.org/10.7358/lcm-2019-002-brre>

Brambilla Ageno, Franca, 'Periodo ipotetico', Appendix to *Biografia, Lingua e stile, Opere*, in *Enciclopedia Dantesca*, ed. by Umberto Bosco, 6 vols (Rome: Istituto dell'Enciclopedia Italiana, 1970–1978), VI (1978), pp. 408–24

Brilli, Elisa, 'Dante e la storia: gli studi storici nelle *Letture Classensi* (12 dicembre 2020)', in *Cinquant'anni di letture classensi: lingua, storia e modernità di Dante*, ed. by Giuseppe Ledda, special issue of *Letture Classensi*, 49 (2021), pp. 69–88

—— 'Dante's Biographies and Historical Studies: An Ouverture', *Dante Studies*, 136.1 (2018), pp. 133–42

Brilli, Elisa, and Giuliano Milani, *Dante's Lives: Biography and Autobiography* (London: Reaktion, 2023)

Brownlee, Kevin, 'Pauline Vision and Ovidian Speech in *Paradiso* I', in *The Poetry of Allusion: Virgil and Ovid in Dante's 'Commedia'*, ed. by Rachel Jacoff and Jeffrey T. Schnapp (Stanford: Stanford University Press, 1991), pp. 202–13 <https://doi.org/10.1515/9781503623422-017>

Brugnoli, Giorgio, 'Ancor che fosse tardi', in Brugnoli, *Studi danteschi*, 3 vols (Pisa: Edizioni ETS, 1998), I, pp. 133–39

Brundage, James A., 'Rape and Seduction in the Medieval Canon Law', in *Sexual Practices and the Medieval Church*, ed. by Vern L. Bullough and James A. Brundage (Amherst, NY: Prometheus Books, 1982), pp. 141–48

Bruni, Leonardo, *The Humanism of Leonardo Bruni. Selected Texts*, trans. by James Hankins (Binghamton, NY: Medieval & Renaissance Texts & Studies in conjunction with the Renaissance Society of America, 1987)

Bufano, Antonietta, 'Smagare', in *Enciclopedia Dantesca*, ed. by Umberto Bosco (Rome: Istituto della Enciclopedia Italiana, 1970) <https://www.treccani.it/enciclopedia/smagare_(Enciclopedia-Dantesca)/> [accessed 31 May 2025]

Burke, Kenneth, *The Rhetoric of Religion: Studies in Logology* (Berkeley: University of California Press, 1970) <https://doi.org/10.1525/9780520352025>

Burr, David, *The Spiritual Franciscans: From Protest to Persecution in the Century after Saint Francis* (University Park: The Pennsylvania State University Press, 2001)

Caferro, William, *Petrarch's War: Florence and the Black Death in Context* (Cambridge: Cambridge University Press, 2018) <https://doi.org/10.1017/9781108539555>

Callegari, Danielle, *Dante's Gluttons: Food and Society from the 'Convivio' to the 'Comedy'* (Amsterdam: Amsterdam University Press, 2022) <https://doi.org/10.1515/9789048550036>

Calvino, Italo, 'Sul tradurre', in Calvino, *Mondo scritto e mondo parlato* (Milan: Mondadori, 2002), pp. 47–59

——— 'Tradurre è il vero modo di leggere un testo', in Calvino, *Mondo scritto e mondo parlato* (Milan: Mondadori, 2002), pp. 85–91

Cambon, Glauco, 'Examples of Movement in the *Divine Comedy*', *Italica*, 40.2 (June 1963), pp. 108–31 <https://doi.org/10.2307/477570>

Canaccini, Federico, *1289: la battaglia di Campaldino* (Bari: Laterza, 2021)

Carpi, Umberto, *La nobiltà di Dante* (Florence: Polistampa, 2004)

Casadei, Alberto, 'Ancora sui canti fiorentini dell'*Inferno* (e ancora sul Veltro)', *Italianistica*, 52.2 (2023), pp. 11–32

——— *Dante oltre l'allegoria* (Ravenna: Longo, 2021)

Cassell, Anthony K., 'Santa Lucia as Patroness of Sight: Hagiography, Iconography, and Dante', *Dante Studies*, 109 (1991), pp. 71–88

Casteen, Elizabeth, 'Rape and Rapture: Violence, Ambiguity, and Raptus in Medieval Thought', in *The Sacred and the Sinister: Studies in Medieval Religion and Magic*, ed. by David J. Collins (University Park: The Pennsylvania State University Press, 2019), pp. 91–116 <https://doi.org/10.5325/j.ctv14gp00v.8>

Cattani, Paola, Matteo Fadini, and Federico Saviotti, 'In principio fuit interpres', *Ticontre. Teoria Testo Traduzione*, 3 (2015), pp. 3–12 <https:

//teseo.unitn.it/ticontre/article/view/957/957> [accessed 23 April 2025]

Cecco d'Ascoli (Francesco Stabili), *L'Acerba* (*Acerba etas*), ed. by Marco Albertazzi, 3rd edn (Lavis: La Finestra, 2016)

Cestaro, Gary P., *Dante and the Grammar of the Nursing Body* (Notre Dame, IN: Notre Dame University Press, 2003)

—— 'Sodomite, Homosexual, Queer: Teaching Dante LGBTQ', in *Approaches to Teaching Dante's 'Divine Comedy'*, ed. by Christopher Kleinhenz and Kristina Olson, 2nd edn (New York: Modern Language Association of America, 2020), pp. 103–09

Chace, Rebecca, 'Edith Grossman, Who Elevated the Art of Translation, Dies at 87', Obituary, *The New York Times*, 4 September 2023 <https://www.nytimes.com/2023/09/04/books/edith-grossman-dead.html> [accessed 24 April 2025]

Cherchi, Paolo, 'Geryon's Downward Flight; the Usurers', in *Lectura Dantis. Inferno. A Canto-by-Canto Commentary*, ed. by Allen Mandelbaum, Anthony Oldcorn, and Charles Ross (Berkeley: University of California Press, 1998), pp. 225–37 <https://doi.org/10.1525/9780520315808-018>

Cherubini, Giovanni, 'L'approvvigionamento alimentare delle città toscane tra XII e XV secolo', in Cherubini, *Firenze e la Toscana (Scritti vari)* (Pisa: Ospedaletto, 2013), pp. 39–55

—— 'Gargonza', in *Enciclopedia Dantesca*, ed. by. Umberto Bosco (Rome: Istituto della Enciclopedia Italiana fondata da Giovanni Treccani, 1970) <https://www.treccani.it/enciclopedia/gargonza_(Enciclopedia-Dantesca)/> [accessed 19 May 2025]

Chida, Nassime, 'Dante and the legacy of Montaperti', *Studj Romanzi*, n.s., 19 (2023), pp. 163–74

—— 'Guido da Montefeltro and the Tyrants of Romagna in *Inferno* 27', *Romanic Review*, 112.1 (2021), pp. 97–119

Cioffi, Caron Ann, 'The Anxieties of Ovidian Influence: Theft in *Inferno* 24 and 25', *Dante Studies*, 112 (1994), pp. 77–100

Cogan, Marc, *The Design in the Wax: The Structure of the 'Divine Comedy' and its Meaning* (Notre Dame, IN: University of Notre Dame Press, 1999) <https://doi.org/10.2307/j.ctvpj7dm5>

Colella, Gianluca, *Costrutti condizionali in italiano antico* (Rome: Aracne, 2010)

Coleridge, Samuel Taylor, *Biographia Literaria*, in *The Collected Works of Samuel Taylor Coleridge*, 16 vols (Princeton: Princeton University Press, 1969–2001), VII (1985), pp. 1–856

—— 'Lecture X', in *Coleridge's Miscellaneous Criticism*, ed. by Thomas Middleton Raynor (Cambridge: Harvard University Press, 1936), pp. 131–90

Compagni, Dino, *Dino Compagni's Chronicle of Florence*, trans. by Daniel Bornstein (Philadelphia: University of Pennsylvania Press, 1986)

Conte, Gian Biagio, *Il genere e i suoi confini* (Turin: Stampatori, 1980)

Contini, Gianfranco, 'Cavalcanti in Dante', in Contini, *Un'idea di Dante* (Turin: Einaudi, 1976), pp. 143–57

—— 'Dante come personaggio-poeta della *Commedia*', in Contini, *Un'idea di Dante* (Turin: Einaudi, 1976), pp. 33–62

—— 'Filologia ed esegesi dantesca', in Contini, *Un'idea di Dante* (Turin: Einaudi, 1976), pp. 133–42

—— *Letteratura Italiana delle origini* (Florence: Sansoni, 1985)

—— *Un'idea di Dante* (Turin: Einaudi, 1976).

Cook, William R., and Ronald B. Herzman, '*Inferno* XXIII: The Past and Present in Dante's Imagery of Betrayal', *Italica*, 56.4 (Winter 1979), pp. 377–83 <https://doi.org/10.2307/478665>

Cooper, Mariah L., *Representations of Rape and Consent in Medieval English Laws and Literature* (Leeds: Arc Humanities Press, 2024) <https://doi.org/10.1515/9781802702170>

Cornelis de Boer, *Ovide moralisé; poème du commencement du quatorzième siècle* (Amsterdam: Müller, 1915)

Corrado, Massimiliano, 'Omai si scende per sì fatte scale. Il volo di Gerione e di Dante', in *Lectura Dantis romana. Cento canti per cento anni*, ed. by Enrico Malato and Andrea Mazzucchi, 3 vols (Rome: Salerno, 2013–15), I.1: *Inferno. Canti I–XVI* (2013), pp. 526–72

Coulson, Frank T., 'Literary Criticism in the Vulgate Commentary on Ovid's *Metamorphoses*', in *Medieval Textual Cultures: Agents of Transmission, Translation and Transformation*, ed. by Faith Wallis and Robert Wisnovsky (Berlin: De Gruyter, 2016), pp. 121–32

Coulson, Frank T., and Piero Andrea Martina, eds, *Commentaire Vulgate des 'Métamorphoses' d'Ovide. Livres I–V*, trans. by Piero Andrea Martina and Clara Wille (Paris: Classiques Garnier, 2021)

Crasta, Fabrizio, 'Gli angeli neutrali da Dante a Matteo Palmieri', *Lettere Italiane*, 67.1 (2015), pp. 5–25

Crisafi, Nicolò, *Dante's Masterplot and Alternative Narratives in the 'Commedia'* (Oxford: Oxford University Press, 2022) <https://doi.org/10.1093/oso/9780192857675.001.0001>

Cristaldi, Sergio, 'Un ipotesto biblico: l'Apocalisse', *Lettere Classensi*, 37 (2008), pp. 83–117

Croce, Benedetto, *La poesia di Dante*, 2nd rev. edn (Bari: Laterza, 1921)

Curran, Leo C., 'Rape and Rape Victims in the *Metamorphoses*', *Arethusa*, 11.1–2 (1978), pp. 213–41

Dameron, George, 'Feeding the Medieval Italian City-State: Grain, War and Political Legitimacy in Tuscany, c. 1150–c. 1350', *Speculum*, 92.4 (October 2017), pp. 976–218 <https://doi.org/10.1086/693379>

—— *Florence and its Church in the Age of Dante* (Philadelphia: University of Pennsylvania Press, 2005) <https://doi.org/10.9783/9780812201734>

Dante's Inferno, dir. by Sean Meredith (Ricochet Releasing, 2008)

The Dartmouth Dante Project, 2025 <https://dante.dartmouth.edu/> [accessed 2 June 2025]

Davidsohn, Robert, *Storia di Firenze*, trans. by Giovanni Battista Klein, 5 vols (Florence: Sansoni, 1960)

de Lauretis, Teresa, 'Queer Texts, Bad Habits, and the Issue of a Future', *GLQ: A Journal of Lesbian and Gay Studies*, 17.2–3 (2011), pp. 243–63

de Rooy, Ronald, ed., *Divine Comedies for the New Millennium: Recent Dante Translations in America and the Netherlands* (Amsterdam: Amsterdam University Press, 2003) <https://doi.org/10.1017/9789048505241>

del Lungo, Isidoro, *Dino Compagni e la sua Cronica*, 3 vols (Florence: Le Monnier, 1879–87)

Dell'Oso, Lorenzo, 'L'*Inferno* a Firenze? Su alcuni elementi teologici dei primi canti della *Commedia* (*Inf.* 1–4)', *Italianistica: Rivista di letteratura italiana*, 53.3 (2024), pp. 12–26

Delmolino, Grace, 'Fraudulent Counsel: Legal Temporality and the Poetics of Liability in Dante's *Inferno*, Boniface VIII's *Liber Sextus*, and Gratian's *De penitentia*', *Speculum*, 98.3 (2023), pp. 727–62

DeVun, Leah, *The Shape of Sex: Nonbinary Gender from Genesis to the Renaissance* (New York: Columbia University Press, 2021) <https://doi.org/10.7312/devu19550>

Di Sabato, Bruna. 'Tradurre il testo non letterario', in *I confini della traduzione*, ed. by Bruna Di Sabato and Antonio Perri (Limena: Libreriauniversitaria.it, 2014), pp. 47–69

Dionisotti, Carlo, 'Scuola storica', in *Dizionario critico della letteratura italiana*, ed. by Vittore Branca, 3 vols (Torino: Unione Tipografico-Editrice Torinese, 1973), III, pp. 352–61

Eco, Umberto, *Dire quasi la stessa cosa. Esperienze di traduzione* (Milan: Bompiani, 2003)

—— *Experiences in Translation* (Toronto: Toronto University Press, 2001)

—— *Mouse or Rat? Translation as Negotiation* (London: Phoenix, 2002)

Eliot, T. S., 'Dante' [1929], in Eliot, *Selected Essays* (London: Faber and Faber, 1972), pp. 237–77

Elliott, Dyan, 'Raptus/Rapture', in *The Cambridge Companion to Christian Mysticism*, ed. by Amy Hollywood and Patricia Z. Beckman (Cambridge: Cambridge University Press, 2012), pp. 189–99 <https://doi.org/10.1017/CCO9781139020886.013>

Ellrich, Robert J., 'Envy, Identity, and Creativity: *Inferno* 24–25', *Dante Studies*, 102 (1984), pp. 61–80

Enenkel, Karl, 'Salmacis, Hermaphrodite, and the Inversion of Gender: Allegorical Interpretations and Pictorial Representations of an Ovidian Myth, ca. 1300–1770', in *The Figure of the Nymph in Early Modern Culture*, ed. by Karl Enenkel and Anita Traninger (Leiden: Brill, 2018), pp. 53–148 <https://doi.org/10.1163/9789004364356_004>

Faedda, Barbara, *From Da Ponte to the Casa Italiana. A Brief History of Italian Studies at Columbia University* (New York: Columbia University Press, 2017) <https://doi.org/10.7312/faed18593>

Falzone, Paolo, 'Per Dante virgiliano', in *Dante e l'eredità dei classici*, ed. by Stefano Carrai, special issue of *Letture Classensi*, 51 (2023), pp. 31–60

Federici, Theresa, 'Dante's Davidic Journey. From Sinner to God's Scribe', in *Dante's 'Commedia': Theology as Poetry*, ed. by Vittorio Montemaggi and Matthew Treherne (Notre Dame, IN: Notre Dame University Press, 2010), pp. 180–209 <https://doi.org/10.2307/j.ctvpg862d.13>

Ferrante, Gennaro, 'Il paradosso di Gerione', *Rivista di studi danteschi*, 20 (2020), pp. 113–33

Ferrante, Joan M., *Dante's Beatrice: Priest of an Androgynous God* (Binghamton, NY: State University of New York Press, 1992)

Ferrucci, Franco, 'The Meeting with Geryon', in Ferrucci, *The Poetics of Disguise. The Autobiography of the Work in Homer, Dante, and Shakespeare*, trans. by Ann Dunnigan (Ithaca and London: Cornell University Press, 1980), pp. 66–102

Folena, Gianfranco, *Volgarizzare e tradurre* (Turin: Einaudi, 1991)

Fortuna, Sara, and Manuele Gragnolati, 'Allattamento e origine del linguaggio tra la *Commedia* dantesca e *Aracoeli* di Elsa Morante', in *Parole di donne*, ed. by Francesca Maria Dovetto (Ariccia: Aracne, 2009), pp. 271–303

—— '*Attaccando al suo capezzolo le mie labbra ingorde*: corpo, linguaggio e soggettività da Dante ad *Aracoeli* di Elsa Morante', *Nuova Corrente*, 55 (2008), pp. 85–123

—— 'Between Affection and Discipline: Exploring Linguistic Tensions from Dante to *Aracoeli*', in *The Power of Disturbance: Elsa Morante's 'Aracoeli'*, ed. by Manuele Gragnolati and Sara Fortuna (Oxford: Legenda, 2009), pp. 8–19 <https://doi.org/10.4324/9781315085531-2>

Fosca, Nicola, Commentary to the *Inferno*, in The Dartmouth Dante Project, 2025 <https://dante.dartmouth.edu/> [accessed 9 June 2025]

Francesco da Buti, *Commento di Francesco da Buti sopra La Divina Commedia di Dante Allighieri*, ed. by Crescentino Giannini (Pisa: Fratelli Nistri, 1858–62)

Frank, Joseph, 'Spatial Form in Modern Literature: An Essay in Two Parts', *The Sewanee Review*, 53.2 (Spring 1945), pp. 221–40

Freccero, John, 'Infernal Irony: The Gates of Hell', in Freccero, *Dante: The Poetics of Conversion* (Cambridge, MA: Harvard University Press, 1986), pp. 93–109

—— 'The Neutral Angels', in Freccero, *Dante: The Poetics of Conversion*, ed. by Rachel Jacoff (Cambridge, MA: Harvard University Press, 1986), pp. 110–18

Fritz, Jean-Marie, with the collaboration of Cristina Noacco, ed., *Ovide moralisés latins: Arnoul d'Orléans, 'Allegoriae'; Jean de Garlande, 'Integumenta'; Giovanni del Virgilio, 'Allegoriae'* (Paris: Classiques Garnier, 2022), pp. 132–33

Fumagalli, Maria Cristina, *The Flight of the Vernacular: Seamus Heaney, Derek Walcott, and the Impress of Dante* (Amsterdam: Rodopi, 2001) <https://doi.org/10.1163/9789004486249>

Fumo, Jamie C., 'Commentary and Collaboration in the Medieval Allegorical Tradition', in *A Handbook to the Reception of Ovid*, ed. by John F. Miller and Carole E. Newlands (Hoboken, NJ: Wiley, 2014), pp. 114–28 <https://doi.org/10.1002/9781118876169.ch8>

Gardini, Nicola, *Tradurre è un bacio* (Borgomanero: Giuliano Landolfi, 2015)

Gerber, Amanda J., 'Rethinking Ovid: The Commentary Tradition', in Gerber, *Medieval Ovid: Frame Narrative and Political Allegory* (New York: Palgrave Macmillan, 2014), pp. 11–50 <https://doi.org/10.1057/9781137482822_2>

Gillen, Katherine, and Kathryn Vomero Santos, 'Shakespeare and the Politics of Tradaptation', *PMLA*, 138.3 (May 2023), pp. 715–20 <https://doi.org/10.1632/S0030812923000391>

Giusti, Giuseppe, *Proverbi toscani*, ed. by Gino Capponi (Florence: Capponi, 1873)

Glăveanu, Vlad P. , ed., *Palgrave Encyclopedia of the Possible* (Cham: Palgrave MacMillan, 2022) <https://doi.org/10.1007/978-3-030-90913-0>

Gogarty, Oliver St John, *The Poems and Plays of Oliver St John Gogarty* (Gerrards Cross, Bucks: Colin Smythe Limited, 2002)

Goldthwaite, Richard, *The Building of Renaissance Florence: An Economic and Social History* (Baltimore: Johns Hopkins, 1980)

Goodison, Lorna, *Collected Poems* (Manchester: Carcanet, 2017)

—— *Redemption Ground: Essays and Adventures* (Brighton and Hove: Myriad Editions, 2018)

Gragnolati, Manuele, *Amor che move. Linguaggio del corpo e forma del desiderio in Dante, Pasolini e Morante* (Milan: Il Saggiatore, 2013)

—— 'Authorship and Performance in Dante's *Vita nova*', in *Aspects of the Performative in Medieval Culture*, ed. by Manuele Gragnolati and Almut Suerbaum (Berlin: de Gruyter, 2010), pp. 123–40 <https://doi.org/10.1515/9783110222470>

—— 'Diffracting Dante's *Paradiso*: Transformation, Identity, and the Form of Desire', in *Cultural Reception, Translation, and Transformation of Italian Literature: Essays in Honour of Martin McLaughlin*, ed. by Guido Bonsaver, Brian Richardson, and Giuseppe Stellardi (Oxford: Legenda, 2017), pp. 352–66 <https://doi.org/10.2307/j.ctv16kkxtz.29>

—— 'Eschatological Anthropology', in *The Oxford Handbook of Dante*, ed. by Manuele Gragnolati, Elena Lombardi, and Francesca Southerden (Oxford: Oxford University Press, 2021), pp. 447–63 <https://doi.org/10.1093/oxfordhb/9780198820741.013.30>

—— *Experiencing the Afterlife: Soul and Body in Dante and Medieval Culture* (Notre Dame, IN: Notre Dame University Press, 2005)

—— 'Gluttony and the Anthropology of Pain in Dante's *Inferno* and *Purgatorio*', in *History in the Comic Mode: Medieval Communities and the Matter of Person*, ed. by Rachel Fulton and Bruce W. Holsinger (New York: Columbia University Press, 2007), pp. 238–50 <https://doi.org/10.7312/fult13368-022>

—— *Identity, Pain and Resurrection: Body and Soul in Bonvesin da la Riva's 'Book of the Three Scriptures' and Dante's 'Commedia'* (doctoral thesis, Columbia University, 1999)

—— 'Insegnare con un classico. La complessità di Dante e lo spirito critico', in *In cattedra. Il docente universitario in otto autoritratti*, ed. by Chiara Cappelletto (Milan: Cortina, 2019), pp. 177–214

—— 'Ombre a abbracci. Riflessioni sull'inconsistenza nella *Commedia* Dante', *Chroniques italiennes web*, 39 (2020), pp. 30–43 <https://hal.sorbonne-universite.fr/hal-03787182v1>

—— '*Paradiso* XIV e il desiderio del corpo', *Studi Danteschi*, 78 (2013), pp. 285–309

Gragnolati, Manuele, and Elena Lombardi, 'Autobiografia d'autore', *Dante Studies*, 136 (2018), pp. 143–60

Gratian, *Decretum*, in *Corpus iuris canonici*, ed. by Emil Friedberg, 2 vols (Leipzig: B. Tauchnitz, 1879–1881; repr. Graz: Akademische Druck- und Verlagsanstalt, 1959), I

Gregory the Great, *The Book of the Morals of St. Gregory the Pope, or an Exposition on the Book of Blessed Job*, trans. and ed. by John Henry Parker, 3 vols (London: Rivington, 1844)

Gregory XIII, ed., *Corpus juris canonici emendatum et notis illustratum*, 4 vols (Rome: Gregory XIII, 1582) <https://digital.library.ucla.edu/canonlaw/> [accessed 2 June 2025]

Grossman, Edith, *Why Translation Matters* (New Haven: Yale University Press, 2010), pp. 26–27 <https://doi.org/10.1007/s12109-010-9175-2>

Halberstam, Jack, *The Queer Art of Failure* (Durham, NC and London: Duke University Press, 2011) <https://doi.org/10.2307/j.ctv11sn283>

Halpern, Daniel, ed., *Dante's Inferno: Translations by Twenty Contemporary Poets* (Hopewell, NJ: Ecco Press, 1993)

Havely, Nick R., *Dante* (Oxford: Blackwell, 2007) <https://doi.org/10.1002/9780470690123>

Havely, Nick R., and Bernard O'Donoghue, eds, *After Dante: Poets in Purgatory: Translations by Contemporary Poets* (Todmorden: Arc Publications, 2021)

Hawkins, Peter S., and Rachel Jacoff, eds, *The Poet's Dante* (New York: Farrar, Straus and Giroux, 2002)

Herlihy, David, *Pisa in the Early Renaissance: A Study in Urban Growth* (New Haven: Yale University Press, 1958)

Hexter, Ralph J., 'Medieval Articulations of Ovid's *Metamorphoses*: From Lactantian Segmentation to Arnulfian Allegory', *Mediaevalia*, 13 (1998), pp. 63–82

Hollander, Robert, *Dante: A Life in Works* (New Haven: Yale University Press, 2001)

Holsinger, Bruce W., 'Sodomy and Resurrection: The Homoerotic Subject of the *Divine Comedy*', in *Premodern Sexualities*, ed. by Louise Fradenburg and Carla Freccero (New York: Routledge, 1996), pp. 243–74

Hooper, Laurence E., 'Characterization', in *The Cambridge Companion to Dante's 'Commedia'*, ed. by Zygmunt G. Barański and Simon Gilson (Cambridge: Cambridge University Press, 2019), pp. 43–60 <https://doi.org/10.1017/9781108367769.006>

Horace, *Satires, Epistles and Ars Poetica*, ed. and trans. by H. Rushton Fairclough, Loeb Classical Library, 194 (London: William Heinemann, and Cambridge, MA: Harvard University Press, 1970)

Inglese, Giorgio, *Vita di Dante. Una biografia possibile* (Rome: Carocci, 2015)

Jacobus de Voragine, *The Golden Legend: Readings on the Saints*, trans. William Granger Ryan (Princeton: Princeton University Press 2012) <https://doi.org/10.1515/9781400842056>

—— *Legenda Aurea*, ed. by Johann Georg Theodor Graesse (Vratislavia: Koebner, 1890)

Jacoff, Rachel, 'Dante, Geremia e la problematica profetica', in *Dante e la Bibbia*, ed. by Giovanni Barblan (Florence: Olschki, 1988), pp. 113–23

Jacoff, Rachel, and William A. Stephany, *Lectura Dantis Americana: Inferno II* (Philadelphia: University of Pennsylvania Press, 1989) <https://doi.org/10.9783/9781512817164>

Jakobson, Roman, 'On Linguistic Aspects of Translation', in *The Translation Studies Reader*, ed. by Lawrence Venuti (New York: Routledge, 2004), pp. 138–43

John of Garland, *Integumenta Ovidii*, ed. and trans. with commentary by Kyle Gervais (Kalamazoo, MI: Medieval Institute Publications, 2022) <https://doi.org/10.2307/jj.7941371>

Kirkpatrick, Robin, 'Polemics of Praise: Theology as Text, Narrative and Rhetoric in Dante's *Commedia*', in *Dante's 'Commedia': Theology as Poetry*, ed. by Vittorio Montemaggi and Matthew Treherne (Notre Dame, IN: University of Notre Dame Press, 2010), pp. 14–35 <https://doi.org/10.2307/j.ctvpg862d.7>

Krasiński, Zygmunt, *The Undivine Comedy*, trans. by Charles S. Kraszewski (Lehman, PA: Libella Veritatis, 1999).

Kripke, Saul, *Naming and Necessity* (Malden, MA: Blackwell Publishing, 1981)

Kristeva, Julia, *La révolution du langage poétique: l'avant-garde à la fin du XIXe siècle. Lautréamont et Mallarmé* (Paris: Seuil 1974)

—— *The Revolution of Poetic Language*, ed. by Leon S. Roudiez, trans. by Marguerite Waller (New York: Columbia University Press, 1984)

Kumar, Akash, 'Authentically Speaking: Dante and the Politics of Language in Meloni's Italy', *Dante Notes*, November 21, 2022 <https://www.dantesociety.org/node/176> [accessed 28 May 2025]

Larson, Atria, 'Lucretia (and Lucia) and the Medieval Canonists: Guilt, Consent, and Chastity in the Early Canonistic Jurisprudence of Rape', *Law and History Review* (2025, forthcoming)

—— 'A Note on a Hagiographical Source for Gratian's *Decretum*: The Quotation Attributed to St. Lucy in C. 32 q. 5', *Traditio* (2025, forthcoming)

Le Goff, Jacques, *The Birth of Purgatory*, trans. by Arthur Goldhammer (Chicago: University of Chicago Press, 1984)

Ledda, Giuseppe, *Il bestiario dell'aldilà: gli animali nella 'Commedia' di Dante* (Ravenna: Longo, 2019)

—— *La Bibbia di Dante* (Turin: EMI, 2015)

—— 'Cultura religiosa: ricordi autobiografici di un lettore novecentesco di studi su Dante', in *Now Feed Yourself: Anglo-American and Italian Scholarship on Dante*, ed. by Zygmunt G. Barański, Theodore J. Cachey Jr., and Anna Pegoretti (Oxford: Legenda, 2024), pp. 201–27 <https://doi.org/10.2307/jj.22212195.12>

—— 'Dante Alighieri, Dante-poet, Dante-character', in *The Cambridge Companion to Dante's 'Commedia'*, ed. by Zygmunt G. Barański and Simon Gilson (Cambridge: Cambridge University Press, 2019), pp. 28–42 <https://doi.org/10.1017/9781108367769.005>

—— 'Dante e la tradizione delle visioni medievali', *Letture Classensi*, 37 (2008), pp. 119–42

—— 'La danza e il canto dell'"umile salmista": David nella *Commedia* di Dante', in *Les Figures de David à la Renaissance*, ed. by Elise Boillet, Sonia Cavicchioli, and Paul-Alexis Mellet (Geneva: Droz, 2015), pp. 225–46

—— 'L'esilio, la speranza, la poesia: modelli biblici e strutture autobiografiche nel canto 25 del *Paradiso*', *Studi e problemi di critica testuale*, 90 (2015), pp. 257–77

—— *La guerra della lingua. Ineffabilità, retorica e narrativa nella 'Commedia' di Dante* (Ravenna: Longo, 2002)

—— 'Modelli biblici nella *Commedia*: Dante e san Paolo', in *La Bibbia di Dante. Esperienza mistica, profezia e teologia biblica in Dante*, ed. by Giuseppe Ledda (Ravenna: Centro Dantesco dei Frati Minori Conventuali, 2011), pp. 179–216

—— 'Osservazioni sul contributo di Ezio Raimondi agli studi danteschi: bilanci e prospettive', in *Ezio Raimondi lettore inquieto*, ed. by Andrea Battistini (Bologna: Il Mulino, 2016), pp. 117–23

—— 'Poesia e agiografia nella *Commedia*', in *Dante poeta cristiano e la cultura religiosa medievale. In ricordo di Anna Maria Chiavacci Leonardi*, ed. by Giuseppe Ledda (Ravenna: Centro Dantesco dei Frati Minori Conventuali, 2018), pp. 215–58

Lewis, David, *Counterfactuals* (Cambridge, MA: Harvard University Press, 1973)

—— 'Truth in Fiction', *American Philosophical Quarterly*, 15.1 (1978), pp. 37–46

Livraghi, Leyla M. G., 'Esemplarità del mito e agone con gli antichi in *Inferno* 24–25', in *I classici di Dante*, ed. by Paola Allegretti and Marcello Ciccuto (Florence: Le Lettere, 2017), pp. 59–90

—— 'Raptus e deificatio ovidiani nel sistema della *Commedia*', in *Ortodossia ed eterodossia in Dante Alighieri: atti del convegno di Madrid (5–7 novembre 2012)*, ed. by Carlota Cattermole, Celia de Aldama, and Chiara Giordano (Alpedrete: Ediciones de la Discreta, 2014), pp. 691–709

—— 'Sabello e Nasidio, Cadmo e Aretusa: strategie dell'*aemulatio* dantesca nelle metamorfosi di *Inferno* 25', *Dante: Rivista internazionale di studi su Dante Alighieri*, 14 (2017), pp. 55–66

Lombardi, Elena, '"Che libito fe' licito in sua legge": Lust and Law, Reason and Passion in Dante', in *Dantean Dialogues: Engaging with the Legacy of Amilcare Iannucci*, ed. by Maggie Kilgour and Elena Lombardi (Toronto: University of Toronto Press, 2013), pp. 125–54 <https://doi.org/10.3138/9781442663213-008>

—— *The Wings of the Doves: Love and Desire in Dante and Medieval Culture* (Montreal: McGill Queens University Press, 2012) <https://doi.org/10.1515/9780773586949>

Malato, Enrico, 'Avvertenza del curatore', in Dante Alighieri, *La Divina Commedia*, ed. by Enrico Malato, 3 vols (Rome: Salerno Editrice, 2021–), I: *Inferno* (2021), pp. xix–xxix

Maldina, Nicolò, '"Per poenitentiam factum prophetam". Filigrane davidiche nel prologo della *Commedia*', in *Poesia e profezia nell'opera di Dante*, ed. by Giuseppe Ledda (Ravenna: Centro Dantesco dei Frati Minori Conventuali, 2019), pp. 163–78

Marchesini, Giancarlo, 'Teorie della traduzione e strategie traduttive', in *I saperi del tradurre. Analogie, affinità, confronti*, ed. by Clara Montella (Milan: Franco Angeli, 2007)

Marchionne di Coppo Stefani, *Cronica Fiorentina di Marchionne di Coppo Stefani*, ed. by Niccolò Rodolico (Città del Castello: Lapi, 1903)

Marcozzi, Luca, 'Dante vince la guerra della pietà', in *Lectura Dantis romana. Cento canti per cento anni*, ed. by Enrico Malato and Andrea Mazzucchi, 3 vols (Rome: Salerno, 2013–15), I.1: *Inferno. Canti I–XVI* (2013), pp. 484–525

—— 'Ovidius "regulatus poeta": Dante e lo stile delle *Metamorfosi*', in *I classici di Dante*, ed. by Paola Allegretti and Marcello Ciccuto (Florence: Le Lettere, 2017), pp. 135–55

Markulin, Joseph, 'Dante's Guido da Montefeltro: A Reconsideration', *Dante Studies*, 100 (1982), pp. 25–40

Martinich, A. P., and David Sosa, *The Philosophy of Language*, 6th edn (New York: Oxford University Press, 2013)

Marucci, Valerio, 'Francesco Torraca e Dante', *L'Idomeneo*, 31 (2021), pp. 97–106

—— 'Introduzione', in Francesco Torraca, *Commento alla Divina Commedia*, 3 vols (Rome: Salerno, 2008), I, pp. 9–32

Mates, Benson, 'Leibniz on Possible Worlds', in *Leibniz: A Collection of Critical Essays*, ed. by Harry G. Frankfurt (Garden City, NY: Anchor Books, 1972), pp. 335–64

Mazzotta, Giuseppe, *Dante's Vision and the Circle of Knowledge* (Princeton: Princeton University Press, 1993)

Menzel, Christopher, 'Possible Worlds', in *The Stanford Encyclopedia of Philosophy*, ed. by Edward N. Zalta, Summer 2024 edn <https://plato.stanford.edu/entries/possible-worlds/> [accessed 9 June 2025]

Mercuri, Roberto, *Semantica di Gerione. Il motivo del viaggio nella 'Commedia' di Dante* (Rome: Bulzoni, 1984)

Miłosz, Czesław, *The History of Polish Literature* (London: Macmillan, 1969)

Moevs, Christian, *The Metaphysics of Dante's 'Comedy'* (New York: Oxford University Press 2005) <https://doi.org/10.1093/0195174615.001.0001>

Monti, Johanna, 'Alla ricerca della conoscenza. Quali strumenti per la traduzione saggistica?', in *Tradurre saggistica. Traduttori, traduttologi ed esperti a confronto*, ed. by Clara Montella (Milan: Franco Angeli, 2010), pp. 143–61

Moore, Edward, *Contributions to the Textual Criticism of the 'Divina Commedia'* (Cambridge: Cambridge University Press, 1889)

—— *Studies in Dante, Fourth Series: Textual Criticism of the 'Convivio' and Miscellaneous Essays* (New York: Haskell House, 1917; repr. 1968)

Moynihan, Robert, 'The Development of the "Pseudo-Joachim" Commentary "Super Hieremiam": New Manuscript Evidence', *Mélanges de l'École française de Rome, Moyen-Age*, 98 (1986), pp. 109–42

Müller, Wolfgang P., 'Lucretia and the Medieval Canonists', *Bulletin of Medieval Canon Law*, 19 (1989), pp. 13–32

Murray, K. Sarah-Jane, and Matthieu Boyd, ed. and trans., *The Medieval French Ovide Moralisé: An English Translation*, 3 vols (Woodbridge, Suffolk: Brewer, 2023)

Mussato, Albertino, *Écérinide, épîtres métriques sur la poésie, songe*, ed. and trans. by Jean-Frédéric Chevalier (Paris: Les Belles Lettres, 2000)

Najemy, John, *History of Florence* (Oxford: Blackwell, 2006)

Nasti, Paola, 'Religion and the Religious in Dante Studies', in *Now Feed Yourself: Anglo-American and Italian Scholarship on Dante*, ed. by Zygmunt G. Barański, Theodore J. Cachey Jr., and Anna Pegoretti (Oxford: Legenda, 2024), pp. 167–200 <https://doi.org/10.2307/jj.22212195.11>

—— 'Ri-teologizzare Dante? Percorsi e prospettive per Dante e la cultura del suo tempo', *Letture Classensi*, 50 (2022), pp. 63–121

Newlands, Carole E., 'Violence and Resistance in Ovid's *Metamorphoses*', in *Texts and Violence in the Roman World*, ed. by Monica Gale and J. H. D. Scourfield (Cambridge: Cambridge University Press, 2018), pp. 140–78 <https://doi.org/10.1017/9781139225304.007>

Noakes, Susan, 'From Other Sodomites to Fraud', in *Lectura Dantis. Inferno. A Canto-by-Canto Commentary*, ed. by Allen Mandelbaum, Anthony

Oldcorn, and Charles Ross (Berkeley: University of California Press, 1998), pp. 213–24 <https://doi.org/10.1525/9780520315808-017>

Olson, Kristina M., 'Uncovering the Historical Body of Florence: Dante, Forese Donati, and Sumptuary Legislation', *Italian Culture*, 33.1 (2015), pp. 1–15

Ottokar, Nicola, *Il comune di Firenze alla fine del Dugento* (Turin: Einaudi, 1962)

Ovid, *Amores; Medicamina Faciei Femineae; Ars Amatoria; Remedia Amoris*, ed. by Edward J. Kenney, rev. edn (Oxford: Oxford University Press, 1994)

—— *Change Me: Stories of Sexual Transformation from Ovid*, trans. by Jane Alison (Oxford: Oxford University Press, 2014)

—— *I volgarizzamenti trecenteschi dell'"Ars amandi' e dei 'Remedia amoris'*, ed. by Vanna Lippi Bigazzi, 2 vols (Florence: Accademia della Crusca, 1987)

—— *Metamorfosi*, ed. by Alessandro Barchiesi and Gianpiero Rosati, trans. by Ludovica Koch and Gioachino Chiarini, 6 vols (Milan: Mondadori, 2005–15)

—— *Metamorphoseon Libri XV, Lactanti Placidi Qui Dicitur Narrationes Fabularum Ovidianarum*, ed. by Hugo Magnus (Weidmann, 1914; repr. New York: Arno Press, 1979)

—— *Metamorphoses*, ed. by Richard J. Tarrant (Oxford: Oxford University Press, 2004)

—— *Metamorphoses*, trans. by Stephanie McCarter (New York: Penguin Books, 2022)

Padoan, Giorgio, *Il lungo cammino del 'poema sacro'. Studi danteschi* (Florence: Olschki, 1993)

Pampaloni, Guido, 'Bianchi e Neri', in *Enciclopedia Dantesca*, ed. by. Umberto Bosco (Rome: Istituto della Enciclopedia Italiana fondata da Giovanni Treccani, 1970) <https://www.treccani.it/enciclopedia/bianchi-e-neri_(Enciclopedia-Dantesca)/> [accessed 19 May 2025]

—— 'I primi anni dell'esilio di Dante', in *Conferenze Aretine 1965* (Arezzo: Academia Petrarca; Bibbiena: Società Dantesca Casentinese, 1966), pp. 133–47

Pasquazi, Silvio, 'Il canto II dell'*Inferno*', in *Inferno: letture degli anni 1973–1976*, ed. by Silvio Zennaro (Rome: Bonacci, 1977), pp. 35–65

Pasquini, Emilio, 'Il canto di Gerione', *Atti e memorie*, 3rd ser., 4.4 (1967), pp. 346–68

—— *Dante e le figure del vero. La fabbrica della 'Commedia'* (Milan: Bruno Mondadori, 2001)

Pepin, Ronald E., ed. and trans., *The Vatican Mythographers* (New York: Fordham University Press, 2008)

Pertile, Lino, 'Life', in *Dante in Context*, ed. by Zygmunt G. Barański and Lino Pertile (Cambridge: Cambridge University Press, 2015), pp. 461–74 <https://doi.org/10.1017/CBO9781139519373.029>

——— *La punta del disio: semantica del desiderio nella 'Commedia'* (Fiesole: Cadmo, 2005)

——— 'Works', in *Dante in Context*, ed. by Zygmunt G. Barański and Lino Pertile (Cambridge: Cambridge University Press, 2015), pp. 483–88 <https://doi.org/10.1017/CBO9781139519373.030>

Petrocchi, Giorgio, 'Radiografia del Landiano', *Studi Danteschi*, 35 (1958), pp. 5–27

Piattoli, Renato, ed., *Codice diplomatico dantesco* (Florence: Libreria Luigi Gonnelli e figli, 1940)

Pinto, Giuliano, *Il libro del Biadaiolo. Carestie e annona a Firenze dalla metà del '200 al 1348* (Florence: Olschki, 1978)

Pozzi, Giovanni, *La parola dipinta* (Milan: Adelphi, 1981)

Proto, Enrico, 'Gerione (*La corda – La sozza immagine di froda*)', *Giornale dantesco*, 8 (1900), pp. 65–105

Punzi, Arianna, *Rimario della 'Commedia'* (Rome: Bagatto, 2001)

Purdy Moudarres, Christiana, 'Bodily Starvation and the Ravaging of the Will: A Reading of *Inferno* 32 and 33', *Viator*, 47.1 (2015), pp. 205–28

Quintilianus, Marcus Fabius, *Institutionis oratoriae libri xii*, ed. by Michael Winterbottom, 2 vols (Oxford: Oxford University Press, 1985)

Raimondi, Ezio, *Intertestualità e storia letteraria. Da Dante a Montale* (Bologna: CUSL, 1991)

Repetti, Emanuele, 'Ampinana', in *Dizionario geografico, fisico, storico della Toscana*, 6 vols (Florence: Presso l'autore e editore, 1833–46)

Ricciardelli, Fabrizio, *Il libro del chiodo*, Fonti per la storia dell'Italia medievale, Antiquitates, 9 (Rome: Istituto Palazzo Borromini, 1998)

Richlin, Amy, 'Reading Ovid's Rapes', in *Pornography and Representation in Greece and Rome*, ed. by Amy Richlin (New York: Oxford University Press, 1992), pp. 158–79

Riffaterre, Michael, *Fictional Truth* (Baltimore: Johns Hopkins University Press, 1990) <https://doi.org/10.56021/9780801839337>

Robson, James, 'Bestiality and Bestial Rape in Greek Myth', in *Rape in Antiquity: Sexual Violence in the Greek and Roman Worlds*, ed. by Susan Deacy and Karen F. Pierce (London: Duckworth, 1997), pp. 65–96 <https://doi.org/10.2307/j.ctvd1cb94.7>

Ruggeri, Pietro, 'Poesia e profezia nei canti del Paradiso terrestre', *L'Alighieri*, 65 (2025), pp. 53–75

Rushdie, Salman, *Joseph Anton: A Memoir* (New York: Random House, 2012)

——— *Knife: Meditations After an Attempted Murder* (New York: Random House, 2024)

——— *Languages of Truth: Essays, 2003–2020* (New York: Random House, 2022)

Rushworth, Jennifer, *Discourses of Mourning in Dante, Petrarch, and Proust* (Oxford: Oxford University Press, 2016) <https://doi.org/10.1093/acprof:oso/9780198790877.001.0001>

Russo, Vittorio, *Il romanzo teologico: Sondaggi sulla 'Commedia' di Dante* (Naples: Liguori, 1984)

Ruud, Jay, '"Never Built at All, and Therefore Built Forever": Camelot and the World of P. G. Wodehouse', *Connotations*, 24.1 (2014–15), pp. 105–21

Ryan, Marie-Laure, *Possible Worlds, Artificial Intelligence, and Narrative Theory* (Bloomington: Indiana University Press, 1991) <https://doi.org/10.2979/2675.0>

Saffiotti Bernardi, Simonetta, and Umberto Bosco, 'Ugolino della Gherardesca, conte di Donoratico', in *Enciclopedia Dantesca*, ed. by Umberto Bosco (Rome: Istituto della Enciclopedia Italiana fondata da Giovanni Treccani, 1970) <https://www.treccani.it/enciclopedia/ugolino-della-gherardesca-conte-di-donoratico_(Enciclopedia-Dantesca)/> [accessed 18 May 2025]

Salzman-Mitchell, Patricia B., *A Web of Fantasies: Gaze, Image, and Gender in Ovid's Metamorphoses* (Columbus: Ohio State University Press, 2005)

Santagata, Marco, *Dante. Il romanzo della sua vita* (Milan: Mondadori, 2012)

—— *Dante: The Story of His Life*, trans. by Richard Dixon (Cambridge, MA: Harvard Belknap Press, 2016) <https://doi.org/10.2307/j.ctvjsf5bx>

Sasso, Gennaro, 'L'*ananke* di Ulisse', in Sasso, *Ulisse e il desiderio* (Rome: Viella, 2011), pp. 15–120

Schildgen, Brenda Deen, 'Violence in the Domestic Sphere in the *Commedia*', in Schildgen, *Dante and Violence: Domestic, Civic, Cosmic* (Notre Dame, IN: University of Notre Dame Press, 2021), pp. 55–98 <https://doi.org/10.2307/j.ctv19m63z2.8>

Segal, Charles, 'Il corpo e l'io nelle *Metamorfosi* di Ovidio', in Ovid, *Metamorfosi*, ed. by Alessandro Barchiesi and Gianpiero Rosati, trans. by Ludovica Koch and Gioachino Chiarini, 6 vols (Milan: Mondadori, 2005–15) I: *Libri I–II* (2005), pp. xv–ci

Segre, Cesare, 'Viaggi e visioni d'oltretomba fino alla *Commedia* di Dante', in Segre, *Fuori dal mondo* (Turin: Einaudi, 1990), pp. 25–48

Sermonti, Vittorio, *L'Inferno di Dante* (Milan: Rizzoli, 1993)

Singleton, Charles S., *'Commedia': Elements of Structure* (Cambridge, MA: Harvard University Press, 1954)

—— *Journey to Beatrice*, 2nd edn (Baltimore: Johns Hopkins University Press, 1977)

Sparrow, Katie, 'Dante's Dantes: Self-Characterization in the *Vita nova* and *Commedia*' (unpublished doctoral thesis, University of Notre Dame, 2023) <https://doi.org/10.7274/1j92g735d7f> [accessed 18 April 2025]

Stalnaker, Robert, 'A Theory of Conditionals', in *Studies in Logical Theory*, ed. by Nicholas Rescher (Oxford: Blackwell Publishing, 1968), pp. 98–112

Starn, Randolph, *Contrary Commonwealth: The Theme of Exile in Medieval and Renaissance Italy* (Berkeley: University of California Press, 1982) <https://doi.org/10.1525/9780520312951>

Starr, Willow, 'Counterfactuals', in *The Stanford Encyclopedia of Philosophy*, ed. by Edward N. Zalta, Winter 2022 edn <https://plato.stanford.edu/archives/win2022/entries/counterfactuals/> [accessed 9 June 2025]

Steinberg, Justin, *Dante and the Limits of the Law* (Chicago: University of Chicago Press, 2013) <https://doi.org/10.7208/chicago/9780226071121.001.0001>

Storey, H. Wayne, 'Franciscan Controversies and Paradigms in Dante', *Medieval Perspectives*, 24 (2009), pp. 1–22

—— 'Michele Barbi, curatore di testi danteschi', *Studi Danteschi*, 85 (2020), pp. 45–67

—— 'A Note on Boccaccio's Dantean Categories, or, What's in a Book? *libro, volume, pistole, rime*', *Philology*, 1.1 (2015), pp. 115–19

—— *Transcription and Visual Poetics in the Early Italian Lyric* (New York: Garland, 1993)

Storey, H. Wayne, and Michelangelo Zaccarello, eds, *Dante and the Malaspina Seven Centuries after his Sojourn in Lunigiana (1306–2006)*, special issue of *Dante Studies*, 124 (2006)

Sznura, Franek, *L'espansione urbana di Firenze nel dugento* (Florence: La Nuova Italia, 1975)

Tavoni, Mirko, 'Effrazione battesimale tra i simoniaci (*If* XIX 13–21)', *Rivista di letteratura italiana*, 10 (1992), pp. 457–523

Terlizzi, Sergio, ed., *Documenti delle relazioni tra Carlo I d'Angiò e la Toscana* (Florence: Olschki, 1950)

Tolkien, J. R. R., *The Fellowship of the Ring*, 2nd edn (Boston: Houghton Mifflin, 1966)

—— 'On Fairy-Stories', *The Tolkien Reader* (New York: Ballantine Books, 1966), pp. 31–99

Tomko, Michael, *Beyond the Willing Suspension of Disbelief: Poetic Faith from Coleridge to Tolkien*, New Directions in Religion and Literature (London: Bloomsbury Academic, 2016)

Torraca, Francesco, *Il Canto v dell' 'Inferno'* (Rome: Nuova Antologia, 1902)

Vallone, Aldo, *Strutture e modulazioni nella 'Divina Commedia'* (Florence: Olschki, 1990)

Van Peteghem, Julie, *Intertextual Dante, Digital Dante* (Columbia University Libraries, 2017) <https://digitaldante.columbia.edu/intertexual-dante-vanpeteghem/>

—— *Italian Readers of Ovid from the Origins to Petrarch: Responding to a Versatile Muse* (Leiden: Brill, 2020), pp. 18–26 <https://doi.org/10.1163/9789004421691>

Vandelli, Giuseppe, 'Note sul testo critico della *Commedia*', *Studi Danteschi*, 4 (1921), pp. 39–84; 6 (1923), pp. 45–98; 7 (1923), pp. 47–95

Vasina, Augusto, *I Romagnoli fra autonomie cittadine e accentramento papale nell'età di Dante* (Florence: Olschki, 1965)

Veglia, Marco, 'Una controfigura biblica', in Veglia, *Dante leggero. Dal priorato alla 'Commedia'* (Rome: Carocci, 2017), pp. 111–47

Venuti, Lawrence, *The Translator's Invisibility* (New York: Routledge, 2008)

Vignuzzi, Ugo, 'Se (sed)', in *Enciclopedia Dantesca*, ed. by Umberto Bosco, 6 vols (Rome: Istituto dell'Enciclopedia Italiana, 1970–1978), v (1976), pp. 112–17

Villani, Giovanni, *Nuova Cronica*, ed. by Giuseppe Porta, 3 vols (Parma: Guanda, 1990–91)

Walcott, Derek, *Omeros* (New York: Noonday, 1990)

Weaver, William, 'In Other Words: A Translator's Journal', *The New York Times*, 19 November 1995

—— 'Pendulum Diary', *Southwest Review*, 75.2 (Spring 1990), pp. 150–78

—— 'The Process of Translation', in *The Craft of Translation*, ed. by John Biguenet and Rainer Schulte (Chicago: Chicago University Press, 1989), pp. 117–24 <https://www.gadda.ed.ac.uk/Pages/resources/babelgadda/babeng/weavertranslation.php> [accessed 23 April 2025]

Webb, Heather, *Dante's Persons: An Ethics of the Transhuman* (Oxford: Oxford University Press, 2016) <https://doi.org/10.1093/acprof:oso/9780198733485.001.0001>

Wiles, J. C., '"Se non…" (*Inf* 9.9) and "I vostri mali…" (23.109): Interpretative Issues of Infernal *Aposiopesis*', *Annali d'italianistica*, 39 (2021), pp. 205–27

Wodehouse, P. G. (Pelham Grenville), *The Mating Season* (Woodstock: Overlook Press, 2001)

Woltmann, Suzy, 'How to Make Audiences Suspend Their Disbelief', *Backstage*, 18 April 2023 <https://www.backstage.com/magazine/article/suspension-of-disbelief-75754/> [accessed 11 April 2025]

'Worldbuilding', Wikipedia, 5 April 2025 <https://en.wikipedia.org/wiki/Worldbuilding> [accessed 11 April 2025]

Yowell, Donna, 'Ugolino della Gherardesca', in *The Dante Encyclopedia*, ed. by Richard Lansing (New York: Garland Publishing, 2000), pp. 839–41

Notes on the Contributors

Roberta Antognini is Associate Professor Emerita of Italian Studies at Vassar College. She is the translator of Teodolinda Barolini's *La 'Commedia' senza Dio. Dante e la creazione di una realtà virtuale* (2003). She is also the author of *Il progetto autobiografico delle Familiares di Petrarca* (2008), and co-editor of the collection of essays *Poscritto a Giorgio Bassani* (2012). With Deborah Woodard, she has translated into English several poetic collections by Amelia Rosselli: *Hospital Series* (2015), *Obtuse Diary* (2018), *The Dragonfly* (2022), *Notes Scattered and Lost* (2024), and *Document* (2025). With Peter Robinson, she has translated and edited Giorgio Bassani's *The Collected Poems* (2023).

Roberto Antonelli is the current President of the Accademia Nazionale dei Lincei. Emeritus Professor of Romance Philology at Rome 'La Sapienza', he has been Membre étranger de l'Académie des Inscriptions et Belles Lettres since 2016. He was President of the Société de Linguistique Romane (2016–2019), President of the Ateneo federato delle Scienze umane, delle Arti e dell'Ambiente at Rome 'La Sapienza' (2008–2010) and Dean of the Faculty of Humanities (2004–2008) at Rome 'La Sapienza'. He has published widely in all fields of Romance Studies, from the Middle Ages to the present day.

Zygmunt Barański is Serena Professor of Italian Emeritus at the University of Cambridge and R.L. Canala Professor of Romance Languages & Literatures Emeritus at the University of Notre Dame. He has published extensively on Dante, medieval and modern Italian literature, and modern Italian culture and film. Among his books are *Dante e i segni. Saggi per una storia intellettuale di Dante* (2000), *'Chiosar con altro testo'. Leggere Dante nel Trecento* (2001), *Dante in Context* (with Lino Pertile, 2015), *The Cambridge Companion to Dante's 'Commedia'* (with Simon Gilson, 2019), and *Dante, Petrarch, Boccaccio. Literature, Doctrine, Reality* (2020).

Teodolinda Barolini is Lorenzo Da Ponte Professor of Italian, Columbia University. Fellow of the Accademia Nazionale dei Lincei, Accademia Olimpica, American Academy of Arts and Sciences, American Philosophical Society, and the Medieval Academy of America. Fifteenth President of the Dante Society of America. Author of *Dante's Poets* (1984; It. 1993), *The Undivine Comedy* (1992; It, 2003), *Dante and the Origins of Italian Literary Culture* (2006; It, 2012), *Dante's Multitudes* (2022; It, 2024). Editor of *Rime giovanili* *e della 'Vita Nuova'* (2009; Eng. 2014). Editor-in-Chief, Digital Dante: first on-line commentary on the *Commedia*.

Lina Bolzoni is Professor Emerita of Italian Literature at the Scuola Normale Superiore in Pisa, Global Distinguished Professor at New York University and a fellow of the Accademia Nazionale dei Lincei and the British Academy. Her books include: *La stanza della memoria. Modelli letterari e figurativi nell'età della stampa* (1995), *La rete delle immagini. Predicazione in volgare dalle origini a Bernardino da Siena* (2002), *Il cuore di cristallo. Ragionamenti d'amore, poesia e ritratto nel Rinascimento* (2010), *Il lettore creativo. Percorsi cinquecenteschi fra memoria, gioco, scrittura* (2012), and *Una meravigliosa solitudine. L'arte di leggere nell'Europa moderna* (2019).

Alberto Casadei teaches at the University of Pisa. He researches Italian literature from the fourteenth to the sixteenth century, comparative contemporary literature, and literary theory. Among his most recent studies: *Biology of Literature* (2018), *Dante: Other Ascertainments and Critical Points* (2019), *Dante beyond Allegory* (2021), *A Poem that Becomes Sacred. The Projectuality and Poetics of Dante* (2024).

Nassime Chida is an Assistant Professor of Italian Studies at Wellesley College and an Associate Editor of *Digital Dante*. She has previously taught at Columbia University and Duke University. She specializes in Dante, with a particular focus on the representation of Dante's political and military context in the *Commedia*. Her publications have appeared in *Romanic Review* and *Studi Romanzi*.

George Dameron is Professor Emeritus of History at Saint Michael's College. He is the author of *Episcopal Power and Florentine Society, 1000–1320* (1991), *Florence and Its Church in the Age of Dante* (2005), and co-editor, with Beth Petitjean, of *Charity, Medicine, and Religion in Late Medieval and Early Modern Italy: Essays in Memory of Philip R. Gavitt* (2024). He is also the author of a variety of studies on the history of medieval Italy, particularly Tuscany, as well as an essay on the papacy in Dante's *Divine Comedy*.

Grace Delmolino is Assistant Professor of Italian at the University of California, Davis and Associate Editor of *Digital Dante*. She holds a PhD from Columbia University in Italian and Comparative Literature and Society. Her areas of research are Dante, Boccaccio, canon law, gender studies, and the history of consent. Recent essays have appeared in *Speculum*, *The Decameron Ninth Day in Perspective*, and *Reconsidering Consent and Coercion*. Her first book, on Boccaccio and canon law, reads the *Decameron* as a pioneering text of medieval consent theory.

Laura DiNardo recently received her PhD in Italian and Comparative Literature from Columbia University. Her research focuses on medieval and analytic philosophy of language in relation to the works of Dante, with her dissertation utilizing analytic philosophical methods to more fully excavate the poet's enactment of a language theory in the *Commedia*. She is the Assistant Managing Editor of *Digital Dante*.

Joan M. Ferrante is Professor Emeritus of English and Comparative Literature at Columbia University. Among her publications are *Woman as Image in Medieval Literature: From the Twelfth Century to Dante* (1975), *The Political Vision of the Divine Comedy* (1984), and *To the Glory of Her Sex: Women's Roles in the Composition of Medieval Texts* (1997). She originated the online database of medieval women's correspondence, *Epistolae*.

Manuele Gragnolati is Professor of Medieval Italian Literature at Sorbonne Université, Associate Director of the ICI Berlin Institute for Cultural Inquiry, and Senior Research Fellow at Somerville College, Oxford. He is the author of *Experiencing the Afterlife: Soul and Body in Dante and Medieval Culture* (2005), *Amor che move. Linguaggio del corpo e forma del desiderio in Dante, Pasolini e Morante* (2013), and *Possibilities of Lyric: Reading Petrarch in Dialogue* (with Francesca Southerden, 2020). He has also edited several books, including *The Oxford Handbook of Dante* (with Elena Lombardi and Francesca Southerden, 2021).

Akash Kumar is an Assistant Professor of Italian Studies at the University of California, Berkeley. His research focuses on medieval Italian literature through the lens of Mediterranean and global culture, from the history of science to the origins of popular phenomena such as the game of chess. His book, *Love's Knowledge: Science and Lyric from Giacomo da Lentini to Dante*, is forthcoming from University of Toronto Press. He is an Associate Editor of *Digital Dante* and Editor of Dante Notes, the digital publication of the Dante Society of America.

Giuseppe Ledda is Professor of Italian Literature at the University of Bologna. His main area of research is Dante and medieval literature. He also works on Renaissance and twentieth-century Italian literature. He has published many articles and several books on Dante including: *La guerra della lingua: Ineffabilità, retorica e narrativa nella 'Commedia' di Dante* (2002); *La Bibbia di Dante* (2015); and *Il bestiario dell'aldilà. Gli animali nella 'Commedia' di Dante* (2019). He is a senior editor of the peer-reviewed journal *L'Alighieri*.

Elena Lombardi is Professor of Italian Literature at Oxford and a Fellow of Balliol College. She is the author of five books: *The Syntax of Desire: Language and Love in Augustine, the Modistae, Dante* (2007), *The Wings of the Doves: Love and Desire in Dante and Medieval Culture* (2012), *Imagining the Woman Reader in the Age of Dante* (2018), *Beatrice e le altre. Dante e l'universo femminile* (2021), *and Ulysses, Dante, and Other Stories* (2023), as well as several articles on topics related to the medieval and early modern periods. She is one of the co-editors of the *Oxford Handbook of Dante* (2021).

Kristina M. Olson is Associate Professor of Italian in the Department of Modern and Classical Languages at George Mason University. She is the author of *Courtesy Lost: Dante, Boccaccio and the Literature of History* (2014), and several articles on Dante and Boccaccio. She co-edited four volumes, including *Approaches to Teaching Dante's 'Divine Comedy'* with Christopher Kleinhenz. She has served as Vice President of the Dante Society of America, and as President, Vice President and Treasurer of the American Boccaccio Association. She is the current Editor-in-Chief of *Dante Studies*.

F. Regina Psaki is Professor Emerita of Romance Languages at the University of Oregon. She has published scholarly studies of narrative and authorial voicing in Dante, Boccaccio, and medieval imaginative fictions. She has translated chivalric romances from French and Italian: *Il Tristano Riccardiano* (2006), *Le Roman de la Rose ou de Guillaume de Dole* (1995), and *Le Roman de Silence* (1991). She is currently focusing on misogynous diatribes and defenses of women in Italian and French, and the critical history and future of the *Roman de Silence*.

H. Wayne Storey is the Founding Editor of *Textual Cultures*, former editor of *Medioevo letterario d'Italia* and former president of the Society for Textual Scholarship. One of the leading proponents of material philology in the U.S. and Italy, Storey is a specialist of medieval manuscripts. His collaborations with Barolini have included *Dante for the New Millennium* and *Petrarch and the Origins of Interpretation*. He is currently completing an extensive material commentary for his new 'rich-text' digital edition of Petrarch's Fragmenta (http://petrarchive.org) and 'Petrarch's Italian Book'.

Julie Van Peteghem is Associate Professor of Italian at Hunter College, CUNY, and Doctoral Faculty in Comparative Literature at The Graduate Center, CUNY. She is Managing Editor of *Digital Dante* and the Editor of the Intertextual Dante project on the site. She earned her PhD in Italian and Comparative Literature from Columbia University. She is the author of *Italian Readers of Ovid from the Origins to Petrarch* (Brill, 2020), and her work has appeared in journals such as *Humanist Studies & the Digital Age*, *Italian Studies*, and *Studi Danteschi*.

Index

Abelard, Peter 113
Abrams, Walter 18
Antognini, Roberta 1, 4, 11, 29
    n. 21, 236 n. 21, 261 n. 1
Antonelli, Roberto 6
Arachne 21, 246, 259, 326
Aristotle 36, 176, 187 n. 6, 300
Arnaut Daniel 53, 345
Arnulf of Orléans 271, 272, 274,
    275, 277
Auerbach, Erich 24, 25, 53, 66,
    73, 136, 139, 293, 294
    n. 12, 308, 309
Augustine of Hippo 24, 67, 86,
    137, 185 n. 3, 198 n. 26,
    219, 234, 251, 300
Bang, Mary Jo 10, 319, 325 n. 8,
    327–337
Barański, Zygmunt G. 4, 5, 9, 20
    n. 14, 151 n. 7, 154 n. 11,
    155 n. 13, 157 n. 17, 159
    n. 21, 163 n. 26, 210 n. 3,
    215, 220
Barbi, Michele 57, 59, 165 n. 29,
    219
Barthes, Roland 17
Bassnett, Susan 351 n. 5
Beatrice 2, 3, 37, 42, 43, 70, 71,
    82, 84–92, 141, 143, 157,
    184, 188, 191, 197–202,
    207, 208, 216, 217, 246,
    247, 265, 292, 294,
    304–307, 309, 310, 326,
    334
Bellos, David 356
Benjamin, Walter 351 n. 5
Bernard of Clairvaux 92, 206,
    219, 306, 309, 311
Bersani, Leo 10, 312–314

Bersuire, Pierre 276, 277, 281
Boethius 54, 113, 214, 300
Bolzoni, Lina 9
Bonaventure 60–63
Boniface VIII 60, 76, 93, 94,
    121, 133 n. 17, 143, 154,
    162, 164, 166, 326
Botterill, Steven 95 n. 22, 228,
    235, 238, 306
Boyde, Patrick 226, 227
Brambilla Ageno, Franca 56 n. 8,
    111, 112, 186 n. 4
Brandeis, Irma 1, 2
Brilli, Elisa 125 n. 2, 126, 129
    n. 12, 290 n. 6
Bruni, Leonardo 168, 353
Burke, Kenneth 287 n. 5
Burr, David 59
Cacciaguida 67, 90, 93, 94, 211
Caferro, William 149 n. *
Callegari, Danielle 150, 152 n. 8,
    n. 9, 155 n. 13, 178, 179
    n. 53
Calvino, Italo 351, 352
Carpi, Umberto 126
Casadei, Alberto 7, 8
Cavalcanti, Guido 53, 76, 97,
    129, 162, 196
Cecco d'Ascoli 41–47, 322
Certeau, Michel de 53
Cestaro, Gary P. 278 n. 43, 312,
    312 n. 20
Cherchi, Paolo 358, 359
Cherubini, Giovanni 158 n. 20,
    170
Chiavacci Leonardi, Anna Maria
    75 n. 12, 86 n. 20, 108, 109,

200 n. 28, 240 n. 29, 254
n. 4, 359 n. 28
Chida, Nassime 4, 7
Colella, Gianluca 110, 113
Coleridge, Samuel Taylor 6,
15–19, 22, 23, 30–32, 34,
47, 101 n. 7
Compagni, Dino 161 n. 24, 167
n. 32, n. 33, 171 n. 39,
n. 40, 173 n. 45, 174, 175
n. 49
Conte, Gian Biagio 70
Contini, Gianfranco 70, 75, 95,
97, 139, 210, 212, 226,
227, 286
Cooper, Mariah L. 264
Corrado, Massimiliano 355
n. 20, 358, 359
Coulson, Frank T. 273, 276
n. 41
Crisafi, Nicolò 109 n. 17, 139
n. 3, 290 n. 7
Croce, Benedetto 67
Curran, Leo C. 269, 279 n. 46
Dameron, George 7, 8
David the Psalmist 210, 211,
213, 214, 217, 250, 251
Davidsohn, Robert 153–174
Delmolino, Grace 4, 8, 133
DeVun, Leah 272, 282 n. 54
DiNardo, Laura 4, 6, 7
Dominic 6, 25, 59, 60, 214, 370
Dronke, Peter 137
Eco, Umberto 365, 365 n. 34
Eliot, T. S. 286
Elliott, Dyan 265
Farinata degli Uberti 7, 76, 82,
129, 132, 172, 358 n. 25
Ferrante, Joan M. 3, 4
Forster, E. M. 39, 40
Fosca, Nicola 118
Fra Giordano 187, 191

Francesca da Rimini 16 n. 3, 41,
43, 44, 74–76, 80, 81, 125,
128, 130, 132, 197, 262,
294–296, 326, 358 n. 25
Francis of Assisi 6, 25, 59, 60,
214, 370
Frank, Joseph 321
Freccero, John 24, 144 n. 5, 293,
294 n. 12
Ganymede 203, 204, 266, 267,
280, 282 n. 54
Gardini, Nicola 349
Geryon 5, 11, 19–21, 47, 137,
287, 355–362, 364
Giovanni del Virgilio 98, 140,
275–277, 281
Goodison, Lorna 11, 328, 340,
344–347
Gragnolati, Manuele 4, 10, 39
n. 32, 201 n. 32, 290 n. 6,
292, 345 n. 10
Gratian 8, 133 n. 17, 186, 187,
192–195, 197, 198 n. 26,
203, 204, 208, 264
Gregory the Great 193 n. 18
Guido da Montefeltro 7, 44,
116–121, 128
Guinizzelli, Guido 53, 75, 281,
282
Guittone d'Arezzo 53
Hawkins, Peter 137, 328 n. 15
Hermaphroditus 9, 267–283
Hollander, Robert 24, 137, 154
n. 11, 159 n. 21, 161 n. 24,
162 n. 26, 164 n. 28, 167
n. 32, 168 n. 34, 175 n. 49,
192 n. 15, 230
Holsinger, Bruce W. 266 n. 17,
282 n. 54, 314 n. 23
Homer 147, 288, 343, 344
Horace 19–22, 47, 147
Ibn Rushd (Averroes) 302, 346,
347

Jacobus de Voragine 187–189
Jacoff, Rachel 144 n. 5, 186 n. 4,
    191, 192 n. 15, 215, 265
    n. 16, 318, 328
Jakobson, Roman 353, 365, 366
Jameson, Fredric 39, 127
Joachim of Flora 59, 61–63
John of Garland 272–275, 281
John the Evangelist 60, 67,
    211–215, 217–220, 234
Jonson, Ben 347
Kirkpatrick, Robin 306, 308
Krasiński, Zygmunt 235, 236
Kristeva, Julia 10, 311, 312
Kumar, Akash 4, 10, 11
Larson, Atria 193 n. 17, 194
    n. 19, 195 n. 20
Latini, Brunetto 76, 93, 142, 359
Latini, Pseudo-Brunetto 152,
    178
Le Goff, Jacques 216
Ledda, Giuseppe 8, 45 n. 45,
    125 n. 2, 234 n. 17, 280
    n. 49
Leibniz, Gottfried 101
Lewis, David 31 n. 23, 105 n. 15,
    115 n. 31, 116, 120, 121
Lombardi, Elena 10, 201 n. 32,
    264 n. 12, 265 n. 13, 345
    n. 10
Lucan 147, 268, 275
Lucia 8, 183–208
Malato, Enrico 240 n. 28, 359
    n. 28, 360 n. 29
Marchionne di Coppo Stefani
    157 n. 18
Mary, Virgin 42, 43, 92, 199,
    200, 201 n. 30, 247, 249,
    251, 309, 311
Mazzotta, Giuseppe 224, 233,
    318, 328
McCarter, Stephanie 269, 271
    n. 30, 281 n. 52

Minos 106, 107
Moevs, Christian 306
Montale, Eugenio 1
Moore, Edward 75, 189 n. 10,
    191 n. 12
Mussato, Albertino 97
Najemy, John 157 n. 17, 158
    n. 18, 159 n. 21, 160 n. 22,
    n. 23, 161 n. 24, 162 n. 26,
    167 n. 32, n. 33, 168 n. 34
Nardi, Bruno 8, 24, 65–67, 136,
    137, 139
Newlands, Carole E. 261 n. 2,
    263
Olson, Kristina M. 133, 278
    n. 43
Ovid 9, 23, 24, 147, 229, 230,
    246, 261–283, 289, 363
Padoan, Giorgio 24, 126, 137,
    186 n. 4
Pampaloni, Guido 153, 154
    n. 11, 163 n. 26, 169–173
Pasquali, Giorgio 70
Pasquazi, Silvio 187 n. 7, 191,
    192
Pasquini, Emilio 126, 359 n. 28
Paul, Saint 67, 69, 80, 141, 214,
    215, 217–220, 234, 265
Pertile, Lino 151 n. 7, 154 n. 11,
    155 n. 13, 157 n. 17, 159
    n. 21, 162, 163 n. 26, 164
    n. 28, 167 n. 32, 170 n. 37,
    172 n. 42, 174 n. 48, 175
    n. 49, 176, 233, 241 n. 31,
    306
Peter, Saint 67, 90, 91, 94, 220
    n. 29
Piattoli, Renato 159 n. 21, 162
    n. 26, 164 n. 28, 165 n. 29,
    166 n. 30, n. 31, 170 n. 37,
    172 n. 43, 173 n. 45, 176
    n. 50
Piccarda Donati 187 n. 6, 197,
    198, 208, 262, 265, 369

Pinto, Giuliano 154 n. 11, 155
n. 12, 156 n. 15, 158 n. 18,
n. 19, 160 n. 22, 161 n. 24,
168 n. 34, 170 n. 37, 174
n. 46, 177 n. 52
Pozzi, Giovanni 257
Psaki, F. Regina 4, 10
Quintilian 95 n. 21, 98
Raimondi, Ezio 210, 211
Richlin, Amy 262 n. 4, 269
Ricoeur, Paul 300
Rosselli, Amelia 1
Rushdie, Salman 11, 346, 347
Ruud, Jay 341
Salmacis 9, 267–283
Santagata, Marco 32 n. 24, 126
n. 4, 151–176
Sartarelli, Stephen 1
Schildgen, Brenda Deen 262,
264 n. 12, 265 n. 14
Segre, Cesare 79, 82
Sermonti, Vittorio 359 n. 28,
360 n. 29, 363, 364
Shakespeare, William 18, 30,
330 n. 19, 347
Singleton, Charles S. 8, 24, 36,
66, 67, 70, 136–140, 179
n. 54, 224, 227–230, 233,
241, 286 n. 4
Spitzer, Leo 24, 25
Stalnaker, Robert 113–115, 119,
120
Statius 82, 83, 92, 211, 258, 275,
288, 302, 334
Stephany, William A. 186 n. 4,
191, 192
Storey, H. Wayne 5, 6
Sullivan, Karen 2
Tavoni, Mirko 32 n. 24, 215
Thomas Aquinas 8, 29, 36, 60,
61, 147, 187, 192, 197,
208, 234, 265, 370

Tolkien, J. R. R. 18, 22, 23,
30–34, 47
Tomko, Michael 17, 18, 22, 34
Torraca, Francesco 41, 125, 128,
131, 132
Ugolino della Gherardesca 8, 44,
130, 149–152, 152 n. 8,
n. 9, 153, 173 n. 44, 178,
179, 358 n. 25
Ulysses 5, 32, 76, 96, 204, 207
n. 37, 246, 259, 322, 324,
358, 361 n. 30, 364
Van Peteghem, Julie 4, 9
Vandelli, Giuseppe 55 n. 7, 57
Venuti, Lawrence 351 n. 5, 352,
353 n. 13
Vignuzzi, Ugo 103, 111 n. 20
Villani, Giovanni 157 n. 18, 161
n. 24, 162 n. 26, 168 n. 34,
170 n. 38, 171, 174 n. 46,
175 n. 49
Virgil 37, 47, 53, 69–71, 75,
78–86, 88, 92, 99, 100,
102, 107–111, 117, 122,
138, 145, 147, 149, 199,
200, 200 n. 27, 205, 210,
211, 213, 215, 229, 230,
247, 248, 253, 258, 265,
267, 273, 275, 280, 288,
324 n. 7, 334, 343,
345–347, 359–364
Walcott, Derek 10, 340,
342–345
Weaver, William 1, 350
Wetherbee, Winthrop 318
Wlassics, Tibor 51
Wodehouse, P. G. 340, 341
Wordsworth, William 15

Cultural Inquiry

EDITED BY CHRISTOPH F. E. HOLZHEY
AND MANUELE GRAGNOLATI

VOL. 1   TENSION/SPANNUNG
          Edited by Christoph F. E. Holzhey

VOL. 2   METAMORPHOSING DANTE
          Appropriations, Manipulations, and Rewritings
          in the Twentieth and Twenty-First Centuries
          Edited by Manuele Gragnolati, Fabio Camilletti,
          and Fabian Lampart

VOL. 3   PHANTASMATA
          Techniken des Unheimlichen
          Edited by Fabio Camilletti, Martin Doll, and Rupert Gaderer

VOL. 4   Boris Groys / Vittorio Hösle
          DIE VERNUNFT AN DIE MACHT
          Edited by Luca Di Blasi and Marc Jongen

VOL. 5   Sara Fortuna
          WITTGENSTEINS PHILOSOPHIE DES KIPPBILDS
          Aspektwechsel, Ethik, Sprache

VOL. 6   THE SCANDAL OF SELF-CONTRADICTION
          Pasolini's Multistable Subjectivities, Geographies, Traditions
          Edited by Luca Di Blasi, Manuele Gragnolati,
          and Christoph F. E. Holzhey

VOL. 7   SITUIERTES WISSEN
          UND REGIONALE EPISTEMOLOGIE
          Zur Aktualität Georges Canguilhems und Donna J. Haraways
          Edited by Astrid Deuber-Mankowsky and Christoph F. E.
          Holzhey

VOL. 8   MULTISTABLE FIGURES
          On the Critical Potentials of Ir/Reversible Aspect-Seeing
          Edited by Christoph F. E. Holzhey

VOL. 9   Wendy Brown / Rainer Forst
          THE POWER OF TOLERANCE
          Edited by Luca Di Blasi and Christoph F. E. Holzhey

VOL. 10   DENKWEISEN DES SPIELS
Medienphilosophische Annäherungen
Edited by Astrid Deuber-Mankowsky and Reinhold Görling

VOL. 11   DE/CONSTITUTING WHOLES
Towards Partiality Without Parts
Edited by Manuele Gragnolati and Christoph F. E. Holzhey

VOL. 12   CONATUS UND LEBENSNOT
Schlüsselbegriffe der Medienanthropologie
Edited by Astrid Deuber-Mankowsky and Anna Tuschling

VOL. 13   AURA UND EXPERIMENT
Naturwissenschaft und Technik bei Walter Benjamin
Edited by Kyung-Ho Cha

VOL. 14   Luca Di Blasi
DEZENTRIERUNGEN
Beiträge zur Religion der Philosophie im 20. Jahrhundert

VOL. 15   RE-
An Errant Glossary
Edited by Christoph F. E. Holzhey and Arnd Wedemeyer

VOL. 16   Claude Lefort
DANTE'S MODERNITY
An Introduction to the Monarchia; with an Essay by Judith
Revel. Translated by Jennifer Rushworth
Edited by Christiane Frey, Manuele Gragnolati,
Christoph F. E. Holzhey, and Arnd Wedemeyer

VOL. 17   WEATHERING
Ecologies of Exposure
Edited by Christoph F. E. Holzhey and Arnd Wedemeyer

VOL. 18   Manuele Gragnolati and Francesca Southerden
POSSIBILITIES OF LYRIC
Reading Petrarch in Dialogue

VOL. 19   THE WORK OF WORLD LITERATURE
Edited by Francesco Giusti and Benjamin Lewis Robinson

VOL. 20   MATERIALISM AND POLITICS
Edited by Bernardo Bianchi, Emilie Filion-Donato,
Marlon Miguel, and Ayşe Yuva

VOL. 21   OVER AND OVER AND OVER AGAIN
           Reenactment Strategies in Contemporary Arts and Theory
           Edited by Cristina Baldacci, Clio Nicastro,
           and Arianna Sforzini

VOL. 22   QUEERES KINO / QUEERE ÄSTHETIKEN
           ALS DOKUMENTATIONEN DES PREKÄREN
           Edited by Astrid Deuber-Mankowsky and Philipp Hanke

VOL. 23   OPENNESS IN MEDIEVAL EUROPE
           Edited by Manuele Gragnolati and Almut Suerbaum

VOL. 24   ERRANS
           Going Astray, Being Adrift, Coming to Nothing
           Edited by Christoph F. E. Holzhey and Arnd Wedemeyer

VOL. 25   THE CASE FOR REDUCTION
           Edited by Christoph F. E. Holzhey and Jakob Schillinger

VOL. 26   UNTYING THE MOTHER TONGUE
           Edited by Antonio Castore and Federico Dal Bo

VOL. 27   WAR-TORN ECOLOGIES, AN-ARCHIC FRAGMENTS
           Reflections from the Middle East
           Edited by Umut Yıldırım

VOL. 28   Elena Lombardi
           ULYSSES, DANTE, AND OTHER STORIES

VOL. 29   DISPLACING THEORY THROUGH
           THE GLOBAL SOUTH
           Edited by Iracema Dulley and Özgün Eylül İşcen

VOL. 30   RETHINKING LYRIC COMMUNITIES
           Edited by Irene Fantappiè, Francesco Giusti,
           and Laura Scuriatti

VOL. 31   PSYCHOTHERAPY AND MATERIALISM
           Essays by François Tosquelles and Jean Oury
           Edited by Marlon Miguel and Elena Vogman

VOL. 32   Astrid Deuber-Mankowsky
           QUEER POST-CINEMA
           Reinventing Resistance

VOL. 33   BREAKING AND MAKING MODELS
           Edited by Christoph F. E. Holzhey, Marietta Kesting,
           and Claudia Peppel

VOL. 34   Rosa Barotsi
          TIME AND THE EVERYDAY IN SLOW CINEMA

VOL. 35   Stella do Patrocínio
          FALATÓRIO/CHATTER
          Edited by Iracema Dulley and Marlon Miguel

VOL. 36   PASOLINI
          Dialogues avec la France / Dialoghi con la Francia
          Edited by M. A. Bazzocchi, P. Desogus, M. Gragnolati, A.-V.
          Houcke, H. Joubert-Laurencin, and D. Luglio

VOL. 37   A WORLD OF POSSIBILITIES
          The Legacy of The Undivine Comedy
          Edited by Kristina M. Olson

www.ingramcontent.com/pod-product-compliance
Lightning Source LLC
Chambersburg PA
CBHW030351130626
46549CB00004B/1448